W9-BQM-761

LANDMARKS OF AMERICAN WRITING

LANDMARKS of AMERICAN WRITING

Edited by **HENNIG COHEN**

BASIC BOOKS, INC., PUBLISHERS

New York   *London*

The Authors

GAY WILSON ALLEN is Professor of English at New York University and author of *The Solitary Singer: A Critical Biography of Walt Whitman* and *William James: A Biography.*

WAYNE ANDREWS, Archives of American Art Professor at Wayne State University, is a critic, editor, and photographer. His publications include *Architecture, Ambition and Americans* and *Architecture in Chicago and Mid-America.*

WARNER BERTHOFF is Professor of English at Harvard University. He is the author of *The Example of Melville* and *The Ferment of Realism: American Literature, 1884–1919.*

EDWIN H. CADY is the James H. Rudy Professor of English at Indiana University. He is the author of a biography, *Stephen Crane,* co-editor of a collection of Crane's letters, and has written extensively on William Dean Howells.

HENNIG COHEN is Professor of English at the University of Pennsylvania and editor of *American Quarterly,* the journal of the American Studies Association.

JAMES P. DOUGHERTY, Associate Professor of English at the University of Notre Dame, has published essays on twentieth-century American writers, including E. E. Cummings, and contributes verse to literary magazines.

ARTHUR P. DUDDEN, Professor and Chairman of the Department of History at Bryn Mawr College, is the editor of *Woodrow Wilson and the World Today* and *The Assault of Laughter.*

LEON EDEL is the Henry James Professor of English at New York University. An editor and biographer of James, he received the Pulitzer Prize and the National Book Award for *Henry James: The Middle Years.*

RICHARD HARTER FOGLE is Professor of English at the University of North Carolina. A specialist in the literature of nineteenth-century English and American Romanticism, he is the author of *Hawthorne's Fiction* and *Hawthorne's Imagery.*

ALFRED V. FRANKENSTEIN has been art critic for the *San Francisco Chronicle* for more than thirty years and until recently was music critic as well. He is also lecturer in American Studies at Mills College.

WILLIAM H. GOETZMANN is Professor of History and head of the American Studies Program at the University of Texas. His book, *Exploration and Empire: The Explorer and the Scientist in the Winning of the West* won the Pulitzer Prize and the Francis Parkman Prize.

NORMAN S. GRABO is Professor of English at the University of California at Berkeley. He is the author of a study of Edward Taylor, the Puritan poet and minister, and an editor of Taylor's sermons.

ALLEN GUTTMANN is Associate Professor of English and American Studies at Amherst College. His books include *The Wound in the Heart: America and the Spanish Civil War* and *The Conservative Tradition in America*.

WALTER HARDING is University Professor of English at the State University of New York at Geneseo. He is Secretary of the Thoreau Society and is the author or editor of more than a dozen books on Thoreau.

WILLIAM L. HEDGES is Professor of English at Goucher College and author of *Washington Irving: An American Study, 1802–1832*. He is an editor of the projected edition of the works of Washington Irving.

DANIEL HOFFMAN is Professor of English at the University of Pennsylvania. Among his critical writings are *Form and Fable in American Fiction*. The most recent of his four volumes of verse is *Striking the Stones*.

SAMUEL HYNES is Professor of English at Northwestern University. A reviewer for literary magazines in England and the United States, his books include *The Edwardian Turn of Mind*.

RALPH L. KETCHAM is Professor of American Studies, Public Affairs, and Political Science at Syracuse University. He has served as associate editor of both the *Papers of James Madison* and the *Papers of Benjamin Franklin*.

EVERETT S. LEE is Professor and Head of the Department of Sociology and Anthropology at the University of Massachusetts. Formerly the Director of the University of Pennsylvania Population Studies Center, he is President of the Population Association of America.

DAVID LEVIN is Professor of English at Stanford University. He is the author of *History as Romantic Art* and *In Defense of Historical Literature*.

RAVEN I. McDAVID, JR., is Professor of English at the University of Chicago. He is editor of the *Linguistic Atlas of the United States and Canada* and of H. L. Mencken's *The American Language* and a past president of the American Dialect Society.

JAMES E. MILLER, JR., is Professor of English at the University of Chicago. A former editor of *College English,* he is the author of *A Critical Guide to "Leaves of Grass"* and *Walt Whitman,* and editor of *Whitman's "Song of Myself"—Origin, Growth, Meaning.*

MURRAY G. MURPHEY is Professor of American Civilization at the University of Pennsylvania. He is President of the Charles S. Peirce Society and author of *The Development of Peirce's Philosophy.*

RUSSEL B. NYE is Professor of English at Michigan State University. His biography, *George Bancroft: Brahmin Rebel,* was awarded the Pulitzer Prize. He is a past president of the American Studies Association.

STOW PERSONS is Professor of History at the University of Iowa. He is the author of *American Minds* and editor of *Evolutionary Thought in America.*

BENJAMIN QUARLES is Professor of History at Morgan State College, Maryland. He is the author of the biography, *Frederick Douglass* and editor of *Narrative of the Life of Frederick Douglass.*

EARL H. ROVIT is Associate Professor of English at the City College of the City University of New York. He is the author of an analytical biography, *Ernest Hemingway,* and a novelist.

LOUIS D. RUBIN, JR., is Professor of English at the University of North Carolina. A novelist and critic, his recent books are *The Curious Death of the Novel: Essays in American Literature* and *The Teller in the Tale.*

MARK SCHORER is Professor of English at the University of California at Berkeley. He is the author of many volumes of criticism and fiction, and the biography *Sinclair Lewis: An American Life.*

JOHN SEELYE is Associate Professor of English at the University of Connecticut and an editor of the novels of Melville, Poe, and other nineteenth-century American writers. He edited *Etchings of a Whaling Cruise* by J. Ross Browne.

JOHN WILLIAM WARD is Professor of History at Amherst College. He is the author of *Andrew Jackson: Symbol of Age* and editor of *Society and Manners in the United States* by Michael Chevalier and *The Nature and Tendency of Free Institutions* by Frederick Grimké.

GERALD WEALES is Professor of English at the University of Pennsylvania. An editor, novelist, and critic, he received the George Jean Nathan Award for Drama Criticism in 1966. His most recent book is *The Jumping-Off Place: American Drama in the 1960's*.

MELVIN K. WHITELEATHER is a commentator on political and foreign affairs for the Philadelphia *Evening Bulletin*. He was an Associated Press correspondent in Paris, Berlin, and Rome in the 1930's and a war correspondent in Germany, North Africa, Italy, and Russia during World War II.

Preface

Originally, a landmark was an object used to define boundary lines, whether of personal real estate or of nations. In the sense that the word applies to the definition of the national character, it is appropriate to *Landmarks of American Writing* which draws upon written materials of a literary and quasi-literary sort for information about the nature of the American experience and its effects on the arts, sciences, and society within its boundaries. Subsequently, the term was used by sailors to designate an object that stood out prominently from the landscape and therefore could be used as a guide in navigation. The chapters of this book deal with works of a kind and magnitude that have rendered them conspicuous and in various ways have provided a sense of direction to the course of the national development. In modern and more common usage, a landmark is an event or stage in the historical process that signifies a turning point, the end of one thing and the beginning of another. The essays which follow are also concerned with such turning points in American history.

The choice in the title of the somewhat loose word "writing" is likewise calculated. Beneath this rubric one can decently include the conventional literary genres (the novel, short story, poetry, drama) as well as works that were written for other than primarily literary purposes (biography, history, travel narrative, and essays in philosophy, politics, economics, sociology, philology), though an important aspect of the latter is their literary excellence and their deliberate use of literary devices to enhance their effectiveness. Thus the inclusiveness of the word "writing" permits a wide range of subject matter and form and at the same time recognizes literary qualities. Literature is read both as literature and as history, and history is read both as history and as literature. In short, the influence of the American Studies movement which emphasizes the importance of examining the culture as a totality from multidisciplinary viewpoints and utilizes inter-disciplinary means underlies this attempt at breadth and variety. The chronological arrangement, going forward from the colonial period to the recent past, implies a view of this culture in historical perspective.

There remains one matter regarding which no explanation can be adequate: Why were these particular thirty-two examples of American writing chosen for consideration? Why, for instance, second-bests like Melville's *The Confidence-Man* and Mark Twain's *The Adventures of Tom Sawyer?* Why William James and not Charles Peirce? Why are the fields of education and religion left unrepresented? One could argue that *The Confidence-Man* is less well known than *Moby-Dick* and deserves to be better known, that in its cross-grained way it is remarkably American and timely; or that precisely because *Tom Sawyer* has been relegated to the juvenile bookshelf while *Adventures of Huckleberry Finn* has been raised to the rank of a world classic it deserves reconsideration. But the answer is that there are other landmarks of American writing. They, too, stand as eminences defining the horizons of the national spirit and the nation's creative accomplishment, indicating objectives and pathways, designating changes in the direction of the historical progress. Hence this collection of essays is in its fashion something of a landmark.

These essays were originally prepared for the Voice of America for presentation as lectures to audiences abroad through its *Forum* series.

HENNIG COHEN

July, 1969

Contents

CONTENTS

LANDMARKS OF AMERICAN WRITING

I

WILLIAM BRADFORD:
OF PLYMOUTH PLANTATION

Norman S. Grabo

A nation born of successful and sustained revolution will under-standably at first celebrate its heroes and then venerate them. Can there be any wonder, therefore, that Americans should date their ideals from the period of the American Revolution in the late eighteenth century? Or that they should continue to contemplate and explore the writings of that most formative period? Benjamin Franklin, Thomas Jefferson, James Madison, Alexander Hamilton, George Washington, John Adams—statesmen and men of affairs—architects of a new nation, not only constructed the constitution of a new way of life but put their dreams into words as well as into action. The ideals they personified and taught—a government of laws, not persons; freedom from all forms of tyranny; the advantages of competitive relationships, political as well as economic—may not always be realized in American life as they were originally envisioned, but their grip on the American character has been permanent. They have helped create the image Americans show not only to the world, but to themselves: shrewd, practical, competitive, resourceful, benevolent and humane (whenever possible), and often irritatingly successful.

There is another side to the American character, hidden like the stone in a peach, perhaps, but no less hard and permanent. Non-Americans seem to detect it more readily than Americans, and whether they respond with amusement or disgust or simply bewilderment, they instinctively register the American smugness and pride which is curiously not complacence or satisfaction with material success, but a sense of moral superiority that makes that success and indeed justifies it. One may ignore this aspect of the American character or commend it or decry it, but it is, often unconsciously, there, a shaping, controlling force. That it is a force and not merely a characteristic shows in everything from the American conquest of its western lands in the nineteenth century to the political oratory of John F. Kennedy's New Frontier: Americans are a special people, committed to a great historical mission, and destined to accomplish the most cherished dreams of mankind.

Yet this notion does not belong to its revolutionary leaders. Rather it belongs to the preceding century, finding full and eloquent voice in one of the most curious documents in the history of American writing—William Bradford's *Of Plymouth Plantation*. It is curious not only because of its own peculiar history but because of the improbability of its success in the first place. The likelihood of any contemporary historian writing the inside story of his times so successfully that his account remains the chief authority for three centuries is rare enough. That he should, moreover, describe and embody the principles of those times so exactly as to give them mythic force in a nation's consciousness heightens the improbability. Make him a self-taught country boy, exiled from his native land to a "hideous and desolate wilderness" where he accidentally became the leader of a handful of social outcasts, and the improbable becomes implausible. Yet all this is the case.

Born in Yorkshire, England, in 1590, William Bradford was raised in the tiny village of Austerfield.[1] In his teens he fell under the influence of the radical Puritan preaching at neighboring Scrooby, and by 1608 escaped the wrath of ecclesiastical authorities, joining the Puritan exodus to the Netherlands. In Amsterdam and for a longer time in Leyden, Bradford joined the struggle to maintain pure religious principles in an alien culture, and he succeeded moderately well. Bradford became a weaver, and with the help of an inheritance from England, eventually even bought a small house and married. By 1617, however, it had become clear that this community could never find a permanent home in Holland. A longstanding truce was coming to an end, and Dutch and English alike feared the outbreak of war; bitter theological controversies had codified the Calvinistic beliefs of the English expatriates, but had also sharpened their differences from their neighbors; the community as a whole had not prospered, and now its elders—often made old before their time by hard work and poverty—began to sicken and die while youngsters were bred to foreign language, habits, and sins. There was no choice but to separate from these conditions, and separate they did, arranging in England for financial support and for two ships, the unsound *Speedwell* and the *Mayflower,* to carry them across the ocean to the little-known new world called America.

Separation was no new thing for these people; it had indeed become a fundamental principle among them, and was in large part responsible for both their character and their difficulties. They represented the most extreme views among English Protestants who believed that church reforms since the 1530's had proceeded neither quickly enough nor far enough. Their ideal was what they supposed to have been the state of the primitive Christian churches in the first three centuries after Christ—small independent congregations of people who believed they had experienced signs of God's saving grace in their own souls. Only sanctified people communing together could make such a congregation; to commune with others would corrupt the purity of God's worship as well, perhaps, as contaminate the truly gracious. After 1600 such Puritans increasingly declared that they could no longer worship in the established English Church nor acknowledge the spiritual leadership of the monarch. By refusing to pay either spiritual or temporal duties to the state-connected church they violated both ecclesiastical and civil law, and were prosecuted—they said persecuted—for their action. Moreover, by maintaining publicly that the Church of England was no true church, and by proclaiming themselves Separatists, they provoked the displeasure not only of authorities but of all who were made to feel spiritually inferior by these assertions. Here is the root of that sense of American specialness: a God-conferred righteousness so deeply felt that it needed no visible proofs.

No wonder they met with deceit and ill-fortune in negotiating their voyage. No wonder that they still had the grit to make it. In November of 1620, after sixty-five hard days at sea, a mere one hundred and two passengers stood at anchor off Cape Cod in New England. Men, women, infants, "saints" and laboring "strangers" alike [2] gazed in mingled relief and dismay at the bleak coast, the first permanent settlement in the present United States. By the following year death had reduced that number by half, and Bradford, now thirty-one years old, was elected governor of the small remainder, an office he would hold for a total of thirty-three years with only occasional relief. Having begun so calamitously, the fortunes of these "pilgrims," as Bradford called them, could only improve. Yet the next ten years saw not only improvement but persistent difficulty. Ill-feelings among supporters both in England and Holland, betrayal and stupidity from agents handling their desperate affairs, failed crops, arson, earthquake, unruly visitors, gouging interest rates on borrowed funds, Indian threats, the encroachment of renegade traders, and licentious ministers more than aggravated the natural difficulties of a tiny population subsisting on the margin of three thousand miles of wilderness in one direction and an equal expanse of ocean in the other.

Despite these difficulties, by 1630 the little colony at New Plymouth was on firm footing and showed every sign of succeeding. A clear charter had been secured, enormous debts had been cleared, the economy relatively stabilized, and now reports came in of a massive migration of Puritans under the leadership of John Winthrop to Massachusetts Bay, not fifty miles away. Thus strengthened, Plymouth should have looked forward with pleasure to a prosperous and useful future, for while the Massachusetts Bay colony was well financed and well organized, Plymouth could bring to it the advantage of what Bradford called "the grave mistris Experience." But for Bradford the event seems not to have generated great hopes for the future. Instead, he seems to have sensed a kind of finality in it, for he made that year the occasion to collect his notes and carefully preserved documents into an ordered narrative. There was something prophetic in that act, for the next ten years would see waves of English settlers, most of them Puritans but not Separatists, swell the population of Massachusetts Bay until eventually that colony engulfed New Plymouth.[3]

Writing was not entirely a new endeavor for Bradford, for his description of the settlement itself in 1620 had been printed in England in 1622,[4] and as governor it had been his duty to de-

6

scribe for English investors what difficulties and successes the "plantation" encountered as well as to defend the colony's policies and actions from a variety of attacks. Experience had taught him the necessity of keeping clear and accurate accounts, for the failure to do so had been very dear indeed. But this practical duty was only partly responsible for his care in these matters. Bradford was also a profoundly religious man thrust providentially into a role of leadership to God's favored people. He knew that in some glorious future his stewardship would be called to judgment and that his spiritual accounts must face a divine audit. Like numberless New Englanders after him who registered their lives in diaries, journals, notebooks, autobiographies, and biographies, Bradford sought to set his accounts straight and preserved the evidence for doing so. Between these mercantile and spiritual motives, however, developed another, the consciousness that the experience of his people in the wilderness was important in the course of events, that its historical magnitude deserved telling and that he was in the best possible position to tell that story. In brief, William Bradford now consciously undertook to write history, not merely to keep records.

With self-effacing modesty, Bradford declared his subject in the simple title, *Of Plymouth Plantation,* below that stating his intentions with disarming honesty, dignity, and directness: "And first of the occasion and inducements thereunto; the which that I may truly unfold, I must begin at the very root and rise of the same. The which I shall endeavour to manifest in a plain style, with singular regard unto the simple truth in all things; at least as near as my slender judgment can attain the same." [5] His sense that truth is "simple" is very important, existing as it does in what is at once a concept of history and an act of faith. That sense was not peculiar to Bradford, of course, as he shows fully in his first chapter. History is true when it accurately reflects God's providential will in men's affairs. All of time is seen as a progress toward a predetermined end which is timeless and spiritual and toward which every man and indeed the entire race of man and nature unswervingly tend, a perfect and therefore complete and changeless condition. But the image of history as a progress or pilgrimage of mankind to a holy state was complicated by another image of struggle as pilgrims were hindered from their end

7

by innumerable adversaries both natural and supernatural. If the true history of man was simple, it was not always clear.

Yet by the time Bradford wrote, historians had clearly mapped out the road from the world of affliction and misery to that "more goodly country" of heaven. The Bible itself was one such map; the early Christian church histories of Socrates Scholasticus and Eusebius were others, and Bradford was familiar with them.[6] But for him the clearest guide was John Foxe, whose *Acts and Monuments* (1563) revealed in brilliant strokes the struggles of God's simple truth to manifest itself in a corrupt world. Foxe saw the history of the Christian era falling into six great periods of three hundred years each: the first was the period of primitive purity, followed by three centuries of triumph as Christianity prevailed in a hostile world. The third great period saw the development of internal troubles through monasticism, until in the fourth—the period from 900 to 1200 A.D.—Antichrist triumphed in the supremacy of the church of Rome. This, says Foxe, was the dark and dismal time. It was followed, in the years from 1200 to 1500, by a critical period whose end saw the great Protestant Reformation. That, one might suppose, should inaugurate another great triumphal period for Foxe, a period continuing into Bradford's times. But it did not, for Foxe saw it merely as a final period of continued trial and travail, and so did Bradford.

Over and over again the words *trouble, trial, travail, difficulty,* and *danger* occupy his opening chapters, even as he describes the whole background to this Pilgrim venture—the English persecutions, the expatriation to Holland, the preparations for the voyage—before the weakened company landed in New England. He quotes other cases of suffering people such as the Stoic Seneca at the mercy of the sea and his dread of it, St. Paul shipwrecked among barbarians, Spanish conquistadores of the preceding century starving in their West Indies explorations, and even the Israelites under Moses, with whom Bradford and other Puritans were so fond of identifying themselves, wandering in the wilderness in search of a Mt. Pisgah from which to view the Promised Land. Always the same point is made: the most famous sufferings of man were trivial compared to those of this band of chosen Englishmen. Seneca had merely sailed a few miles along the shores of Italy, while the Pilgrims were buffeted and tossed for months upon the main sea; St. Paul's barbarians "showed them no small kindness in refreshing" him and his company, while the Indians of New England "were readier to fill their sides full of arrows than otherwise"; the Israelites found their Pisgah and their Promised Land whereas the Pilgrims, look where they might, found nothing to "solace or content" them. Did Peter Martyr "magnify" the Spaniards by claiming that "none living which is not a Spaniard could have endured" five days on the meager rations they had? The Pilgrims lived on less, sometimes for two or three months together!

The reason for this persistent emphasis on the trial and travail of "modern" times is not difficult to see. On one hand, Bradford is instinctively responding to and taking advantage of John Foxe's analysis. Nineteen years before Bradford's birth an Anglican convocation declared that a copy of Foxe's great *Book of Martyrs* should be beside every cathedral Bible and that every official of the church should have a copy in his home.[7] Foxe's analysis permeated English Protestant thought, carrying with it almost the authority of Scripture; that reason is deepened by what seems to be a conscious literary strategy on Bradford's part. He dwells on the weakness and littleness of the Pilgrim venture in the face of its troubles in order to magnify the significance of their accomplishment. Shakespeare's Henry the Fifth voices the sentiment immediately before the battle of Agincourt in response to the wish that the English army numbered more men. "No," he says:

> If we are mark'd to die, we are enow
> To do our country loss; and if to live,
> The fewer men, the greater share of honour.
> God's will! I pray thee, wish not one man more.[8]

Bradford, however, shifts the emphasis tellingly, as he comments upon his company's poor, divided, useless condition: "as if the Lord by this work of His providence thought these few too many for the great work He had to do" (p. 53). If, as I take to be the case, there is an element of English national pride in Bradford's attitude, somewhat akin to Henry the Fifth's, it is submerged in

9

the larger conviction that God may use the most humble, unlikely, even contemptible instruments in his glorious work.

By all rational expectations, Bradford suggests, the venture should fail. The virtue that permitted its success did not belong to its participants but to the Lord who prepared their way and nourished them with illustrious providences. These remarkable instances of God's favor can be illustrated by this now famous example, as Bradford records what befell the seasick Pilgrims in mid-ocean:

> And I may not omit here a special work of God's providence. There was a proud and very profane young man, one of the seamen, of a lusty, able body, which made him the more haughty; he would alway be contemning the poor people in their sickness and cursing them daily with grievous execrations; and did not let to tell them that he hoped to help to cast half of them overboard before they came to their journey's end, and to make merry with what they had; and if he were by any gently reproved, he would curse and swear most bitterly. But it pleased God before they came half seas over, to smite this young man with a grievous disease, of which he died in a desperate manner, and so was himself the first that was thrown overboard. Thus his curses light on his own head, and it was an astonishment to all his fellows for they noted it to be the just hand of God upon him. (p. 58)

Such events were not coincidental to Bradford. The natural world to him was a marvelous construction of signs, emblems, and hieroglyphs, a symbolic world in which nothing was truly accidental, though the design of the whole might be difficult to perceive. When therefore on the following page he describes a young Puritan falling overboard, he notes that "it pleased God" that the man caught a rope and so was saved. So it was that the Lord signaled his favor for the Pilgrim cause. By putting the two instances so close together, Bradford attempts to make the design of God's will more visible.

This is a selective process, and Bradford is quite blunt about it. For the sake of brevity, he says, he omits other things, selecting what bears out the "simple truth" promised in his opening words. The pattern of notable providences and divine judgments has often been the most interesting aspect of Bradford's work to later readers, who have sometimes been as interested in what Bradford omitted as in what he includes. Modern historians occasionally worry about his truthfulness in this matter, but the question is not a serious one. When Bradford decides consciously or unconsciously to recount or to reject events and persons, he does so within limits set to his own perceptions. That is to say, in his understanding some matters speak to the "simple truth" he sees while others do not. In a sense Bradford's faith prejudges both events and their importance for him as well as determining the values he will attach to them. To an age that no longer shares his view of the world, Bradford's judgments must frequently seem warped and irrelevant, but his honesty in making them cannot seriously be challenged.

Truth for a man of intense personal conviction, a man of faith, can never be exclusively rational. Truth that matters, said one of his English contemporaries, is the truth of affection, and only a fool would omit the affection of the truth.[9] Bradford not only lets his tone betray his emotional response in a variety of ways, but he consciously constructs his descriptions to involve his readers, to make them participate emotionally in the experience. Consider the magnificent passage in which Bradford muses upon the plight of his little colony as it landed in America:

> But here I cannot but stay and make a pause, and stand half amazed at this poor people's present condition; and so I think will the reader, too, when he well considers the same. Being thus passed the vast ocean, and a sea of troubles before in their preparation . . . , they had now no friends to welcome them nor inns to entertain or refresh their weatherbeaten bodies; no houses or much less town to repair to, to seek for succour. . . . And for the season it was winter, and they that know the winters of that country know them to be sharp and violent, and subject to cruel and fierce storms, dangerous to travel to known places, much more to search an unknown coast. Besides, what could they see but a hideous and desolate wilderness, full of wild beasts and wild men—and what multitudes there might be of them they knew not . . . for which way soever they turned their eyes (save upwards to the heavens) they could have little solace or content in respect of any outward objects. For summer being done, all things stand upon them with a weatherbeaten face, and the whole country, full of woods and thickets, represented a wild and savage

hue. If they looked behind them, there was the mighty ocean which they had passed and was now as a main bar and gulf to separate them from all the civil parts of the world. If it be said they had a ship to succour them, it is true; but what heard they daily from the master and company? But that with speed they should look out a place . . . where they would be, at some near distance; for the season was such as he would not stir from thence till a safe harbor was discovered by them, where they would be, and he might go without danger; and that victuals consumed apace but he must and would keep sufficient for themselves and their return. Yea, it was muttered by some that if they got not a place in time, they would turn them and their goods ashore and leave them. Let it also be considered what weak hopes of supply and succour they left behind them, that might bear up their minds in this sad condition and trials they were under; and they could not but be very small. It is true, indeed, the affections and love of their brethren at Leyden was cordial and entire towards them, but they had little power to help them or themselves; and how the case stood between them and the merchants at their coming away hath already been declared.

What could now sustain them but the Spirit of God and His grace? (pp. 61–63)

The passage typifies Bradford at his best. What he wants is the reader's *appreciation,* not mere knowledge, of the Pilgrims' plight. To secure it he resorts to emotionally charged language— "poor peoples," "no friends," "cruel and fierce storms," "sharp and violent" winters; and he chooses details that spoke to deep English values—inns, houses, towns, civil parts. Nature is more than difficult; it is malignant, coming upon them with a "weatherbeaten face." Associates threaten to abandon them. Their friends back in Holland are helpless to assist them. The reader must feel sympathy for them, and Bradford employs whatever rhetorical devices he can to arouse that feeling—alliteration, balance and antithesis, striking metaphor. In such passages Bradford is consciously literary. Kenneth Murdock has remarked of Bradford's style that his "phrasing is not that of the imaginative artist, ransacking books for illustrations and parallels, but that of the man whose ears were full of the plain speech of English farmers and who was bred to relish simple rhythms and words rich with the sense of familiar life." [10] That is an accurate appraisal, but Bradford does go beyond it. He had an eye for details that expose the emotional significance of events. He recalls, for example, the treatment the Pilgrims anticipated from savage and brutish Indians who "delight to torment men in the most bloody manner that may be; flaying some alive with the shells of fishes, cutting off the members and joints of others by piecemeal and broiling on the coals, eat the collops of their flesh in their sight whilst they live, with other cruelties horrible to be related" (p. 26). He describes Indians suffering from smallpox who "for want of bedding and linen and other helps they fall into a lamentable condition as they lie on their hard mats, the pox breaking and mattering and running one into another, their skin cleaving by reason thereof to the mats they lie on. When they turn them, a whole side will flay off at once . . . and they will be all of a gore blood, most fearful to behold . . . they die like rotten sheep" (pp. 270–271). Or the man so weakened by hunger that while "gathering shellfish was so weak as he stuck fast in the mud and was found dead in the place" (p. 116).

Bradford's details are not all so gruesome, but they all contribute to a single pervasive image. The roistering rebel who got so drunk he ran his guard's sword up his own nose, the lecherous minister who fawned before them "and would have kissed their hands if they would have suffered him," the tearful parting from friends and family in Leyden, so painful that even Dutch bystanders broke into tears, all are designed to evoke pity, sympathy, sorrow. It is not customary to say so, but Bradford, like most Puritan writers, was a great sentimentalist. The corruption of mankind and the instability of all worldly things lie behind this melancholy view of events. Bradford's Pilgrims suffering on the shores of America are an emblem of all mankind in a fallen and deceitful world. His consciousness of that emblematic fact accounts for what Peter Gay has called, not quite accurately, the prevailing sadness of his book.[11] Bradford's vision is a sad one, but its reflection in the incidents he selects and in his tone is rather poignant than simply sad. There is regret and nostalgia even in the opening pages, where John Foxe's image of a period of trial and travail is first recalled. In such a world, Bradford truly cares. That is what distinguishes *Of Plymouth Plantation* from most other equally important political and historical documents: it is a book of love.

Bradford writes as the father of his small community. He is protective of it, jealous for its safety and for its privileges. Americans speak of their revolutionary heroes as "Founding Fathers," but those good men had much less fatherliness about them than had Bradford. In fact, they repudiated that quality intentionally, creating a depersonalized system of laws abstract, efficient, and just that had at its base the equality of all men before it. There would be no difference of persons before that system, for Americans had learned by 1776 that a government based solely on the goodwill of its governors could produce tyranny as readily as public good. Experience had taught Bradford differently, however. His models had been the good pastor in Holland, John Robinson, and his own close friend, almost a father to him, William Brewster. Beyond them, of course, his examples were Moses and the God of Israel Himself. Neither Miles Standish, Thomas Prence, nor Edward Winslow, Bradford's most competent companions, could have fulfilled that role so competently as Bradford.

His first recorded act as governor was the performance of a civil marriage ceremony. Other duties, particularly the punishment and execution of criminals, were not so happy, but Bradford carried them out dutifully and not without relish. He writes at large about Thomas Morton who established a riotous outpost called Merry-Mount, setting up a Maypole and consorting with Indians in a fashion quite unsuited to the social morality of the Plymouth Pilgrims. Bradford squashed that business with all the rigor one commonly ascribes to Puritans. His reason for doing so is that the colony was threatened by Morton's indiscriminate trading of spirits and guns to the Indians. The righteousness of his explanation is compelling; nonetheless, one wonders how much the moral repugnance Bradford clearly felt for Morton determined his policy. Was it really guns and liquor that threatened Bradford? Or the dancing and singing and the relatively successful fur-trading that led to Morton's banishment? Likewise with the hypocritical minister John Lyford. Shortly after his arrival, Lyford was detected spreading malicious rumors about the Pilgrims, especially their religious practices. His letters to England, designed certainly to damage the Pilgrim efforts, were intercepted at sea by Bradford, and became the grounds for a successful trial in which Lyford was severely censured. Lyford's tearful repentance lasted no more than a couple of months, however, and he was soon sent packing to Salem and then to Virginia where he died. As much as his political and religious attacks may have been the direct cause of his dismissal from Plymouth, Lyford's scandalous sexual adventures become a clear part of the justification, in Bradford's telling, of the ungenerous treatment he received from the governor.

To Bradford, people such as Morton and Lyford are not equal to others. They are less than men, beastly in their practices, and not deserving of the same consideration accorded by government to those of the better sort. But Bradford is not content with his own satisfaction regarding their treatment; he wants posterity to know and to justify his actions as well. By preserving the relevant documents, notes, and letters, as well as by incorporating some of them in the history itself, he bears witness to the American respect for the written word and to the ancient English sense of fair play. Even before leaving the *Mayflower,* this band of Pilgrims, in the face of "discontented and mutinous speeches," had bound themselves by a written agreement into a "Civil Body Politic," expressing thereby a rather surprising faith in the efficacy of written agreements among men.

Bradford remarked on the theoretical aspect of such contracts early in the book. The Pilgrims had negotiated for King James's approval of their venture, though not all of them thought the King's seal very reliable, pointing out that "if afterwards there should be a purpose or desire to wrong them, though they had a seal as broad as the house floor it would not serve the turn; for there would be means enow found to recall or reverse it. Seeing therefore the course was probable, they must rest herein on God's providence as they had done in other things" (pp. 30–31). That ultimate reliance on God's favor marks all their dealings among themselves. Sometimes, as with the English who raised the money for their initial voyage, their agents Robert Cushman and Isaac Allerton, their main source of supply, Captain Thomas Weston, and finally, most distressing, their treasurer, James Sherley, they were sadly taken advantage of and their written agreements did not "serve the turn." Other times the issue seemed to warrant the trust these men put in their written agreements. The Mayflower Compact, as it is commonly known, was one such.

In the many such documents that lard this narrative, one cannot help but be impressed with the general forthrightness and fair-mindedness of the Pilgrims, much of it a reflection of Bradford's own temper. His policy, as these documents reveal it, is sage rather than shrewd. He is not a sharp dealer, even when he confesses to have kept some matters from the knowledge of the people he governed. One sees the steady accumulation of experience in his practical solutions to a variety of ticklish diplomatic problems, and discovers that years of exile have given him insight into the ways of communities as well as individuals. The common sharing of production and goods, an experiment forced upon the settlers in the very beginning in Plymouth, failed because it created suspicion among the participants and offered no incentive to individual effort. He is pleased therefore to vindicate his successful capitalistic solution, commenting, "The experience that was had in this common course and condition, tried sundry years and that amongst godly and sober men, may well evince the vanity of that conceit of Plato's and other ancients applauded by some of later times; that the taking away of property and bringing in community into a commonwealth would make them happy and flourishing; as if they were wiser than God" (pp. 120–121). There is a sentiment in that final remark that even modern Americans are reluctant to surrender.

I have suggested that with the arrival of the Massachusetts Bay settlement in 1630, the year Bradford began *Of Plymouth Plantation,* he wrote with a sense of accomplishment, of something finished. His annals continued regularly until 1646, after which he simply recorded two dates, 1647 and 1648, without comment. Following 1630 the story of his colony is even more than earlier a series of troubles. Prosperity had brought more settlers, and with them an economy and civil order much more complex to deal with. Competition for land and for trade increased sharply, and Plymouth was frequently the loser. Indian resentment of the invasion of their lands heightened, and while the Pequod uprising of 1637 was dealt with summarily by the combined colonial forces, the threat of war against the powerful Narragansetts in 1645 was only narrowly averted. The success of the English of Massachusetts Bay and the formation in 1643 of a confederation of New England colonies gave Plymouth additional security, but only at the cost of its own autonomy. Like a father grown old, Bradford saw his family slipping away from him. Some, like William Brewster, by death, others for "better accommodations," and some inexplicably like the sometime Governor Edward Winslow, whose trip to England on behalf of Plymouth marks the final comment in Bradford's book: "he was detained longer than was expected, and afterwards fell into other employments there; so as he hath now been absent this four years, which hath been much to the weakening of this government, without whose consent he took these employments upon him."

If the words are regretful, they are not bitter. They were added four years after Bradford stopped his regular entries, and indicate that the aging governor reviewed his book from time to time. At the death of William Brewster he had written, "I should say something of his life, if to say a little were not worse than to be silent." He then briefly memorialized his friend and teacher. But now, with the departure of Winslow, silence wins. There is pathos in that silence, but it would be an exaggeration to call it tragic, for Bradford knew from the beginning of the book that the Mayflower Pilgrims "should be but even as stepping-stones unto others for the performing of so great a work" (p. 25). If his conviction taught him that Pilgrims were spiritually and morally superior because God had so graced them with his favor, it also gave him a yielding and submissive temper to the inevitability not of fate or time, but of God's will, and that kind of submission is heroic.

There is a final symbolic appropriateness that Bradford would have appreciated in the fate of the book itself. After his death in 1657, the manuscript circulated among historians until the period of the American Revolution, when it disappeared, just at the time many of Bradford's suppositions about the nature of God, man, society, and government were most violently rejected. The book was not rediscovered until 1855, when it was found in the Bishop of London's Fulham Palace and printed in full for the first time in 1856, almost two hundred years after its author's death and upon the eve of the great American Civil War. That

2 BENJAMIN FRANKLIN: *AUTOBIOGRAPHY*

Ralph L. Ketcham

Benjamin Franklin's *Autobiography* is in one obvious sense an unfinished work; it does not include the last thirty years of his life when in England, France, and America he earned fame as a statesman and diplomat. It thus has nothing to say about the American Revolution—just a few reflections on the relevance of early episodes of Franklin's life to that climactic event. Yet the life described, even including the portions Franklin wrote in 1771 while still a subject of George III, is profoundly revolutionary when viewed in the context of its time.

Had one charged Franklin during any part of his life covered in the *Autobiography* with being anything other than a loyal Englishman living in North America, he would have been both dumbfounded and insulted. His earliest boyhood memories were of the sense of salvation in New England at the glorious victories of *old* England over Louis XIV. Franklin thought of his voyages to England before 1776 as "going home," as did nearly all colonials during that period. When he was a bookseller in Philadelphia he took pride in the eager market for Pope, Addison, and other English writers, who were more admired there, Franklin thought, than in London itself. In 1751, he wrote of the British Empire as an harmonious family, growing in power, prosperity, and freedom on both sides of the Atlantic. He grieved at Braddock's defeat before Fort Duquesne and gloried in Wolfe's victory at Quebec as much as William Pitt himself. During the 1760's Franklin praised the British Empire as "the greatest political structure human wisdom ever yet erected," and wrote that in England there were "in almost every neighborhood, more sensible, virtuous, and elegant Minds than we [in America] can collect in ranging 100 Leagues in our vast Forests." The revolution in loyalty, the first conscious phase of the American Revolution, came very gradually for him as English venality, arrogance, and narrow-mindedness loomed ever larger in his mind. Finally, in 1775, he declared from London that "the extream corruption prevalent among all Orders of Men in this old rotten State" was so great that he could not "but apprehend more Mischief than Benefit from a closer Union" between colonies and mother country. It was this change that caused John Adams to declare that the important American Revolution, the revolution in the hearts and minds of the people, took place before 1776, and before a shot had been exchanged between redcoats and continentals.

Equally missing from Franklin's *Autobiography* are more than fleeting glimpses of the second phase of the American Revolution, that in national purpose, which had its culmination in the Declaration of Independence, in the Federal Constitution, and in the rival visions of Jefferson and Hamilton of national growth. Franklin's plan at Albany in 1754 for a partially self-governing union of the colonies, his resistance to proprietary prerogative in Pennsylvania, and his stunned objection in London in 1757 to Lord Granville's doctrine that "the King is the legislator for the Colonies," all described in the *Autobiography,* foreshadow the revolutionary purposes that preoccupied the country in 1776 and afterward; but generally in the *Autobiography* Franklin accepts political principles, structures of government, and even national goals long familiar to him as a Briton. Like most of his revolutionary colleagues, Franklin gave serious attention to reformulations of national purpose only in 1775 when he came "home" (by then meaning North America) bent on independence. His work on the Pennsylvania and Federal constitutions, and his defenses of them, were likewise declarations of purpose, as were his statements from France of the foreign policy guidelines of the new nation. The importance of this phase was so obvious to participant and observer alike that, then and ever since, these formal, structural acts have seemed to embody the Revolution by themselves.

Less apparent, however, and initially at least, less self-

21

conscious, was the need for a new sense of national identity and character. What special qualities would distinguish the citizens of the United States? What would be the habits and attitudes and characteristics of its people? What would they epitomize or stand for in the world? Under the influence of Montesquieu, the Abbé du Bois, and others, the eighteenth century placed great emphasis on delineating national character. The Spanish, for example, were said to be brave, mystical, and cruel; the English practical, phlegmatic shopkeepers; and the French refined, artistic, and immoral. Each nation was thought to have a special significance, a character, evident in its history, the impression made on travelers, its climate, and in the features of its land. Most nations possessed a long, mysterious past from which its character had simply come into being. The new United States, on the other hand, could see its origins clearly and explicitly. Moreover, its people were largely British with minorities of Germans, Dutch, French, and others in some of the provinces. Yet, in curious, unself-conscious ways these transplanted Europeans, even in early colonial days, seemed somehow a different breed of men. The open land, the fact of migration across the Atlantic, the impulse to leave home, *or something,* had given them a new character. As the former colonists achieved independence they joined with Europeans in asking, with increasing insistence and sophistication, Crèvecoeur's famous question: "What then is the American, this new man?" Franklin's *Autobiography,* more than any other work, answered this question and thus helped to explain and ultimately to further define the revolutionary elements in the national character.

Franklin's Quaker friend, Abel James, found the rough manuscript of the first part of the *Autobiography* among Franklin's papers, scattered by British troops during the Revolution. He read it with "great Joy," he said, and urged Franklin to finish "so pleasing and profitable a work, . . . which would be useful and entertaining not only to a few, but to millions." Benjamin Vaughn, a young English friend, thought the manuscript revealed "the internal circumstances [of America] . . . the manners and situation of *a rising* people," and therefore would offer a clear picture of the new ways of the New World. Men on both sides of the Atlantic sought to know what life was, or might be like, in the new United States. And Franklin's life in Boston and Philadelphia during his first fifty years seemed somehow to bear a remarkable stamp, to inaugurate a new epoch in human history. It embodied the characteristics Franklin himself explained in 1782 would be useful "to those who would remove to America." When published, Franklin's *Autobiography* became at once a model and an inspiration for young men anxious to achieve the new way of life. Thomas Mellon, Irish immigrant and founder of the great banking dynasty, read the *Autobiography* in 1827 on the meager acres worked by his father in western Pennsylvania. It was, he later wrote, "the turning point in my life." For Jared Sparks, growing up on a Connecticut farm, the *Autobiography* "first aroused my mental energies . . . prompted me to resolutions, and . . . taught me that circumstances have not a sovereign control over the mind," views that led Sparks to a career as an author and president of Harvard College. A leading Florentine printer once explained that "at the age of 35 I was a lost man. . . . I read again and again the *Autobiography* of Franklin, and became enamored of his ideas and principles to such a degree that to them I ascribe my moral regeneration. . . . Now at the age of fifty-one, I am healthy, cheerful and rich." Franklin's *Autobiography*, translated into dozens of languages and reprinted hundreds of times, more than any other document revealed and propagated the new character which alone could give full meaning to the American Revolution.

The revolutionary significance of the *Autobiography* is implicit in its nature and style. The autobiographical form was popular in the eighteenth century, but the subjects were principally military exploits, court intrigue, and spiritual quests. Elizabethan sea dogs or generals of the War of the Spanish Succession wrote of strenuous campaigns, grand strategy, and gory battles. The memoirs of Louis XIV's great commander, the Prince of Condé, for example, thrilled thousands in Europe and America. Also widely read were the "inside stories" of the nefarious, clandestine doings of the great European courts. The memoirs of the Cardinal De Retz, telling of the Machiavellian intrigues of French government during Louis XIV's minority and of the cabal behind the election of a Pope, captivated a wide audience.

Even more titillating were personal accounts of the boudoir escapades of noblemen and their mistresses. Nell Gwyn, Madame Pompadour, and even the fictitious Fanny Hill were legends if not idols in their day. More edifying but no less marvelous were the autobiographies of spiritual pilgrimage—graphic accounts like those of Loyola, John Bunyan, and the Quaker George Fox. Their mystical experiences and miraculous deliverances filled readers with awe and wonder.

Franklin's story, on the other hand, dealt with no heroics in the conventional sense, spilled no blood, told of no backstair trysts, and chronicled no mysterious path to sainthood. Rather than telling of a courtly world foreign and remote to most men, Franklin described a life begun in a humble station easily recognized by millions, not hundreds. Furthermore, he rose not by superhuman strength, seductive liaison, or even amazing grace, but by application of character traits accessible to anyone. His *Autobiography* is deliberately plain and homely. The picture throughout is not that of events most men could know only from the outside by fantasy, but of a world familiar to them and with which they could readily identify. His language, moreover, suited the life he described, simple, direct, down-to-earth, and vernacular. Though Franklin's story is in its own way marvelous and majestic, like any account of human dignity and potentiality, it nonetheless meets its reader on his own ground, telling him on every page that what the author had done anyone else might do by forming the habits he describes. If life in the new world was indeed like this, then a most profound revolution had taken place that somehow depreciated every courtly life story ever told.

Critics of Franklin's *Autobiography,* and of life lived according to "Poor Richard's tags" as D. H. Lawrence put it, often find it mundane, unaesthetic, and bourgeoise. In one sense, though, they miss the point that Franklin intended to emphasize precisely those qualities as most likely to show the common man, mired in his workaday world, the way to prosperity and dignity. The *Autobiography* meant to teach practical first steps and then—in describing Franklin's retirement from business at age forty-two, devotion to science and literature, and long service to the public —to indicate the vast potentiality of the *means* exemplified by Poor Richard. Despite the almost scheming calculus of Franklin's little dots-in-squares method of achieving virtue, and even its ultimately shallow assumptions about human nature, the overall quality of the life described in the *Autobiography* is neither mean, ignoble, nor insensitive. It was to the mass of men, uplifting, challenging, relevant, and therefore revolutionary.

The youthful reading Franklin records in the *Autobiography* as influential further suggests both the parts of Western culture that formed his character and their special meaning in the new world. Bunyan's *Pilgrim's Progress,* for example, despite Franklin's early repudiation of Puritan theology, was for him a graphic dramatization of the habits and qualities that made life meaningful and good, that would serve an earnest man in a secular as well as a religious pilgrimage. Vanity, sloth, dissipation, timorousness, and hypocrisy were to be shunned, while intrepidity, honesty, prudence, and charity were worthy. From Plutarch's *Lives* Franklin gleaned more lessons about virtuous character. In addition to extolling such personal earnestness as Demosthenes' learning to speak with pebbles in his mouth to cure stuttering, or shouting while running uphill to give volume to his voice, Plutarch gave greatest praise to men who served the public well. Pericles, Publicola, Fabius Maximus, and Cicero, lawgivers and builders of the commonweal, were held up as model leaders. Alexander the Great and Julius Caesar, though praised for their courage and vigorous leadership, were condemned finally for becoming tyrants who deluged the world in blood. In remembering Bunyan and Plutarch as he did, Franklin took from his heritage precepts that had a special meaning in the new nation he would one day help found.

Of more particular relevance were works by Daniel Defoe and Cotton Mather on methods of community self-improvement. Living in London and embodying the ebullient bourgeois spirit at its best, Defoe wrote an *Essay upon Projects* to offer practical ways to cure social problems. Cooperative effort and simple organization could save sailors' widows from destitution, make English roads the best in the world, and take money squandered on beer to provide old-age security. Defoe, in many respects an English Franklin in background, talents, and outlook, assumed always that reason and common sense could serve community needs. Cotton Mather's *Essays to do Good* applied Defoe's methods to encourage habits of piety and altruism in small neighborhood groups. Young men, by associating together, concerning themselves with each other's weaknesses and problems, accepting responsibility for community welfare, and resolving to practice Christian charity, could improve their own lives and induce remarkable social progress.

As Franklin read the new, rational thought of his day, he found further encouragement to come to grips with the world in which he lived. Locke's empirical philosophy, insisting that each man was the product of his sense impressions and therefore a unique individual responding to the world around him, heightened Franklin's interest in his environment. Locke's belief that education should be personal, practical, and down-to-earth and his insistence that the unique character of each man's spiritual experience made religious toleration not only right but necessary for social peace became cornerstones of Franklin's own philosophy. Then, when he read *The Spectator,* described in the *Autobiography* as so influential, his world-view came into focus. Seeking to temper Puritan fanaticism with Augustan urbanity and to root out Restoration degeneracy with a new moral earnestness, *The Spectator* seemed to tell Franklin that he could have the best of his father's world and Locke's as well, joined in a way of life both suited to him temperamentally and of clear meaning as he landed penniless on Market Street wharf in Philadelphia. The traditions and philosophy of the Old World, sifted and blended in Franklin's creative mind and tempered by the unsettled opportunities of the New World, had achieved a new synthesis and a new relevance. Though the *Autobiography* underscores Franklin's connection with the past, it dramatizes as well new implications and revolutionary projections. Unself-consciously, Franklin had acquired a character so pregnant with meaning that in old age it called for a wholly novel autobiography in both style and content.

When Franklin began his career as a printer, the lessons of Defoe and Mather were immediately useful. Furthermore, Philadelphia, a growing city less than fifty years old, stood ready to be guided and organized by eager, able young men. The Junto, Franklin's club of young tradesmen, did exactly what Defoe and

Mather suggested, and soon its members had not only greatly improved their own fortunes but had provided Philadelphia with an array of useful institutions: a lending library, a fire company, a learned society, a college, an insurance company, a hospital, and an efficient city watch. Though the direct, visible results were impressive in their own right, the implications in personal terms were even more remarkable and portentous. Somehow the environment of the New World and the enterprising qualities Franklin had come to exemplify, when brought together, created unprecedented prospects. Social problems long thought insoluble suddenly seemed to yield to amazingly simple stratagems. Books could be made available to thousands, medical care furnished to all, and education made relevant to community needs. Fire loss, fear on the streets, and death by plague could be sharply reduced, apparently, by human effort and organization. Set beside fatalistic bromides hallowed from time immemorial about the grim and tenuous prospects of human life, Franklin's story not only underscored the outlook Defoe had expressed in London, but it showed *how* it could be made a reality. This transforming possibility, made real and believable in a concrete example, again revealed that life in the New World had a compelling, distinct character.

Another way in which Franklin's *Autobiography* conveyed its sense of relevance to the common man was in its easy movement from the personal to the social to the political. Great questions of public affairs, instead of appearing in a separate realm remote and inaccessible to most men, are dealt with through the skills and attitudes Franklin had taught common men how to achieve. Values impressed upon Franklin in his youth proved highly valuable as he began his ascent in life. The sober, honest, industrious ways of his father and of the Puritan catechisms were just the qualities a tradesman needed to prosper. Poor Richard's aphorisms and little schemes, like the plan for virtue, were practical, meaningful advice for rising young men. This obvious connection was the compelling message of Franklin's life story. Then, as Franklin looked beyond his own affairs, and considered community problems with like-minded men, it seemed apparent that the same virtues, practiced cooperatively, were exactly the prescription needed. There is nothing the least bit mysterious or miraculous about the Junto projects. Franklin's tone throughout emphasizes how obvious and simple all the enterprises were. Witness, for example, the manifest benefits of systematic, cooperative efforts to keep the streets clean or to maintain a sober, zealous night watch.

Part of the ease of success, of course, arose from the relative absence in a new city of the ancient prerogatives and vested interests that always oppose innovations. No foot-dragging guilds of firemen or academicians were there to resist Franklin's plans for a fire company or a college. He could succeed as a printer, and even expand his business the length of the Atlantic coast, because monopoly franchises or other hoary devices to keep out newcomers were not yet generally established. Everywhere Franklin and his friends turned their restless energy they found opportunity rather than opposition. Comparison with Defoe is instructive. He as much exemplified the enterprising spirit as Franklin, had at least as much originality in proposing projects, and was the more skillful writer, but London confronted him at every turn with immovable establishments. The very nature of the New World itself, unformed, indeterminate, and beckoning, encouraged ideas to become realities.

Franklin's gradual, unpremeditated departure into politics was a simple extension of his personal and community activities. He became public printer and clerk of the Pennsylvania Assembly to advance his business. Then, as described so graphically in the *Autobiography*, he organized a militia in a Quaker province. He was unimpressed with pacifist dogma and felt that sharing the burden of self-defense had obvious utility: it would, probably with little bloodshed, keep French or Spanish warships from destroying Philadelphia. Then, he easily gained a seat in the Assembly in order to further the plans for the hospital and academy by attracting public support and funds. His intention was straightforward: to use the government of the province itself, as the most broadly effective agency, for promoting institutions of public benefit. That, after all, he had learned from Locke and others, was the only legitimate purpose of government.

This laid the groundwork for Franklin's opposition to proprietary privileges and ultimately set him on the course to political revolution. In entering politics, Franklin had no thought, of course, of resisting the mother country, but the *Autobiography* reveals that the habits and values he had acquired living in the New World were not always going to suit the authorities. The governor of Pennsylvania could not understand why Franklin sided with "these damned Quakers" when the proprietor was perfectly willing to give him a lucrative office in return for his support. To Franklin it was equally unthinkable to turn against a group he thought had given Pennsylvania "good and useful" government. Having in mind privileges common in Europe, the proprietors sought unashamedly to exempt their vast lands in Pennsylvania from taxation. Franklin thought it "incredible meanness" for them to place the whole burden of defense on smaller landholders. Franklin told another governor who tried to bribe him that he would support zealously measures for "the Good of the People," without sweeteners, but that otherwise he would have to oppose whatever the rewards or inducements. Franklin and a British commander in North America, Lord Loudoun, found themselves in a hopeless misunderstanding when Loudoun insisted that of course Franklin was profiteering on war supplies like everyone else in His Majesty's service. For Franklin, simple precepts and habits of life were beginning to have fateful implications for the very nature of the British Empire. There is no more instructive insight into the origins of the American Revolution than the contrasts in Franklin's *Autobiography,* in accounts set side by side, between the *means* of his rise to fame and prosperity, and the *means* proprietary governors and Royal commanders assumed would be used to manage the public business.

Though it took Franklin twenty years or more (until 1776) to realize the ultimate meaning of these impasses with proprietary and royal officials, he had in fact been leading a revolutionary life almost from the moment of his birth. The great public deeds of Franklin's later life, not described in his *Autobiography,* fulfill the commitment and promise of his first half-century. His indignation at Lord North's highhandedness would be expected from one who had left Boston rather than suffer the petty tyranny of a brother. His tactical skill in diplomatic negotiations in Paris would not have surprised Philadelphia neighbors who had seen him carry through a dozen civic projects. Marvelously effective and witty essays defending American rights were second nature to Poor Richard, who had learned from boyhood how to use words to propound plain precepts of justice and common sense. A full understanding of the life-style of Franklin's first fifty years, the point of the *Autobiography,* makes the events of 1763–1789 much less startling than they appear otherwise. Once the life Franklin had lived in Boston and Philadelphia was a reality, not only for him but less only in degree for thousands of men, revolt against hereditary privilege and the impulse to found a new nation were not only possible but probably inevitable.

The very character of the *Autobiography* itself, a perfectly credible, dramatically simple life story, enhanced its meaning, of course, beyond anything a mere abstract statement of revolutionary principles could do. He had been reared in a family whose status and material well-being, at least, was indistinguishable from the common lot. In Philadelphia he was a runaway of unknown origin who nonetheless found the resources within himself, and a sufficiently open society, to make a decisive impact. The confidence this experience produced and the way of life thus implanted were the prime revolutionary forces behind both the dramatic events of 1776 and the only slowly realized identity of the new nation thus created.

As American writers struggled self-consciously to bring into being a national literature and to convey to the world a sense of the national character, the popularity of Franklin's *Autobiography* played a key role. Reading it, the world, and Americans themselves, sensed the answer to Crèvecoeur's question, "What is an American?" In a twinkling, apparently timeless and eternal patterns of life seemed outmoded. If one wanted to know what Americans were like, what their national aspirations were, one had but to read Franklin's *Autobiography.* Utterly swept aside were dynastic or mystical conceptions of national purpose. America's purpose was to nourish lives like Franklin's, and her character was that embodied in his life story. Systems of government and foreign policy, as Franklin showed in the last fifteen years of his life, were to be framed to serve that purpose and that character. The measure of the United States' uniqueness was the contrast between his life-style and that prevalent in the rest of the world. The mission of America was to offer it as an example to mankind. Though critics at home and abroad, from Mark Twain to D. H. Lawrence, would expose scathingly the limitations of this way of life (or at least the limitations of their caricatures of it), it has remained worthy and compelling to millions. It has been as well a persistent reminder, whenever American society tends to stratify and stagnate and vulgarize, of what is being lost or betrayed.

In a world full of new nations, Franklin's *Autobiography* has meaning not only to remind his own country of its juster purposes, but to suggest elements of nationality relevant anywhere. Though physically Franklin's world has disappeared and, indeed, in many parts of the globe it never existed, the wider meaning of his life story can nevertheless be projected. It is a reminder that personal qualities, the character of the people, must somehow underlie the more conscious, formal aspects of nation-building. It also offers a pattern not confined, theoretically at least, within national boundaries. Franklin's way of life does not exclude Englishmen or Japanese any more than many traditions and insights of other cultures, East and West, exclude Americans. In fact, the warm reception of the *Autobiography* all over the world is evidence that other ways of life, such as that contained, for example, in the Confucian ethic, have long embodied some values similar to Franklin's. His *Autobiography* urges, then, that nations, including Franklin's own, conceive of themselves in terms of the everyday lives of their citizens and that they shun metaphysical, overweening, or imperial notions of their destiny.

MICHEL-GUILLAUME ST. JEAN DE CRÈVECOEUR:
3 *LETTERS FROM AN AMERICAN FARMER*

Russel B. Nye

America existed as a state of mind long before it separated from Europe by act of revolution. Thomas More's *Utopia,* in 1515, only a few years after Columbus' first voyage, held out the promise of this bright, fresh world across the sea. The accounts of Renaissance explorers encouraged the growth of the myth of America as a land of pearls and plenty where, as the first English visitors to the Carolinas wrote, a simple primitive people lived happily "after the manner of the golden age." Michael Drayton, Shakespeare's contemporary, his imagination touched by the Virginia Company's expedition of 1606, spoke of the new colony as "Earth's only Paradise"; to John Donne, preaching on the meaning of English settlement in America, it was a land destined to be put "to great uses," where future generations might see "the growth thereof to perfection." The settlers who followed the explorers found nothing like this, of course, but the myth persisted. Bishop Berkeley, nearly a century after the first settlement, could still speak of America as that "happy clime . . . , the seat of innocence, where nature guides and virtue rules."

To this myth the Age of Reason added another—the myth of America as Hope, of man's opportunity to escape for once and all the errors of a corrupt, and weary Old World. The Calvinist settlers of New England saw America as a Land of Canaan, to which God directed them as He once directed the Children of Israel. Edward Johnson, who came to Massachusetts with the first wave of settlers in 1630, believed it "the place where the Lord will create a new Heaven, and a new Earth, new Churches, and a new Commonwealth altogether." America represented to these men a new Eden wherein Adam could have his second chance; subsequent generations cherished and perpetuated the hope that it might be so, come the millennium. By the time of the American Revolution, British and French philosophers (especially the French) had constructed a model of what an ideally rational society ought to be. America furnished an opportunity both to construct and to test it against actuality. Locke's remark, "In the beginning all the world was America," summarized the Enlightenment's faith that man now might build, in this new and uncontaminated environment, the kind of society he should have made in the beginning. The United States, then, seemed to provide a place where what Europe had failed to do might still be done.

These two myths, pervasive and persistent, of America as Paradise and America as Hope had already combined to control Europe's thinking about the New World when Michel-Guillaume Jean de Crèvecoeur, soon to become famous as "The American Farmer," settled in Orange County, New York, then a British North American colony. Crèvecoeur was born at Caen, in Normandy, in 1735. At sixteen he was sent to England, where he spent six years in school and acquired a deep interest in North America. He arrived in Canada about 1754 as a lieutenant in the French army, specializing in cartography. He traveled through the Great Lakes country, fought at the Battle of Quebec in 1759, and then came to the American colonies. Making his way through Pennsylvania and New York as a merchant and surveyor, he took out New York citizenship in 1765, adopting the Anglicized name of John Hector St. John. Four years later he married Mehitabel Tippet, the daughter of a Yonkers merchant, bought a farm in Orange County, and settled down to the management of his estate.

The memory of "the sweet and pleasant days" of the next ten years spent at his farm, "Pine Hill," never left him. Here Crèvecoeur's three children were born, and here he wrote the essays which were to make up *Letters From an American Farmer.* "I never was but a simple surveyor of lands, a cultivator of my own grounds, or a wanderer through the forests of the country," he told the Duke de la Rochefoucauld, which was true after a fashion, except that as a French aristocrat with a wealthy wife and prosperous estate he was not quite the simple, modest farmer he pretended to be.

The revolutionary controversy, however, soon thrust itself into his rural retreat. Though Crèvecoeur had certain reservations about revolutionary agitators who, he said, were "perpetually bawling about liberty without knowing what it was," he preferred not to take sides, arousing the enmity of Tory and radical alike once the fighting broke out. His farm was twice overrun by troops and by 1780 the hostility of his neighbors made his position in the community untenable. He obtained British permission to sail from New York to London in 1780, carrying with him a small trunk of manuscripts. However, he was detained as a spy, imprisoned for three months, and finally allowed to depart late that year. He sold his manuscripts for thirty guineas to a London publisher who in 1782 brought out his book (dedicated to the French philosopher Raynal) under the title *Letters From an American Farmer, describing certain Provincial Situations, Manners, and Customs, and Conveying some idea of the state of the People of North America: written to a Friend in England, by J. Hector St. John.*[1]

Crèvecoeur's *Letters* was an immediate success in London and on the Continent, and he was welcomed into the sophisticated salons of Paris as a celebrity. The Rousseauistic attitudes expressed in his book appealed to the popular fancy, while his account of his idyllic pastoral existence at Pine Hill seemed the perfect illustration of physiocracy in practice. The French government sent him back to New York as consul general in 1783, after the peace, to find his wife dead, his home burned in an Indian raid, and his children in the hands of a kindly stranger in Boston. Picking up the pieces of his life, Crèvecoeur stayed in New York for seven years, doing much to keep Franco-American friendship alive during the difficult period of postwar diplomacy. "There is nobody who understands more perfectly the interests of the two countries," said Jefferson's secretary, William Short, "as they relate to each other, and none more zealous to promote them mutually." He helped to establish a commercial shipping service between New York and Lorient, wrote for the press in the United States and France, and took great interest in scientific agriculture, an interest he shared with Jefferson. He introduced new methods of potato culture into Normandy and alfalfa into the United States, tested seeds, experimented with crops, and was elected both to the Société Royale d'Agriculture and the American Philosophical Society. He became close friends with Washington, Franklin, and especially with Thomas Jefferson, who attended his daughter's wedding. In 1790 he returned in ill-health to France and his estate near Rouen, occupying his leisure with a three-volume account of his American travels, published in 1801 as *Voyages in Upper Pennsylvania and New York State*. Continued illness forced him into retirement, and he died in 1813.

Crèvecoeur's *Letters*, which are of course really essays, were cast in the popular epistolary form of eighteenth-century fiction, no doubt because he could by this stratagem both generalize and personalize his comments on his American experience. The letters are presumably written by an American farmer named James, in response to a series of questions put to him by a "Mr. F. B.," a cultured English visitor who wishes to learn more of America.[2] James is third-generation American, an honest, unassuming yeoman of admittedly "limited power of mind," but possessed of "a tolerable share of sense . . . , some perspicacity, a warmth of imagination, *and* a tender and well-meaning heart." Although he describes himself as "neither philosopher, politician, divine, or naturalist," James, serving as Crèvecoeur's *persona,* deals in ideas far from simple and can write, on occasion, sophisticated, Gallic-flavored prose. Actually, beyond the first three letters the question-and-answer device begins to fade, until, by Letter V, James is overtly replaced by the author. It is not until the last letter that Crèvecoeur once more takes up the mask of "James the Farmer."

The twelve *Letters* vary widely in length and organization, reflecting what must have been some hasty editorial decisions by Crèvecoeur and his London publisher. Letter I, after introducing the characters and situation, responds to "Mr. F. B.'s" implied question, "What is American life like?" James's description coincides precisely with what the Enlightenment expected it to be—a paradisiacal life of reason, close to nature, orderly, peaceful, healthy, prosperous. What James emphasizes as the virtues of American society are in exact contrast to European vices—a government of "simple and just laws" which demands little of the "industrious farmer," who in turn makes few demands upon it. "Here we have had no war to desolate our fields," writes James in obvious reference to Europe. "Our religion does not oppress the cultivators; we are strangers to those feudal institutions which have enslaved so many." America, he explains, is a land of unparalleled opportunity, providing a "great field of action" for the "energy of future generations."

The second letter is a reply to the question, "What is the life of an American farmer like, in comparison to that of a European?" The chief difference, James finds, is the American's independence. "The instant I enter my land," he writes, "the bright idea of prosperity, of exclusive right, of independence, exalts my mind." The American owns his land, in fee simple and outright, under a government whose power over him is severely limited. The law in America, explains James, "is to me precisely what I am in my barnyard, a bridle and check to prevent the strong and greedy from oppressing the weak." He then proceeds to draw in greater detail the portrait of an emergent agrarian democracy, comprised of a "people of cultivators . . . , possessing freedom of action and freedom of thought" under a "substantial system of felicity." The name "American," he concludes, "is the most fortunate that any man can possess. . . . Thank God my lot is to be an American farmer, instead of a Russian boor, or an Hungarian peasant."

Letter III, in answer to the question, "What is an American?" is the longest and most complex, since this is not a question to be answered easily. Effusive, rambling, and repetitive, it is nonetheless the most thoroughly considered of all the essays and Crève-coeur's most important statement. It has three general concerns: first, it explores the differences between American and European society; second, it analyzes American regional groupings, recognizing for probably the first time the unique significance of the American frontier; and third, it interprets the process of assimilation by which the European becomes "this new man," an American.

In the first instance, Crèvecoeur—through James—explains that American society is energetic, dynamic, "animated with the spirit of an industry which is unfettered and unrestrained, because each person works for himself." It is also "a modern society," built of new materials on a new continent. Not for the New World is the spectacle of "great lords who possess every thing, and a herd of people who have nothing"; instead Americans are a people "of middle means . . . , of decent competence," united "under the silken bands of a mild government . . . , possessors of the soil they cultivate, members of the government they obey, and the framers of their own laws." Theirs is, in fine, a society in which "man is as free as he ought to be . . . , the most perfect society in the world."

While it "does not afford that variety of tinges and gradations which may be observed in Europe," American society, Crèvecoeur explains, has differences of its own kind. There are distinguishable types of Americans because different environments produce different men. "Men are like plants," he continues (in an extended botanical metaphor far too sophisticated for James), which differ among themselves "from the peculiar soil and exposition in which they grow." An American environment, therefore, produces Americans whose distinctive nature derives from "the air we breathe, the climate we inhabit, the government we obey, the system of religion we possess, and the nature of our employment." Seacoast society, he explains, has bred "a bold and enterprising class" of sailors, merchants, and city dwellers— aggressive, cosmopolitan, resourceful, even obstinate. The next line of settlement has produced farmers, "independent freeholders" such as James himself. Beyond them, at the "extended line of frontiers," are the lawless, violent, improvident frontiersmen, those "off-casts" of society—a "mongrel breed, half-civilized, half-savage," Crèvecoeur calls them—who in making the first penetration of the wilderness are themselves touched by its wildness. Yet it is these "ferocious, gloomy, licentious" people, ironically, who provide the necessary first step toward the evolution of the stable, agrarian society which follows them. They open the path for "the arrival of a second and better class, the true American freeholders . . . , more industrious people who will finish their improvements, convert the loghouse into a convenient habitation, and . . . change in a few years that hitherto barbarous country into a fine fertile, well-regulated district."

But whatever may be the regional differences among Americans, they disappear as all are "melted into a new race of men." In a long and carefully organized passage in Letter III, Crèvecoeur details the psychological changes which turn Europeans into Americans. The immigrant comes, with Europe's past clinging to him, to a huge, lovely country, empty, open, quite unlike Europe "where every place is overstocked." "He no sooner breathes our air," writes James, "than he forms schemes and embarks on designs he never would have thought of in his own country." His first step, then, toward Americanization, is his rejection of Europe's "ancient prejudices and manners"; his next comes with his realization of the opportunities the country offers to him. "Has he a particular talent, or industry?" asks James. "He exerts it in order to procure a livelihood, and it succeeds." He finds independence, higher wages, plentiful food, and, most important of all, he "alters his scale . . . ; he now feels himself a man, because he is treated as such." He begins to think in different terms, American terms, since he has become "a new man, who acts upon new principles; he must therefore entertain new ideas and form new opinions."

So out of this "promiscuous breed," this "mixture of English, Scotch, Irish, French, Dutch, Germans and Swedes . . . , that race called Americans has risen." The change from European to American, as Crèvecoeur describes it, rests on that second chance, the opportunity to begin again, that lay at the center of the American myth. It is significant that the word "new" appears seventeen times in Letter III, often in company with such words as "metamorphosis," "regeneration," and "resurrection." These Americans, men born again in a New World Eden, Crèvecoeur sees as the hope of the world, "western pilgrims, who are carrying along with them that great mass of arts, sciences, vigour, and industry which began long since in the east; they will finish the circle . . . , and one day cause great changes in the world."

The theme of America as land of opportunity and hope winds through Letter III and imposes unity upon it. Crèvecoeur constantly emphasizes the openness of American society, its mobility and fluidity. There is in America, he repeats, quite literally "room for everybody"—thousands of acres of untaxed, uncultivated land, a prospect which exerted a tremendous appeal to land-hungry Europe. In this "great American asylum," the "poor of Europe" may find peace and prosperity; the good things of life, lacking for the mass of Europeans, are here for the working and asking. Here "servant may rise to master . . . , the slave of some despotic prince become a free man," writes James; he who has hitherto been a cipher now finds "for the first time in his life, he counts for something." To the industrious immigrant, America says,

> Welcome to my shores, distressed European; bless the hour in which thou didst see my verdant fields, my fair navigable rivers, and my green mountains! If thou wilt work, I have bread for thee; if thou wilt be honest, sober and industrious, I have greater rewards to confer on thee,—ease and independence. I will give thee fields to feed and cloathe thee; a comfortable fireside to sit by, and tell thy children by what means thou hast prospered; and a decent bed to repose on. I shall endow thee beside with the immunities of a freeman . . . Go thou and work and till; thou shalt prosper, provided thou be just, grateful, and industrious.

As illustration Crèvecoeur appends the tale of Andrew the Scotsman, who came to Pennsylvania with nothing, took up land on the frontier, and within a few years owned a house, six cows, two horses, and numerous tools and utensils, all worth six hundred forty dollars—ample proof of "the happy effects which constantly flow from sobriety and industry, when united with land and freedom."

The next two letters, IV and V, in which James reports on a trip to the island of Nantucket, mark a change to a much less emotional mood. In them he introduces another question into his discussion of the factors of success in the American system. The hardy Nantucketers live by fishing. If this society of fishermen, living on a barren, rocky island, is as open, happy, and stable as his own prosperous community of New York farmers, it will prove that the success of American society depends not upon occupational circumstances alone, but rather on underlying fundamental economic principles. This turns out to be the case, for in Nantucket James sees much the same elements at work as in New York; both societies place few restrictions on individual enterprise. Both allow free rein to that "native industry and perseverance common to all men" by providing for them "a system of rational laws founded on perfect freedom"; both give their citizens "the full rewards of their industry . . . , and allow them to enjoy the fruit of their labor . . . , unshackled and free." Though the term "laissez faire" was not yet current in American usage, it is this principle that James finds clearly to be the common component of success in both societies.

In Letters VI, VII, and VIII, which continue the survey of Nantucket and nearby Martha's Vineyard, Crèvecoeur virtually abandons the character of James. The letters take on the conventional mannerisms of the contemporary travel narrative, until in Letter IX Crèvecoeur abruptly shifts the locale to Charles-Town in Carolina, a commercialized, contentious, slaveholding society dominated by lawyers, planters, and merchants. (Significantly, there are no lawyers in James's community, only one in Nantucket, but a whole battery of them in Charles-Town.) His sketch of the city is not an attractive one. Built on slavery, to Crèvecoeur a system of "the most diffusive misery and wretchedness," Charles-Town appears to him a misdirection and perversion of the American ideal. There is nothing here of the balance and moderation of James's agrarian New York democracy, none of the industrious harmony of seafaring Nantucket.

The discussion of American society, initiated by "Mr. F. B.'s" first question, ends at Charles-Town. Crèvecoeur has presented to his readers three aspects of the developing American civilization: a rural agrarian democracy, independent and self-sufficient; a nonagricultural society with a complicated set of internal dependencies and set on a different economic base; and finally an urbanized, commercialized, dehumanized society, tainted with the evil of slavery, far removed from nature's sources and implicitly denying its values. His final comments are, he admits, "melancholy reflections" brought on by his sudden confrontation with a Negro slave left to die in a cage as punishment for disobedience; but if this is Crèvecoeur's view of America's ultimate destiny, it is a bitter and disillusioned one.

At this point the book reflects its hasty preparation for editing and publication, for Letters X and XI bear little relation to its major themes. Letter X contains some observations on snakes and hummingbirds for readers interested in natural history, including a highly colored account of a snake fight; Letter XI is an interpolated account of a Russian traveler's visit to the home of John Bartram, the Pennsylvania Quaker naturalist. But in Letter XII, the last, Crèvecoeur assumes once more the character of James, who returns to speak of his experiences in the American Revolution. How can a lover of peace and freedom choose, he asks through James, between such contending foes? "He who governs himself according to what he calls his principles," he ruefully concludes, "may be punished either by one party or the other for those very principles." So, discouraged and disillusioned with his own divided society, James decides to join the Indians who live "in the great forest of nature . . . , with more ease, decency, and peace than you can imagine." Here, Crèvecoeur closes his book. With Farmer James he moves into the simple, unspoiled society of the Indian with mixed melancholy and optimism, hoping that he may find there the safety, harmony, and order that war and civilization destroy. If James's commonwealth of enlightened freeholders cannot survive in the world of revolution, or if even in peace it must eventually change into another Charles-Town, a flight to the forest, Crèvecoeur seems to imply, may be the only answer.

Crèvecoeur was an admirer of Rousseau and a child of French romanticism. "Sentiment and feeling," he once wrote, "are the only guides I know." He found in American society what the physiocrats of the Enlightenment prepared him to find, that is, a land of happy husbandmen, living in a free, egalitarian society close to benevolent nature. His portrait of America, as it appears in the first five letters, at least, is idealized and sentimentalized, but it is nonetheless a perceptive, sympathetic articulation of the feeling that underlay the myths of America as Paradise and America as Hope, as they appeared in the first generation's version of the American dream.

Yet Crèvecoeur's view of this ideal pastoralized society should not be construed as simply that of an Arcadia. He is well aware, even in the early letters, of the frailties of human nature, and equally aware that imperfect men will never create a perfect society, not even in the favorable atmosphere of America. "Good and evil," he remarks in Letter III, "I see to be found in all societies, and it is vain to seek for any spot where these ingredients are not mixed." The good life he sought, and which at first he lived at Pine Hill, lay between the tainted, authoritarian society of Europe, where "great lords . . . possess every thing," and the anarchistic, carnivorous society of the frontier. As a man of the Enlightenment, Crèvecoeur believed that the ideal level of life existed somewhere between the primitive and the oversophisticated, close enough to nature to receive its influences and sufficiently removed from the corruptions of too much civilization. Here, on this middle ground, men might join together to lead orderly lives: the good in human nature have free rein, the destructive element be checked and controlled. Such a society could never be constructed in Europe, which had insufficient resources to sustain it and centuries of tradition to overcome. But in America it was possible—or at least it seemed so to Crèvecoeur in James's time.

Here lies the anomaly of Crèvecoeur's *Letters,* which read as a whole, exhibit a curious inconsistency of beginning in hope, ending in equivocation. They close with a reluctant admission, implied but evident, that the American dream is perhaps only a dream, that the rational society of free men it promises is the substance of things to be hoped for rather than attained. The rural peace of James's farm so movingly described in the early letters is balanced by the rapacity of Charles-Town; the honest yeomen of Orange County and the sturdy fishermen of Nantucket are set against the half-savage frontiersmen and Carolina's cruel slaveholders; the harmonious commonwealth of freeholders is eventually torn apart by dissension and war. "Man is an animal of prey," Crèvecoeur writes in Letter XI, "with rapine and bloodshed implanted in his heart," and one can expect little good from him. From this fact there is no escape, either in forest or city, in Old or New World:

> Where do you conceive then that nature intended we should be happy? Would you prefer the state of men in the woods, to that of

men in a more improved situation? Evil predominates in both; in the first they often eat each other for want of food; and in the other they often starve each other for want of room. For my part I think the vices and miseries to be found in the latter, exceed those of the former, in which the real evil is more scarce, more supportable, and less enormous. Yet we wish to see the earth peopled; to accomplish the happiness of kingdoms, which is said to consist in numbers. Gracious God: to what end is the introduction of so many beings into a mode of existence in which they must grope amidst as many errors, commit as many crimes, and meet with as many diseases, wants, and sufferings.

Thus "we must pay very dear," Crèvecoeur sadly concludes, "for what little share of political felicity we enjoy," since it cannot last. James's final rejection of the society in which he once held so much confidence is an admission of failure. He can do no more than hope that his final prayer—"Permit, I beseech thee, O Father of nature, that our ancient virtues, and our industry, may not be totally lost"—will be heard, and, as he asks, "our ancient tranquillity" restored.

The importance of Crèvecoeur's *Letters From an American Farmer* to American literature lies in the fact that in company with Franklin's *Autobiography,* John Woolman's *Journal,* Samuel Sewall's *Diary,* and Jefferson's *Notes on Virginia,* it is one of those authentic American artifacts which first gave expression to the national consciousness. The book stands, without a doubt, at the beginning of an American literary tradition.

First, it views the American scene directly, through non-European eyes; the land and the people appear not as Europe transplanted or transformed, but as elements of a rising nation with a quality of its own. Crèvecoeur had a gift for the vivid vignette—a snowstorm in the forest, a crowded country inn—and a gift for narrative incident—the sudden terror of an Indian raid, a contest between two snakes in his garden—which embody valid *American* experience. True, the *Letters* contain a great deal of accurate information about conditions of life in the later eighteenth century, but Crèvecoeur possessed an emotional commitment to the American society and landscape that made his book something more than reliable reporting. He perceived the artistic possibilities of native themes and materials; because he was so deeply involved with the American experience, he made literature out of it.

Second, Crèvecoeur helped to create the original self-reliant, self-sufficient, independent Yankee as an American character, as the man who takes care of himself and his own, stands on his own two feet, and confronts life on equal terms. Though Crèvecoeur undoubtedly saw in the American character what French romantic individualism conditioned him to see, this provided reinforcement for a prototype already being shaped by English, Calvinistic, and frontier forces. James, Andrew the Hebridean, and the Nantucket sailors made their society work on the principle of enlightened self-interest. They made their way not by fortune, but "by the gradual operation of sobriety, honesty, and emigration," going where the opportunities were. They belong in the honorable tradition that includes ambitious young Ben Franklin, Jackson's Young Americans, and Horatio Alger's self-made heroes, down to the Junior Chamber of Commerce's most recent young-men-of-the-year.

Third, Crèvecoeur began to explore what soon became a major American literary theme, the theme of self-analysis. American literature has been tremendously introspective, more so perhaps than that of any other western culture. Crèvecoeur posed for the first time the great question, "What is an American?" and its corollary, "What does it mean to *be* an American?" Tocqueville, Mrs. Trollope, Dickens, Lord Bryce, Laski, Maurois, Myrdal, and an army of observers have asked these questions since Crèvecoeur's time, but as outsiders. He asked from within, and replied in American terms, as Emerson, Whitman, Henry James, Mark Twain, and William Faulkner have done after him. In a general sense, the whole of American literature is an attempt to answer the query first put to Farmer James.

Finally, in finding no answer, Crèvecoeur located the central, enduring problem of American life, that of somehow bridging the gap between America as fact and America as ideal. The combination of doubt and trust, of faith and disillusion, so clear in Crèvecoeur's book, is distinctively American. As Cotton Mather could not find in his America the realization of the saintly commonwealth the Puritan founders planned, so Crève-

coeur could not find in post-revolutionary America the kingdom
of reason the Enlightenment expected it to be. From the beginning American writing has been characterized by this tension, so
deeply felt in *Letters From an American Farmer,* between the
distant ideal of America as man's Paradise and Hope, and the
constant, unremitting struggle to realize it, here and now, in
actuality. This is as true of our time as it was of Crèvecoeur's.

Notes

1. Written in English, the book was translated in an expanded version by Crèvecoeur for a French edition in 1787. A previous translation
appeared in 1784. Some of the *Letters* which were critical of the revolutionary party in America were not published in the 1782 London
edition. A few were included in the 1787 French edition, but the rest
remained in manuscript until the American edition of 1925. The original English version was reprinted five times in the next ten years, the
enlarged French edition three times, and there were two editions of a
German and a Dutch translation.

2. Jefferson, of course, was writing at the same time what later became his *Notes on Virginia,* published in Paris in 1784, in response to a
similar request for information on Virginia from the Marquis de Barbe-
Marbois, Secretary of the French Legation in Philadelphia.

4 *THE FEDERALIST*

Melvin K. Whiteleather

The Federalist Papers are political tracts that have been lifted above their level by subsequent developments. They were written as campaign literature, tailored specifically to influence adoption of the new United States Constitution. Had the Constitution been rejected, or had it failed to work, they would be today little more than a historical curiosity familiar only to experts in the field.

But this was not to be their fate. The Federalist Papers are as alive now as they were in 1787–1788 when they first appeared, indeed as alive as the United States Constitution itself. Reference is frequently made to them in interpreting the Constitution, the United States Supreme Court itself cites them, and they have entered the realm of literature. It is almost impossible for the constitutionalist, the historian, or the political philosopher delving into the communal behavior of man to ignore them. This is true far beyond the confines of the United States, as well as within this country.

As literature, the Papers have their faults. The wonder is that they have so few, given the conditions under which they were written and their purpose. They are repetitious in part and bear marks of inconsistency. They are long and scholarly to a point beyond the understanding of the popular audience for which they were intended. One need not look far to find explanations of the faults. The Papers were written not by one man, but by three with different backgrounds and often different outlooks, although the signature was the same on all of them—Publius. None of the three saw the essays of the others before publication;

often the last pages of a manuscript were rushed to the waiting printer and were set with only elementary editing. Moreover, there were eighty-five articles, and they were spread over a seven-month period in no fewer than four different New York newspapers. This foolhardy procedure reveals that the authors thought they were engaging in pamphleteering.

A partial collection of the Papers appeared in book form under the title of *The Federalist* in the spring of 1788, while the series was still running in the newspapers. The most prolific of the three authors wrote an introduction to that first edition in which he gave the reader fair warning about what to expect with respect to style.

"The particular circumstances under which these Papers have been written," he said, "have rendered it impracticable to avoid violations of method and repetitions of ideas which cannot but displease a critical reader.

"The latter defect has even been intentionally indulged in order the better to impress particular arguments which were most material to the general scope of reasoning. Respect for public opinion, not anxiety for the literary character of the performance dictates this remark."

Who was this Publius or, more correctly, who were Publius?

Authorship was not formally acknowledged until the first edition of *The Federalist* was brought out in Paris in 1792. Then it was revealed that Publius was Alexander Hamilton, James Madison, and John Jay—all men of consequence in the early history of the United States. It remained for scholars in this century to ferret out precisely which of the three wrote which of the Papers. The scholars differ in their selections. If we are to accept Douglass Adair's thorough research, Hamilton wrote fifty-one of the eighty-five Papers and was the author of the introduction to the first edition. Madison wrote twenty-six of them, Jay five, and three were the joint effort of Hamilton and Madison.[1] Since we know that there was so little collaboration in the undertaking, it is a little surprising that three are attributed to a joint effort. Still, to have only three out of eighty-five Papers composed jointly does not destroy the image of the three men working together but each independently.

The Founding Fathers of the United States were remarkable

men. When *The Federalist* was written Hamilton was only thirty years old, Madison was thirty-six, and Jay forty-two. Hamilton and Madison concentrated on the internal affairs sections of the Constitution while Jay treated foreign affairs. The latter had had diplomatic experience and favored conciliation with England rather than independence. Yet, with Benjamin Franklin and John Adams, he had negotiated the treaty of independence with Britain in 1783 and then served as minister to Spain under the Articles of Confederation. He was Secretary for Foreign Affairs at the time of the Constitutional Convention in Philadelphia.

These men were strikingly different. Hamilton and Jay were prominent New York lawyers. Madison, a Virginia philosopher from a family of the old landed aristocracy, received a Princeton education. Jay belonged to conservative society in New York and enjoyed a social status which Hamilton acquired only through marriage.

Hamilton was born on the island of Nevis in the British West Indies under unfortunate circumstances that made him technically illegitimate. He early set out for the mainland, managed to get an education at King's College—now Columbia University—in New York, and to become a lawyer. He was General George Washington's private secretary for four years during the Revolution, and later commanded a regiment at Yorktown. As the first Secretary of the Treasury, he set financial and economic policies that have influenced the country ever since. His aggressive political career came to an end in his duel with Aaron Burr. Madison, of course, was to become the fourth President of the United States, serving two terms from 1809 to 1817. Jay was to become the first Chief Justice of the United States. Different as these men were, they had this in common: they were widely read in the classics and were well grounded in political philosophy. They were familiar with Cicero and Hobbes, Plutarch and Locke, Grotius and Rousseau.

The Confederation of thirteen colonies formed after independence was won from Britain was not functioning at all as a "United States." Under the Articles of Confederation, each state retained all but a small portion of its sovereignty; the federal government had no power to enforce its laws and resolutions; there were no guaranteed relationships among the several states.

A quota method of financing left the federal establishment in constant pecuniary difficulties.

Having just emerged from a war, all of the thirteen states were anxious about foreign threats; the territory around them was still under European control. Yet these threats, real or imaginary, became less dangerous than the bickering and even bloodshed among themselves. Maryland and Virginia had a fierce commercial dispute. New York, New Hampshire, and Massachusetts spilled each other's blood over Vermont. Pennsylvania and Connecticut fought over the Wyoming Valley. Conflicting claims to lands lying immediately west of the Confederation were a constant source of friction among New York, Connecticut, and Massachusetts in the north, and Georgia and South Carolina in the south. There were boundary disputes between Georgia and South Carolina, between North Carolina and Virginia, and Virginia and Maryland. New York and Massachusetts, and Pennsylvania and New York also had boundary quarrels. To top it off, there were disputes even among districts within states, and on a larger scale, the southern tier of states felt that the northern tier was tyrannical—a foretaste of things to come in the next century. Serious proposals were made in Massachusetts to secede and take all New England along. The Bay State felt put upon by both New York and Pennsylvania.

The fact was that the Confederation government was ridiculed at home and laughed at abroad. It became abundantly clear that the Articles of Confederation had to be amended if the thirteen states were to remain together. Several state delegations in Congress became alarmed and pushed through a resolution calling for a Constitutional Convention to meet in Philadelphia on May 14, 1787. The resolution was in a minor key. It did not come close to stating what the actual situation was. It said only that experience had shown the Articles of Confederation to possess some defects.

Convention delegates were to be appointed by the states, and Congress gave them explicit instructions as to what they were to do: they were to revise the Articles of Confederation, making them "adequate to the exigencies of government and the preservation of the union."

Revise the Articles of Confederation, said the instructions, not write a new Constitution. Nevertheless, the convention devised an entirely new document, in clear violation of the power granted it by Congress.

Madison tried to get around this violation by arguing that the Constitution retained the principles of the Articles of Confederation; all the convention did, he said, was to put the principles into practice and "invigorate them." But he was not able to persuade many of his colleagues in the convention that his argument would carry much weight. The prohibition against going further than amending forbid "any alteration . . . unless such alteration is agreed to in a congress of the United States, and be afterwards confirmed by the legislatures of every state." This rule the convention delegates did not dare follow. They knew very well that no legislature would accept the Constitution they had drawn. So they recommended to Congress that their work be submitted to especially elected state conventions, and that the Constitution go into effect when nine of the thirteen states had ratified it.

The delegates returned to their states to argue for ratification, or against it. Hamilton had a heavy load. The New York delegation in Philadelphia had split over the Constitution, some members having gone home before the document was completed. Hamilton took it upon himself to sign in the name of New York.

Once back home, he plunged immediately into the fight for ratification. Letters addressed "To the People of the State of New York" soon began to appear in the New York City press signed "Publius." Other letters on the Federalist–Anti-federalist battle also appeared. There was a collection of "Caesars" and "Catos" and "Constant Readers" but "Publius" seems to have been the favorite, possibly because he wrote so much. It is strange that he should have been for his style was scholarly and long-winded, not at all what could be expected to reach broad sections of the population. One of the letters signed "Countryman," a man or woman with seemingly above-average intelligence, wrote:

"As to Mr. Publius, I have read a great many of his papers and I really cannot find out what he would be at; he seems to me as if he was going to write a history, so I have concluded to wait and buy one of his books when they come out."

"Countryman" and others like him may not have been able to understand what Publius "would be at"; nevertheless, he had tremendous influence with the delegates to the New York convention and with the delegates to the Virginia convention. The Papers provided the Federalists with a systematic analysis of the Constitution and enabled them to document their arguments in convincing manner. Hamilton personally argued so brilliantly in the New York convention that he is credited with having been the deciding force that put the Constitution over in that state by a very narrow margin. There is irony in this, for after all the work done by Publius and Hamilton personally, when New York ratified, it had no effect on the fate of the Constitution. Ten of the thirteen states had already ratified, and since only nine were required, the Constitution was in force.

But love's labor was not lost. Although it was not their intention, Hamilton, Madison, and Jay found an audience far beyond the thirteen American states. The Papers had an immediate impact in Europe and Latin America when they became available in book form. They were quoted in the French Constituent Assembly debates and Germans seeking unification of the German states in freedom found them inspiring. *The Federalist,* in fact, became a guide to liberty and constitutional government.

The three men were concerned with getting the new Constitution adopted, so they naturally addressed themselves to the weaknesses of the Articles of Confederation and showed how the proposed new basic law would provide cures. Each letter had a central theme and the reader was warned what that was by the title, such as: "The Dangers from Foreign Force and Influence"; "The Dangers from Dissension Between the States"; "The Consequences of Hostilities Between the States"; "Union as a Safeguard Against Domestic Faction and Insurrection"; "The Utility of Union in Respect to Commercial Relations, to a Navy, to Revenue, to Economy in Government"; "The Powers Necessary for Common Defense"; "Militia and Taxation"; "The Conformity of the New Constitution to Republican Principles"; "The Powers of the New Government"; "The Separation of Powers," and so on.

The benefits of union was the theme that ran through them all. While arguing specific points to meet existing circumstances, the authors larded their reasoning with philosophical observations that had universal application. They took theories and put them to work. There were interesting innovations in the new Constitution such as the federal state, the presidential system, the organization of the judiciary, and judicial review.

A French jurist's preface to a 1902 Paris edition called *The Federalist* a work on the theory of federalism as well as the practice of it. Max Beloff, a British authority, has written that the authors were acutely aware that they had been given a chance to construct a new political society, of proving by experiment what had been only abstract speculations: namely, that the social contract was no mere anthropological figment of logical abstraction, but the actual basis of the American union. Thomas Jefferson, who was serving as minister to France when the Papers were written, called *The Federalist* "the best commentary on the principles of government which has ever been written."

Hamilton and Madison did not see eye to eye on these principles. That is another extraordinary aspect of their curious collaboration. Hamilton was really a nationalist rather than a federalist, but he loyally argued the federalist case just the same. He did not believe that the Constitution gave the national government nearly enough power. When he subsequently became the first Secretary of the Treasury, he moved promptly to gather power to that office. He set precedents that became the roots of political divisions, and in the modern United States his views of federal power are prevailing over those favoring states' rights. Democracy was a radical creed in 1787. Hamilton was very much afraid of it. The Constitutional Convention spent considerable time discussing the "tyranny and follies" of democracy. The problem was to devise a system of government that would preserve liberty. We speak freely today about democracies, but democracy is not what the Founding Fathers created. They created a representative government with safeguards *against* democracy.

What were these safeguards? Hamilton explains them in No. IX as the separation of powers, a system of checks and balances, lifetime tenure of judges during good behavior, and representative and federal government. Madison in No. LI explains at some length that keeping the power of the three branches of government—the legislative, executive, and judicial—strictly separate preserves liberty because the danger of one branch getting the upper hand over another is dissipated.

The liberty Madison and Hamilton talked about so much was only indirectly individual liberty. Individual liberty was not uppermost in their minds because they were arguing for the Constitution. The new basic law was not concerned with reforming man, but with erecting a structure that would handle man and all of his feebleness. They were thinking about political liberty. The experience under colonialism showed through clearly. But immediately after the Constitution began to function, it was recognized that the absence of specific safeguards for individual liberty was a grave defect. Madison then took the lead in the very first Congress, meeting in New York, to get a people's charter adopted. The result was the Bill of Rights contained in the first ten amendments to the Constitution.

The First Amendment guaranteed that Congress shall make no law respecting the establishment of religion or prohibiting the free exercise thereof, abridging the freedom of speech or of the press, or of the right of the people peaceably to assemble and to petition the government for a redress of grievances. From this solid rock, the amendments went on to prohibit unreasonable search and seizure, and the denial of life, liberty, or property without due process of law, and concluded with the Tenth Amendment that went back to the Constitutional structure. It stated flatly that "the powers not delegated to the United States by the Constitution, not prohibited by it to the states, are reserved to the states respectively, or to the people."

This amendment reflected an uneasy feeling that perhaps the document prepared in Philadelphia was not, after all, specific enough to protect the rights of states as against the federal government. Yet Madison in No. XLV expressed no doubts, although he was a states' rights man. He wrote that the power of the federal government was limited and defined, while the powers of the states were many, residual, and indefinite. "The power reserved to the several states," he wrote, "will extend to all the objects which, in the ordinary course of affairs, concern the lives, liberties and properties of the people, and the internal order, improvement and prosperity of the state." But in spite of Madison's opinion expressed in *The Federalist*, the first Congress thought it necessary to clarify the states' rights versus powers of the federal government issue in the Bill of Rights.

Historians generally agree that No. X, written by Madison, stands out among the eighty-five Papers but they do not all agree on why they believe that is so. Charles A. Beard has called it "one of the ablest statements of the economic basis of politics ever written." Edward Meade Earle inclines toward the same belief and adds that it is also one of the ablest examples of the economic interpretation of history. Others challenge this economic interpretation. Douglass Adair, quoted earlier, and Benjamin F. Wright are among the critics. Adair says Beard fit No. X into the 1913 political atmosphere in which he wrote and found in Madison's words proof of Beard's theory of the doctrine of class struggle. Wright argues that the universal element in *The Federalist* is its recognition of the importance of human nature in politics, together with its remarkably penetrating analysis of the motives and the behavior of men in a free society.

What did Madison say that might warrant the conclusion that he was an economic determinist?

"Those who hold and those who are without property have ever formed distinct interests in society," he wrote,

> Those who are creditors and those who are debtors, fall under a like discrimination. A landed interest, a mercantile interest, a moneyed interest, with many lesser interests, grow up of necessity in civilized nations, and divide them into different classes, actuated by different sentiments and views. The regulation of these various and interfering interests forms the principal task of modern legislation, and involves the spirit of party and faction in the necessary and ordinary operations of the government.

In this quotation Madison puts his scalpel to history and uncovers different classes, but also many factions, even among propertied persons, which hardly fall into a rigid category. The factions may be religious or even, as Madison said, "frivolous and fanciful." Madison went on to add that if these various conflicting interests were passed through the medium of a chosen body of citizens, the wisdom of that body might "best discern the true interest of the country" and be least likely to sacrifice it to "temporary or partial considerations."

It is true that the framers of the Constitution were deeply

concerned with the protection of property rights, but they were also deeply concerned about many other things as well. The Constitution, says Wright, did not attempt to imprison human nature; it established a government likely to work satisfactorily for man's good, taking into account his behavior. That is what Madison was explaining in No. X and it is the basis for regarding that paper as outstanding. The economic interpretation was accepted theory in the 1920's and 1930's but has since been discarded in favor of the much broader meaning.

Clearly, it was union—the blessings of union, the benefits of union, union for defense from the outside and against dissension inside—which provided the central theme running through *The Federalist*. Hamilton, in No. VI, said that the purpose of union was for security "from the arms and arts of foreign nations," the prevention of "dissensions between the states themselves" and for protection "from domestic factions and convulsions." The thirteen states were all on the Atlantic seaboard. Behind them lay a vast continent, sparsely settled, over which they had no control, but on which they had designs. There were still Indians to contend with, and Europeans—British, French, Spanish—still were capable of creating trouble on land and on sea. There was uncertainty which it was hoped could be overcome by stronger united action. The Constitution framers decided to try to bring this unity about by putting political theories into practice, and profiting by the experience of Greeks, Romans, and existing monarchial systems. They created a new form of government and the authors of *The Federalist* explained it all in universal as well as specific terms.

Thus the Federalist Papers became the outstanding American contribution to the literature on constitutional government and federalism, and a classic of western political thought. And this classic came from the pens of three men writing letters to New York City newspapers, in a casual kind of collaboration, for a local and immediate political purpose.

Note

1. "The Authorship of the Disputed Federalist Papers," *William and Mary Quarterly,* I, 3rd Series (1944), 97–122.

5 THE SKETCH BOOK OF GEOFFREY CRAYON, GENT.

William L. Hedges

Not the best but the most famous and popular of Washington Irving's works, *The Sketch Book of Geoffrey Crayon, Gent.,* first appeared in the United States as a series of booklets or pamphlets in 1819. It was in England that Irving had written the stories, essays, and sketches of which the book is composed. He had shipped the material section by section to one of his brothers at home to be put through the press. Before all the installments were published, however, English periodicals began pirating some of the contents. To protect himself, Irving brought out about half the work in a volume in England, at his "own risk." His publisher failed, but the book succeeded, whereupon John Murray, the eminent London publisher, took it over and issued *The Sketch Book* complete in two volumes.

This was the beginning of Irving's celebrity. From then on he was able to make a living solely by his pen, something no American had done before him. It was the acclaim in Britain that counted most. Americans still largely lived under the literary domination of England. American writers were at an initial disadvantage because printers in the United States could publish English books without paying royalties to the authors. Furthermore the American public, even forty years after the Declaration of Independence, still tended to assume that books by American authors could not be very good. British reviewers on the whole said so, often in a hostile or condescending tone. Finally, however, in *The Sketch Book* British critics found an American whom they believed to be a genuine writer. Encouraged by this judgment, his own countrymen could take Irving more seriously. When he returned to the United States twelve years and six books later, he was received as something of a national hero.

Before *The Sketch Book* he had been uncertain of his professional identity. He had burst into print exuberantly in his early twenties and earned a reputation in New York City as one of a group of brash young wits. In 1807 he had collaborated on the comic periodical *Salmagundi* with one of his brothers and a young writer named James Kirke Paulding. The magazine offered irreverent comment on local manners, fashions, culture, and politics, while at the same time it lampooned the tradition of the periodical essay from which it was derived. Two years later the burlesque *History of New York,* ostensibly the work of the addlepated antiquarian, Diedrich Knickerbocker, climaxed this semiprofessional phase of Irving's career. Although his family were not averse to having a writer in their midst, their ability or willingness to support him financially was limited. He had trained for the law, but his heart was not in it. Nor, though he helped out from time to time, was he happy in the importing business which his father and brothers had developed.

He went to England in 1815 to begin an extended European stay and was confronted almost immediately by the twin emergencies of the imminent bankruptcy of the Liverpool branch of the family enterprises and the grave illness of his brother Peter, who was in charge there. Irving's work on *The Sketch Book,* which began a couple of years later, was a flight from such experiences as the one in the Liverpool office, that is, from business, which he had once called a "soul killing way of life." But the typically American conception of literature as nothing more than a polite avocation had held him back a long time. He was thirty-six years old when *The Sketch Book* began to appear.

Ironically it may well have been his unsettledness, projected through the subdued, quietly whimsical and self-mocking voice of Geoffrey Crayon that made *The Sketch Book* a success. The comedy of *Salmagundi* and *Knickerbocker* has a crude energy, more obviously reflective of certain essential qualities of American experience than *The Sketch Book.* But the style of Crayon, with its easy grace and subdued humor, on the whole immediately pleased the British and ultimately won so much admiration at home that generations of school children in the United States were trained to imitate it. It is a familiar style, still basically formal but not academic or complex, fond of homely English and American nouns and verbs. It is symmetrical without seeming to strain; it runs naturally to abundant metaphor. Neither pretentious nor overly rhetorical, the style suggests that Irving did not have to work hard at being literary—which is something that cannot be said of much American writing between 1776 and 1820.

Irving's basic talent was closer to caricature than to celebration. Had he remained in the United States he might have exercised that talent with less restraint, but he was three thousand miles away from the social types he knew best. And even though he was still writing primarily for an American audience, he knew well enough that his work would eventually be scrutinized by English readers. In his earlier work he had poked fun with comparative impunity not only at *arrivistes,* like his own family, but at the old Dutch aristocracy of New York, but, older now, less sure of himself, and in England, he was more cautious.

For the English reader there was little in *The Sketch Book* that was new. Crayon hedges himself about with scraps of verse and prose culled from British authors, both famous and forgotten, which he uses for epigraphs or as illustrations in footnotes and text. In fact much of the work is *about* literature, "The Boar's Head Tavern, Eastcheap," for instance, which Crayon calls a "Shakespearian Research," or its companion piece, "Stratford-on-Avon," or "The Royal Poet," a sketch which resurrects a long verse narrative written by James I of Scotland during his imprisonment in Windsor Castle. In "The Art of Book-Making" Crayon falls asleep in the British Museum and has a nightmare about authors borrowing from works of obscure predecessors, a fantasy which is virtually continued in "The Mutability of Literature" as he commiserates with a little quarto volume in the library of Westminster Abbey on what the passage of time does to literary reputations. Furthermore, even when he is not talking about an author or talking to an old book, Crayon may remind the reader of earlier British literature. In "Westminster Abbey," for instance, he suggests Goldsmith or Addison; on a trip to the country, he slightly resembles the Spectator visiting Sir Roger de

Coverley. Indeed, his very sound has affinities with the language of Addison and Goldsmith. This is in part what it meant for Irving to be hailed as the first literate American—that he had mastered a familiar English prose style.

The Sketch Book does not challenge England. The humorous side of English character which Crayon observes is, as he points out, essentially what the English have seen for themselves in creating the image of John Bull. Bull is England's loyalty to England exaggerated, rendered a bit blind and provincial. At its worst, Bull-ism is "an apology for . . . prejudice or grossness" or for "an unreasonable burst of passion about trifles," but it has its charms, and it is generally redeemed by qualities such as heartiness, courage, and frankness. Speaking of John Bull, who in *The Sketch Book* is both a typical English gentleman and, allegorically, the whole nation, Crayon says, "The secret of the matter is, that John has a great disposition to protect and patronize. He thinks it indispensable to the dignity of an ancient and honorable family, to be bounteous in its appointments, and to be eaten up by dependents; and so, partly from pride, and partly from kind-heartedness, he makes it a rule always to give shelter and maintenance to his superannuated servants."

There is something of John Bull in most of the Englishmen in *The Sketch Book*. Squire Bracebridge, for instance, whose country estate Crayon visits at Christmas time and who becomes the subject of several sketches, is a variation or refinement of the type. A "bigoted devotee of the old school," the Squire believes that there is "no condition more truly honorable and enviable than that of a country gentleman on his paternal lands." Crayon sees the old gentleman partly as a whimsical eccentric but is nonetheless essentially sympathetic with his desire to keep up "holiday observances" such as mistletoe, Yule logs, wassail bowls, Christmas masques, and old games like "hoodman blind" and "shoe the wild mare."

Squire Bracebridge, of course, is an anachronism, a largely fictitious throwback to an era closer to feudalism. On the whole it is vestiges of the English past that catch Crayon's eye rather than the English present, about which *The Sketch Book* has nothing to say that compares with the perceptiveness of, say, Hawthorne's *Our Old Home* or Emerson's *English Traits* a generation later. Irving's fondness for old England may have disarmed criticism there and thus contributed to the success of his book. But for all the merits of "Rip Van Winkle," "The Legend of Sleepy Hollow," and two or three other individual pieces, the book would not be worth reading as a whole were it not for the fact that the curiosity about England, embodied in Geoffrey Crayon, reflects a particularly American emotional need.

"The Author's Account of Himself" presents *The Sketch Book* as a portfolio of observations made by Crayon in the course of his travels abroad. But Irving did not quite trust his basic structural scheme. He must have sensed that to hold his audience he had to have occasionally a more pronounced dramatic interest than Crayon could provide alone. We read only a few sketches before encountering, without apology or explanation, a story about America, "Rip Van Winkle," which, instead of being attributed to Crayon, is presented as "A Posthumous Writing by Diedrich Knickerbocker." Three other narratives in the original edition of *The Sketch Book*—it was slightly expanded later—have little or nothing to do with Crayon's trip to England. Otherwise, however, the book adheres to the stated format. And as Crayon's personality emerges, a unity of interest and feeling develops which compensates for Irving's casualness about the structure, so much so that one finally wants to read "Rip Van Winkle" and "The Legend of Sleepy Hollow," if not as stories told by Crayon instead of Knickerbocker, then at least as stories that have touched Crayon almost personally.

Like many of his forebears in the periodical essays of the eighteenth century Crayon is neither married nor young, but whereas bachelorhood had simply underlined the original Mr. Spectator's detachment and independence as an observer of human manners, in Crayon it combines with the inclination to travel to indicate restlessness, homelessness, and loneliness. He strikes the pathetic note early. His account of his Atlantic crossing virtually becomes a meditation on disaster. His mind dwells on storms and signs of shipwreck. When the ship lands at Liverpool, he watches the reunion of a young wife and her fatally stricken sailor husband, who has come home to die. Of his own debarkation, Crayon observes, "I stepped upon the land of my forefathers—but felt that I was a stranger in the land."

This is not an ordinary homesickness any more than his trip to England is ordinary sightseeing. He has already described himself as a lover of the picturesque, more interested in "nooks, and corners, and by-places. . . . cottages, and landscapes, and obscure ruins" than in famous spectacles and attractions. His tour of England gradually reveals itself as an unconscious quest for order and stability. He finds what he is looking for in "neat cottages, with their trim shrubberies and green grass plots." Rural English scenery, he says, is "associated in the mind with ideas of order, of quiet, of sober well-established principles, of hoary usage and reverend custom." In their adherence to tradition John Bull and Squire Bracebridge give Crayon a self-assurance he lacks himself. Their large old houses stand for him as sanctuaries for the wayworn traveler.

He also sees literary culture as enhancing the stability of English life, tying present to past and giving it meaning. As he walks about Stratford-on-Avon, the recollection of scenes from Shakespeare seems to heighten and even transform the reality of the town. He marvels at "the singular gift of the poet; to be able thus to spread the magic of his mind over the very face of nature; to give to things and places a charm and character not their own, and to turn this 'working-day world' into a perfect fairy land." This may be the first expression of what came to be the escapist attitude toward literature dominant in the United States after the Civil War in the culture known as the genteel tradition, an attitude which offered stiff resistance to the growth of realism and naturalism. The temptation of this attitude for an American in 1820 in the face of the strong tendency to judge literature by strict moral and utilitarian criteria is understandable. Crayon tends to make fun of the bourgeois citizen as a social climber, but in the figure of William Roscoe, an eminent historian and Liverpool banker, he finds a grand example of the "union of commerce and . . . intellectual pursuits," an example especially pertinent to the United States, that "young and busy country" which is dependent for literature and culture on "hours and seasons snatched from the pursuit of worldly interests. . . ."

Crayon obviously has not felt completely at home in what he calls "the common-place realities of the present" in the United States. To appreciate him, one has to imagine what it was like to grow up in a country relatively barren of native belles-lettres, of fine arts, or of a meaningfully formulated history, a country in which practical considerations were apt to undermine cultural aspiration, a country frequently sneered at by Europeans as intellectually backward. Crayon sneers back in observing the "swelling magnitude of many English travellers" to America, and in his essay "English Writers on America" he makes clear the resentment felt in his country against European criticism. He also makes fun (by pretending to accept it) of the pseudo-scientific view of Buffon and other Europeans that animal life deteriorates in America, man included. Crayon goes to England, he says, to see "the gigantic race" from which he has "degenerated." But the exaggeration may mask a fear that there is some truth in the theory.

At any rate, through Crayon, Irving becomes the first of a series of major American writers to make an issue of the contrast between the drabness, the plainness, the ordinariness, the newness of America and life in Europe as he sees it, encrusted with "the accumulated treasures of age." James Fenimore Cooper, Nathaniel Hawthorne, and Henry James were to speak explicitly of the hardship which the American writer labored under in a society destitute of the monuments and works of art, the traditional rituals and symbols, the long established institutions and customs that to those authors gave interest to the surface of life in Europe.

A sense of the barrenness of the American scene was increasingly after 1820 to help turn the attention of the native writers to history—a tendency encouraged by the example of Sir Walter Scott, with whom Irving discussed literary strategy while preparing *The Sketch Book*. Cooper, Hawthorne, William Gilmore Simms, John P. Kennedy and others, drawing on history for picturesque material, gradually developed a tradition of American romance and in the process often gave poetic or mythical, if not precisely historical, meanings to portions of the American past. Several of Irving's American stories also utilize the past, while in Crayon he almost literally depicts the American writer searching for values in culture and tradition.

Yet the quest for a meaningful past constantly verges on graveyard rumination. Mutability is the most persistent note of *The*

Sketch Book. Crayon cuts a ludicrous figure occasionally, as when he speaks of himself as eager to "loiter about the ruined castle—to meditate on the falling tower" and "lose" himself in the past. To look at vestiges of the past is sooner or later to be reminded of the process of decay. Interpreting the floral imagery of English funerals and burials, Crayon seems to sense how naturally and deeply rooted in a culture poetry and symbolism can be—a vital realization for an American. But in reaching it he reveals openly his own anxiety about death. Funeral rites and monuments to the dead only partly distract the living from awareness of the inevitability of decay and oblivion.

It is no wonder that the accumulation of memorial plaques and statues seems to turn Westminster Abbey into a vast tomb. Crayon, wandering alone there near dusk, overwhelmed by the silence, is as though momentarily immured with the dead, lost to the living. Poets' corners there may be, but Crayon also knows about the dust gathering on the forgotten books in old libraries. With his penchant for exploring dark Gothic passageways, he sometimes seems a haunted figure, like Knickerbocker poking around in the "rubbish of years." If his subdued fear of old things reflects an American suspicion that the past is basically irrelevant to the present—a suspicion paradoxically coupled with a desire for connection with the past—much of Crayon's musing on mutability must also reflect Irving's personal insecurity, his uncertainty about his professional future, his partial estrangement as an American in England, his bachelorhood. His notebooks in this period show his sense of himself as a soul gone astray, shipwrecked. In spite of his awareness of the danger of mawkishly indulging in pathos, he sentimentalized parts of *The Sketch Book* beyond anything that modern taste can bear. Crayon gives disquisitions on broken hearts and maidens dying of disappointed love. His sketch "The Widow and Her Son" weeps for bereaved motherhood. The prospect of economic failure and the breaking up of homes and families repeatedly looms before Crayon, a negative manifestation, doubtless, of the same need which impels Irving to find houses and traditions in which Crayon can at least temporarily feel at home.

Curiously, however, certain pieces of fiction in *The Sketch Book* undercut the sentimentality, just as Crayon's fantastic confrontations with forgotten books mock his literary aspirations. Woman's devotion, the wife as guardian angel, home and marriage as refuge from the vicissitudes of the world—these are the daydreams of Geoffrey Crayon. His book includes, however, not only the extravagantly idealized bride of the sketch called "The Wife" but the termagant Dame Van Winkle as well. "Rip Van Winkle" is the story of a husband's unconscious flight from a bad marriage. Sleeping out the best twenty years of his life on the breast of a green knoll in the Catskill Mountains, Rip wakes up at last old and impotent. But though initially terrified, he is free (his wife has died) and soon happy (his daughter can mother him now and he can be an idler with impunity).

The other well-known American story, "The Legend of Sleepy Hollow," makes fun of a bookish bachelor who dreams of a comfortable marriage and is unable to provide it for himself. A tale called "The Spectre Bridegroom" presents a young couple defying with great resourcefulness a stupid and destructive prejudice which family pride has maintained as an honorable tradition. *The Sketch Book* appears finally as the work of a somewhat self-mocking sentimentalist. Irving's comic perspective is largely responsible for the success of "Rip Van Winkle" and "The Legend of Sleepy Hollow," which mark the beginning of the short story as a separate authentic literary form. These stories are partially derived from German legends and tales—which is another instance of Irving's interest in traditional lore. Scott was the stimulus for his German readings. Nonetheless the American stories are rooted in the landscape and customs of the Hudson River Valley, which is their setting. Given local habitation, the characters in them begin to seem human even while they remain to a degree legendary. And Irving's half-comic, half-pathetic tone, leaving the reader uncertain whether to laugh or feel sorry, to dismiss the characters as grotesques or accept them as hints of something in himself, enhances the strangeness of characterization and gives the figures of Rip Van Winkle and Ichabod Crane slightly mythic overtones.

We associate sensibility, graveyard melancholy, and the vogue for ruins with the era of Gray, Goldsmith, and Sterne, but *The Sketch Book* in 1820 gave impetus in America to a wallowing in soft emotion that lasted at least another forty years. Following

Geoffrey Crayon, the figure of the idle daydreaming bachelor became a literary commonplace. The emotional binge was sustained by a vast subliterature of gift-books, annual publications produced largely for female readers, though it is clear that the American male was also susceptible to sentimentality. There was a soft-heartedness next to the hard-headed matter-of-factness which in this period was subduing the American continent. The avidity for sentimentalism suggests a national need for relief from the grinding pursuit of success and fear of failure, from tensions and anxieties known not only to Irving but to such writers as Hawthorne, Poe, and Melville. The dread and longing that underlie the haunted characters of these writers are not very different from the emotions which generated the sentimentalism of American literature in this period.

Irving's rhetoric distorts and greatly oversimplifies the strains to which a competitive economy subjects marriage, but, less sentimentalized, his ideal image of "The Wife" is a central force in Hawthorne, the symbol of man's need for a love that will bring him out of himself and out of an isolation into which pride, ambition, or greed tends to thrust him. Home, sweet home, the humble hearth, the comfortable pipe, the wife, the child, the old oaken bucket, the cottage in the valley, the green grassplot sheltered from commercial traffic, the oasis in the desert, the green isle in a savage sea—these images express a longing which informs American literature both at its worst and at its best in the first half of the nineteenth century. But at its best that literature is also obsessed with the man who consumes his life in longing, who refuses or is unable to settle down, who leaves home, who wastes his maturity in a lonely futile quest or who simply withdraws from life, who somehow destroys his house, his estate, or his wife and in the process brings about his own destruction. And this grotesque composite personage is in part the legacy of Crayon, Rip Van Winkle, Ichabod Crane, and a handful of characters in subsequent stories by Washington Irving.

6 JAMES FENIMORE COOPER: THE PRAIRIE

William H. Goetzmann

Whether the genteel critics and the newspaper reviewers knew it or not, the most important literary event of 1823 was the publication of Dr. Edwin James's *Account of an Expedition From Pittsburgh to the Rocky Mountains in the Years 1819, 20. . . .*[1] Dr. James was a New York botanist who accompanied United States Army Major Stephen H. Long on a sweeping reconnaissance of the vast frontiers of the American Trans-Mississippi West just as it was being opened to the horde of settlers who would, in succeeding decades, complete the march across the continent. Major Long's mission, coming at this strategic time, was only partially military. His main purpose, not unlike that of the moon-bound astronauts of today, was to report back to the nation all of the advantages, disadvantages, and dangers of the new country. Dr. James's task was to cast Major Long's rough field notes and those of his scientific and military assistants into a sober narrative of scientific exploration. Few writers have had more dramatic material. Dr. James's account took the Major and his men out across the rolling prairies along the dramatically broken banks of the Platte River to the Front Range of the Rocky Mountains, then south paralleling the mountain wall, past Pikes Peak, to the Royal Gorge of the upper Arkansas River on the very edge of Spanish territory in New Mexico. At this point the party split. One detachment went down the Arkansas directly through hostile Pawnee country. The other swung south to the Canadian River, and thinking it the Red River (which now separates Texas and Oklahoma), headed

66

back down its course to the Arkansas and eventually the Mississippi.

On the march, the explorers passed through Indian lands, including the dangerous village of the "Bad Hearts," through buffalo herds strung out for miles, climbed towering Pikes Peak for the first time, and gazed with scientific detachment on the weirdly contrasting topography of the High Plains—where rising out of nowhere, like a ship on the sea, stand Scott's Bluff, Courthouse Rock, and other strange eminences. They saw rivers that cut suddenly into the rolling plains, raging fires on the sea of grass, thickets of willows and dwarf trees in the river bottoms that afforded oases for Indian nomads, and the Cross Timbers —a forest standing for no apparent reason out on the bald prairie. Most of all, they were struck with the fact that this fantastic country resembled nothing so much as a "Great American Desert." To them it was a moonscape. The "lost pathfinder," Zebulon Pike, had been right when, ten years earlier in his own published account, he had described it in this exotic fashion. Any would-be settler who ventured out of the familiar forests of the Mississippi Valley, across the infinite and terrible spaces of the High Plains, clearly left most of the possibilities for civilization behind. In their view, he was entering upon what could only be a somber and disheartening enterprise.

James Fenimore Cooper followed Major Long's adventures by means of Dr. James's narrative which he read while taking his ease in Paris. A dreamer and aristocratic armchair adventurer, who was never to see the West himself, Cooper was clearly fascinated by the possibilities which Dr. James's story afforded for the writer of fiction, especially the romantic fiction then so much in fashion in France. Cooper had already read with some care Nicholas Biddle's recasting of the notebooks of Lewis and Clark, and very possibly he had read Zebulon Pike's account as well. In short, he kept up with the basic literature of the westward movement and had even known an Indian or two—surviving relics of a lost world of pristine freedom who dwelt on his father's baronial Otsego estate in northern New York. In his father's day, at the end of the eighteenth century, Otsego Hall had been carved out of the forest where the fierce Mohawks once lived.

Now the wilderness was tamed, just as it had been over a century earlier to the eastward as the Puritans drove out the Pequots, Mohicans, and other tribes. Though he seemed remote from it—certainly in Paris—the frontier experience touched Cooper deeply and personally. It was the great theme of his life, standing always in the forefront of his imagination. Though the frontier theme can be seen in some fashion in virtually all of his books: the sea novels, the Revolutionary War works, the Chainbearer series, the Littlepage trilogy, the Utopian fantasies, even offstage in his European books and works of social criticism, it rose to major prominence in his Leatherstocking Tales for which he is chiefly remembered.

The Prairie, which Cooper wrote in 1826–1827 in Paris, was the third book in the Leatherstocking saga which chronicled the adventures of Natty Bumppo, a forest hunter and frontiersman who resembled Daniel Boone, immortalized by John Filson in a biography in 1784. It was apparently to be the third and last volume of a trilogy which was artfully structured. The first volume, entitled *The Pioneers,* Cooper had published in 1823. It introduced Natty Bumppo as "Deerslayer," a relatively old man who, in killing a deer on Judge Marmaduke Temple's New York estate, violated civilized law and was punished. From the beginning, it was clear that Natty Bumppo had a past, and a rather noble one at that, consisting of adventures with the Indians in the forest wilderness, and going back beyond the Revolution to the French and Indian War. Cooper thus placed his major character just beyond the middle of life. In so doing, he began his epic classically *in medias res.* The next volume, *The Last of the Mohicans* (1826), is a flashback that pictures Natty in the prime of life, in the midst of his glorious past. *The Prairie,* written right on the heels of the previous book and suggesting that Cooper was rapidly spinning out the conclusion to his woodsman's odyssey, is clearly a finale—the grand curtain scene of Leatherstocking, now an old man well past eighty, and waiting serenely for death out in nature beyond the reaches of civilization. From a point just past the center of his hero's life, Cooper had thus flashed backward and forward. He had, through the medium of Leatherstocking, told the story of frontier America.

Critics, preoccupied with apologizing for his stilted language, have generally missed the skill and subtlety with which the trilogy was structured. Over all three books hangs a cloud of mortality, of inevitable death and change with its inescapable sadness and elegiac tone. In the first book, the deer is killed, but even worse, possessed as property under law. The trees are cut down and the forest is rapidly disappearing. Mighty Deerslayer himself is tried and convicted of the humiliating crime of poaching, and hence suffers spiritual death at the hands of Judge Temple, the agent of civilization. Leatherstocking's day, like that of the wilderness he loves so much, is clearly past. One can only leave it to the Freudian critics to decide whether Judge Temple was meant to be Cooper's own father, and if this is then a novel of emotional rebellion as well as a novel of social commentary.

The Last of the Mohicans, a story of Leatherstocking's prime years, also tells a tale of dying and thus sustains the tone, if not the theme of the first book. This time, of course, the victim is the noble Uncas, last of his tribe which had been virtually wiped out by vicious New Englanders years before. Thus we have a sequence of doom: first the Indian, then the forests, then the hunter. *The Prairie* is the last in this somber sequence. It is entirely a novel of death, but appropriately enough, death and resurrection, for it ends on that ambiguous Easter note of sadness and hope. It chronicles the death of one way of life and the birth of another which is not altogether bad.

At this point, Cooper had created a subtle structural master-piece; then, as D. H. Lawrence so astutely but only halfway perceived, Cooper began the "sloughing of the old skin." [2] He went back in 1840 and 1841 and wrote two more books in the Leatherstocking series, *The Pathfinder* and *The Deerslayer,* which took Natty Bumppo back by successive stages through young manhood to youth and the beginning of his career. The spell of death was broken. In a different sense, another resurrection had occurred, and Leatherstocking once again roamed the forests and the glimmerglass lakes. These books had a place, certainly, in proportion to Natty's very long life, and they did make clear to the reader in the age of Manifest Destiny and march of empire just what the attractions of the unspoiled wilderness had been. They also recalled the pioneering exploits of an older heroic generation that had given hard birth to the country and which was in danger of being forgotten except in the formalistic orations of Daniel Webster.

There was something so basic about Cooper's five Leather-stocking tales that they received the supreme accolade. They were taken up by the generations and read as children's books for nearly a hundred years. They sustained themselves on the magic level of story and character down through all the years when Americans lost their self-consciousness in a preoccupation with work, industrial development, and the growth of great cities where the forest and the longhouse once stood. They outlasted the dime novel and hundreds of imitations which blossomed into a whole new genre called "westerns." They survive even today in the era of the cinema and the "horse opera," holding their own against the best of John Ford.

But since 1950, at least, with the work of Henry Nash Smith in *Virgin Land, The American West as Symbol and Myth,* literary critics and students of culture have begun to see the larger meaning of Cooper's work. Cooper now stands forth clearly as the great novelist of changing America, and at the heart of his work stands the ambivalence and paradox that are central to the American historical experience. Cooper, along with many other Americans, could never make up his mind whether he preferred nature or civilization. Nature was God's pure handiwork. It was beauty, the vast, silent sublimity of forest and lake and prairie. It was innocent and noble and free. It was America's one great spiritual and material resource, and it set us off during a crucial period of national self-identification from the feudal, class-ridden industrial society of "civilized" Europe. On the other hand, nature was crude, lawless, the home of violence, danger, and terror. Most of all it stood in the way of progress. Over and over again in his Leatherstocking tales, Cooper posits the contrast between nature—time stood still—and progress—the relentless, and in many ways inviting, wave of the future. The problem was to tame nature and bring it under control for good without degenerating into the callous over-civilization of Europe. This was the mission of America, to create a new society, efficient and orderly and civilized, but based closely upon the beneficent laws of nature and hence free. So Cooper, like most Americans, while always aware of the nature versus progress dilemma, invariably had it both ways.

In his books he celebrated *both* nature and civilization; time *and* progress stood still. The Leatherstocking saga catches all of this so perfectly because it is a myth or story of heroic proportions that chronicles the emerging historical identity of the American people. Cooper knew, as some social scientists of the present appear to have forgotten, that individual and collective identities can only be derived from history. His great achievement was to render the historical process of change during a period of cultural genesis somehow timeless and permanent while at the same time capturing all of the ambiguities, dislocations, and anomalies of a culture in the throes of a process of acceleration more rapid than any ever seen before. It was because he was so sensitive to the historical process bound up in the frontier movement that Cooper, of course, found Dr. Edwin James's narrative of the cutting edge of civilization on the prairies so utterly fascinating.

The Prairie, as befitting the final act of a great drama, has most of Cooper's symbolic characters onstage in a vastly greater panorama than any of his other books. The tone and many of the characters in the book are reminiscent of Shakespeare's valedictory play, *The Tempest.* There is never any doubt but that this is to be the finale. The landscape, Mark Twain notwithstanding,[3] is a real landscape derived from James's careful account, but it is bizarre and skillfully managed by Cooper. It is a "bleak and solitary place" with "bruised and withered grass," offering little "that was flattering to the hopes of an ordinary settler of new lands." It was colored by the "hues and tints of autumn," suggesting age, and the great fortress rock which was to shelter the Bush family stood out upon the autumnal prairie like a tombstone.

Leatherstocking, wrinkled and old, makes his sudden appearance on the prairie silhouetted against the setting sun, an awe-inspiring nature god about to pass from the face of the earth:

> The sun had fallen below the crest of the nearest wave of the prairie, leaving the usual rich and glowing train on its track. In the center of this flood of fiery light, a human form appeared, drawn against the

gilded background, as distinctly, and seemingly as palpable, as though it would come within the grasp of any extended hand. The figure was colossal, the attitude musing and melancholy, and the situation directly in the route of the travellers. But embedded, as it was, in its setting of garish light, it was impossible to distinguish its just proportions or true character.

The effect of such a spectacle was instantaneous and powerful. The man in front of the emigrants came to a stand, and remained gazing at the mysterious object with a dull interest, that soon quickened into superstitious awe.

Throughout the book, this godlike quality of Leatherstocking is maintained. His wisdom, constantly thrust before the reader and the other characters in the story, is a function of his great age and long experience. His powers, now no longer physical (even his "hawkeye" has grown dim), derive from his great intuitive understanding of nature and men. But so great are these powers, especially those of intelligence and morality, that he largely influences the actions of all the others in the story.

More important than his powers, however, are his values for they denote what he represents in Cooper's myth of America's beginnings. The twin keys to Leatherstocking's values are freedom and a reverence for nature. Having been arrested by Judge Temple for making free use of nature's bounty when he killed a deer, Natty rejects "the law of the clearings" for the most part, favoring instead the freedom of nature's laws—even as applied to the Indians who make "free" with the settlers' horses because, being natural beings, they have little feeling for or need of private property. Leatherstocking does not, however, violate nature or nature's laws, and, embodying Cooper's basic ambivalence in this matter, he does not entirely scorn civilization's laws. Speaking to Ellen Wade, he declares, "The law—tis bad to have it, but I sometimes think it is worse to be entirely without it. Age and weakness have brought me to feel such weakness at times. Yes-yes, the law is needed when such as have not the gifts of strength and wisdom are to be taken care of." Here Cooper gets at the heart of his theme, and for that matter the theme of most "westerns" down to the present day. This is the role of law and order which is synonymous with the best aspects of civilization in that it provides justice and protection for the weak against the vicious, the violent, and the rapacious—in short the spoiler who is in Cooper's terms the unnatural man. The good law is, by implication, Jeffersonian law which is in harmony with nature, indeed derives from it, but which nevertheless allows a man to be as free as possible without injury to his fellow creatures. It depends fundamentally upon tolerance and mutual respect.

These qualities are sadly lacking in Ishmael Bush who might be considered the main character in the story. Bush is a brute who has killed a man back in "civilization" in a fight over land. Gathering his numerous brood about him like some tribal leader, he has set out on his exodus across the forbidding prairie to get as far as possible beyond the restraints of law for which he has only contempt. As evidence of this, he has added kidnapping to his crimes. In partnership with his evil brother-in-law, Abiram White, he has abducted Inez de Certavallos, daughter of a decadent but rich Spanish colonial grandee. Improbable as it seems at first reading, Bush and White expect to collect a ransom for Inez out in the wilderness. On this point the reader might possibly be deceived by a geographical "elipse" in Cooper's story, since if the emigrant band were heading across the prairie on or near the Spanish trail from Santa Fe to St. Louis, they might well have been, by Cooper's (and James's) logic, in a position to contact Spanish authorities in the matter of the ransom. Cooper simply neglected to mention the occasional Spanish outposts along the way such as those near the base of the southern Rockies, on the Red River between Oklahoma and Texas, and the trading camps along the Platte River as well as the temporary camps of the comancheros operating out of Santa Fe.

Bush's important role, however, is not that of kidnapper. He is Ishmael the outcast and outlawed wanderer. He is a kind of gypsy Caliban of brutish and powerful strength doomed to suffer in his own private dungeon of ignorance, unless he learns. We first see him crashing across the prairie in one of Cooper's best descriptive passages:

> He was a tall, sunburnt man, past the middle age, of a dull coun-
> tenance and listless manner. His frame appeared loose and flexible;
> but it was vast, and in reality of prodigious power. It was only at
> moments, however, as some slight impediment imposed itself to his

loitering progress, that his person, which in its ordinary gait seemed so lounging and nerveless, displayed any of those energies which lay latent in his system, like the slumbering and unwieldy, but terrible, strength of the elephant.

Resorting to then fashionable phrenological description, Cooper adds, "The inferior lineaments of his countenance were coarse, extended and vacant; while the superior, or those nobler parts which are thought to affect the intellectual being, were low, receding and mean." He dresses like a gypsy, absurdly loaded with the plunder of a hundred brushes with hated civilization: a silken sash, a silver-hafted knife, a marten's-fur cap, Mexican coins for buttons, three worthless watches slung around his neck, a rifle with a mahogany stock banded in precious metal; and he carries the prime symbol of evil—the spoiler's axe. Like Lennie in Steinbeck's *Of Mice and Men,* he is ignorant, but possessed of terrible and menacing potential for destruction which he can barely control. He stands for the great barbarian melting pot of America, unleashed, in Cooper's aristocratic view, upon the prostrate body of nature.

Cooper's story, however, is really the story of how Ishmael Bush learned to value the ways of civilization, how he redeemed himself and rose up out of his brutishness to wisdom and sanity and maturity, how out in nature he exchanged the role of Caliban for that of Prospero who in the end puts all things right. *The Prairie* is therefore very much Bush's story, though it is again a measure of Cooper's ambivalence that Bush is forced to compete throughout with Leatherstocking for the reader's attention because Cooper cannot finally make up his mind about nature versus civilization. In a sense, Bush and the bee hunter, Paul Hover, of the next generation, are to be seen as Leatherstocking's successors in a maturing America, with all the sad and sentimental connotations that that condition brings with it.

Despite twists and turns of plot, the course of Bush's education is relatively simple. One of his stalwart but stupid sons is mysteriously murdered. Bush thrashes about in a thicket of accusations and misdirected Old Testament tribal wrath. First he believes the Indians did it, then poor, good Leatherstocking.

Finally, however, he learns that it was Abiram White, his own brother-in-law. Since there is no law out in the wilderness (some say, west of the Pecos) he is forced to create his own court of justice, conduct a trial, convict, condemn, and hang Abiram White. It is as a result of this experience that the tribal patriarch repents his own evil ways, learns the value of law, and civilization comes at last to the prairie. He is finally seen as the dispenser of justice, setting free Inez, giving his ward, Ellen, to Paul Hover, freeing Captain Middleton, coming to terms with the Indians, and in general making peace with civilization.

The Indians form a counter-story to that of Ishmael Bush. Both Pawnee and Sioux, though fierce, no-quarter fighters, have codes of honor and justice. This is symbolized by the dramatic passage of arms between Mahtoree and Hard-Heart on an island in the river between the two warring Indian armies that so much resembles the chivalric duel between Richard the Lion-Hearted and Saladin in Walter Scott's *The Talisman*. Cooper also goes to great lengths, some say absurd lengths, to indicate how the Indian's closeness to nature and his intuitive grasp of its ways makes him the supremely appropriate inhabitant of the great prairie no-man's land. He repeats, on several occasions in the book, Dr. James's conclusion that the Great American Desert should form a permanent and healthy barrier to American expansion. It should be left to nature's noblemen, the wild, free, yet honorable redmen with whom Leatherstocking elects to spend his declining years. But alas, the reader realizes sadly that Leatherstocking and his Indian friends are destined, like Uncas the last Mohican, to vanish before the march of empire—however good that empire may be.

The two pairs of younger characters in the book deserve further mention. Inez de Certavallos and her sleepy Spanish father represent, of course, decadent Europe and its feeble colonial culture in America. Captain Middleton, full of youthful excitement bordering on hysteria, is nonetheless a brave representative of the upper-class military aristocracy, making him a fit companion in Cooper's blue book for Inez who is of gentle birth. Ellen Wade and Paul Hover are the rising energetic middle-class generation. Little orphan Ellen is a girl scout, a combination Tess Trueheart and Doris Day, brave, bubbly-clean, and reverent who neverthe-less works her "womanly wiles" on the naive bee hunter who has followed her halfway across the continent with an only vaguely defined purpose in mind. Paul Hover, of course, finds happiness. He has his Ellen in the end, he has his bee business, and best of all, he is Leatherstocking's designated successor. He receives the magic laying on of hands. On the latter point, however, Cooper somehow fails to convince. One is left to wonder if Paul Hover represents a truly apostolic successor, especially since Cooper did not continue *his* story (as a "son of Leatherstocking," so to speak) in 1840, but rather went back to the young manhood of Natty Bumppo himself. And further, in *The Pathfinder* Cooper created a similar character, still unsatisfactory as a surrogate— the young sailor, Jasper Western. The aristocratic Cooper, it seems, never could really reconcile himself emotionally to the middle class.

With most of the characters accounted for, we are left with only the ridiculous Dr. Obed Bat. The good doctor is clearly Cooper's attempt to write one of Shakespeare's "low" or comic characters into his story. Dr. Bat is a distant kin to Justice Shal-low, Ancient Pistol, perhaps even in some ways to Doll Tear-sheet. In his great pretension and corresponding lack of wisdom or common sense, he slightly resembles Falstaff, though Cooper's character falls far short of any such lofty literary attainment.

Yet, Dr. Bat adds an important dimension to Cooper's story that is commonly overlooked. For one thing, the impractical naturalist very probably reflects Cooper's personal reaction to Dr. James's overly scientific account of Major Long's adventure. The James narrative is studded with official and sober scientific de-scriptions that do not enhance the belletristic quality of the story and are real-life counterparts to Dr. Bat's penchant for Linnean nomenclature on any and every occasion. Dr. James's businesslike descriptions of bizarre, potentially colorful phenomena must be ranked with Dr. Bat's obtuseness in mistaking his own donkey (Asinus domesticus) for a buffalo (Vespertilio horribilis). Con-sider for instance this absurd visual image so soberly presented by Dr. James as a typical scene in the "Bad Heart" village: " 'I saw one mother,' Dr. James carefully recorded, 'apparently thirty years of age and of usual stature, suckling her infant who *stood* upon the ground. She found it necessary to stoop but little and stood observing us almost erect while the child of about two years was nursing.' " But Dr. Bat was not intended solely as a figure of humor, nor simply as a vehicle for Cooper's impatience. He also embodies Cooper's comment on science and the validity of the abstract scientific view of nature as opposed to Leatherstocking's common-sense intuitive outlook. Major Long's staff, preoccupied with measuring Pikes Peak, overlooked its grandeur. Dr. Bat errs in the same direction: " 'I made my own base, knew the length of the perpendicular by calculation, and to draw the hypotenuse had nothing to do but to work my angle,' said the busy Dr. Bat describing how he was rescued after being lost from camp. 'I supposed the guns were fired for my benefit, and changed my course for the sounds—not that I think the senses more accurate or even as accurate as a mathematical calculation, but I feared some of the children might need my services.' "

Dr. Bat sees nature only in the abstract. He is a collector out of context, a systematizer, a classifier. He does not know true nature and he is consequently a virtually helpless tenderfoot. And he does not learn. He misses life itself. In Cooper's view, he is the most ignorant of all, beyond even the redemption afforded Ishmael Bush. Clearly Cooper, the artist and romantic, detested the world of science and abstract reasoning. As early as 1827, out on the boundless prairies of Cooper's imagination, the "two cultures" stood unalterably opposed.

One could not arrive at truth through science, but one could do so in the most profound sense through history, the literary imagination, romance, and myth. Though Leatherstocking faded away into the sunset, broken twig, toothless hound, and all, Cooper could never forget him. He was too much a part of Cooper's own, and changing America's, basic experience. He lives on today, out of time, out of space, far out of the course of ordinary "realistic" experience, perhaps in the realm of what J.R.R. Tolkien called "Faërie," but in any case ever so much more historical than history itself. Whatever "literary offenses" Fenimore Cooper committed, lack of insight, broad vision, profundity, imagination, and genius were not among them.

Notes

1. The most accessible version of Dr. James's narrative can be found in volumes XIV–XVII of Reuben Gold Thwaites, *Early Western Travels Series* (Cleveland, 1905). This is a reprint of the edition published in 1823 by Longman, Hurst, Rees, Orme, and Brown in London, and by H. C. Carey and I. Lea in Philadelphia.

2. See D. H. Lawrence, *Studies in Classical American Literature* (New York, 1966), p. 53.

3. This reference and the reference in the concluding sentence of the present article are to Mark Twain's essay "The Literary Offenses of Fenimore Cooper" which appears in *How To Tell A Story and Other Essays* (New York, 1897), pp. 78–96. In this essay Mark Twain attacks Cooper in considerable detail for not being a close observer either of nature or of human behavior and language.

7 FRANCIS PARKMAN:
THE OREGON TRAIL

David Levin

In the spring of 1846 an aristocratic young Bostonian named Francis Parkman set out with a friend to experience life among the western American Indians, a thousand miles beyond the frontier. Parkman had graduated from Harvard College two years earlier and had spent some time studying law, but now he was dedicated to writing history, and he wanted to study Indian life at firsthand. In 1847 he published in *The Knickerbocker Magazine* the sketches that he later collected under the title *The California and Oregon Trail*. This book, written when Parkman was only twenty-four years old, remains in print in several editions nearly one hundred fifty years later. It is a remarkably representative book. Some reasons for its original success and its continuing interest may help us to appreciate its value.

The date of Parkman's adventure is of central importance, both from a literary and from a historical point of view. A number of excellent contemporary writers, not all of them known to Parkman, were turning their adventurous experience into literary art. Richard Henry Dana, Jr., narrated the experiences and pleaded the cause of ordinary sailors in *Two Years before the Mast* (1840). Washington Irving followed his famous books on travels in England and Spain with narratives from his tour of the American West, in a volume entitled *A Tour on the Prairies* (1835). And in the very year of Parkman's journey to the West two of the best American writers of the century occupied themselves with the literature of personal experience in nature: Herman Melville published *Typee*, a narrative based on his life among cannibals in the Marquesas Islands; and Henry

Thoreau, in residence at Walden Pond, was already recording his experiment in confronting the essential facts of life—an experiment on which he would report a few years later in one of our great books, *Walden; or, Life in the Woods* (1854).

Every one of these books profits from a commitment to study the manners of others, to report on a life close to nature, and to use the author's new perspective as a means of revealing new truths about American civilization. Melville's protagonist is surprised to learn that a society of cannibals lives without internal strife because it lives without money, and he concludes that western civilized man (observed through his historic influence on primitive cultures such as the Marquesas and the Sandwich Islands) is "the most ferocious creature on the face of the earth." Henry Thoreau, hoeing beans near Concord, hears the music of a military band and comments not about life in the Sandwich Islands but about Americans who are "said to live in New England."

Francis Parkman begins his journey, then, at a time of great literary concern with American character and destiny, in the year Bernard DeVoto later called The Year of Decision. His adventure coincides with the opening of the war between the United States and Mexico. In the West he meets emigrants bound for the Pacific Coast, and persecuted Mormons on their way to Utah. Before returning East to the "settlements" he meets soldiers both going to and returning from Mexico. The whole country seems at times to be full of movement toward the West. For better or worse, American destiny seems to be manifest. The Indian nations and the buffalo, wandering together across the Great Plains, are doomed.

Parkman, of course, already knew before setting out for the West that the Indians' way of life was doomed. His entire book, like many others of the time—from James Fenimore Cooper's romances to the histories to which Parkman himself devoted his later career—is steeped in nostalgia for a primeval world that is fated to change drastically. Parkman arrives not only prepared to study strange manners and natural phenomena but also convinced that they will very soon disappear.

The Oregon Trail is therefore filled with pictures that express a remarkable intensity, as if the narrator were at once resolved to suffuse his life with experience and to preserve the experience in images against the immediate threat that similar experience will no longer be possible. He must see the Indians before their way of life vanishes. He longs to experience the buffalo hunt, an Indian war, the summer migration of an Indian village. He rejoices to hear that the Dahcotah nation plans war against the people called Snakes, and he is deeply disappointed when he misses the action. Struck with a debilitating illness, he acts out what might be considered an allegory of his entire scholarly life as he defies sickness and forces himself onward over a vast landscape in a desperate effort to find the Indians in their genuine martial condition. Ill and alone, he wanders over dry hills and plains in futile search of a large Indian army. With him he carries three books, the Bible, the works of Shakespeare, and the works of Byron, but it is only the last of these that he mentions reading during his long adventure. Lonely endurance in the face of hardship is his test of manhood.

The excellent pictures that result from these attitudes express some of the best qualities of romantic writing in nineteenth-century America. Among contemporaries only Thoreau and Melville can match the exactness of Parkman's pictures: the prairie teeming with animal life, snakes, owls, prairie dogs, wolves, antelope; a bullfrog, a turtle, and snakes in a pond; the "level monotony of the plain" when it is empty of movement and Parkman can see "not a tree nor a bush nor a living thing"; the moon rising in a prairie sky; a group of "squalid" Indians with shaved heads and mounted on "meagre little horses" laden with buffalo meat; a wagon train seemingly motionless ("the tall white wagons and the little black specks of horsemen" in the "tall rank grass" of the prairie); a sudden prairie thunderstorm turning the woods purple and "levelling the tall grass"; ox-wagons fording a treacherously swift stream; "a long procession of buffalo . . . walking in Indian file, with the utmost gravity and deliberation," on the crest of a distant hill.

In depicting the buffalo, Parkman takes care to communicate the experience of wild terrain, as well as the massive numbers of buffalo, before he concentrates on what it is like to shoot a single buffalo bull. On his first hunt, for example, he follows his guide through the tall, rank grass toward the base of the hills:

From one of their openings descended a deep ravine, widening as it issued on the prairie. We entered it, and galloping up, in a moment were surrounded by the bleak sand-hills. Half of their steep sides were bare; the rest were scantily clothed with clumps of grass, and various uncouth plants, conspicuous among which appeared the reptile-like prickly-pear. They were gashed with numberless ravines; and as the sky had suddenly darkened and a cold gusty wind arisen, the strange shrubs and the dreary hills looked doubly wild and desolate.

In almost every chase, with Indian hunters and with his few traveling companions, Parkman reminds us of the immensity of western space, the changeable terrain, the correction of illusion as one rides at full speed over rough but seemingly level ground and then suddenly loses perspective when the land dips between two hills. Repeatedly the chase takes the hunter miles away from his companions, and he must find his solitary way back to camp after a lonely separation, sometimes overnight.

This kind of experience leads Parkman to anticipate some of the techniques of impressionism, as in the passage I have just quoted, and it also leads him to stress the versatility of human vision. The painter's eye, restricted a moment ago by the sudden entry into the ravine, can now, in the open country, hold in view a massive number of animals:

We had gone scarcely a mile when we saw an imposing spectacle. From the river bank on the right, away over the swelling prairie on the left, and in front as far as the eye could reach, was one vast host of buffalo. The outskirts of the herd were within a quarter of a mile. In many parts they were crowded so densely together that in the distance their rounded backs presented a surface of uniform blackness; but elsewhere they were more scattered, and from amid the multitude rose little columns of dust where some of them were rolling on the ground. Here and there a battle was going forward among the bulls. We could distinctly see them rushing against each other, and hear the clattering of their horns and their hoarse bellowing.

From that distant perspective Parkman takes us with him in chase of the herd until, "half suffocated by the dust and stunned by the trampling" sound, he gives us a sharp impression from the center of the mass as the herd rushes into a ravine: "Suddenly, to

my amazement, the hoofs were jerked upwards, the tails flour-
ished in the air, and amid a cloud of dust the buffalo seemed to
sink into the earth before me."

The climactic picture of the buffalo, however, is a clear portrait
of an individual creature confronted by the lone hunter, who lies
in wait by a river and watches the buffalo come to drink. Except
for a few more adjectives and some uncertainty about the point
of view, Parkman gives us here the literary method and the attitude toward nature that have become associated in our century
with the name of Ernest Hemingway:

[The hunter] sits down quietly on the sand. Listening intently, he
hears the heavy monotonous tread of the approaching bull. The moment after, he sees a motion among the long weeds and grass just at
the spot where the path is channeled through the bank. An enormous
black head is thrust out, the horns just visible amid the mass of tangled mane. Half sliding, half plunging, down comes the buffalo upon
the river-bed below. He steps out in full sight among the sands. Just
before him a runnel of water is gliding, and he bends his head to
drink. You may hear the water as it gurgles down his capacious
throat. He raises his head, and the drops trickle from his wet beard.
He stands with an air of stupid abstraction, unconscious of the lurking danger. Noiselessly the hunter cocks his rifle. As he sits upon the
sand, his knee is raised, and his elbow rests upon it, that he may level
his heavy weapon with a steadier aim. . . . The bull, with slow deliberation, begins his march over the sands to the other side. He advances his foreleg, and exposes to view a small spot, denuded of hair,
just behind the point of his shoulder; upon this the hunter brings the
sight of his rifle to bear. . . . The spiteful crack of the rifle responds to his touch, and instantly in the middle of the bare spot appears a small red dot. The buffalo shivers; death has overtaken him,
he cannot tell from whence; still he does not fall, but walks heavily
forward, as if nothing had happened. Yet before he has gone far out
upon the sand, you see him stop; he totters; his knees bend under
him, and his head sinks forward to the ground. Then his whole vast
bulk sways to one side; he rolls over on the sand, and dies with a
scarcely perceptible struggle.

The same kind of pictorial skill helps Parkman to give his
human pictures a depth not merely visual but also historical. At
the very beginning he shows us a remarkably varied collection of

people preparing to leave the frontier settlements. When he arrives at Fort Laramie after weeks of travel, he encounters a migrant Indian village and a large group of emigrants headed West. He depicts the emigrants sharply as "a crowd of broad-brimmed hats, thin visages, and staring eyes. . . . Tall, awkward men, in brown homespun; women, with cadaverous faces and long lank figures, came thronging in together, and, as if inspired by the very demon of curiosity, ransacked every nook and corner of the fort." Parkman shrewdly notices the indiscriminate thoroughness of their invasion, the depth of their anxiety and mistrust for strangers, and their bewilderment before the immensity and desolation of the country through which they slowly travel: "They seemed," he says, "like men totally out of their element; bewildered and amazed, like a troop of schoolboys lost in the woods." He catches the determination, the unpreparedness, and the misery of these migrant families in one symbolic picture that makes them the last pilgrims in a three-hundred-year-old westward movement. He notices along the trail beside the river Platte

> the shattered wrecks of ancient claw-footed tables, well waxed and rubbed, or massive bureaus of carved oak. These, some of them no doubt the relics of ancestral prosperity in the colonial time, must have encountered strange vicissitudes. Brought, perhaps, originally from England; then, with the declining fortunes of their owners, borne across the Alleghanies to the wilderness of Ohio or Kentucky; then to Illinois or Missouri; and now at last fondly stowed away in the family wagon for the interminable journey to Oregon. But the stern privations of the way are little anticipated. The cherished relic is soon flung out to scorch and crack upon the hot prairie.

The pictures of migrant Indian villages have the same strong historical quality, but here Parkman does not need to comment so explicitly on their symbolic meaning. From his first encounter outside Fort Laramie through his sojourns among the Ogillallah and among the Dahcotah in the Black Hills, he gives us numerous pictures of the nomadic village that travels all day, establishes itself quickly in tents at evening, and then disappears in the morning as fast as these fated Indians and the buffalo on which they thrive will disappear from the face of the Great

Plains. Throughout his description of Indian customs and manners, the suddenness of their arrival and departure, with imagery of swarms, reinforces our sense of their impermanence.

Yet Parkman's tone in describing Indian life rings with the condescension of the genteel New Englander's gilded conception of progress. As he moves among the Indians Parkman sounds very much like Tommo, the narrator of Herman Melville's *Typee*, but unlike Melville's narrator Parkman never learns to respect the people whose life he observes. He speaks in the tone of the civilized New Englander observing inferior beings, and his language is full of allusions to savages, superstition, cutthroats, half-breeds. When concentrating on the ugliness or the harshness of Indian life, he creates vivid, often comic pictures which many readers have welcomed as a correction of sentimental fiction about the noble savage. Consider, for example, his description of an eighty-year-old Ogillallah squaw:

> The moving spirit of the establishment was an old hag of eighty. You could count all her ribs through the wrinkles of her leathery skin. Her withered face more resembled an old skull than the countenance of a living being, even to the hollow, darkened sockets, at the bottom of which glittered her little black eyes. Her arms had dwindled into nothing but whip-cord and wire. Her hair, half black, half gray, hung in total neglect nearly to the ground, and her sole garment consisted of the remnant of a discarded buffalo-robe tied round her waist with a string of hide. Yet the old squaw's meagre anatomy was wonderfully strong. She pitched the lodge, packed the horses, and did the hardest labor in the camp. From morning till night she bustled about the lodge, screaming like a screech-owl when anything displeased her.

Here and in more pleasant delineations of Indian clothing and customs Parkman gives us vivid information from an uncomprehending outsider whose self-criticism never extends beyond good-humored reminiscences of the discomforts of travel. He is a faithful reporter and a brave man, but limited by a very narrow conception of Indian culture. He can describe an Ogillallah hero who looks like "an Apollo of bronze" and speaks in the "deep notes of an organ"; but he must remind us that "after all [the hero] was but an Indian." Indian hospitality, the nomadic life, and Indian religion thus come to us in Parkman's pages as an ill-

comprehended experience, and Indian thought, like Indian conversation, seems empty, to be judged by the standard of technological and Unitarian progress. "They were thorough savages,"
Parkman says of the Ogillallah. "Neither their manners nor their
ideas were in the slightest degree modified by their contact with
civilization. They knew nothing of the power and real character
of the white men, and their children would scream in terror
when they saw me. . . . They were living representations of the
'stone age.' "

It is just after this introduction to Ogillallah life that Parkman
predicts the decline of the buffalo and therefore the ruin of the
"large wandering communities who depend on them for support. . . . The Indians," he says, "will soon be abased by whiskey and overawed by military posts; so that within a few years
the traveller may pass in tolerable security through their country.
Its danger and its charm will have disappeared together." Parkman understands the direction of history but not the nature of
Indian life. For him that exists only as danger and charm, as
experience and image but not as value.

In this regrettable limitation, as in his strength, Parkman represents American literary culture in his time. Of course, the western Indians in those days were often a genuine threat to any
stranger moving across the landscape, but Parkman seems unable
to connect the Indians' hostility with the threat posed to their
life by white emigration. He cannot transcend the "white man's"
point of view. He repeatedly comments on the need to treat
Indian offenses severely in order to avoid contemptuous attacks
in consequence, and although he never does encounter real danger from Indians he describes many near misses and narrates
several tales of murder.

Despite his criticism of sentimental portrayals of Indians, then,
Parkman achieved in *The Oregon Trail* one of the most lively
accounts we have of Indian and emigrant life on the Great
Plains. He does not underestimate the misery caused by insects,
oppressive heat, violent storms, runaway horses, disagreeable
companions, and enervating illness. His portrayal of a starving
Negro who has wandered for thirty-three days on the prairie,
barely subsisting on crickets and lizards, gives us a view of the
wonders encountered in the West, and a terrifying glimpse of

loneliness that is just as powerful as Melville's portrait of a young cabin boy driven mad by his solitary immersion in the vast calm of the Pacific Ocean. Even in some of the descriptions of his own loneliness, when his illness is most distressing, Parkman lets us experience both the misery and the heroism attendant on adventure in the West.

Here, as I have already suggested, Parkman's narrative tends toward allegory, for he will spend the rest of his life in a literary quest for genuine historical Indians, and will fight against an illness more completely debilitating than the one that afflicted him during this journey. Among all the motley characters and types portrayed in *The Oregon Trail,* Parkman is almost unique in his capacity to understand the historical significance of the experience. Both the merits and the defects of his reflections on actual Indian life owe something to his interest in legendary Indians, and when he encounters the grandsons of Daniel Boone among the bands of emigrants he is alert to the legend of the frontiersman. In the characterization of his guide Henri Chatillon, Parkman finds legend justified in reality.

Henri Chatillon is an illiterate hero, schooled in the ways of the Indian and the prairie, possessed of "a natural refinement of mind"; his face is "a mirror of uprightness, simplicity, and kindness," and he has a naturally shrewd perception of human character. When Parkman meets him he has just returned to St. Louis after four years in the Rockies, and he is prepared to set forth almost immediately again. He has fought the grizzly bear, he is thoroughly at home among the Indians, and he is loyal to his Indian wife, whose grievous death occurs during the narrative. Parkman depicts him only a few times, but with unforgettable effect when Chatillon moves easily among a herd of buffalo, who "seem no more to regard his presence than if he were one of themselves." He regards the buffalo as "a kind of companions," and he tells Parkman that he never feels alone when they are around him. Like Cooper's Leatherstocking, he cannot abide the wanton shooting of wild creatures. He acts most forcefully in Parkman's narrative as the virtuous antagonist of a self-indulgent soldier who has joined the party for the journey back to the settlements.

The return to those secure communities is for Parkman a re-

turn from the "arid deserts, meagrely covered by the tufted buf-
falo-grass," to Arcadian plains "carpeted with rich herbiage
sprinkled with flowers," to the green prairies "of the poet and
novelist." As Parkman expresses relief over his return to the settlements, he remains true to the call of the wilderness, to which
he looks back regretfully. It is Henri Chatillon, at the end of
the book, who represents that attraction in the final paragraph.
Parkman depicts him there in plain city clothes that express his
"native good taste"; and we are asked at the end to imagine him
riding the gift horse of Parkman's comrade and firing Parkman's
rifle in the Rocky Mountains. There, in Parkman's fancy, Henri
Chatillon rides as a living testimony to the possibility of interchange between the doomed past and the inevitable future, and
Parkman himself heads East on railroad coaches and steamboats
to memorialize that possibility in a book.

Chatillon thus resembles not only Cooper's Leatherstocking,
whose virtues he embodies, but also Melville's Bulkington, the
sailor in *Moby-Dick* who, having just returned to Nantucket
from a three-year voyage, immediately embarks on another.
Chatillon cannot stay long in the settlements; he must return to
the mountains. And the overwhelming effect of Parkman's book
is an impression of the grandeur in which men like Chatillon
and more uncouth, typical trappers live their exciting, dangerous, hardy lives. Sometimes the empty prairie is "an impersona-
tion of Silence and Solitude." Once, at sunset, it looks like "a
turbulent ocean, suddenly congealed when its waves were at the
highest, and it lay half in light and half in shadow as the rich
sunshine, yellow as gold, was pouring over it. The rough bushes
of the wild sage were growing everywhere, its dull pale-green
overspreading hill and hollow." Soon afterward, the hill country
nearby is filled with violent action as Ogillallah hunters kill
buffalo with bow and arrow, and Parkman gives us an unforgettable view of some young men cracking huge buffalo thighbones
and devouring the marrow. It is the rich, wild variety of life and
the vast size of the continent that Parkman celebrates in dozens
of landscapes, portraits, catalogs. He brings experience to his
eastern readers, and he also brings them a joyful report of the
great country over which the invasion, with more of his cheers

than his regrets (and regardless of both cheers and regrets), inexorably moves.

The consequences of his heroic journey may be properly said to have remained with Parkman for the rest of his long life, for he was never again thoroughly free of sickness, and he was even forced to dictate much of the narrative to Quincy Shaw, the friend who had accompanied him. Parkman's permanent place in American letters may well have been established by this book of his youth, but he returned often to this experience in the great histories that form his major achievement. Over the next forty years he composed his *History of France and England in North America,* celebrating the achievements and sufferings of explorers, missionaries, and soldiers in the centuries from the first French settlements to the Anglo-American conquest of Canada in 1763. During the forty years of Parkman's struggle to complete that history, the American frontier was extended to the Pacific Coast, and Parkman died soon after the United States Census reported that the frontier no longer existed.

8 NARRATIVE OF THE LIFE OF FREDERICK DOUGLASS

Benjamin Quarles

The *Narrative of the Life of Frederick Douglass,* a slim volume of one hundred twenty-five pages appearing in the spring of 1845, was a landmark in the literary crusade against slavery. It took first rank among the nearly one hundred slave narratives of book-length compass, just as its author took the foremost place among the Negro Americans who made a career of striking at slavery. The wide sale and distribution of the Douglass narrative marked it as one of the most influential pieces of reform propaganda in American literature. For it bore upon the matter at hand— human bondage—an issue potentially explosive in its power to divide the nation along sectional lines, with the northern states, where slavery no longer existed, arrayed against the southern states, where black laborers were needed to produce cotton and other agricultural staples.

As a literary classic, the Douglass *Narrative* comes as a bit of a surprise, its author's antecedents being what they were. Up to the time of the book's publication, most of Douglass' life had been spent in the obscure shadowland of slavery. Born in 1817 in Maryland, Douglass had just turned twenty-one when he fled from his master to New Bedford, Massachusetts. Here for four years he turned his hand to odd jobs, facing discrimination in getting work as a ship calker, but otherwise having no trouble in taking the giant step from slavery to freedom.

A turning point in his life came in August 1841 at Nantucket, Massachusetts, when he attended a meeting of the abolitionists, a band of earnest men and women whose denunciation of slavery was hardly less harsh than their castigation of slaveholders.

While sitting in the audience watching the proceedings, Douglass was asked to say something about his experiences before he ran away. His words were halting, but he spoke with conviction, whereupon the Massachusetts Anti-Slavery Society hired him as a full-time lecturer. For the next four years the young former slave proved to be one of the prize speakers of the Society, often touring the reform circuit with the two best-known abolitionists in New England, the fiery William Lloyd Garrison and his colleague and close friend, the peerless orator, Wendell Phillips. Indeed the signed statements of Garrison and Phillips appear in the opening pages of the Douglass volume, the former writing the book's preface, and the latter furnishing an introductory letter.

The publication of his *Narrative* brought to Douglass widespread publicity on two continents. This was all he needed; henceforth his own considerable abilities as an orator and a writer would suffice to keep his name before the public. His was among the most eventful of American personal histories. In 1847, after nearly two years traveling throughout the British Isles, he returned to America and became editor of an antislavery weekly which he brought out for sixteen years. In 1848 he took a prominent part in the Seneca Falls Convention in New York which formally inaugurated the woman's rights movement in America. During the war between the North and the South he recruited troops for the former, and he urged President Abraham Lincoln to strike forcefully against slavery. After the war he received high appointive positions from three successive presidents, becoming in turn Marshal of the District of Columbia, Recorder of Deeds for the District, and United States Minister to Haiti.

The autobiography which furnished Douglass with his passport to prominence belonged to a distinctive genre, the "heroic fugitive" school of American literature. Written by or about slaves, these narratives in some cases tended to be overdrawn, relying heavily upon the pathological. Their pages ran to stock figures, such as sadistic masters and brutal overseers. Not many narratives failed to speak of the harsh treatment and cruel punishments which befell the slaves, and fewer still failed to tell of at least one instance of the separation of families, particularly of a slave mother from her child.

Unquestionably slave narratives were propagandistic. They

were, after all, a weapon in the warfare, their avowed intention being to loose the bonds of the enchained. A contribution to social history, these autobiographies and biographies of former slaves loomed large in the campaign literature of abolitionism, making an emotional impact of considerable proportions in the northern states. The *Narrative* is much like the others in its general approach. It was designed as a plea for human freedom. Describing the author's experiences in slavery, it is primarily storytelling in tone, one incident serving as a springboard for the next. But in the Douglass *Narrative* there are many points of distinction, qualities which from the viewpoint of the literary historian give his volume its pre-eminent spot. It was an arresting book on many counts.

To begin with it was written wholly by Douglass himself. It was one of the total of sixteen put down on paper by former slaves themselves, the others being ghost-written, mainly by white abolitionists. The antislavery reformers much preferred to have the former slaves write their own stories, thereby striking at the notion of Negro inferiority. Hence such a work as the Douglass *Narrative,* one that had not been filtered through someone else's mind, was doubly welcome in reformist circles.

Douglass had become literate without a day of formal schooling. While he was still a slave, his mistress had begun to teach him his letters, in response to his importunities and in the hope that he might come to know the Bible. When his master put a stop to this instruction, fearful that it might undermine his control, Douglass, as he tells it in his *Narrative,* bribed white boys on the streets of Baltimore to teach him. By the time Douglass joined the abolitionist ranks he could read and write, and he was quick to improve upon his somewhat elementary skills. The antislavery platform was a school for the training of writers no less than of orators. His close contact with well-educated men like Wendell Phillips was a stimulus to the former slave who was not completely untouched by the literary flowering in New England. Within a few months after he joined the abolitionists, he was sending letters to their weeklies, particularly William Lloyd Garrison's *Liberator.* Hence after nearly four years as a full-time abolitionist, Douglass was equipped to express himself intelligibly.

The Douglass autobiography had another asset, that of credibility. Obviously slave narratives were short on formal documentation, being put together without benefit of diaries, letters, plantation records, county archives, or a revisit to the old homestead for an on-the-spot rechecking. But if slave narratives were to be believed, and this was crucial to their success, they had to be as accurate as possible. Hence, aside from a handful of hoaxes, slave narratives strove for authenticity.

Certainly this was true of the one produced by Douglass. Soundly buttressed with specific data on persons and places, not a single one of them fictitious, the book conveys a sense of sincerity which gives it much of its strength. Indeed, one reason that Douglass wrote the book was to refute the charge that he was an impostor, that he had never been a slave. And shortly after the book was published he took a trip to the British Isles, lest his former master, now no longer in the dark as to his whereabouts, would seek to repossess him.

A man of veracity, Douglass took pains to be as accurate as his memory and his knowledge permitted. With few exceptions the white persons who entered his pages were readily identifiable. His first master, Captain Aaron Anthony, was a well-known figure on Maryland's Eastern Shore, being the general overseer for the most distinguished family in the county, the Lloyds of Wye. The name of every white person whom Douglass mentions while he was at the second place of his residence—St. Michael's— can be found in the county records located at the Easton Court House. For the years when Douglass was a slave in the city of Baltimore, his *Narrative* mentions six whites, five of whom were listed in the city directory for the period of which Douglass speaks. In a few instances Douglass has not caught the name clearly or he has misspelled it. But it is significant that no one ever seems to have questioned the existence of any person mentioned in the *Narrative*.

Douglass invites the confidence of the critical reader by his avoidance of verbatim remarks from the lips of his cast of characters. Feeling that truth, however unadorned, beggars fiction, he shunned the use of reconstructed dialogue, of contrived conversations—exchanges remembered word for word. Among the *Narrative's* special points of merit is its readability. Douglass writes in simple and direct prose, free of literary allusions, and almost without quoted passages, other than a stanza from John Greenleaf Whittier, two lines from *Hamlet,* and one from William Cowper. The details are concrete, an element of style established in the opening lines, to wit:

> I was born in Tuckahoe, near Hillsborough, and about twelve miles from Easton, in Talbot County, Maryland. I have no accurate knowledge of my age, never having seen any authentic record containing it. By far the larger part of the slaves know as little of their age as horses know of theirs, and it is the wish of most masters within my knowledge to keep their slaves thus ignorant. I do not remember to have ever met a slave who could tell of his birthday. They seldom came nearer to it than planting-time, harvest-time, cherry-time, spring-time or fall-time.

Contributing to the literary effectiveness of the *Narrative* is its pathos. Douglass scorns pity, but his pages are evocative of sympathy, as he meant them to be. Deeply affecting is the paragraph on his mother, creating its mood with the opening sentence and heightening it with every line:

> I never saw my mother, to know her as such, more than four or five times in my life; and each of these times was very short in duration, and at night. She was hired by a Mr. Stewart, who lived about twelve miles from my home. She made her journeys to see me in the night, traveling the whole distance on foot, after the performance of her day's work. She was a field hand, and a whipping is the penalty of not being in the field at sunrise. She would lie down with me, and get me to sleep, but long before I waked she was gone. Very little communication ever took place between us. Death soon ended what little we could have had while she lived. . . . She died when I was about seven years old.

The *Narrative* is not given to flights of introspection, but it clearly reveals that its author had a reflective turn of mind. The sight of a fleet of Chesapeake Bay ships moving out to the open sea on a Sunday morning could provoke in the young slave a bitter apostrophe:

You are loosed from your moorings, and are free; I am fast in my chains, and am a slave. . . . You are freedom's swift-winged angels, that fly around the world; I am confined in bands of iron! . . . The glad ship is gone; she hides in the dim distance. I am left in the hottest hell of unending slavery.

The *Narrative* is without humor or light touches. Its tone is steadily condemnatory, all roads converging to this end. For example, Douglass presents a graphic description of the holiday week, from Christmas to New Year, in which the slaves indulged in sports and merriment. But he views these holidays as a gross fraud, attributing them not to the benevolence of the masters but solely to their effectiveness in dampening the spirit of rebellion. Similarly the *Narrative* holds that singing among the slaves was not an evidence of their contentment, but a measure of their unhappiness. In perhaps the most moving passage in the volume, Douglass portrays these songs as furnishing a testimony against slavery and offering a prayer for deliverance. "The mere recurrence of those songs, even now, afflicts me," ran one passage, "and while I am writing these lines, an expression of feeling has already found its way down my cheek."

The *Narrative* is too brief and episodic to develop any single character other than that of the chronicler. But it presents a half-score or so of sharply etched portraits, among them Austin Gore, an overseer of whom we are both told and made to feel "was just the man for such a place, and it was just the place for such a man." In Edward Covey, a slave-breaker whose business it was to discipline the unruly, we have a cruel and cunning figure worthy of Dickens.

For all his criticisms of the slaveholders and their hirelings, Douglass did not fail to take note of certain human weaknesses among the slaves themselves. Never given to avoiding unpleasant facts, a hallmark of his public career, Douglass tells of the quarrels between the slaves of Colonel Lloyd and those of Jacob Jepson:

Slaves are like other people, and imbibe prejudices quite common to others. They think their own better than that of others. Many, under the influence of this prejudice, think their own masters better than the masters of other slaves. . . . It was so on our plantation. When

95

Colonel Lloyd's slaves met the slaves of Jacob Jepson, they seldom parted without a quarrel about their masters; Colonel Lloyd's slaves contending that he was the richest and Mr. Jepson's slaves contending that he was the smartest. These quarrels would almost always end in a fight. . . . The slaves seemed to think that the greatness of their masters was transferable to themselves. It was considered as being bad enough to be a slave; but to be a poor man's slave was deemed a disgrace indeed!

If the *Narrative* goes into detail about Douglass' experiences as a slave, it tells us nothing about his manner of getting away. This omission was deliberate. Douglass was highly critical of slaves who divulged publicly their techniques of escape. In his opinion such a practice played into the hands of the enemy, making the underground railroad an upperground railroad. "I would," he wrote, "keep the merciless slaveholder profoundly ignorant of the means of flight adopted by the slave." Douglass' own manner of escape was not particularly dramatic or novel; he rode a train from Baltimore to Philadelphia, using as his passport the borrowed "free papers" of a Negro friend who was not a slave. But however prosaic his method of escape, Douglass did not reveal it until after the Civil War.

The literary qualities of the *Narrative,* combined with its strong story line, made for excellent sales. As far as antislavery journals were concerned, the Douglass autobiography was the literary event of the season during its first weeks of publication. The *Narrative*'s initial edition of five thousand copies was sold in four months. Within a year four more editions of two thousand copies each were published. In the British Isles five editions appeared, two in Ireland in 1846 and three in England in 1846 and 1847. Within five years after its appearance, a total of some thirty thousand copies of the *Narrative* had been published in the English-speaking world. In 1848 a French edition, a paperback, was being sold in the stalls. The brisk sales of the book reflected its good press notices. The antislavery journals described it in superlatives, frequently taking the liberty of reprinting extended passages. But it also got a lengthy front-page review in the New York *Tribune,* unstinted in its praise: "Considered merely as narrative, we have never read one more simple, true, coherent and warm with genuine feeling."

Across the Atlantic the response was much similar. The London *Atlas* found it a "very remarkable little volume . . . and one of the most thrilling and absorbing imaginable." In the opinion of the Bristol *Mercury* "a more deeply interesting NARRATIVE than Douglass's can hardly be conceived." The influential *Chambers' Edinburgh Journal* was struck by its ring of truth, noting that it would "help considerably to disseminate correct ideas respecting slavery and its attendant evils." Mary Howitt, coeditor of *Howitt's Journal*, found the *Narrative* "most beautiful and affecting." *Littell's Living Age,* an American periodical, gave an estimate of its sweep in the British Isles after one year's circulation: "Taking all together, not less than one million persons in Great Britain and Ireland have been excited by the book and its commentators."

The wide circulation of the *Narrative* stamped it as a work of major influence, changing many minds and leaving its impress on public opinion. In America it struck a particularly sensitive nerve. It came upon the scene in an age characterized by reformist movements—woman's rights, peace, temperance, prison improvements, public school education, and experiments in communal living, among others. In the front rank of these schemes of human betterment stood the abolitionist crusade. In an age of reform it became the most unsettling and revolutionary of all reforms.

The primary role of the abolitionist movement resulted from its emphasis on civil rights and moral obligation. During the middle decades of the nineteenth century, antislavery sentiment was widespread in the western world, but in the United States more distinctively than anywhere else, the abolitionists assumed the role of championing civil liberties—freedom of speech, freedom of the press, and the right of petition. Thus they identified themselves with a great tradition of freedom which they proposed to translate into a universal American birthright. The abolitionists insisted that slavery was the great moral issue of the times, a veritable sin against God and man. In an age more influenced by the church than ours, the abolitionists contended that slavery was un-Christian, Jesus having taught a doctrine of universal brotherhood. In the hands of some of its stalwarts, the abolitionist movement took on the tone and sometimes the substance of a religious revival. It was in this reformist milieu that the Douglass *Narrative* found its niche, at once reflecting and deepening a mood then rife. Hence in theme, in emphasis, and in spirit the *Narrative* was an American book. It reaffirmed this country's heritage of liberty by holding a mirror up to its citizens and urging them to look at themselves, but not with rose-colored glasses. The manifesto of a typical American reformer, the *Narrative* voiced a creed of liberty that all who listened would find hard to deny.

Although Douglass was not a churchgoer, his *Narrative* reflects an undertone of retributive justice, that one reaps what he sows. The passing of his grandmother who, when her usefulness ended, had been put out in a little hut in the woods to fend for herself moved him to a rhetorical question, "Will not a righteous God visit for these things?" As short as it is, the *Narrative* devotes eight of its pages to an appendix correcting any misapprehension that its author was an opponent of religion. Douglass distinguishes two kinds of doctrine. "I love the pure, peaceable, and impartial Christianity of Christ," he wrote. "I therefore hate the corrupt, slaveholding, women-whipping, cradle-plundering, partial and hypocritical Christianity of this land."

Slave narratives like that of Douglass made a deep impression in the North, most readers finding their testimony quite persuasive. Outside the South, most people got their impressions about slavery from having read the life stories of runaways like Douglass. Thus when Harriet Beecher Stowe wrote *Uncle Tom's Cabin* in 1852 its sales quickly reached flood proportions mainly because a receptive audience had already been created by its previous exposure to slave narratives like that of Douglass. Hence if President Abraham Lincoln could greet Mrs. Stowe as "the little lady who made this big war," certainly some of this credit might be shared by those former slaves who dinned their stories into the public mind and created an adverse image of slavery that helped make possible the emergence of a Mrs. Stowe and an Abraham Lincoln.

The influence of the *Narrative* extended across the Atlantic, engulfing the British Isles. Here too the soil was already fertile. In the summer of 1845 when Douglass and his *Narrative* arrived simultaneously in the British Isles, both were heartily received.

For twenty months Douglass was lionized, whether in England, Ireland, or Scotland, whether in large cities or at quiet cross-roads. Mayors presided over assemblies gathered to hear him. He dined with the great abolitionist Thomas Clarkson a month before his death. He spent an evening with the economist-statesman John Bright and his sister.

In his tour of the British Isles, Douglass had often carried a supply of books for display and sale. When he left England to return home, his *Narrative* continued to exert its influence, strengthening antislavery sentiment wherever it circulated. British hostility to American slavery became an important factor during the Civil War in the United States, making it impossible for the South to win diplomatic recognition in London. Former slaves and their writings had done much to create this antislavery mood across the Atlantic, and in this company we must number Frederick Douglass and his *Narrative*.

For a final evaluation of the outreach of the *Narrative* we may turn to our own times. The slim volume has been reprinted four times in the past half-dozen years, a period in which a bridge in the nation's capital has been named after Douglass; his homesite in the same city has been taken over as a national shrine by the United States Department of the Interior and a twenty-five-cent Frederick Douglass stamp of general issue has been circulated by the United States Post Office. Interest in Douglass has mounted in the past decade as the problem of Negro-white relations has taken on a new urgency. For his long career against discrimination, Douglass has been dubbed the "Father of the Civil Rights Movement."

And, of course, the *Narrative* does speak to the role of the Negro in American life, a role compounded of a struggle and, however incomplete, an overcoming. A scripture for the black man, the *Narrative* was a clear and passionate utterance of his protest and of his aspiration. But the *Narrative* does not address itself to Negroes alone or to Americans alone. It appeals to the conscience of mankind, and therein lies much of its power well over a hundred years after its initial appearance.

In a long lifetime of seventy-eight years, the prolific Douglass would turn out two additional autobiographies, plus a spate of formal lectures, magazine articles, newspaper editorials, and personal letters. These later writings would be marked by a constantly increasing factual scope and an ever-deepening social sagacity. But none of them surpassed the *Narrative* in moving eloquence and moral explicitness. It takes its place as one of the most arresting autobiographies in the entire catalog of American reform.

9 EDGAR ALLAN POE: *TALES OF THE GROTESQUE AND ARABESQUE*

John Seelye

We are all aliens in America, seeds blown from afar, and perhaps for this reason are too insistent on being true-born Americans. So much of what we call the American Renaissance, despite the bugle calls of literary nationalism, was alien also. Unlike their European counterparts, American romantics were not able to draw sentimentally upon a dead culture but were forced to seek materials elsewhere. Irving described his Hudson River grotesques in the language of Addison and Steele; Cooper transferred Scott's border wars to the American frontier; Emerson viewed nature through Coleridge's spectacles; Thoreau spent long winter evenings carving himself into a wooden image of Rousseau; Melville had an early love affair with Byron; and Hawthorne built seven-gabled castles copied from the Gothic model. The culture of nineteenth-century America was thoroughly secondhand, like its architecture, bastardized Empire crossed with miniaturized Gothic, and encrusted with the exuberant productions of that ingenious import, the jigsaw.

Most alien and most skillful in jigsaw literature was Edgar Allan Poe, a blowing seed that never lodged. Being most alien, Poe was perhaps the more "American," a perpetual nomad. Born of an English mother in Boston, the child of wandering players, Poe was early orphaned, and spent the rest of his life a restless outcast, the Ishmael that Melville, secure in his family circle, liked to imagine himself. Having been raised in England by foster parents, the John Allans of Scotland, England, and Virginia, Poe early lost his heart to the idea of aristocracy: not to the responsibilities of peerage, but to the theatrical posturings of

Lord Byron and the regency dandies made famous by the novels of Bulwer-Lytton. Once again transplanted, this time to Virginia, he assumed the Cavalier's resentment of modern progress, and came to equate democracy with mob rule. Expelled from the University of Virginia for indulging in the Byronic excesses which were eventually to make that institution notorious, Poe next enlisted in the army, then as now a haven for the alien consciousness. With its poetry of regulations and orders-of-the-day, the army satisfied Poe's need for system, but it left his aristocratic thirst unquenched. He attempted to satisfy his thirst by entering West Point, but his Byronic impulses once again undid him, and he was drummed out.

By 1831, when Poe was dismissed from West Point, he had already published two volumes of poetry—*Tamerlane* and *Al Aaraaf*—and at the relatively early age of twenty-two had learned that poetry is not a dependable means of support. Disinherited by his foster father, Poe was forced to adapt his aristocratic, romantic temperament to the popular fiction market, entering the world of magazine editing and writing which he did not leave until his death sixteen years later. It was a peculiar environment for Poe, and yet his talents as an editor were impressive. The adjustment was difficult, however, and despite his success in boosting circulation, he was in constant trouble with his successive publishers because of his periodic fits of alcoholism and his unsteady habits. Some measure of comfort and stability was provided by his aunt, the motherly Mrs. Clemm, and her daughter, Virginia, who became Poe's bride at the age of fourteen. But this haven became in turn a torment when Virginia contracted tuberculosis and died by slow degrees.

In spite of these tensions, made worse by the miserable salaries paid him, Poe managed to come to his own in the magazine world. By means of his editorial authority, as well as by his stories, poems, and essays, Poe was able to satisfy his aristocratic yearnings and his rage for order as well. A glance at an issue of one of Poe's magazines, either the *Southern Literary Messenger* or *Graham's,* reveals how successful he was at preserving his alien identity while purveying entertainment to middle-class Americans. There, amidst turgid fiction submitted by amateur writers —usually professional men with a taste for artistic production—

and the sentimentally poetic maunderings of bored housewives, with perhaps a pompous outline of moral philosophy (in four parts) reluctantly submitted by some professor of a female seminary, the slashing colors of Poe's genius stand out like a sapphire set in lead. Poe came to inhabit a bizarre region of the mind, concocted out of memory and imagination, and blurred by the dimness of that state which exists between sleep and consciousness. On this exotic, inner coast, though a castaway, Poe could be lord of all he surveyed.

Successful as an editor of popular magazines, in his own contributions to those same periodicals Poe always assumed a contrary stand. Disappointed in his poetic ambitions, he took a peculiar revenge, expressing his genius by constructing jigsaw puzzles of ratiocination, solving cryptograms, writing meticulously nonsensical theories of composition, fooling his readers with hoaxes, shocking their middle-class sensibilities with his morbid tales of putrefaction and death, savagely attacking writers who had talent and praising those who had none, taking refuge in the arcane and ignoring the popular issues of the day, he assaulted society with an impish perversity. Poe defined himself by contraries, constructing a literary personality which was at constant odds with so much that was in fashion, a cultural, eclectic Frankenstein's monster. Poet, philosopher, painter, musician, he is the type of all romantic genius, with the satanic egotism of Byron and the encyclopedic lore of Coleridge.

It is this created consciousness which marks Poe as particularly alien to the American experience, for his frantic, surely obsessive cosmopolitanism is antithetical to the rampant nationalism of his day, in which domestic matters, however much screened through European tastes, were the chief concern. Like his daemonic heroine, Ligeia, the voice of Poe's writing is an example of the will triumphing over the inadequacies of mere matter, conditions, circumstances. In an age dominated by adulation of Washington Irving's genial mannerisms and admiration of Fenimore Cooper's adventure stories (as opposed to his political opinions), Poe's insistence on using the themes and voices of madness, sin, and death, brought perversity to a fine art.

In 1840 Poe published a collection of his sketches and stories, the work of the nine previous years. It was in 1840 also that

Cooper brought Natty Bumppo back to life in *The Pathfinder,* emphasizing his hero's muscular Christianity, and thereby betraying at last that his frontiersman was nothing more than a Methodist missionary clothed in Dan'l Boone's castoff coonskins. In that same year, Richard Henry Dana, Jr., published *Two Years Before the Mast,* a masculine, realistic, no-nonsense account of his cruise to California and back. And Margaret Fuller founded her periodical *Dial,* which registered the sunshine of Transcendental optimism. Poe's collection was called *Tales of the Grotesque and Arabesque,* and by its title alone the book shrieks its idiosyncrasy. Next to it the titles of most American books have a homespun, linsey-woolsey look, and its contents verified that initial impression. It was not, needless to say, a best seller. The *Tales* did not appeal to the readers who rushed to buy Cooper's new Leatherstocking novel, nor were those reviewers who had been struck by the verisimilitude and sinewy style of young Dana much impressed by Poe's lush mannerisms. And unlike Margaret Fuller, Poe could not even count on a minority cult of disenchanted Unitarians.

Even today, *Tales of the Grotesque and Arabesque* is seldom read in its entirety. Few of Poe's best-known stories are in the collection—they were to be written in the seven years left to him—and most of the "grotesques" are slight, pitiable tours de force of wit and scrapbook erudition, spiced with French epithets and Latin epigrams. Only "William Wilson" and "The Fall of the House of Usher," both of them written at the end of the decade, barely in time for inclusion, fall into the class of later masterpieces like "The Cask of Amontillado," "The Pit and the Pendulum," and "The Murders in the Rue Morgue." For the rest, a bare handful of memorable experiments remain. In the arabesques, "Berenice," "Ms Found in a Bottle," "Morella," and "Ligeia," we find Poe working out his claim in the only frontier that interested him, the perilous outpost of the nearly sane.

If Poe's contrived cosmopolitanism points up his alien consciousness, if his obsession with sin, madness, and death reveals his cultural perversity, it is his virtual boycott of the western frontier which cuts him off totally from the brotherhood of American letters. Except for the sardonic "The Man Who Was

Used Up," the 1840 *Tales* is completely lacking in any material alluding to the greatest of American experiences, and save for his abortive imitation of Irving's *Astoria,* "The Journal of Julius Rodman," Poe's later work is likewise deficient. At a time when America was looking westward, Poe kept his back to the frontier, as if to deny the existence of that terrifying immensity, that raw, unimaginable territory where great forces were locked in combat. Like a man dangling from a rising balloon, Poe clung to the eastern seaboard, his eyes fixed on the continent beyond. Like that dangling man, he seems to have abhorred the idea of pure, unlimited space.

Space consciousness fills the literature of the American Renaissance. Whether it is the prairies of Cooper's novels, Emerson's ever-expanding vista of opportunity, Melville's great ocean of metaphysical contingencies, or the windy immensity of Whitman's *Leaves of Grass,* the idea of space for Poe's contemporaries was somehow linked to the opening country, to the westward movement of empire, to the staggering breadth of land that was America's promised destiny. With the possible exception of Hawthorne, who shared with Poe an interest in the inner territory, most American writers saw space as an endless opening up of possibilities. They may have viewed it with fear, like Melville, caution, like Cooper, hope, like Emerson, or exultation, like Whitman, but they saw it always as expansiveness, breadth, infinity.

Perversely, as with so many other things, Poe saw space otherwise. Though he kept his back to the frontier, he could not ignore the ocean, and a number of his stories and his only novel, *Arthur Gordon Pym,* are seaborne, a circumstance which only emphasizes his peculiar consciousness. For Poe's ocean is always a gigantic helix, drawing the hapless voyager toward some vast, central maelstrom. It is never Cooper's bounding, athletic main, or Melville's great symphony of metaphysical contrasts. Spacious, it is nevertheless an ever-closing space, a claustrophobic phenomenon much like the pits, descending pendulums, walls, coffins, and heavy masonry of his other tales. Significantly, Arthur Pym spends much of his time hidden under hatches or marooned on a capsized hull. And once he gets moving southward, he is caught in a mighty current which carries him toward an unknown destiny.

Whereas Poe's theatrical cosmopolitanism, his delight in mystification and madness provide the decoration, the furniture of his grotesques and arabesques, it is his peculiar spatial consciousness which lends them their form. In *Eureka!*, completed just before his death, Poe attempted to come to terms with the idea of pure space, and the implications of his theory of the universe have direct equivalents in his stories. Much more than his pretentious, half-fraudulent "Philosophy of Composition," the anti-transcendental *Eureka!* is a diagram of Poe's unique, perverse art, and to some extent explains the peculiar effect that his great tales, commencing with "Fall of the House of Usher," have on the reader even today. For Poe's theory of unity, of oneness, unlike that of Emerson and the Transcendentalists, was a theory of dissolution, of ultimate annihilation, claustrophobically realized. Having sprung from nothingness, the universe would return to nothing, and was held in atomic diffusion only as an effort of thought by the Supreme Being. According to Poe, the atomic particles were held apart by forces of mutual attraction and repulsion, but they were at the same time in a state of gradual return to the origin of their being, pulled by gravity toward ultimate annihilation. These tensions and their fatal resolution have counterparts in Poe's fiction as early as "Ms Found in a Bottle," the prototype of *Arthur Gordon Pym*.

"The Universe," wrote Poe in *Eureka!*, "is a plot of God," and though he added that unlike the plots of God, the plots of men are never perfect, he also noted that there are definite correspondences between the art of fiction and the design of the universe. In the world, he observed, there is an "absolute *reciprocity of adaptation*," of creatures to environment, environment to creatures. The pleasure given mankind by a display of his own ingenuity, furthermore, "is in the ratio of the approach to this species of reciprocity. In the construction of a plot, for example, in fictitious literature, we should aim at so arranging the incidents that we shall not be able to determine of any one of them, whether it depends from any other or upholds it." Poe's language here contains an architectural metaphor, suggesting that the incidents in a plot are like building stones, each participating in the general structure without calling particular attention to itself. This variation on the organic theories of Coleridge is of particular significance, considering Poe's emphasis on architecture in "Fall of the House of Usher," the best demonstration in *Tales of the Grotesque and Arabesque* of his spatial theory.

Poe wrote by the rule of two. This rule is manifest in *Eureka!* with its emphasis on attraction and repulsion, one and many, matter and spirit, body and soul. Along with his claustrophobia, it is the secret of the concentered energy, the compressed, closed-in quality of his art. Important also is Poe's style of plenitude, with his delight in luxurious description, and his tendency to lavish attention on the interior decoration of his many gloomy settings. Then there is his air of hushed urgency, the confession of author to reader, of dark secrets imparted in a tense, perhaps slightly mad interview. Author and reader are the basic two, the assumed couplet which is the foundation of the pairs to follow. In "Metzengerstein" there are the rival families, who become a single rider and his steed, engulfed in a final holocaust; in "Berenice" there is the obsessed narrator and his cataleptic cousin, and in "Morella" and "Ligeia" we are given examples of soul-transference in which the play of couplets receives a metempsychotic finale. Attraction and repulsion are the great forces in Poe's universe, and his diseased, crazed heroines have just that double quality—they attract by the same qualities which repel.

Perhaps the most memorable of Poe's couples is William Wilson and his alter ego, his conscience, whose final encounter kills them both. " 'You have conquered, and I yield,' " William Wilson is told in a voice which echoes his own, " 'Yet henceforth art thou also dead—dead to the World, to Heaven, and to Hope! In me didst thou exist—and, in my death, see by this image, which is thine own, how utterly thou hast murdered thyself.' " As in *Eureka!* the reuniting of the pairs, body and soul, matter and spirit, result in annihilation for both, for duality is but oneness exemplified and oneness is death. The rule of two is the rule of separateness, of falling apart, of echo. And yet it is the principle of joining, of multiples, of paradox welded into completed irony. The closing of the circuit electrocutes, because absolute unity is a circle of nothingness, is death. Only by keeping the pairs diffused can life go on. Togetherness is annihilation.

Of all the stories in *Tales of the Grotesque and Arabesque,* "The Fall of the House of Usher" best exemplifies the phenomenology of Poe's *Eureka!* Again it is a matter of twos, commencing with the narrator and his former schoolmate, Roderick Usher, and concluding with Roderick and his twin sister, Madeline, who die in one another's arms, the last of their family, a deathly union which brings their ancestral house crumbling down. The "house," at once a physical structure and a symbol of the Usher family, is pictured in terms which prophesy the dreadful outcome of the tale. Set in a wasteland of gray sedges and white, decaying trees, it stares down into the dark tarn by which it is surrounded with "vacant eye-like windows." The phrase is Poe's, and he repeats it twice, as the sedges, the trees, and the eye-like windows are reflected in the tarn.

When the narrator first views the decaying house, he is convinced that there hangs about it an atmosphere peculiar to the place, "a pestilent and mystic vapor, dull, sluggish, faintly discernible and leaden-hued." This singular vapor of decay enhances the fungus-covered exterior of the building, from which "no portion of the masonry had fallen," and yet which seems to present "a wild inconsistency between its still perfect adaptation of parts and the crumbling condition of the individual stones." Still entire, still standing, the building nonetheless has "a barely perceptible fissure . . . extending from the roof . . . in front" and making "its way down the wall in a zig-zag direction, until it became lost in the sullen waters of the tarn."

This condition of universal decay and imminent collapse is shared between the house with the "eye-like" windows and its inhabitant, Roderick Usher, whose physical frame and mental control are declining rapidly. Overcome with a constant terror of the future, an apprehension of his own imminent destruction, Usher attributes his condition to the effect upon him of the building, convinced that "the mere form and substance of his family mansion" has had a destructive effect "over his spirit"—matter over mind, body over soul. His sister Madeline shares in this general malaise, the victim of a lingering disease, approaching dissolution. Dwelling on the duality of his self and his decaying house, Usher paints abstractions of luminous, subterranean passageways, and has written a poem, "The Haunted Palace," in which the human mind is depicted in architectural terms. One recalls again the "eye-like" windows which stare into the tarn. Roderick Usher suffers from the terror that the walls of his house, unified as they are by decay and the overspreading fungus, possess a sentience, a life of their own. The decline of his family and his own debility he blames on the "silent yet importunate and terrible influence" of the house.

The catastrophe of the story, in which the prematurely entombed sister returns to confront her brother, toppling upon him and sending them both at last to their deaths, as a whirlwind howls about the phosphorescent walls of the outer house, seems to bear out Roderick's intimations of mortality, for with the death of the twins, the house itself collapses in a terrifying finale:

> The storm was still abroad in all its wrath as I found myself crossing the old causeway. Suddenly there shot along the path a wild light, and I turned to see whence a gleam so unusual could have issued; for the vast house and its shadows were alone behind me. The radiance was that of the full, setting, and blood-red moon, which now shone vividly through that once barely-discernible fissure, of which I have before spoken as extending from the roof of the building, in a zig-zag direction, to the base. While I gazed, this fissure rapidly widened— there came a fierce breath of the whirlwind—the entire orb of the satellite burst at once upon my sight—my brain reeled as I saw the mighty walls rushing asunder—there was a long tumultuous shouting sound like the voice of a thousand waters—and the deep and dank tarn at my feet closed sullenly and silently over the fragments of the "House of Usher."

This conclusion, so catastrophic in its violence and cosmic in its implications, is echoed in a sketch which Poe wrote the same year, "The Conversation of Eiros and Charmion." In the conclusion of that story there is the same "wild, lurid light alone, visiting and penetrating all things," the same "shouting and pervading sound," but here it is the destruction of the world, not a single "house," and the sound seems to come from the mouth of God, "while the whole incumbent mass of ether in which we existed burst at once into a species of intense flame, for whose surpassing brilliancy and all-fervid heat even the angels in the high Heaven of pure knowledge have no name. Thus ended all."

The House of Usher collapses into its own dread reflection,

worlds collide into nothingness, for the sum of two is one, the unity that is a void, compounded of parts equally, and held apart only by the will of the artist, be he God or Man. In stories and poems, essays and philosophical tracts, the principle remains the same, spun from the consciousness of Poe the claustrophobic, sitting in his room and looking out into a mirror at himself sitting in his room. His universe could have been bounded by a nutshell were it not for his bad dreams, whose whirling spirals of terror provided the only reality he could depend upon. Writing too quickly, trying somehow to preserve a threadbare dignity and a sane mind in a turmoil of debts and alcoholic fits, and yet out of it all, out of disinheritance and dismissal, out of his wretched feuds with editors and fellow writers, out of his absolute sense of abandonment—of being crushed between the walls of debt and rejection—out of all this Poe managed to construct the materials of his alien craft. Small wonder that for him the real world and the world of art were one, that existence depended upon a tenuous balance of forces, that all things were moving inexorably toward a perfect unity of annihilation, that oneness for him, as for his creation, Roderick Usher, meant death, an unbearable harmony, like music amplified a hundred thousand times.

NATHANIEL HAWTHORNE:

IO THE HOUSE OF THE SEVEN GABLES

Richard Harter Fogle

Nathaniel Hawthorne's *The House of the Seven Gables* was published in 1851. Like its predecessor, *The Scarlet Letter,* its origin is in the history of the Puritans of Massachusetts; in this later book there is Hawthorne family history as well, in the story of the Pyncheon family over some two hundred years in Salem. The time is Hawthorne's day, overshadowed by the past. The story is, in the words of the Preface, "a legend prolonging itself, from an epoch now gray in the distance, down into our own broad daylight, and bringing along with it some of its legendary mist. . . ." The actual House is the material symbol of the Pyncheon fortunes, an old mansion now in decline, built upon property usurped from the original owner, Matthew Maule, by the original Pyncheon, a hard, stern Puritan. This act of Colonel Pyncheon, the "founder of the house," still grips the Pyncheons of today: Judge Pyncheon, a reincarnation of the Colonel; Hepzibah, a melancholy relic of the past, and the unfortunate Clifford, her brother. Significantly, Phoebe, the Pyncheon who redeems the family, has not been reared within the shadow of the ancient House. One other person, Holgrave, dwells in the House as a lodger. We eventually discover that he is the last survivor of the injured Maules. His life, too, has been darkened, but he has a freedom not permitted to the Pyncheons.

Posterity has not agreed with him, but Hawthorne preferred this second novel to *The Scarlet Letter.* He thought the *House* better balanced, more various, more representative of his whole mind, which contained humor and delicate sentiment as well as tragic gloom. He considered it, in fact, more fully harmonious; it possessed more colors, completely blended into a satisfying aesthetic whole.

Anyone who has considered Hawthorne's theory of composition, especially his theory of the prose romance, has undoubtedly noticed his pictorial analogies for his verbal art. Perhaps, indeed, they are so numerous and obvious that we tend to overlook them as not requiring discussion. At first glance, too, they are commonplace and traditional. They call to mind both the Horatian *ut pictura poesis* of neoclassicism and the "picturesque" of the English Romantics. But, as is also true of his symbols, which are also apparently conventional, the difference with Hawthorne is that he *means* his figure of picture. He uses it consistently and responsibly. It is assimilated in his critical discourse, and fully operative in his fiction.

This contention has an important relation to a crux of Hawthorne criticism, his treatment of character. Looked at individually, Hawthorne's people do not satisfy us. They seem too abstract, too allegorical; they are all imperfect, mutilated, incomplete. They pretend to life, and like most nineteenth-century novelists Hawthorne wants to be conceded his *donnée* of reality. Conscious of a certain thinness, he nevertheless rather wistfully aspires to the illusion of verisimilitude. Thus if we go wrong, and we generally do on this point, our author himself is considerably to blame. He is trying to deceive us, and he is covering his weakness instead of playing from his strength.

His strength lies in his total conception of the art of fiction as picture, in which individual characters function not as individuals, but in relation to each other and to his total design. Thus Hawthorne's people should not be studied in isolation. Of themselves the characters of *The House of the Seven Gables* are all inadequate. Phoebe is too sweet, Hepzibah and Clifford Pyncheon are nearly ludicrous, and a little contemptible in their defenselessness. The formidable Judge is too melodramatic, too openly hateful, and the young photographer Holgrave too lightly drawn. Taken together, however, as parts or colors of the picture, as shading and contrast, they make up a design.

There are doubtless other reasons for the nature of Hawthorne's characterization. His view of life does not ordinarily permit of the dominant hero and heroine, or the dominant villain either. He believes in good and evil, but these are states not permanently identified with people; there is always the possibility that different circumstances would have produced different results. Even Judge Pyncheon, that iron-hearted hypocrite, is victim as well as tyrant. Again, Hawthorne does not believe in success, nor in lasting significance in objective action. In his major romances his principal characters appear in groups of four or five.

Further, *The House of the Seven Gables* is thoroughly relevant to the social, the psychological, and the religious history of colonial America and the young republic. It is family history as well, since the successful Pyncheons and the defeated Maules are simply two faces of the Hawthorne generations in Salem, Massachusetts. Issues arise: the Judge is the American materialist; and in the fortunes and the aspirations of the Pyncheons we see the principles of aristocracy and democracy in conflict in a young and growing society. Out of the American scene and problem we see emerging, too, more universal themes. The history of the Pyncheons repeats the Original Sin and the Fall of Man in indigenous Yankee terms; it issues from the crime of the original Pyncheon against the original Maule. One discerns in it, also, the immemorial tragedy of a house, like Aeschylus' *Oresteia,* or the Oedipus trilogy, or in modern American terms Eugene O'Neill's *Mourning Becomes Electra* or Faulkner's tales of the Sutpens and Compsons of Mississippi.

In their setting of time and place the characters of the book are recognizable social, historical, and moral types. The Judge is the modern reincarnation of the Original Puritan, and in himself the modern financial magnate, town father, and politician. Hepzibah is the aristocratic spinster with pathetic pretensions to gentility, in a relatively democratic society which is also strongly materialistic. She is slow to realize that without money her values are impotent, and at the beginning of the story we see her learning a cruel lesson in reality—she is forced to keep a "cent-shop," the equivalent of the twentieth-century corner confectionery. Clifford Pyncheon is the paradoxical but inevitable product of material success, the refined dilettante, who at a later date would have resorted to Henry Jamesian expatriation. Phoebe is the flower of

New England provincial democracy, a new and hopeful type for the American future. She is "ladylike" without being a "lady." The more ambiguous Holgrave is, with perhaps an ironic glance at the doctrines of the Fall and Redemption, the "new man" American style, a sort of New England Mark Twain, rootless, free, mobile, and versatile; and like the others, a product of a particular society.

In *The House of the Seven Gables* Hawthorne's Preface announces the theme. The romancer may, if he think fit, "so manage his atmospherical medium as to bring out or mellow the lights and enrich the shadows of the picture." The story "is a legend prolonging itself, from an epoch now gray in the distance, down into our own broad daylight, and bringing along with it some of its legendary mist, which the reader, according to his pleasure, may either disregard, or allow it to float almost imperceptibly about the characters and events for the sake of a picturesque effect." Here is of course a fourth dimension of time, and it is well to remind ourselves of the limitations of analogy. A novel is not literally a picture, though it may profitably be compared to one. Nevertheless, time merges with the pictorial: the distant past is "gray," the present is "broad daylight," and the "legendary mist" is an imaginative atmosphere, itself a sort of total lighting or aerial perspective.

The author, as he says, does not choose to mar the harmonies of his picturesque story by didacticism. He will not impale it "with its moral as with an iron rod,—or, rather, as by sticking a pin through a butterfly,—thus at once depriving it of life, and causing it to stiffen in an ungainly and unnatural attitude." The moral, however, may itself become an element of the harmony of the picturesque, by the gradations of its light. "A high truth, indeed, fairly, finely, and skillfully wrought out, brightening at every step, and crowning the final development of a work of fiction, may add an artistic glory. . . ."

Hawthorne asks of his reader and critic that he place himself at the proper distance for viewing his picture. Consequently he regrets the closeness of his work to "an actual locality." "Not to speak of other objections, it exposes the romance to an inflexible and exceedingly dangerous species of criticism, by bringing his fancy-pictures almost into positive contact with the realities of the moment." These realities would constitute, that is, an over-strong and generally inappropriate light for viewing. In his sketch "Main Street," in which a showman exhibits more than two centuries of Salem history in a "shifting panorama," a spectator damns the exhibition. The showman defends his art: " 'But, sir, you have not the proper point of view. . . . You sit altogether too near to get the best effect of my pictorial exhibition. Pray, oblige me by removing to this other bench; and, I venture to assure you, the proper light and shadow will transform the spectacle into quite another thing.' "

With "the proper point of view," then, Hawthorne trusts that "the proper light and shadow" will appear. Seen thus, the too-simple and sunny Phoebe becomes a study in harmony; and, as good, the fullest contrast with Judge Pyncheon, the embodiment of Pyncheon evil, who is a study in disharmony and excess. Phoebe "shocked no canon of taste; she was admirably in keeping with herself, and never jarred against surrounding circumstances. . . . She was very pretty; as graceful as a bird, and graceful much in the same way; as pleasant about the house as a gleam of sunshine falling on the floor through a shadow of twinkling leaves, or as a ray of fire-light that dances on the wall while evening is drawing nigh." Her primary image is sunshine, pleasantly tempered, a golden mean. Though delicately tanned, she is never fully exposed to the heat of the sun and everyday experience: on one occasion we find her using a sunshade. The key to her character, as to Hawthorne's moral and aesthetic values, is moderation. When the unfortunate Clifford almost involuntarily tries to throw himself out of a window into the street, "Phoebe, to whom all extravagance was a horror, burst into sobs and tears."

Judge Pyncheon's falsity, on the other hand, is manifested in excess and extremity. He is basically discordant. At his first introduction (in terms of portraiture, incidentally) he is a counterfeit of decorum and "keeping," always a little awry because he has no corresponding inner sense:

It was the portly, and had it possessed the advantage of a little more height, would have been the stately figure of a man considerably in the decline of life, dressed in a black suit of some thin stuff, resembling broadcloth as closely as possible. A gold-headed cane, of rare Oriental wood, added materially to the high respectability of his aspect, as did also a neckcloth of the utmost snowy purity, and the conscientious polish of his boots. His dark, square countenance, with its almost shaggy depth of eyebrows, was naturally impressive, and would, perhaps, have been rather stern, had not the gentleman considerately taken upon himself to mitigate the harsh effect by a look of exceeding good humor and benevolence. Owing, however, to a somewhat massive accumulation of animal substance about the lower region of the face, the look was, perhaps, unctuous, rather than spiritual, and had, so to speak, a kind of fleshly effulgence, not altogether so satisfactory as he doubtless intended it to be. A susceptible observer, at any rate, might have regarded it as affording very little evidence of the general benignity of soul whereof it purported to be the outward reflection. And if the observer chanced to be ill-natured, as well as acute and susceptible, he would probably suspect that the smile on the gentleman's face was a good deal akin to the shine on his boots, and that each must have cost him and his bootblack, respectively, a good deal of hard labor to bring out and preserve them.

The Judge, then, like a bad portrait is compact of harsh and glaring disharmonies. His height is not quite proportionate to his build, his suit not quite broadcloth, his linen too white, his boots too well polished. His look of benevolence is *exceeding*, and clashes with his natural sternness. He is *unctuous*, with a *fleshly effulgence*, where he intends to express spirituality.

The harmonious Phoebe, intuitively sensing his aesthetic and moral wrongness, draws back from the Judge's cousinly kiss on their first meeting. For a moment the true Judge appears, at the opposite extreme, hard and deadly cold. "It was quite as striking, allowing for the difference in scale, as that betwixt a landscape under a broad sunshine and just before a thunderstorm; not that it had the passionate intensity of the latter aspect, but was cold, hard, immitigable, like a day-long brooding cloud." In an effort to right the balance, the Judge shortly turns upon Hepzibah "a smile, so broad and sultry, that, had it been only half as warm as it looked, a trellis of grapes might at once have turned purple under its summer-like exposure."

The Judge and Hepzibah are mirror-images of each other, with attributes reversed. Hepzibah is dark, and even in her voice is a thread of blackness. Her habitual expression is a scowl, an echo of the dark-browed house of the seven gables in whose shadow she lives. But within is light, for she has a soft and loving heart. Her darkness has been impressed upon her, while it is the reality of the outward-smiling Judge. There is no blackness in the delicate hedonist Clifford, but with a difference in shading he also is the obverse of the Judge, with a certain resemblance on the other hand to Phoebe.

Clifford readily showed how capable of imbibing pleasant tints and gleams of cheerful light from all quarters his nature must originally have been. He grew youthful while she sat by him. A beauty—not precisely real, even in its utmost manifestation, and which a painter would have watched long to seize and fix upon his canvas, and after all, in vain—beauty, nevertheless, that was not a mere dream would sometimes play upon and illuminate his face.

One notes again the portrait motif. But Clifford's hold on reality is so precarious, his connection so tenuous, that he can hardly be pictured at all.

It is remarkable, however, that the characters of *The House of the Seven Gables* have been conceived very largely as pictures. Critics have often mentioned the role of the actual portraits in the House, and the more subtle function of its mirrors. Most central is the Colonel, the original Pyncheon and "founder of the house":

In one sense, this picture had almost faded out into the canvas, and hidden itself behind the duskiness of age; in another . . . it had been growing more prominent, and strikingly expressive. . . . For, while the physical outline and substance were darkening away from the beholder's eye, the bold, hard, and, at the same time, indirect character of the man seemed to be brought out in a kind of spiritual relief.

Hawthorne reflects that "In such cases the painter's deep conception of his subject's inward traits has wrought itself into the essence of the picture, and is seen after the superficial coloring has been rubbed off by time."

This picture includes and focuses a good deal. It is the dark aura of the House, the mystic center of its evil. It contains within it the dimension of time. Most important, it interplays with and is a commentary upon the Judge, the Pyncheon of today. The Judge, as we have seen, is himself a portrait, but his essence is obscured by external detail. At his first introduction it is said of him that "He would have made a good and massive portrait; better now, perhaps, than at any previous period of his life, although his look might grow positively harsh in the process of being fixed upon the canvas."

There is likewise a portrait of Clifford as a young man, a Malbone miniature. "It is a likeness of a young man, in a silken dressing gown of an old fashion, the soft richness of which is well adapted to the countenance of reverie, with its full, tender lips, and beautiful eyes, that seem to indicate not so much capacity of thought as gentle and voluptuous emotion. Of the possessor of such features we shall have a right to ask nothing, except that he would take the rude world easily, and make himself happy in it." We see this picture again, but idealized by the loving mind of Hepzibah as she awaits the actual Clifford, many years older and just released from prison. It is "painted with more daring flattery than any artist would have ventured upon, but yet so delicately touched that the likeness remained perfect. Malbone's miniature, though from the same original, was far inferior to Hepzibah's air-drawn picture, at which affection and sorrowful remembrance wrought together." Finally, Clifford appears himself, but sadly changed. He is wearing the same dressing gown as in the Malbone miniature, but it has changed correspondingly. "At first glance, Phoebe saw an elderly personage, in an old-fashioned dressing gown of faded damask, and wearing his gray or almost white hair of an unusual length."

Two pictures more comprehensive than these illustrate Hawthorne's characteristic sense of composition and unity. The first is a kind of genre painting, Vermeer with Rembrandt shadows. The scene is a breakfast table, awaiting the first appearance of the long-banished Clifford:

Phoebe's Indian cakes were the sweetest offering of all—in their hue befitting the rustic altars of the innocent and golden age—or, so brightly yellow were they, resembling some of the bread which was changed to glistening gold when Midas tried to eat it. The butter must not be forgotten—butter which Phoebe herself had churned, in her own rural home, and brought it to her cousin as a propitiating gift—smelling of clover blossoms, and diffusing the charm of pastoral scenery through the dark-paneled parlor. All this, with the quaint gorgeousness of the old china cups and saucers, and the crested spoons, and a silver cream jug . . . set out a board at which the stateliest of old Colonel Pyncheon's guests need not have scorned to take his place. But the Puritan's face scowled down out of the picture, as if nothing on the table pleased his appetite.

By way of contributing what grace she could, Phoebe gathered some roses and a few other flowers, possessing either scent or beauty, and arranged them in a glass pitcher, which, having long ago lost its handle, was so much the fitter for a flower vase. The early sunshine— as fresh as that which peeped into Eve's bower while she and Adam sat at breakfast there—came twinkling through the branches of the pear tree, and fell quite across the table.

This quaint and mellow scene is carefully shaded, from the bright gold of the Indian cakes and the butter and the paler gold of morning sun to the dark-paneled walls and the scowling portrait of the Colonel. It is a chiaroscuro effect, but unobtrusive, gently lighted with the dominant gold, and given motion by the gentle stir of the pear-tree branches. As elsewhere, the gray mist of time plays its part in the portrait and the battered glass pitcher, and merges with the sense of poor, misty, time-battered Clifford, who is on the verge of appearing.

Finally, there is the Pyncheon garden by moonlight, Hawthorne's symbol for the light of imagination. It is at this moment that the sunny Phoebe falls in love, becoming a woman:

By this time the sun had gone down, and was tinting the clouds towards the zenith with those bright hues which are not seen there until some time after sunset, and when the horizon has quite lost its richer brilliancy. The moon, too, which had long been climbing overhead, and unobtrusively melting its disk into the azure . . . now began to shine out, broad and oval, in its middle pathway. These silvery beams were already powerful enough to change the character of the lingering daylight. They softened and embellished the aspect of the old house; although the shadows fell deeper into the angles of its many gables, and lay brooding under the projecting story, and within the half-open door. With the lapse of every moment, the garden grew

119

more picturesque; the fruit trees, shrubbery, and flower bushes had a dark obscurity among them. The commonplace characteristics—which at noontide, it seemed to have taken a century of sordid life to accumulate—were now transfigured by a charm of romance. A hundred mysterious years were whispering among the leaves, whenever the slight sea breeze found its way thither and stirred them. Through the foliage that roofed the little summer house, the moonlight flickered to and fro, and fell silvery white on the dark floor, the table, and the circular bench, with a continual shift and play, according as the chinks and wayward crevices among the twigs admitted or shut out the glimmer.

The picture presents Hawthorne's most complex harmonies of light, color, shading, blending, and motion, along with his gift of unobtrusive but significant emphasis. The moonlight deepens Phoebe's perceptions, and adds a new tone to her character. It represents the essential truth of Hawthorne's favorite art, and illuminates his definition of his own romance, managing, as he says, "his atmospherical medium [so] as to bring out or mellow the lights and enrich the shadows of the picture." It represents the aesthetic theory of *The House of the Seven Gables,* and, rightly observed, it goes far toward explaining the nature, the interrelations, and the functions of his characters.

I I   HERMAN MELVILLE:
THE CONFIDENCE-MAN

Warner Berthoff

Herman Melville's strange and puzzling prose "masquerade,"
The Confidence-Man—in Elizabeth Foster's words his "valedictory as a professional novelist"—is one of those books that makes
of the reader's own bafflement a part of its essential subject matter. It openly teases us with its apparent inconsequence, and
then, in flashes of insight that have the abrupt simplicity of an
authoritative and final wisdom, it teases our impatient expectation of an order and sequence that we would hardly think to demand of our own behavior, our own habit of consciousness. It
teases our frivolity, our deep-rooted bad faith as critically princi-
pled readers, in seeking the reassurance of stable and, so to speak,
manageable argument without giving up the privilege of being
richly diverted and entertained. Or, as Melville himself dryly puts
the matter in one of those penetrating remarks that we find scattered through *The Confidence-Man* on the nature of fiction and
our absorption in it, it catches us, too, looking "not only for more
entertainment, but, at bottom, even for more reality, than real
life itself can show."

The book before us is simply "a work of amusement," so Melville tells us in the same passage: strange then that we should lay
any sort of aggressive critical demand upon it, that we should require of it a higher consistency, a more perfect rationality. Almost in the same breath, however—and with a breath-taking
access of seriousness that typifies the book's uneven rhythm of
demonstration—the uncertainty of the whole enterprise, for
writer and reader alike, is suddenly joined to the profoundest
mysteries of our life and our consciousness as spiritual and imaginative beings. How shall novel-writing itself escape this very rest-

lessness, this infinite duplicity of human consideration, in equal parts self-deceiving and self-transcending? A negative answer is inescapable, but Melville, in this book, is beyond exclaiming over it. He makes his point quietly: "It is with fiction," he remarks, "as with religion; it should present another world, yet one to which we feel the tie."

A writer who has come to see his occupation in these extraordinary terms is either on the verge of an extraordinary final mastery or is himself near the breaking point. And it has in fact been hard to separate the special impression *The Confidence-Man* makes on us from our knowledge that its publication early in 1857 marked the end of Melville's life as a writer of books and the beginning of the withdrawal and resignation of his later years. *The Confidence-Man* is the last extended work of prose narrative that Melville published in his lifetime; the last, therefore, in that astonishing succession of writings that fill out the brief, brilliant decade of his public career as an American author. When it appeared he was still a young man, not yet thirty-eight. Yet how much he had already written. Between the Polynesian traveler's tale of *Typee* in 1846 and the frantic allegorical romance of *Pierre* in 1852, he had published seven full-length books, one of them his masterpiece, *Moby-Dick,* and between *Pierre* and *The Confidence-Man* he had been hardly less prolific, filling *Putnam's* and *Harper's* magazines with a vividly imagined series of tales and sketches. (It might be noted that by 1857 Walt Whitman, born the same year as Melville, was only just past the beginning of his career as an American poet.) If Melville had reached a point of professional exhaustion, there was good reason.

Various outward circumstances also played their part in bringing his career to a crisis. A fire at Harper's in 1853 that destroyed the whole undistributed stock of his earlier work was more than just a symbolic check; it made more difficult any significant recovery from the loss of popularity and cash profit he had suffered with *Moby-Dick* and *Pierre.* And publication of *The Confidence-Man,* the reviews of which were not wholly discouraging, was immediately overtaken by the financial panic of 1857; Dix and Edwards, his new publishers, failing within the month. These causes, however, seem incidental. The real trouble was inward.

Melville's family knew it, and sent him on a European tour in the fall of 1856 to regain his health and balance. Hawthorne knew it when they talked in Liverpool that November, and saw also that there would be no easy recovery for him. But the book itself—as it has been impossible for readers not to feel—may be the strongest testimony of all.

For of all Melville's books *The Confidence-Man* is in every way the most problematical, a remarkable claim in the case of an author whose most ambitious earlier work had been greeted by some reviewers as presenting evidence of serious derangement. In the first place nobody is even sure that the book is finished. It doesn't distinctly end; it appears only to break off, all too much like its author's career for the analogy to escape notice. On the other hand nobody is sure that this makes much difference. *The Confidence-Man* seems the kind of book that has one great thing to say and that says it, through an ingenious yet oddly repetitive series of incidents, over and over again. We may not be able to agree on what precisely this message is, but we feel formally the single-mindedness with which it is delivered. We become conscious that what we are observing is the repetition of one consistent species of action, the forced renewal of one uniform perspective. The actual narrative does in fact show a certain progression forward. One scene does more or less prepare another. The mystifying man of confidence drops hints and pointers that ready his victims for his next manifestation in a new disguise and that establish these successive disguises as familiar and expected before he reemerges wearing them. But to say even this may be assuming too much. For it is not at all clear whether there is indeed just one such confidence man, wearing different disguises, or a whole boatload of confidence men distinguished only by an increasing subtlety of performance. The succession of figures who come before us does not match exactly the list offered in Chapter Three by the black cripple who begins the main sequence of episodes, the list of those who will declare their faith in him. And some of the personages he names resemble characters who appear later as antagonists of the confidence man and as, eventually, his further victims.

Indeed there is a sense in which everybody on board the Mississippi steamboat where the action of the book takes place appears as both confidence man and victim—purveyor-dupes all of some visionary distortion of the enterprise of life, some interior hallucination, in which each has persuaded himself to invest heart, soul, and mind (not to mention cash in hand) beyond any margin of security. The progression of the book is as arbitrary and mechanical as a dream, and there is a dreamlike stammering and obsessiveness in the conversation of its characters. The steamboat itself, ironically named the *Fidèle,* is a ship of fools (it sails on the first of April)—"a piebald parliament," Melville writes, continually receiving "additional passengers in exchange for those that disembark; so that, though always full of strangers, she continually, in some degree, adds to, or replaces them with strangers still more strange"; all moving, whether they know it or not, toward a common end, or—as Melville obliquely puts it—"involuntarily submitting to that natural law which ordains dissolution equally to the mass, as in time to each member."

This haunting, slow-motion confusion of human movement and impulse, as of blind men bumping against blind men (not even "battering" each other, as in Yeats's more heroic vision), is the substance of every scene; it takes the place of a plot. An impression grows, becomes dominant, of mankind milling slowly about in a state of hypnosis, self-enchanted, under the compulsion of a seedy, shabby regimen of petty fraudulence and distrust. The confidence man himself is strangely content to play his games and tricks for very small stakes. His elaborate operations as agent for phantom coal companies and charitable funds, selling nostrums called the "Samaritan Pain Dissuader" or the "Omni-Balsamic Reinvigorator," are the more mystifying in having no other tangible motive than "two or three dirty dollars." Yet those few characters who may appear for a time morally superior to the rest, like Pitch, the bluff, cynical, self-reliant Missouri bachelor, or the mystical philosopher Mark Winsome, embodiment of a smug version of the Transcendentalist ethic of self-serving optimism, seem, before we are through with them, fools or knaves of an even deeper dye, since it is presumably a greater potential for virtue that has been corrupted in them. And we are offered no escape from this heavy-footed masquerade of human fraud and folly. The two figures in the book who stand wholly outside its floating theater of action—we are told about them in stories within the main story—are far more terrifying than any who appear on board: the coldly ferocious Goneril, jealous and vindictive, more cuttlefish than woman, whose very touch both stabs and freezes; the Indian-hater, Colonel John Moredock, sober, upright, citizenly devotee of a murderous private religion of unending vengeance. The moral world of *The Confidence-Man* is of a twilight obscurity. To become involved in it is to be drawn into a slowly darkening whirlpool where all conventional wisdom is sucked down and obliterated; and all the paired opposites by means of which we customarily conspire to keep balance—reason and insanity, folly and wisdom, drunkenness and sobriety, enthusiasm and lethargy, sincerity and charlatanism, honesty and deceit, love of man and hatred of man—become synonyms and meaningless jargon. It is a world from which the blessings of grace and of moral certitude appear to have been withdrawn, for we are conscious more of the absence of certain virtues, or elements assumed to be necessary to virtue, than of the power of malign alternatives. It seems fitting that the book's terminal image should be that of an extinguished lamp.

Now, that there are contradictions and loose ends in the fabric of the narrative is something to be kept in mind. Melville *was,* apparently, ill and in low spirits while writing it. We can imagine how, even as he carried forward his caustic general scheme, he might have begun to turn away in self-disgust from the effort to complete it, from the sheer vanity of composition. One's very absorption in writing, all that effort to improvise new images and figures of a pattern of human conduct that never finally varied, might itself seem a confidence game of the most absurd kind. Yet everywhere the vision that is projected appears uniform and complete. We seem to have been introduced into an autonomous civilization that in some queer way is in harmony with itself, however melancholy and distressing that harmony may be. But it is a civilization to which we cannot easily find the vital key—and I am speaking now not of the dense outward particulars of the book's action, which compose a clear enough moral satire on the degradations of a wholly commercial and entrepreneurial society, but of the character of this vision itself, this way of representing humanity that confronts us at every turn.

For the deepest meaning of the book is the atmosphere of mind it registers and proceeds from. Deeper than the satirical "comedy of action" with which we are outwardly occupied—and here, again, I borrow terms from Melville's own commentary—lies the "comedy of thought" that, for one thing, never tells us, as such comedies customarily do, what ground of fictive abstraction the events and characters are meant to occupy. *The Confidence-Man* is full of colorful, seemingly emblematic figures of essential human behavior, yet it is a book which can also casually raise doubts "whether the human form be, in all cases, conclusive evidence of humanity," and whether the basic attributes by which we identify humanity—feeling, reason, natural sentiment—may not be quite unsuitable to the conduct, the plain endurance, of life as we know it.

The total instability of human character and behavior is a basic premise, governing fictional form as well as moral knowledge. The talk of the confidence man himself is full of oblique warnings on this score. "Don't be too sure what I am," he tells one supposedly self-possessed cynic. "You can conclude nothing absolute from the human form." And to another he defines the mind itself as, first of all, "ductile." "We are but clay, sir, potter's clay, as the good book says, clay, feeble, and too-yielding clay." Hence "the mystery of human subjectivity in general," from which all lesser mysteries and dubieties follow; and hence the common possibility of such freakish manifestations as the friend and aider of men, the true philanthropist, who is always surly and cynical in the extreme, or of his even more freakish opposite, the "genial misanthrope"—"a new kind of monster," as the confidence man coolly defines him, made possible by the sinister general advance of "refinement and softness" in modern life. Inconsistency and mutability are the laws of life; they are, for example, the single truth revealed by the otherwise mystifying little story of Charlemont, in Chapter Thirty-Four—and therefore must also be the rule for human discourse and communication. The great masters of narrative and dramatic literature excel, Melville notes, in nothing so much as this rendering of irreducible inconsistency. Shakespeare is the model for all in being at one and the same time "enlightening and mystifying"; to those intent on full clarification he has a strange power to "open . . . eyes and corrupt . . . morals in one operation," though the wiser reader will say no more than, with conscious redundancy, "This Shakespeare is a queer man."

All such turns and spirals of argument indicate, we can say, a further intensification of that general picture of human behavior which characterizes all of Melville's writing, more or less, at first mostly to comic but increasingly (though never exclusively) to tragic ends. Man is a creature subject to galloping contagions, a creature whose very vitality takes the form of a surrender to the epidemic distemper of the moment. In *The Confidence-Man* it is the contagion of suspicion and distrust, erupting periodically in fits of violent misanthropy or the self-hatred of true melancholy; a distemper that is made the more significant because it is also shown to be not at all unwarranted or irrational. But there is, to repeat, a curious lack of dramatic emphasis and concentration in developing this general picture. If there is critical agreement on anything about *The Confidence-Man* it is on this point: that the style rather than the story is the surest measure of what the book has to say, and the chief indicator—more than the broken, enigmatic narrative sequence—of its general import. It is a strange, halting, self-referential style, full of hesitation and qualification, yet now and then flashing out with aphorisms, slogans, obscurely symbolic images and descriptive figures, that do fleetingly light up the moral perplexity of the whole. The movement of the writing thus typifies the procession of events and the vacillation and instability of the characters involved in them. The line between irony and sheer doubletalk, between grim insight and palpable absurdity, is sometimes drawn very fine. "He who comes to know man, will not remain in ignorance of man": by the time we reach this sentence late in the book we may, as baffled as the character who speaks it, be hard put to decide whether it is evasive nonsense or oracular wisdom.

The confidence man himself is the principal exemplar of this style, and questions about the meaning of the book are questions finally about his identity and mission. Who is the confidence man and what does he propose? The book is prodigal of clues, hints, obscure proto-definitions, though a great many of these reflect not the confidence man's own character so much as the character, the distorted and suspicion-ridden incomprehension, of the crowd that judges him. He is, to others, a quack, a fool, a knave

—yet perhaps also, so one on-looker remarks, noting that certain money dispensed by the fellow was, after all, "good money," an "original genius"; in any case "a queer and dubious man" (and therefore the likelier candidate for being some kind of Everyman); a stranger in motley, in his jaunty final disguise as the fantastically costumed "cosmopolitan"; a "man-charmer," so one of his befuddled victims, the crusty barber of the steamboat's business deck, afterward remembers him. Insofar as he persistently offers a doctrine for men to live by that flies in the face of worldly experience, presenting himself as "the Happy Man" in a world where disaffection is so reasonable an attitude, he is an "extraordinary metaphysical scamp," preaching benevolence, charity, and trust in a way that somehow tempts men into an even deeper disbelief in them. "I am Philanthropos, and love mankind," he tells the barber—but the barber's reply to his blandishments carries equal weight: "Sir, you must excuse me. I have a family." Nothing disturbs understanding more than the confidence man's own way of identifying his purposes. "I am for doing good to the world," he says, "once for all and having done with it"; here, a certain audible violence of idiom and the grammatical ambiguity of the pronoun combine in a way giving support to a later charge that this confidence man is the most treacherous of all dealers in truth: one who "puns with ideas as another man may with words."

Or is he something worse than a punster and scamp? In her excellent edition of *The Confidence-Man* Elizabeth Foster has set out a carefully assembled case for seeing this character as the devil and for understanding the book as a demonstration of how Antichrist has wholly superseded Christ as the ruler of this world and how "the devil makes use of Christian idealism for his own ends." This black "allegory," as Professor Foster is willing to call it, is the means by which Melville develops his satirical attack on the whole range of optimistic philosophies, religious, humanitarian, commercial, flourishing in his century. Such a reading of the book is entirely plausible, and so for that matter is the considerably more dogmatic view advanced by Newton Arvin, that *The Confidence-Man* is "one of the most *infidel* books ever written by an American; one of the most completely nihilistic, morally and metaphysically."

The evidence is abundant, and a reader who thinks otherwise may be driven to the dubious expedient of saying only, "It just doesn't read that way to me." Certainly if the mysterious man of confidence *is* the devil, the cynical gentleman-prince of this world of dogs and foxes, he is a very ingenious and aesthetically pleasing addition, truly original, to the whole gallery of modern fictional devils. Yet it can also be argued that, far from tempting the world and its citizens into any fall from grace or leading it into unrighteousness, the confidence man merely adapts himself to it for the duration of the voyage. He does not himself give direction to the world's custom. He simply falls in with it and plays its games—and more than once he is struck and abused for his pains; when occasionally he takes some small measure of material revenge, it is invariably in a way that satisfies us, for he does so by tricking his opponent into some appropriate self-contradiction and the loss at most of only a few coins or bills; the pettiness of the retaliation is nicely proportioned to the essential meanness of the offense.

At the same time he talks far more than he tricks, and far in excess of any cash return. He talks, talks, talks. He functions in the book as essentially a promoter of discourse, a "talking man" as one of the characters calls him, and thus a teacher in his way—for, he immediately replies, "it is the peculiar vocation of a teacher to talk." "What's wisdom itself," he goes on, "but table-talk?" [1] What he offers, however, is not doctrine, in the ordinary manner of teachers. Rather, it is the image of a way of life, but one that, far from beguiling men into evil ways, is so austere and forbidding when you see the point of it that those few who begin to understand it retreat from it even more violently than those who merely greet it with their ordinary suspiciousness. The name for it may be "confidence," but it is a confidence in circumstances and prospects that is only to be maintained by an unending process of testing, a constantly open-eyed examining of all signs and indications, a process of engaged watchfulness that has no resolution and from which there is, in life, no release.

Moreover, as a proposed way of life it comes guarded with warnings that, worst of all, are directed against itself as well as all other things; for it is the confidence man himself who, in the last chapter, speaking words from the Apocryphal Son of Sirach, seems to connect the teacher of confidence with the spirit's sub-tlest enemies. Perhaps the purest definition of this way of life comes (Chapter Sixteen) as a paraphrase of the teaching of St. Paul in I Thessalonians 5:21: "Prove all things; hold fast to that which is good." (Typically this scriptural verse follows closely after another notable warning about the false teachings of the children of night.) Those who see the consequences of this teach-ing must be truly appalled; and though it is not the kind of teaching we usually associate with the devil, the impulse of those who hear of it is to curse it. "But to doubt, to suspect, to prove," a sick man grasping for cures dolefully protests, *"to have all this wearing work to be doing continually*—how opposed to confi-dence. It is evil."

Perhaps so, but I would myself write this man down as the first modern critic and garbler of the book's projected meaning. For what can also be said on this score is that characters unambigu-ously identified as doers of evil, devils in human shape, do in-deed enter the book—I have already mentioned them: the wife Goneril and the hunter Moredock—but they are not brought aboard the *Fidèle* and do not participate in its running action. We note that they are given, as described, the distinctive char-acteristic of Melville's other "devils," in both earlier and later work: that is, the absolute single-mindedness or monomania, and the pure, helpless, vindictive malice that Melville would eventu-ally specify, in a late poem, as the one unpardonable human affliction. The immediate world of *The Confidence-Man* is the mid-world of common, circumstantial human weakness. For all the book's opening out toward spiritual horror and darkness, it occupies the ground of comedy; in style, in narrative design (or the lack of it), in its ultimately monotonous substance of demon-stration, it holds itself back from the kind of meaning claimed for it by the interpretations mentioned above.

Here again our critical appeal is in part to the curious struc-ture of the book. We feel throughout that the confidence man is not only a character of a different order from the others in the story as, to be sure, the devil would be, too, but that he remains apart in his own self-conscious being from the mid-world of the *Fidèle* and his own passing complicity with it. He remains apart just as, formally, the first and last chapters (and thus our first and last glimpses of him) stand apart from the central mass of the narrative. These chapters enclose the book like the supernatural framing chapters of one of the great panoramic Chinese chronicle-novels, chapters which evoke directly the larger context of meaning of the often chaotic events of the main narrative. In these framing chapters in Melville's book the confidence man plays a different part from that of his usual masquerade, though one obviously germane to it.

We see him first, in the opening chapter, as the mute lamblike "stranger" going about the deck of the *Fidèle* displaying on a slate the great legends about charity from St. Paul's letter to the Corinthians: that charity thinketh no evil, suffereth long and is kind, endureth all things, believeth all things, and never faileth. Like one of Silone's mysterious heroes he is described as having "come from a very long distance," with still some further way to go. His aspect is taken to be "somehow inappropriate to the time and place," and he is treated by the other passengers with a hostility that progresses from annoyance and jeering to shoves and punches until, having gone through his series of inscriptions about charity, he withdraws into "motionless" privacy. We do not see him again in this manifestation; and in the forty-odd chapters that follow, on the rare occasions when charity is urged as a rule for mankind, it is savagely mocked. "To where it belongs with your charity! to heaven with it!" one paragon of suspicion cries out; "here on earth, true charity dotes, and false charity plots." And in the next breath he mocks the great avatar of charity himself: "Who betrays a fool with a kiss, the charitable fool has the charity to believe is in love with him. . . . "

But the speaker here—a gimlet-eyed, sour-faced, wooden-legged cynic, a "shallow unfortunate" whose speech is a surly croak—is not a character likely to be entrusted with the last word. With regard to subsequent episodes he is right enough; through most of *The Confidence-Man* charity is honored only in the breach. Yet it seems to me that the singular brilliance and vividness of that pageant-like opening chapter are never positively dispelled. The bearer of the inscriptions may, in his more usual performance as confidence man, be dubious and equivocal, but the inscriptions themselves are not touched by this change of style. The command to charity so remarkably erected stands over the whole book and carries through it with positive force. Mere improvised fictions, however ingenious in their tracing out of an epidemic demoralization, cannot overthrow the claim it makes on the germ of humanity within us. Surely Melville did not intend them to; nothing we know about the courage of his intelligence, his power as a writer to hold contradictory ideas and feelings in expressive balance, requires us to suppose so. No mere pattern of words can put down the force of true charity, for it is of that order of things, like "true religion" (Chapter Eleven), that is "in some sort independent of words." Man is clay, feeble, ductile, too yielding, but charity is not. It is itself a mysterious stranger and pilgrim in its passage through men's consciousness; it is a force superior to its daily betrayals and bides its time. In this it is like providence; if our conviction of it "were in any way made dependent upon such variabilities as everyday events," this conviction would fluctuate, Melville writes, like "the stock exchange during a long and uncertain war." But it is not so dependent.

Feeling the force of this term, a force undiminished by all the frauds practiced in its name, we are required to ask whether the bearer of it, the confidence man himself, is indeed the double-dealing devil or Great Beast that our apocalypse-minded criticism has pretty regularly assumed him to be. It is possible that he, too, bides his time, in a world which does not encourage him to do anything else. In the last chapter he leaves the public quarters of the boat (for the first time since Chapter One) and goes into the semi-obscurity of the gentlemen's cabin, where he finds an old man sitting alone "in peace" reading a Bible. The old man is such a one as we have not seen before in the book, one who makes no effort to impose himself on the world and who looks out on it not with fixed suspicion or hostility but with a kind of muddled and ingenuous trust that seems very near to foolishness. A man of seventy, he is described as looking "fresh-hearted" as a boy of fifteen, doubtless (the passage insists) because he has somehow remained "ignorant" of what the world really is. But seeing him, the confidence man abruptly changes his usual manner; he "tones himself down." Talk follows, and it is as riddling as elsewhere. The old man is confused and made sad by new reports of uncertainty and deception, and credulously buys a traveler's lock and a money belt from a preternaturally sly and worldly-wise boy-peddler. But through this scene the confidence man acts with a restraint, and a kindliness, different in tone from what has gone before. He eyes the old man "with sympathy," and answers his declaration of an ultimate trust in the power of God with a remarkably straightforward commendation of the worth and true comfort of such trust, for him who can maintain it. And at the last, as the cabin lamp burns low and is extinguished, he "kindly" leads the old man away, out of the obscurity of the place to the haven of his stateroom.

Is there a possibility that this kindness and sympathy are, at last, real kindness and real sympathy, plainly given and plainly received? Have we not come finally upon a meeting free of the tension and combativeness (though not of the equivocality) of all that has preceded? The turn the narrative has taken is not heroic or dramatically momentous; it will not be the basis for a new affirmation that will sweep over the domain of the book and resolve all its multiplying duplicity. Nevertheless it is a turn. An act of kindness *has* been done; charity, strangely untouched by everything that has happened since the deaf-mute first raised his slate, has been asserted. The long pageant in which a quite rational self-interest and misanthropic suspicion have played at graceless, sour odds with the simple instinct of fellow-feeling that makes men seek the comfort of one another's company, has come to an end; and we are left with these two—the cosmopolitan stranger and the old, befuddled figure of trust—in a relation of kindness and mutual consideration: a hopeful, benignant ending after all. It, too, is a "masquerade," but there may be more comfort and cheer in it, or at least less terror, than we quite dare to think.

Note

1. The sentence that follows makes clear the allusion here to the great case of the Last Supper: "The best wisdom in this world, and the last spoken by its teacher; did it not literally and truly come in the form of table-talk?"

HENRY DAVID THOREAU:

12 *WALDEN; OR, LIFE IN THE WOODS*

Walter Harding

Henry David Thoreau's *Walden* (1854) is perhaps the most widely read book-length work of nonfiction in nineteenth-century American literature. It has appeared in nearly two hundred different editions and has been translated into virtually every major modern language. Yet, oddly enough, in the lifetime of its author it was generally considered an imitative work and a failure. It took five years to sell out the first edition of only two thousand copies and it was not brought back into print again until after the author's death. This radical change in its critical reception over the past century is worthy of exploration.

Thoreau was born in Concord, Massachusetts, on July 12, 1817. He graduated from Harvard College in 1837, one of the honor students in his class, and returned to his native Concord to teach. But by 1841 he had concluded that writing, not teaching, was his vocation. Under the aegis of Ralph Waldo Emerson, his Concord neighbor and fellow Transcendentalist, Thoreau turned to the writing of poems and essays, first for the Transcendentalist *Dial* and then for a gradually widening circle of newspapers and periodicals.

In 1845, when he was twenty-eight, he built a cabin on the shores of Walden Pond about two miles from the center of Concord and lived there for two years while writing the two books that he was to publish in his lifetime: *A Week on the Concord and Merrimack Rivers* and *Walden*. It was while he was at Walden that he was arrested for refusing to pay his poll taxes as a protest against Negro slavery and spent a night in jail.

Returning to the village to live in 1847, he spent the remainder of his all-too-brief life in writing, lecturing, and observing the flora and fauna of the region, leaving Concord only on the occasional brief excursions which were to be the bases of his posthumously published travel books, and earning, by occasional surveying and manufacturing pencils in his father's factory, what little money he needed to follow a life patterned on the principles of simplicity. He died on May 6, 1862, at the age of forty-four, still generally considered by his contemporaries to be little more than an obscure eccentric and a minor imitator of his friend and neighbor Emerson. He did not begin to attain any widespread recognition until the turn of the century, and it is only in the past twenty-five years that he has really come into his own.

As for his masterpiece, *Walden,* it is ostensibly an account of the two years, two months, and two days he spent living in his cabin at Walden Pond. On February 4, 1846, while still at Walden, Thoreau delivered a learned lecture on "Thomas Carlyle and His Works" before his fellow townsmen at the Concord Lyceum. When the lecture was over, his audience informed him that they would much rather have heard about his own life at the pond than about an obtuse and difficult Scotsman. Taking their hint, he prepared a lecture entitled "The History of Myself" and delivered it at the Concord Lyceum on February 10, 1847. To his delight, it was received with unprecedented enthusiasm and he was asked both to repeat it a week later and to expand upon it. This lecture and the others similar to it that followed it were the genesis of the book *Walden.*

Reasoning that since the lectures had proved so popular, there would be a market for a book on the subject, Thoreau decided to expand the lectures for publication. Before he left the pond in September of 1847 he had completed a rough draft of the book, and by 1849 he was announcing it as ready for publication. The complete failure of his first book, *A Week on the Concord and Merrimack Rivers,* published at his own expense in 1849, frightened away any potential publishers of *Walden.* Instead of being dismayed by the turn of events, though, Thoreau set about reworking *Walden* to better it. In the course of the next five years Thoreau completely rewrote the book over and over again—a total of eight separate times—revising, adding, modifying, subtracting, and moving sentences and sometimes even whole paragraphs from one chapter to another. The result is obvious to anyone who has examined the fragments of the earlier drafts that are now in the Huntington Library; it is a greatly expanded but much more tightly organized and vastly improved book. Had the first version been the one published, there seems little likelihood that Henry Thoreau would have achieved his present-day fame.

The book is, ostensibly, an account of his life at Walden Pond, written, as he states on the opening page, in answer to "very particular inquiries . . . made by my townsmen concerning my mode of life." We learn of his choosing a site at the pond, cutting the necessary trees, erecting the cabin, moving in, appropriately enough on Independence Day, 1845, planting a garden for food and income, weeding and eventually harvesting it, preparing his cabin with plastered walls and fireplace for winter, and so on. Thus the book can be read as a sort of nineteenth-century *Adventures of Robinson Crusoe*. As such, it has a sort of idyllic, getaway-from-it-all charm that has proved enticing enough to lead many a reader into retreating to his own woods and building a cabin in open imitation of the sage of Walden Pond. It would be interesting to know just how many such imitators of Thoreau there have been. Over the years they must certainly number in the hundreds if not thousands. But it is more interesting to note that Thoreau, apparently foreseeing such literal disciples, went out of his way in *Walden* to say specifically, "I would not have any one adopt *my* mode of living on any account."

Walden may also be read as an account of the flora and fauna of Concord. A large portion of the time Thoreau spent at the pond, and, indeed, a large portion of his life, was spent in observing and studying the birds, the animals, the flowers, the trees, and the progress of the seasons, and a proportionately large part of the book is devoted to reporting his observations. Most of Thoreau's contemporaries thought these sections were the only worthwhile parts of the book, and more than one nineteenth-century reviewer advised his readers to skip the more philosophical parts of *Walden* and concentrate on the nature writing. Actually Thoreau was making a real literary contribution therein. Although there had been other writers about nature before him, such as Gilbert White and John James Audubon, it was Thoreau who is rightly credited with creating the nature essay as such. Earlier nature writers had produced "letters," "episodes," and "journals" reporting their discoveries, but Thoreau was the first to be concerned with craftsmanship and thus the first to make the nature essay a definite, separate literary form. One need only, for example, compare Thoreau's famous passage on the loon in *Walden* with Audubon's report on loons accompanying the *Birds of America* to see the difference. The latter is scientific reporting; the former, artistic.

Let us then consider *Walden* as art. It is often pointed out as the earliest example of modern American prose. The significant difference in its style from that of its contemporaries—even the works of men as gifted as Hawthorne, Melville, and Emerson—is that its prose has the air of the twentieth century about it. Granted that the subject matter is sometimes obviously nineteenth century, as when he speaks of farmers driving their cattle to market or of townsfolk riding past the pond in carriages, yet the styling of the sentences and the word choice is twentieth century. The sentences are straightforward, concise, and to the point. There is no mid-Victorian rambling and the words are precise, sensual, and concrete, not vague and abstract. There is surprisingly little difference between Thoreau's nineteenth-century prose and Ernest Hemingway's, or Henry Miller's, twentieth-century prose, except that his style is less monotonous.

Thoreau's use of figurative language should be emphasized. One can find in *Walden* examples of virtually every type of figure of speech known, from epizeuxis to meiosis, or to choose less exotic figures, from similes to puns. Thoreau, as any reader of *Walden* knows, delighted in puns, and there are so many of them scattered through the book that no one yet has succeeded in cataloguing all of them. As an example, let me point out a favorite. When in "The Ponds" he speaks of the unsuccessful fisherman at Walden Pond being a member of the C-O-E-N-O-B-I-T-E-S, he is not only suggesting that the fisherman was a member of a contemplative order, but if we pronounce the word carefully we will also see that Thoreau was saying, "See, no bites."

Puns, in turn, lead us to the subject of humor in *Walden*. James Russell Lowell, in his famous essay on Thoreau published in 1865, rather pontifically stated that Thoreau had no sense of humor. That statement really only served to prove that it was Lowell and not Thoreau who lacked the sense of humor, for it seems almost inconceivable that anyone could read through *Walden* without seeing the sparkle of Thoreau's wit on every page. The humor is not always of a blatant, slapstick variety, though at times it is that, as when Thoreau speaks of sawing the ice on the pond pit-fashion, that is, with one man underneath the ice, but wit is present everywhere in the book. It is a "critical humor"; it is not there simply to lighten the pages and make us laugh; as with the humor of Jonathan Swift or Voltaire or Mark Twain or Bernard Shaw, it is there to make us think. We may laugh when we read that "the head monkey at Paris puts on a traveller's cap, and all the monkeys in America do the same," for example, but our laughter is tinged with the knowledge that Thoreau, in more ways than one, is making monkeys of us all. In this line, and in many, many others, Thoreau is using humor to point out "What fools we mortals be."

Closely related to Thoreau's use of humor is his use of exaggeration. He placed an epigraph at the beginning of the first edition of *Walden* that has unfortunately been dropped from many of the more recent editions. It read, "I do not propose to write an ode to dejection, but to brag as lustily as chanticleer in the morning, standing on his roost, if only to wake my neighbors up." It was there as a warning that Thoreau often deliberately overstated his case simply to get the attention of his readers. Once he had startled his audience sufficiently to arouse their interest, he then usually modified his position to more reasonable terms. A superb example of this technique can be found in his essay on "Civil Disobedience" which he opens with the statement, "I heartily accept the motto,—'That government is best which governs least'. . . . Carried out, it finally amounts to this, which also I believe,—'That government is best which governs not at all.' " But two paragraphs later he has modified this deliberately outrageous position to "I ask for, not at once no government, but *at once* a better government." And many similar examples can be found in *Walden*.

Thoreau is also a social critic. One of his major aims is to point out the foibles of his times. In fact, it is because these very foibles that he chose to criticize most harshly have become more exaggerated in our time that he seems to speak more pertinently to our age than to his own. His contemporaries rarely saw the point when he complained of their overly complicated lives, when he suggested the "mass of men" were leading "lives of quiet desperation," when he asserted that what we call "progress" was not always necessarily progress, nor "success" always success, when he pronounced that we often confused ends with means and means with ends; or when he claimed that perhaps primitive man led a happier and fuller life in some ways than ours. But now we, a century later, are finding ourselves face to face with the very problems he foresaw and we recognize him as a prophet for our times.

It is perhaps important at this point to correct the widespread but erroneous impression that Thoreau was a primitivist who advocated everyone's abandoning civilization and taking to the woods. In the first place one should realize that he spent only a little over two years, that is, about five per cent of his life, at Walden Pond, that Walden Pond was not out in the wilderness but a mere two miles from the center of Concord, and that rather than living a life of solitude there, he not only had a constant stream of visitors but he himself made almost daily journeys into the village to see his family and his friends. More important, as already suggested, he went out of his way to state specifically that he did not want imitators following him to the woods. Since he personally was interested in observing and writing about nature, it met his personal needs to go to Walden Pond to live. But, he asserts, one can live the simple life anyplace, if one has the mind to. Thoreau continued to live just as simply when he returned to Concord as he had at the pond. So we too, if we wish, can live the simple life in the village, the town, or the city. We can create our own Walden in the heart of New York, London, Bombay, or Tokyo. In that Walden we can live more purposeful, more meaningful, more joyous lives. That is the real essence of *Walden*.

Neither did Thoreau advocate the abandonment of the physical advantages produced by modern science. Quite to the contrary, he pointed out that we were not making the best possible use of them. They have often turned out to be, as he said, but "improved means to unimproved ends." We go to great lengths to install a cable across the Atlantic Ocean and then use it to inquire whether "Princess Adelaide has the whooping cough," rather than to communicate great ideas. We build a railroad to get to the city an hour faster and then waste the hour when we get there. One can well imagine what Thoreau might have said had he lived to see the advent of the television set and the jet plane. He could surely find better uses for them than we are putting them to.

It is important, however, to realize that he is not simply a negative critic, a destructive critic. He is far more positive and constructive. He does not hesitate to point out the problems of our society, but more importantly, he points out the solutions. If we feel overwhelmed by the complexities of present-day society, there is a way out. "Simplify, simplify, simplify" is his byword. Society may be complex, but our lives need not be if we only have the intelligence to select from that complexity that which is important to us, and if we only have the courage to ignore the rest no matter what our contemporaries think or say of us. We squander our lives in futile conformity to the wishes of our neighbors. As Thoreau says over and over, we waste too much of our lives in getting a living, or, trying to "keep up with the Joneses." If we would only reduce our wants, we would correspondingly reduce the percentage of our lives we devote to earning a living and increase the proportion of time spent doing that which we really want to do.

Thoreau, at his college commencement in 1837, stated that he wanted to reverse the Biblical saying and instead of working six days a week and resting the seventh, he would work one day a week and rest six. That is exactly the program he put into effect at Walden Pond. By simplifying his life to its very essentials, he found he could build a home for twenty-eight dollars, twelve and a half cents, and live on twenty-seven cents a week. He easily earned enough to cover these expenses in six weeks out of a year; the remaining forty-six weeks were his to do with as he pleased. He did not then waste those forty-six weeks but devoted them to writing and studying nature. Before anyone is tempted to chastise Thoreau as lazy, he should note that he in his short life created more than twenty volumes of first-rate prose—a formidable accomplishment indeed. Our economy has changed enough over the past century that it is pointless to try to achieve Thoreau's exact figures for income and outgo, but the validity of the principle is still there.

Thoreau is not only a positive and constructive critic, he is an optimistic critic. He is completely convinced that would man only put his mind and heart to it, he could create a heaven right here on earth, and he is just as completely convinced that mankind will indeed someday do exactly that. Thoreau was a Transcendentalist, perhaps the most consistently Transcendental of that whole group of authors. At the heart of Transcendentalism is a belief that each man has within him a God-given ability to choose between right and wrong. Unfortunately man has too often ignored that inner voice and has become so calloused to its word that he no longer hears it. Would he but wittingly strive to revert to the godlike innocence of childhood, he could renew that voice and through it himself.

Recognizing the moral progress man has made since the days of the caveman, Thoreau was convinced that even greater moral progress was to be made in the future through what he thought was an inevitable widespread adoption of Transcendentalist precepts—a spiritual renewal of mankind. It is important to note that one of the major themes of *Walden* is that of renewal. Although he lived at the pond for more than two years, he purposefully telescoped the two years into one in his book not only for artistic unity, but far more so that through the cycle of the seasons he could emphasize the theme of renewal. *Walden* starts with Thoreau's going out to the pond in the spring and then follows him through the summer, the autumn, and the winter, ending with the renewal of life in the spring. That is the major pattern of the book, and woven into it are all sorts of embellishments of that design, as for example when he speaks in "Economy" of the American Indians who through their busk fire regularly destroyed their dross so that they could begin anew. Or when in "Conclusion" he speaks of the strange insect that buried itself in the wood of an apple-tree table for sixty years and then suddenly came to life, or of the pond itself which each year went dormant under its winter covering of ice only to come alive again each spring. Each time Thoreau reiterates the image of renewal he emphasizes his hope and belief that mankind will inevitably renew his spirit and be led to greater accomplishments—not physical accomplishments, necessarily, but spiritual. Such a belief is the very epitome of Transcendentalism.

Thoreau's essay on "Civil Disobedience" has been mentioned several times. It is not an integral part of *Walden,* though it is referred to briefly in the chapter on "The Village," and it is so close to *Walden* in spirit that it can almost be considered one with it. In fact, it is almost impossible to discuss one without the other. Like *Walden,* "Civil Disobedience" was written at the request of his fellow townsmen who in this case wondered why anyone would deliberately not pay his taxes to the state, and seek out an "opportunity" to go to jail. The background of the essay is this: Thoreau so strongly opposed slavery that he determined to pay no taxes to support it. Inevitably he was eventually arrested and placed in jail, though he was freed the next morning because someone, without his permission, paid his taxes for him and apparently continued to pay them for the rest of his life. It had been his intention to arouse the consciences of his fellow men by his arrest, leading them either to abolish slavery or to make it unworkable by joining him in jail in sufficiently large numbers to clog the machinery of government until the unjust laws were repealed. His unwanted release from jail prevented his personally carrying out his protest, but the explanatory lecture he wrote for his townsmen has been spread to the four corners of the earth and has inspired such world leaders as Mahatma Gandhi and Martin Luther King, Jr. It too is the epitome of Transcendentalism, for it urges each man to follow his conscience to lead mankind on to a better world. No one should read *Walden* without also reading the equally important essay on "Civil Disobedience." Fortunately more and more publishers nowadays are printing the two together in one volume.

Despite Henry James's famous statement to the contrary, there is little or nothing parochial about Thoreau's work. True he spent almost his entire life in a tiny New England village, but the themes he wrote on were universal rather than provincial, a fact adequately documented by the translation of his works into so many languages. On the other hand, there is much about his work that is typically American in flavor. There is unquestionably the pioneering spirit of the American frontiersman, even if

Thoreau did choose to create his frontier in his own home town rather than head for the Wild West. The flora and fauna he describes are inevitably American—though he writes about them in such universal terms that one does not need field guides to the birds and flowers of the northeastern United States to appreciate his work. There is a rugged, manly quality about his word choice and styling that seems typically American. Most significant is the fact the themes of his work, both of *Walden* and "Civil Disobedience," are basically the logical developments of the philosophy innate in the American Declaration of Independence.

13 WALT WHITMAN: "SONG OF MYSELF"

James E. Miller, Jr.

Standing near the beginning of Walt Whitman's masterpiece, *Leaves of Grass*, are two lines that sum up Whitman's sense of his own limited but vital achievement:

I myself but write one or two indicative words for the future,
I but advance a moment only to wheel and hurry back in the darkness.

No one has yet figured out for certain just what his "one or two indicative words" mean. Since we are now the future to whom he offered his limited lexicon, perhaps we ought to peruse his book for whatever clues it contains. But we shouldn't keep our eyes simply on the book. Whitman also said:

I bequeath myself to the dirt to grow from the grass I love,
If you want me again look for me under your boot-soles.

Many attempts have been made to confine Whitman to a particular niche, carefully defined and labeled. He has been called Poet of Democracy, Poet of Science, Poet of Religion, Poet of Sex, Poet of Mysticism, Poet of Materialism. And the astonishing truth is that his book can be quoted, like Scripture, to support any of these epithets. He allowed for this multiplicity when he said:

Do I contradict myself?
Very well then I contradict myself,
(I am large, I contain multitudes.)

There is less irresponsibility than at first seems in this passage. Whitman could easily embrace contradictions, but he was ruthless in his consistency with the self. He expressed outwardly conflicting views in order to remain honest to an inner vision.

The vision in Whitman that remained constant, through youth and old age, through exaltation and despair, was a vision of the inviolate self, a strong, unshakable sense of identity that is life's most prized possession. The opening line of *Leaves of Grass* expresses it plainly: "One's-self I sing, a simple separate person."

In making the theme of identity the foundation on which he would erect the superstructure of his poetry, Whitman was taking up the greatest poetic challenge of his time. Less than fifty years before Whitman was born, America had declared her independence. But though she had won her freedom, she had not yet discovered a soul. The poets who gazed enraptured on her lands and horizons saw with an alien sight and spoke with a voice from the past. Whitman would see with his own eyes and speak in the modern tongue.

The search for an American identity had begun many years before, probably with the first settler who came to the New World wilderness possessed only of his dream. In 1782 Michael Guillaume St. Jean de Crèvecoeur had written, "The American is a new man, who acts upon new principles; he must therefore entertain new ideas, and form new opinions." But deep into the nineteenth century, the old ideas and opinions clung to the new nation. Whitman observed in the opening of his 1855 preface to the *Leaves* that "the slough still sticks to opinions and manners and literature while the life which served its requirements has passed into the new life of the new forms."

The conventional poet of Whitman's day took the easy way out of stating again the old conceptions from abroad and affirming anew the outworn affirmations of the past. William Cullen Bryant's "To a Waterfowl," or Henry Wadsworth Longfellow's "A Psalm of Life," or Oliver Wendell Holmes's "The Chambered Nautilus" jarred nobody's comfortable beliefs and disturbed no one's delicate sensibilities. Whitman said of the past:

> Regarding it all a long while, then dismissing it,
> I stand in my place with my own day here.

Whitman's choice was deliberate. He could have written the pretty, sentimental verses popular during his time, as "O Captain, My Captain" proves. Had he fixed his gaze on the past, he could have produced a respectable body of verse conventional in both idea and form—which would have been long since forgotten. Had he contemplated only the future, he might have drowned the interest of the reader in a torrent of abstractions and ideals.

As it was, Whitman chose to look deeply into his own nature and moment, to make profound discoveries of the self and spirit there, and to dramatize his discoveries in a language surging with energy and charged with a life of its own. The origin of his strategy was simple, as he explained at the end of his career in "A Backward Glance o'er Travel'd Roads": "This was a feeling or ambition to articulate and faithfully express in literary or poetic form, and uncompromisingly, my own physical, emotional, moral, intellectual, and aesthetic personality, in the midst of, and tallying, the momentous spirit and facts of its immediate days, and of current America."

In short, Whitman assumed that to discover himself was to discover America. Behind this assumption lay the realization that the identity of America existed not in her geography—in her mountains and lakes, her plains and her coasts—but in the interior of her new democratic man. Whitman knew himself to be such a man, and his simple faith was that in exploring the labyrinths of his own being, he would discover there the mysteries of the American soul. To the opening line of *Leaves:* "One's-self I sing, a simple separate person," he added: "Yet utter the word democratic, the word en-masse."

If *Leaves of Grass* is America's epic, the epic hero is Walt Whitman as representative democratic man. The form of the poem, free verse, reflects in its long, flowing lines the theme of liberty basic to the book. In bursting the bonds of stanzaic form and metrical pattern, Whitman was reiterating the freedom he discovered in himself and his country. In introducing into his poetry a diction as free and easy as his rhyme and rhythm, he was asserting the poetic rights of the language of the street and the market place.

Whitman's language had the immediacy of sweaty, hot-breathed life, and it had moments of illumination as vivid as bolts of lightning on the American prairie. He asked:

> Who goes there? hankering, gross, mystical, nude;
> How is it I extract strength from the beef I eat?
> Stout as a horse, affectionate, haughty, electrical.
> I and this mystery here we stand.

And he said:

> Divine am I inside and out, and I make holy whatever
>   I touch or am touch'd from.
> The scent of these armpits aroma finer than prayer.

And he said:

> You there, impotent, loose in the knees,
> Open your scarf'd chops till I blow grit within you,
> Spread your palms and lift the flaps of your pockets,
> I am not to be denied, I compel, I have stores plenty and to spare,
> And anything I have I bestow.

The astonishing language of Whitman's poetry is a language that is essentially unpoetic, or even antipoetic, in a day when poetic language generally was stilted and stale; Whitman's language emerged not by accident or through ignorance, but rather out of a strongly held belief in the democracy of language. In an important little essay, "Slang in America," Whitman wrote: "Language be it remember'd, is not an abstract construction of the learn'd, or of dictionary makers, but is something arising out of the work, needs, ties, joys, affections, tastes, of long generations of humanity, and has its bases broad and low, close to the ground. Its final decisions are made by the masses, people nearest the concrete, having most to do with actual land and sea." In defining slang, Whitman in effect described the linguistic make-up and impact of his own poetry. He wrote: "Slang, profoundly consider'd, is the lawless germinal element, below all words and sentences, and behind all poetry, and proves a certain perennial rankness, and protestantism in speech. . . . Considering language then as some mighty potentate, into the majestic audience-hall of the monarch ever enters a personage like one of Shake-speare's clowns, and takes position there, and plays a part even in the stateliest ceremonies." Whitman's language, like the clown in court, was unexpected and unrefined, and at times even impudent and impolite. He could say with justification: "I sound my barbaric yawp over the roofs of the world."

Whitman's barbaric yawp shocked his contemporary audience, but today's poet enjoys the linguistic liberty that he pioneered. Carl Sandburg, such Beats as Allen Ginsberg and Lawrence Ferlinghetti, Karl Shapiro in his recent book, *The Bourgeois Poet*—these are a few of the writers who have enjoyed the freedom of language that Whitman so vigorously proclaimed. Whitman turns up in a variety of guises in today's literature, both at home and abroad.

But with all Whitman's experimentation with the language of poetry, there seem to be remarkably few lapses in his taste. With all the "advances" in literary liberty since he wrote, we might expect now to find him a bit prim and old-fashioned, as we sometimes find James Russell Lowell and Longfellow. On the contrary, his diction strikes our ear as modern and natural, and his verbal pyrotechnics appear easy and relaxed.

More important than his enduring style is the modern relevance of his substance, of his passionate commitment to the self. The fashionable contemporary stance for the poet is one of alienation and despair, typified by the spiritual paralysis of T. S. Eliot's J. Alfred Prufrock. The modern malaise is anonymity in a mass culture, the individual deprived of his humanity and reduced to a statistic.

For the man who feels the nausea of emptiness within, a hollowness at the being's very center of gravity, there is no better antidote than to follow Whitman's example in that remarkable celebration of individuality, "Song of Myself":

> I loafe and invite my soul.
> I lean and loafe at my ease observing a spear of summer grass.

In this poem Whitman deliberately planned a rendezvous and consummated an affair with his soul. The affair was passionate and prolonged, and the spiritual progeny remarkable. He asked, "To be in any form, what is that?" And he exclaimed, "Is this then a touch? quivering me to a new identity?"

"Song of Myself" is one of the great mystical poems of the English language, but it is also (and paradoxically) at the same time one of the most deliberately physical of all poems ever written. Near the beginning of this long poem Whitman wrote:

> Urge and urge and urge,
> Always the procreant urge of the world.
> Out of the dimness opposite equals advance, always substance
>   and increase, always sex,
> Always a knit of identity, always distinction, always a breed
>   of life.

This sexuality, this physicality, this fundamental materiality furnishes the substratum and bone-structure of this soaring poem, an anchor for the spirit that seems ready at times for total release and departure.

For "Song of Myself" is not, as was once thought, a chaotic outpouring of half-digested poetic materials: it is a poem written in advance of its time, bearing less relation structurally to *Hiawatha,* Longfellow's narrative poem also published in 1855, than to such modern poems as T. S. Eliot's *The Waste Land* or Ezra Pound's *The Cantos* or William Carlos Williams' *Paterson.* In its structure, "Song of Myself" is a visionary poem which presents a drama—the drama of the poet himself as he goes into a mystical trance, proceeds on a mystical journey, and, finally, emerges exhausted from the mystical state. The journey he takes is a journey of discoveries, and he reports the discoveries as he goes.

This skeleton of a narrative of mystical experience provides the frame of the poem—a frame on which the poet is enabled to hang a multitude of emotions and feelings, assertions and ideas, probings and certainties, suggestions and intuitions. "Song of Myself" has fifty-two sections (some critics have seen an oblique reference to time, to the fifty-two weeks of the year), and early in the poem, in Section 5, the poet enters the threshold of mystical ecstasy by consummating an embrace with his soul:

> Loafe with me on the grass, loose the stop from your throat,
> Not words, not music or rhyme I want, not custom or lecture,
>   not even the best,
> Only the lull I like, the hum of your valvèd voice.
>
>
> I mind how once we lay such a transparent summer morning,
> How you settled your head athwart my hips and gently turn'd
>   over upon me,
> And parted the shirt from my bosom-bone, and plunged your
>   tongue to my bare-stript heart,
> And reach'd till you felt my beard, and reach'd till you held
>   my feet.

The suggestion of ecstatic paralysis cannot be missed in these lines, lines which mix inextricably the physical and spiritual in a bewildering way. They are immediately followed with lines of a different sort, lines of insight and certainty:

> Swiftly arose and spread around me the peace and knowledge
>   that pass all the argument of the earth,
> And I know that the hand of God is the promise of my own,
> And I know that the spirit of God is the brother of my own,
> And that all the men ever born are also my brothers, and the
>   women my sisters and lovers,
> And that a kelson of the creation is love. . . .

In Section 5 of "Song of Myself" Whitman appears to be dramatizing himself as entering the mystical state, a state that immediately brings knowledge and certainty about the cosmos and about the world. The large remaining part (forty-seven out of the fifty-two sections) of "Song of Myself" turns out to be a kind of journey into knowing, a journey initiated in this Section 5. The way of knowing is not straight but cyclic, not logical but intuitive, not simplistic and reductive, but complex and expansive, not a single moment's insight but a series of endless discoveries, not an exclusive path reserved for an aristocratic few, but a public road open to all men alike.

Further along in the poem, in Section 17, the poet pauses in his journey to exclaim:

These are really the thoughts of all men in all ages and lands,
    they are not original with me,
If they are not yours as much as mine they are nothing, or
    next to nothing,
If they are not the riddle and the untying of the riddle they
    are nothing,
If they are not just as close as they are distant they are nothing.

We do not move very far into "Song of Myself" without realizing
that we, the readers, are a part of the drama of the poem. There
are two main characters, the "I" and the "You," and as the poem
moves along an intimacy develops between poet and reader, the I
and the You, that proves by the end of the poem to be almost
embarrassingly complete. It is as though the speaker in the poem,
Walt Whitman, were swimming in the sea of words that make up
the mystical experience and poem, and that frequently he surfaces from the depths to look the shore-bound reader in the eye
to let him know his deeper discoveries. Or to shift metaphors, the
poet seems to soar out on ecstatic flights and to return as swiftly
to the side of the reader to report the wonders of his vision. But
whether diving or soaring, "Song of Myself" appears to be a
narcissistic poem, watching its own least move, observing its own
behavior, reporting its own state of health and insight periodically to the reader. In short, it seems to be a poem that watches
itself get outlined and written.

In Section 33 the poet seems to have reached a vital stage of
his journey into knowing:

Space and Time! now I see it is true, what I guess'd at,
What I guess'd when I loaf'd on the grass,
What I guess'd while I lay alone in my bed,
And again as I walk'd the beach under the paling stars of the
    morning.

My ties and ballasts leave me, my elbows rest in sea-gaps,
I skirt sierras, my palms cover continents,
I am afoot with my vision.

Here in the middle of "Song of Myself," a halfway point on the
journey, the poet has penetrated barriers, space and time, that

have separated him from the ultimate knowledge that he seeks. These lines, with their exhilarated announcement of release and freedom, launch a new phase of the mystical journey—a phase that leads finally to transcendent discovery, assurance, and certainty.

Such discovery and intuitive vision lead the poet, beginning in Section 44, to attempt some kind of summary, a symbolic description of his knowledge. He says:

> It is time to explain myself—let us stand up.
>
> What is known I strip away,
> I launch all men and women forward with me into the Unknown.
>
> The clock indicates the moment—but what does eternity indicate?

The remaining sections of "Song of Myself" are an elaboration of the insights gathered on the mystical journey. Such knowledge is the kind that is felt in the bones rather than held in the head, and such knowledge cannot be measured, circumscribed, and placed precisely in pat definitions. Indeed, such knowledge each man must gather for himself on his own journey, and he can then cry out with the poet: "I know I have the best of time and space, and was never measured and never will be measured."

As in Section 5 of "Song of Myself," the poet enters into the mystical trance through an intimate affair with his soul, so in Section 50 he emerges, fulfilled but exhausted, from the mystical journey:

> There is that in me—I do not know what it is—but I know it is in me.
>
> Wrench'd and sweaty—calm and cool then my body becomes,
> I sleep—I sleep long.
>
> I do not know it—it is without name—it is a word unsaid,
> It is not in any dictionary, utterance, symbol.

Something it swings on more than the earth I swing on,
To it the creation is the friend whose embracing awakes me.

Perhaps I might tell more. Outlines! I plead for my brothers
and sisters.

Do you see O my brothers and sisters?
It is not chaos or death—it is form, union, plan—it is eternal
life—it is Happiness.

All the signs of the deep mystical trance are present. The poet is "wrench'd and sweaty," and at last he becomes "calm and cool," and he needs the restorative of sleep, long sleep. This is the physical state of a man who has been emotionally or spiritually drained by staggering feats of the imagination, hard labor of the spirit. And moreover, he comes out of the mystical experience groping for the language that will hint at what he has discovered —a language that "is not in any dictionary, utterance, symbol." The words that he finally, in his groping, hits upon—form, union, plan, eternal life, happiness—all are pale copies of the reality, the real reality, that is inexpressible, known only in the depths of the mind and soul where language does not penetrate.

This frame of an experience essentially mystical, described above in rough outline, serves as the basic structure of "Song of Myself." But to look only at the frame is like studying man by looking only at his skeleton. "Song of Myself" is a poem rich in passages of rare delicacy, tenderness, and beauty. Here, for example, is an account of a love affair with the earth:

I am he that walks with the tender and growing night,
I call to the earth and sea half-held by the night.

Press close bare-bosom'd night—press close magnetic nourish-
ing night:
Night of south winds—night of the large few stars!
Still nodding night—mad naked summer night.

Smile O voluptuous cool-breath'd earth!
Earth of the slumbering and liquid trees!
Earth of the departed sunset—earth of the mountains misty-
topt!

Earth of the vitreous pour of the full moon just tinged with
    blue!
Earth of shine and dark mottling the tide of the river!
Earth of the limpid gray of clouds brighter and clearer for
    my sake!
Far-swooping elbow'd earth—rich apple-blossom'd earth!
Smile, for your lover comes.

This astonishing passage in effect is a love poem to the world
from the poet become lover: a universal or cosmic lover whose
embrace can encircle the globe and all its varied and voluptuous
landscapes. The lines are an ecstatic affirmation of the joys of
aware physical existence in a dynamic physical world.

Each reader of "Song of Myself" will find passages that fix
themselves firmly in the imagination, lines that leap from the
page with an energy and vitality that overpower and overwhelm.
In Section 44 appears one of the greatest statements of individuality ever made, a ringing assertion of the uniqueness, the pre-
ciousness, the miraculousness of the self in all its glorious selfhood:

I am an acme of things accomplish'd, and I am an encloser of
    things to be.

My feet strike an apex of the apices of the stairs,
On every step bunches of ages, and larger bunches between
    the steps,
All below duly travel'd, and still I mount and mount.

Rise after rise bow the phantoms behind me,
Afar down I see the huge first Nothing, I know I was even
    there,
I waited unseen and always, and slept through the lethargic
    mist,
And took my time, and took no hurt from the fetid carbon.

Long I was hugg'd close—long and long.

Immense have been the preparations for me,
Faithful and friendly the arms that have help'd me.

Cycles ferried my cradle, rowing and rowing like cheerful
  boatmen,
For room to me stars kept aside in their own rings,
They sent influences to look after what was to hold me.
Before I was born out of my mother generations guided me,
My embryo has never been torpid, nothing could overlay it.

For it the nebula cohered to an orb,
The long slow strata piled to rest it on,
Vast vegetables gave it sustenance,
Monstrous sauroids transported it in their mouths and
  deposited it with care.

All forces have been steadily employ'd to complete and
  delight me,
Now on this spot I stand with my robust soul!

Perhaps the most striking element of this passage is the joyful
placement of the self in the natural unfolding of evolution, in a
pre-Darwinian vision of the evolution of life in the world. All the
energy and dynamism and vitality of these lines seems to accumulate and funnel down to charge with rare life that last line as
it comes into dazzling focus: "Now on this spot I stand with my
robust soul!"

Whitman's fundamental discovery in "Song of Myself" was
that the American identity was none other than the "new identity" of the self—the simple, separate person that we all can be in
a free society. But the self that Whitman celebrated was a being
that had to be sought on an interior, primeval journey—an identity that had, in short, to be created by the mystic imagination.
Discovery was open to all. Whitman suggested:

Shoulder your duds dear son, and I will mine, and let us
  hasten forth.
Wonderful cities and free nations we shall fetch as we go.

Since Whitman's day, man has discovered the means of extin-
guishing himself and his planet, and such a catastrophe casts its
shadow over our daily lives. But where is the horror of the loss of

a wasteland both without and within? A nuclear holocaust can hold no terror unless it threatens to destroy something of value. Where is that value, if not in the self, however atrophied, hidden within—a vision of fertile creation and a heightened sense of life's joyous vitality? Whitman's song of the self is a call to reclaim this precious inner possession. We might well confront our day in the way he encountered his, that is, with the equanimity of men who have discovered their own and their country's identity: now on this spot we stand with our robust souls.

At the end of "Song of Myself," Whitman bade farewell to the reader, but it was a farewell that was in effect a greeting and a preparation for personal encounter. He said:

> The spotted hawk swoops by and accuses me, he complains of
> my gab and my loitering.
>
> I too am not a bit tamed, I too am untranslatable,
> I sound my barbaric yawp over the roofs of the world.
>
> The last scud of day holds back for me,
> It flings my likeness after the rest and true as any on the
> shadow'd wilds,
> It coaxes me to the vapor and the dusk.
>
> I depart as air, I shake my white locks at the runaway sun,
> I effuse my flesh in eddies, and drift it in lacy jags.
>
> I bequeath myself to the dirt to grow from the grass I love,
> If you want me again look for me under your boot-soles.
>
> You will hardly know who I am or what I mean,
> But I shall be good health to you nevertheless,
> And filter and fibre your blood.
>
> Failing to fetch me at first keep encouraged,
> Missing me one place search another,
> I stop somewhere waiting for you.

14 MARK TWAIN: *THE ADVENTURES OF TOM SAWYER*

Louis D. Rubin, Jr.

It may seem strange that anyone might feel any need to defend a novel which has sold in the millions of copies, been translated into most of the written languages of the world, and become part not merely of the literature but of the very folklore of childhood. The author's description of it as "simply a hymn, put into prose to give it a worldly air" scarcely stretches the truth too far.

Yet for all such success as that, *The Adventures of Tom Sawyer* has been the subject of comparatively little critical attention, and when it is discussed it is usually viewed as a stage in its author's progress toward *Adventures of Huckleberry Finn,* and not Tom's book but Huck's is generally considered Mark Twain's masterpiece. *"Tom Sawyer,"* declares Lionel Trilling, "has the truth of honesty—what it says about things and feelings is never false and always both adequate and beautiful. *Huckleberry Finn* has this kind of truth, too, but it also has the truth of moral passion: it deals directly with the virtue and depravity of man's heart." Few readers would quarrel with this evaluation; certainly I do not. All the same, the chief importance of *Tom Sawyer* is not as a harbinger of *Huckleberry Finn*. Let us pretend that Samuel L. Clemens did with the manuscript of *Huckleberry Finn* what he did with so many manuscripts: put it away after writing the opening chapters, but never returned to it, so that nothing exists after the incident in which the steamboat overruns the raft. Given Clemens' method of composition, this could have taken place all too easily. What then would be the place of *The Adventures of Tom Sawyer* in the Mark Twain canon?

Surely it would be Mark Twain's best novel. And although the author's reputation would not then be so high as it is, it would still be very high. *Tom Sawyer* would of itself have been enough to make a writer's reputation and keep it secure. So if this is so, it seems only proper to pay more attention to it in its own right, and not merely because it was followed by *Huckleberry Finn*.

One of the explanations for *Tom Sawyer's* subordinate status and reputation is that it happens to be notable as a book which children can read and enjoy. One customarily makes its acquaintance at the age of ten or twelve or thereabouts. It is first encountered at approximately the same stage in one's life at which one reads *Treasure Island, The Swiss Family Robinson, Robin Hood and His Merry Men, Hans Brinker and the Silver Skates, Twenty Thousand Leagues Under the Sea,* and *Captains Courageous,* or, if one is a girl, *Heidi* and *Little Women. Huckleberry Finn,* on the other hand, is often disturbing and is not really a book for children; I recall that in my own instance I found it quite disturbing, and I stopped reading it at the point at which Pap Finn begins beating Huck, and did not pick it up again and read it all the way through until my college years. *Tom Sawyer* contains disturbing episodes, too, but they are disturbing in a different way. It can be read and enjoyed by a child, and can continue to be enjoyed ever afterward—in which characteristic it is quite unlike most or all of the other children's books previously mentioned. This is because the plot of *Tom Sawyer,* while quite fascinating to a child, is not the chief attraction of the novel. Thus, instead of the book's appeal being diminished as soon as one discovers how it comes out, it becomes stronger. After we once know what will happen, our attention is liberated, so to speak, from close attention to the adventure story line, and we are free to take in the characterization, the setting, and the imaginative meaning of the story.

Clemens was right when he insisted to his friend William Dean Howells that it was *not* a children's book, so much as a book about childhood, written for adults. As he declares in his Preface, "part of my plan has been to try to pleasantly remind adults of what they once were themselves, and of how they felt and thought and talked, and what queer enterprises they sometimes engaged in." Yet neither is *Tom Sawyer* a book of simple nostalgia. It largely avoids the sentimentalities of so many books about childhood written for adults, in that the author takes Tom quite seriously, and can describe Tom's experience with the same gravity as Tom would view it. He does not condescend to Tom by "writing down."

Tom Sawyer's world has considerable unpleasantness in it, and there is a great deal about his life that involves terror, violence, and even evil. We have only to consider what happens to Tom and to Huck during the course of the novel. They go out to a cemetery at night and they watch three men robbing a grave and then fighting among themselves, until one of them is stabbed to death. It is Injun Joe who commits the murder, but the blame is fastened upon Muff Potter. So terrified is Tom of what Injun Joe might do if he informs the authorities of what really happened that he talks and moans in his sleep. When eventually he does tell what took place, Muff Potter is freed, but henceforth Tom lives in fear of Injun Joe's revenge. Later he and Huck listen from the second story of an abandoned house as Injun Joe, disguised as a deaf-and-dumb Spaniard, and an accomplice discover buried treasure; there is a frightening moment when Injun Joe starts upstairs to look around, but fortunately for the boys a rotten staircase plank collapses, and Joe gives up the search. Next Tom goes off with Becky Thatcher on an excursion into a cave, and the two become lost and wander around in the darkness for several days before Tom finds a way out. Meanwhile Huck hears Injun Joe plotting to slit the Widow Douglas' nostrils and notch her ears; he warns some nearby citizens of the widow's imminent peril, whereupon there is shooting, and the terrified Huck runs for his life. As for Injun Joe, that unfortunate returns to the cave, and when Judge Thatcher has the cave entrance locked and sheathed after Tom and Becky are rescued, the half-breed dies of starvation and thirst while trapped within.

Whatever might be said about *Tom Sawyer,* then, it can hardly be described as a nostalgic idyl, at least so far as Tom and Huck are concerned. Yet the violence and fear, of which there is a considerable supply in the story, do not have the same kind of horror about them that one finds in *Huckleberry Finn.* There is nothing in *The Adventures of Tom Sawyer,* for example, to match Huck's description of his father in the fifth chapter of

Huckleberry Finn: "There warn't no color in his face, where his face showed; it was white, not like another man's white, but a white to make a body's flesh crawl—a tree-toad white, a fish-belly white." Such a passage as that, which in its own way reminds one of Ishmael's remarks on the whiteness of the whale in *Moby-Dick,* far exceeds in sheer horror and evil any description of Injun Joe that the author ventures in *Tom Sawyer.* The reason, of course, is that *Huckleberry Finn* is told by its author *through* Huck, with the liberation of vernacular language involved thereby, while *Tom Sawyer* is told by the adult author in his own words. And while this difference is one of the reasons why *Huckleberry Finn* is the great novel it is, it is the reason why *Tom Sawyer* succeeds on its terms very well, too.

Let us therefore consider the technique whereby *Tom Sawyer* is told, beginning with an examination of the very first paragraphs of the story:

"Tom!"
No answer.
"Tom!"
No answer.
"What's wrong with that boy, I wonder? You, TOM!"
No answer.
The old lady pulled her spectacles down and looked over them about the room; then she put them up and looked out under them. She seldom or never looked *through* them for so small a thing as a boy; they were her state pair, the pride of her heart, and were built for "style," not service—she could have seen through a pair of stove lids just as well. She looked perplexed for a moment, and then said, not fiercely, but still loud enough for the furniture to hear:
"Well, I lay if I get hold of you I'll——"
She did not finish, for by this time she was bending down and punching under the bed with the broom, and so she needed breath to punctuate the punches with. She resurrected nothing but the cat.
"I never did see the beat of that boy!"
She went to the open door and stood in it and looked out among the tomato vines and 'jimpson' weeds that constituted the garden. No Tom. So she lifted up her voice at an angle calculated for distance, and shouted:
"Y-o-u-u, *Tom!*"

There was a slight noise behind her and she turned just in time to
seize a small boy by the slack of his roundabout and arrest his flight.

Notice what is happening. We begin with Aunt Polly calling
to Tom. The immediate relationship, then, is between the old
lady and Tom, and this is the beginning of the basic dramatic
involvement of the novel, which will concern itself with Tom
Sawyer's activities and his relationships with various people living in the town of St. Petersburg, Missouri. At this point, of
course, we do not yet know that it is Tom, and not the old lady,
who will matter most, and that the passage is chiefly important
for its depiction of Tom *hiding* from the old lady, though since
the book is entitled *The Adventures of Tom Sawyer,* we are naturally on the watch for Tom Sawyer to appear. The fact that he
makes his entry upon the stage in this particular fashion tells us
something about him right away. The role that Tom plays in the
very first scene is one in which he will be cast throughout the
story—that of a child engaged in an attempt to outwit the adult
world.

This, however, is only part of what is going on in these opening paragraphs. There is also a description of the old lady,
mainly having to do with the way she wears her spectacles. She
does not, we are informed, look through them, but over or under
them, because she cannot see through the lenses themselves, and
wears the eyeglasses only for purposes of show. She is also a rather
harassed old lady, and she is given both to talking to herself and
to shouting quite loudly. We also see her energetically poking
the broom under the bed to dislodge Tom, and succeeding only
in disturbing the meditations of a cat. So we get an idea, and a
humorous one at that, of what sort of person the old lady is.

We receive this idea, be it noted, not from either the old lady
or from Tom, nor do we see her as she sees herself or as Tom sees
her; rather, it is as the author sees her, from above as it were. Not
only does he describe her, but he comments humorously on what
he is describing. He exaggerates for comic effect: surely the old
lady's spectacles are not really as opaque as stove lids, and obviously the furniture cannot hear her shouting. Nor does she literally lift up her voice "at an angle calculated for distance"; that is

the author's amusing way of putting it, the metaphor being that of sighting a piece of artillery. It is the storyteller's manner, and we enjoy it.

The direct presence of the storyteller, therefore, is very important to the humor of this opening passage, and indeed in most of what follows in the novel. It is the active role of this authorial impresario telling the story to us that accounts for the distance between the reader and the events of the novel, and this distance is very important, for it is the method whereby the novel is given much of its meaning. We do not see Tom and Huck in action; they are described for us by the storyteller. I do not mean, of course, that our attention is drawn to the storyteller's presence at every moment in the novel. But Mark Twain reasserts himself often enough to force us to keep him well in mind (though we are seldom *aware* of our doing so). Consider, for example, Chapter Fifteen, which begins with a terse, Hemingway-like description of Tom leaving Jackson's Island while his fellow pirates are asleep:

A few minutes later Tom was in the shoal water of the bar, wading toward the Illinois shore. Before the depth reached his middle he was halfway over; the current would permit no more wading, now, so he struck out confidently to swim the remaining hundred yards. He swam quartering upstream, but still was swept downward rather faster than he had expected. However, he reached the shore finally, and drifted along till he found a low place and drew himself out. He put his hand on his jacket pocket, found his piece of bark safe, and then struck through the woods, following the shore, with streaming garments. Shortly before ten o'clock he came out into an open place opposite the village, and saw the ferryboat lying under the shadow of the trees and the high bank. Everything was quiet under the blinking stars. He crept down the bank, watching with all his eyes, slipped into the water, swam three or four strokes, and climbed into the skiff that did "yawl" duty at the boat's stern. He laid himself down under the thwarts and waited, panting.

Presently the cracked bell tapped and a voice gave the order to "cast off." A minute or two later the skiff's head was standing high up, against the boat's swell, and the voyage was begun.

In its precision and economy the passage has the ring of authority, and the storyteller does not make any remarks or invent any unusual metaphors to call attention to himself. He focuses our gaze on the events themselves, and continues to do so as Tom goes ashore in the town, makes his way along back alleys to his aunt's house, sneaks inside, and takes up his position under the bed. Next we hear his aunt and Mrs. Harper conversing, grieving for the missing boys. There is no interpretation; it is straight dialogue. Finally Aunt Polly speaks as follows:

> "Yes, yes, yes. I know just how you feel, Mrs. Harper, I know just exactly how you feel. No longer ago than yesterday noon Tom took and filled the cat full of Painkiller, and I did think the cretur would tear the house down. And God forgive me, I cracked Tom's head with my thimble, poor boy, poor dead boy. But he's out of all his troubles now. And the last words I ever heard him say was to reproach——"
>
> But this memory was too much for the old lady, and she broke entirely down.

At this juncture the story threatens to get away from Tom's viewpoint, and in thus making us realize how very unfunny the boys' adventure of being pirates on Jackson's Island is to their elders, who think the boys have been drowned, Mark Twain is in danger of losing control of his narrative. By directly showing Tom returning home from the island, and the two old ladies as they grieve, without placing himself as storyteller in the role of intermediary, Mark Twain has permitted the situation to come close to pathos. Therefore the author hastily interposes himself, and continues his description as follows:

> Tom was snuffling, now, himself—and more in pity of himself than anybody else. He could hear Mary crying, and putting in a kindly word for him from time to time. He began to have a nobler opinion of himself than ever before. Still, he was sufficiently touched by his aunt's grief to long to rush out from under the bed and overwhelm her with joy—and the theatrical gorgeousness of the thing appealed strongly to his nature, too, but he resisted and lay still.

The potentiality for pathos is thus decisively removed, and we smile at Tom engaging in silent histrionics under the bed in the best romantic fashion. This has been made possible because of the storyteller's comic interpretation of what is going on; he takes us away from Tom's evaluation of the scene, and we look down upon him from above, along with the author. Had the storyteller not reasserted his presence and his attitude, we might have become so concerned with how much the elders back in St. Petersburg are suffering that we would be unable to enjoy the adventures of the runaway boys on Jackson's Island, and at the climactic scene in the church we would view their triumphal return during the memorial services as a cruel and thoughtless bit of posturing, rather than as a dramatic coup for Tom Sawyer.

In short, the conscious presence of the performing storyteller, with his exaggerations, his jokes, and his philosophizing, creates the distance and detachment needed to make us view Tom Sawyer's exploits in the proper way. The perspective thereby achieved is that of an adult looking at Tom's childhood. While we are able to see things as Tom sees them, and Tom is a very acute and discerning observer, we also view Tom as he sees and thinks, from the vantage point of an adult. It is the dual relationship that gives the book its form and meaning. The distance is one of time: an adult looking back at childhood. The events that are happening while we are reading are "over"; they have already happened, back in the past. And especially since the storyteller is obviously mostly good-humored and rather fond of Tom, and enjoys looking back at a child's world, we are never allowed to take things so seriously that they begin to seem pathetic or tragic. The whole narrative is filtered, as it were, through a haze of time: it is in the past.

It is the existence of this perspective, the vantage point of an adult storyteller playing an active and very self-conscious role in the unfolding of the story, that so mutes and softens the violence of much of Tom Sawyer's experience that it does not affect us in the same way that similar violence in *Huckleberry Finn* does. The immediacy of the passage about Pap Finn's white flesh, quoted earlier, is due to its directness, to its impact on Huck's sensibilities and, through his chilling description, on ours. The use of Huck's language—and Mark Twain begins to discover its possibilities toward the end of *Tom Sawyer*—meant for the author that he could confront the experience of his boyhood along the river directly, without the need to maintain the attitude of the cultured adult observer. The result was the great moral drama of *Huckleberry Finn*. In *Tom Sawyer* this was impossible for him to do; he is the genial storyteller reminiscing about a Missouri childhood.

Yet while the presence of that adult storyteller makes some important discoveries impossible for Mark Twain in *Tom Sawyer*, it has its compensating advantages. For by working with that adult perspective, with its built-in dimension of past and present time, Mark Twain is able to tell a story *about* time: a "hymn," as he put it, to boyhood. The account of the summer months in St. Petersburg that constitutes *The Adventures of Tom Sawyer* is by no means one of uncomplicated joy and happiness; as we have seen, Tom Sawyer has his troubles, and sometimes his life is quite unpleasant. Hymns are not necessarily joyful. They are, however, comforting, and so, finally, is *Tom Sawyer*. It is comforting because, for better or worse, it has *happened*; it is the story of a boy's life, and the very fact that it has been lived, and been experienced, and is over, is in itself satisfying, both to the adult storyteller and to the adult reader. The sense of the passage of time is of the first importance in this novel. Tom grows up. Mark Twain recognizes the importance of his having done so in his epilogue, in which he remarks that "it being strictly a history of a *boy*, it must stop here; the story could not go on much further without becoming the history of a *man*." The novel describes a period of about four months in Tom's life during which he reaches the end of his childhood and verges upon adolescence, and the events of the story are directed toward that end.

This is true not only of the immediate adventure plot but of the larger form and direction of the novel as well. Doubtless it is the plot that most interests younger readers, and rightly so, for as adventure stories go, this is an exciting one. It involves a hunt for buried treasure, in which Tom and Huck run away and play at being pirates, and then begin hunting for treasure, which finally they discover in a cave. En route to this discovery they engage in many perilous activities, involving graveyard vigils, corpses, haunted houses, sinister half-breeds, and, for Tom, a near-fatal entombment in a cave. There are also subplots, notably one involving Tom's romance with Becky Thatcher, perhaps the least satisfactory part of the novel. On the level of straight adventure, then, *Tom Sawyer* has much to offer.

Yet the adventure plot is not the chief progression in the novel, though it becomes increasingly prominent as the story moves along. The larger and more important development of *Tom Sawyer,* the growing up of Tom, is what gives Mark Twain's story its lasting interest. The adventure plot exists primarily as a catalyst toward that result. More importantly, what Mark Twain does is to show us the nature of Tom Sawyer's imagination and place it in the society which he inhabits, so that through Tom's doing and thinking the things he does, that relationship is developed. Tom Sawyer and the town of St. Petersburg are the two chief subjects of Mark Twain's book, and the events of the story serve to establish and ultimately define the relationship between them. When we first encounter Tom in the novel he is, as noted, in flight from Aunt Polly; thereafter he continues to exist at cross-purposes with the adult community. Though not so dissociated from his community as Huck Finn is in his novel, Tom is nevertheless no conformist. The extent to which Tom accepts the values of the community has been exaggerated by most commentators; Henry Nash Smith, the most discerning of all critics of the Mark Twain novels, cites the concluding paragraphs of the scene in which Tom and his friends triumphantly walk into the church while their funeral service is being held, as an example of Tom's (and Mark Twain's) acceptance of the community's mores and ideals:

> Suddenly the minister shouted at the top of his voice: "Praise God from whom all blessings flow—Sing!—and put your hearts in it!"
>
> And they did. "Old Hundred" swelled up with a triumphant burst, and while it shook the rafters Tom Sawyer the Pirate looked around upon the envying juveniles about him and confessed in his heart that this was the proudest moment of his life.
>
> As the "sold" congregation trooped out they said they would almost be willing to be made ridiculous again to hear "Old Hundred" sung like that once more.
>
> Tom got more cuffs and kisses that day—according to Aunt Polly's varying moods—than he had earned before in a year; and he hardly

knew which expressed the most gratefulness to God and affection for himself.

"Here," Smith says, "Tom is fully integrated with the community (which is identical with the congregation in the church): the community is completely harmonious within itself; and the general exultation finds expression in the singing of a Christian hymn at the command of the minister. The official culture of St. Petersburg could hardly receive a more absolute affirmation."

But is this harmony quite so complete as Smith would have it? Tom has achieved a positively splendiferous triumph, but surely not by approved methods. He has run away, thrown the community into turmoil, and made possible his "proudest moment" only through deception and, in respect to his frantic aunt and family, almost ruthless cleverness. His way of gaining recognition and renown is certainly not that of his brother Sid, who is a complete conformist; he is by no means a Model Boy, either; earlier, his cleverness at assembling enough tickets to win a Bible without having to memorize the texts required to earn the tickets legitimately ended in acute shame and embarrassment, with the visiting dignitaries and the Sunday school scholars looking on. As for the hymn singing, whatever it may signify about the adult community's religious ideals and beliefs, so far as Tom is concerned it is a purely secular triumph. For Tom the whole thing is simply a good show. Of course it is undeniable that the very show itself, the desire to stage so dramatic a coup as a return to life at his own funeral service, is emblematic of a basic concern with the approval of the community, while Huck Finn in his novel places no value whatever upon the approval of the community. Certainly Tom's dissociation from the community and its values is not nearly so complete as Huck's. Even so, if Tom does seek community sanction, it is very much on his own terms, not the community's. Throughout *The Adventures of Tom Sawyer* he maintains his distance, and accepts plaudits and rewards only on his conditions.

In the end, of course, Tom triumphs completely: he comes back from the cave a hero, and shortly thereafter he wins the town's ultimate accolade by becoming wealthy. As Justin Kaplan remarks in his excellent biography of Samuel Clemens, *Tom Sawyer* "ended with the establishment of a trust fund for Tom and Huck; to have money out at six per cent meant to be a part of the fabric of organized, acquisitive society." This is quite true, but again a qualification must be entered, to the effect that here too Tom secures the community's approval on his own terms. It is *buried treasure* that he produces, discovered in a cave under the sign of the cross; furthermore, its value for Tom is not as wealth for its own sake, but for the occasion it affords for the big scene, the heroic gesture, the dramatic revelation before the assembled townsfolk. What mattered most to him, in that episode as in all others, is the opportunity for "the theatrical gorgeousness of the thing." If Tom is a capable entrepreneur, as demonstrated in the fence-painting episode and in his cornering of the Bible-ticket market, his ultimate objectives are never mercenary. The chief attainment in the affair of the whitewashed fence is not the acquisition of boyhood wealth so much as the satisfaction of having tricked Aunt Polly; in the Bible-ticket exploit it is not the Bible that he wants, but the renown that goes with being called up to the pulpit and being awarded the prize.

The difference is subtle, perhaps, but it is important. Throughout the novel Tom is engaged in a conspiracy, just as he is in *Huckleberry Finn*. The object of his scheming is always the same: romantic heroism. He is on Don Quixote's side, not Sancho Panza's. In *Tom Sawyer* he resists the efforts of family and town to make him conform, and will not take his satisfaction from belonging to the community and accepting its humdrum, pedestrian ways. He *pretends* that the little Missouri town is really a place of high adventure, that Cardiff Hill is Sherwood Forest, that Jackson's Island is a pirate stronghold, that McDougal's Cave is the den of a band of robbers where captives can be held for ransom, that in the middle-class community he inhabits the heroic possibility exists. At the outset of the novel he is an insignificant little boy; at its conclusion he is a hero. And not only that: he has indeed converted St. Petersburg into a place of pirates, glory, and buried treasure. Instead of conforming to the adult values, he has made the adult community conform to his. As we learn in the final chapter, "Every 'haunted' house in St. Petersburg and the neighboring villages was dissected, plank by plank, and its foundations dug up and ransacked for hidden treasure—and not by boys, but men—pretty grave, unromantic men, too, some of them."

Of course the triumph is only temporary. The reader knows that, and so does the storyteller. There will be no more discoveries of buried treasure in St. Petersburg, though later there may be other kinds of treasure, in their own way more impressive even than pirate gold. I think T. S. Eliot is mistaken, for once, when he predicts that Tom "will one day become an eminently respectable and conventional member" of "conventional respectable society." I do not doubt for a minute that Tom will manage to stay in the limelight, discover numerous opportunities for theatrical gorgeousness, and win the esteem of communities far larger than St. Petersburg; but that he will do it conventionally, and be as one with them and their ideals, I very much doubt. What is sufficient for the belief and imagination of the adult townsfolk of St. Petersburg is not likely to prove sufficient for Tom Sawyer. At the age of twelve or thereabouts, he has already attained the pinnacle of St. Petersburg's esteem; it will not be long before he will want new fields to conquer, and it is highly improbable that he will be content with the kind of career that Judge Thatcher has in mind for him. The Judge, as we know, "hoped to see Tom a great lawyer or a great soldier someday. He said he meant to look to it that Tom should be admitted to the National Military Academy and afterward trained in the best law school in the country, in order that he might be ready for either career or both." Somehow I doubt that this is what Tom has in mind. It is more likely, I think, that he will eventually become a novelist, and one who will be capable of writing both *Tom Sawyer* and *Huckleberry Finn*. Neither book is finally an affirmation of the official culture.

Tom Sawyer, to repeat, takes place in the past; when told by the storyteller it is already far back in time, in the long ago. So that if *The Adventures of Tom Sawyer* is a success story, about a little American boy who becomes rich and famous, resembling in this respect the Horatio Alger tales, the success is to a certain extent bittersweet. For in his triumph over his village circumstance, Tom Sawyer is losing something as well. There are various names one can give to it: innocence; boyhood; nature; the tranquil ways of a little village on the river before the railroads came; small-town life back when the Republic was young and its high hopes had not yet come up against the realities of wealth, privilege, injustice, want, deprivation. The world beyond St. Petersburg was waiting in the wings, and all unknowingly, Tom Sawyer was doing his best to bring it onstage. So that the adult storyteller, looking back at that long-ago time and at the boy who lived in it, could see not only what the restless imagination of Tom Sawyer had accomplished, but what had been lost as well.

Early in the novel Mark Twain describes Tom as he leaves the town:

> Half an hour later he was disappearing behind the Douglas mansion on the summit of Cardiff Hill and the schoolhouse was hardly distinguishable away off in the valley behind him. He entered a dense wood, picked his pathless way to the center of it, and sat down on a mossy spot under a spreading oak. There was not even a zephyr stirring; the dead noonday heat had even stifled the songs of the birds; nature lay in a trance that was broken by no sound but the occasional far-off hammering of a woodpecker, and this seemed to render the pervading silence and sense of loneliness the more profound. The boy's soul was steeped in melancholy; his feelings were in happy accord with his surroundings. He sat long with his elbows on his knees and his chin in his hands, meditating.

Everything that happens in *Tom Sawyer* takes place in the imagination of the storyteller who tells us that. And though Huck Finn later escaped from the town by fleeing down the river on a raft, his creator did not. He tried Huck's method, to be sure: in the pilot house of a Mississippi River steam packet, out West in the Nevada Territory, in the Sandwich Islands, in San Francisco, in a palatial mansion in Hartford, in England and on the continent, on excursions to the Holy Land, around the equator, all the way to Australia even. But it was only in his mind that Sam Clemens ever really came close to the freedom he coveted.

Of Tom Sawyer, Huck Finn says, in his own book, that "I reckoned he believed in the A-rabs and the elephants, but as for me I think different." The A-rabs and the elephants—the imagination: that was Tom Sawyer's way. At the close of *The Adven-*

tures of Tom Sawyer Tom finds Huck hiding out among the old empty hogsheads down behind the slaughterhouse, and persuades him to return to the Widow Douglas' house and conform for a while, but only, he says, so that later they can become outlaws and form a robber band. Samuel L. Clemens never formed a robber band; instead he formed a publishing house, and eventually he lost most of his fortune on it. But neither did he rest content on his income let out at six per cent. He wrote books, including two which are among his country's and the world's literary treasures. One of them, in its moral ferocity and its audacity, is as subversive of complacency, smugness, and injustice as any book ever written. The other is a tale of time, about a summer's season long ago, filled with honesty and truth, and if gentler and less daring than its sequel, it is even so in its own way a marvelous story too, a classic if ever there was one.

15   STEPHEN CRANE: *MAGGIE, A GIRL OF THE STREETS*

Edwin H. Cady

Stephen Crane was born in 1871, the same year as Theodore Dreiser, in the same decade with Gertrude Stein, Robert Frost, Upton Sinclair, Carl Sandburg, and Wallace Stevens. The marked difference between Crane and his contemporaries was that his star blazed out so early, so intensely, and was quenched so quickly. World-famous at twenty-five, he was dead at twenty-eight, in 1900. We think of his contemporaries as writers of our century, moderns, almost our contemporaries. Sinclair lived till 1969. Millions of us saw or heard Frost and Sandburg in person or on television. Had Crane lived as long, we might have known him too. He is thus uniquely a man of two ages, the last of the nineteenth century, the first of the moderns. *Maggie, A Girl of the Streets* was Crane's first book. It combined the literary impulses of the past and prophesied experimental things to come. It is a landmark book. Given all these circumstances, it surprises one to realize how little we actually know about the conception, composition, revision, and reception of *Maggie*.

In contrast with his contemporaries, there is doubtless a great deal we are never going to know certainly about Stephen Crane. At Indiana University, for instance, we have nine tons of the papers of Upton Sinclair. It is shocking to discover what one can't exactly know about Crane, what's not available, although students might be interested to hear that new Stephen Crane material will yet appear. This leaves, however, the question of what we can certainly know concerning *Maggie*. There has been extraordinary disagreement in statements by Crane critics concerning what may be found in *Maggie*.

If we look at the book we see that it is short, not much over twenty thousand words. It could be called a novella, even a long short story, like Crane's work entitled *The Monster. Maggie* was broken up by the author into a number of short chapters which tend not to consist of ordinary narrative development. To compare it with, say, a novel by James Fenimore Cooper, reveals that Crane worked by flashes. Frank Norris, Crane's contemporary, in reviewing *Maggie* noticed that it seemed to have been made on the principle of a photographer working in the dark. *Maggie* unfolds in a succession of brief, intensely lit pictures. It works according to the method Henry James labeled *scenes* and *pictures.* Instead of narrative development, Crane's flashes yield *pictures,* by which James meant the representation of views communicating atmosphere, circumstance, condition, setting, perhaps symbols. Less frequently Crane wrote *scenes* as in a play, where people conversing or acting demonstrate something representationally.

Chapter One shows little Jimmy Johnson playing king of the hill on a gravel heap in the slums, fighting for the honor of Rum Alley against the kids from Devil's Row. Fighting, losing, getting beaten up: this communicates the insight that goes all through Stephen Crane's work that the essence of the human condition is a state of war. Enter Pete, who breaks up the fight and rescues Jimmy; enter Jimmy's father who, cursing, takes him home. Chapter Two carries us to the tenement, a reeking, crowded, dismal place which is home for the Johnsons. Enter Maggie as little sister, with the baby Tommy as brother, and then the monstrous mother with the dreadfully ironic name, "Mary." Immediately there is a family fight with smashing furniture and vitriolic cursing, a terror to the children.

In Chapter Three the "old woman" enters, misshapen and mean, the tenement neighbor. The father (whose name we never know, he's just "old Johnson") goes on a spree, which leads to a decisive domestic fight won by Mary. In three flashes we have been shown the environment. As much as anything, *Maggie* is an ecological study. Scientifically, ecology is the study of environment, of the total relationship of an organism to its condition. Crane has established the ecological situation of the slum child.

In the fourth chapter, events become foreshortened. Henry James thought it useful to talk about fiction in terms of painting, and he liked to show how sometimes it is necessary to foreshorten perspectives. There is a good deal of foreshortening of time, technically very interesting, in *Maggie*. Tommy, the baby, dies in one short paragraph and is gone, carrying the flower Maggie stole from an Italian fruit vendor. Then comes a study of Jimmy and the process by which, as Crane says, he became a young man of leather, a youth whose sneer was chronic.

Chapter Five begins with the most intriguing statement in the book. As she grew, Maggie became a pretty girl, a flower which "blossomed in a mud puddle." This, as James would have said, constituted Crane's *donnée*. Presumably James was recalling plane geometry, where every problem begins with a "given." An author must also start with his "given," and there is a sense in which we must not presume to look behind it. The given in *Hamlet* is that Hamlet has come home from Wittenberg; and it does no good to inquire into what Wittenberg was like for Hamlet or his relationships there with Rosencrantz and Guildenstern. A lot of nonsense passing for literary study has been written about non-questions like that. The *donnée* is precisely Hamlet's given situation when the play begins.

The *donnée* in *Maggie* is that, in defiance of Rum Alley, Maggie "blossomed in a mud puddle." It has been doubted by critics whether it is possible to blossom in mud puddles. We are not sure what an expert sociologist would say to this. Is it possible to become a blossom, a pretty and innocent girl on Rum Alley in the Johnson household? Regardless of doubts, still that was Crane's *donnée* and, having blossomed, Maggie is forced to go and work in a sweatshop by Jimmy, her brother, the young man of leather, who makes a significant remark: "Yeh've edder got teh go teh hell or go teh work!" She goes to work. In the same chapter Crane studies the decline of Mary so that at the end of this chapter the reappearance of Pete, whom Maggie finds fascinating, is loaded with irony.

Chapter Six starts with a typical speech by Pete. "Say, Mag, I'm stuck on yer shape, it's outa sight!"—a real Galahad. Nevertheless, Pete conjures up for Maggie images of splendor. Her illusions contrast with the squalor of home and the sweatshop. She begins for the first time to see herself as a woman. She begins to primp.

Chapters Seven and Eight introduce Maggie to the world in a marvelous succession of scenes. The world, the wonderful world, to which Pete introduces Maggie is the world of Bowery theater saloons, with their drunkenness, roughness, cheapness, squalor, and tawdry sentimentality which passes for entertainment.

Chapter Nine reaches a crisis pivotal to the book. We see Mary Johnson disgraced in a series of public sprees, clashing physically with Jimmy but losing to him where she had won over the dead father. In the midst of her defeat, with all its horror, she tells Maggie: "Go teh hell. . . . Damn yeh, git out!" And Pete is right on hand to show her the way. In the next chapter comes the second pivot of the novel, enforcing the central theme of its irony. The thing almost never sufficiently appreciated in *Maggie* is the profundity of its irony. The mean old woman meets Jimmy coming home and gloatingly informs him that his sister is ruined, she *has* gone to hell. Jimmy tells Mary, and her response establishes the other aspect of her character. One side is the drunkenness, the riotousness, the violence. The other side is her love and her talent for sentimental personal melodrama. She launches into a gorgeously self-satisfying portrayal of the crucified mother whose disobedient, ungrateful child has run off to be ruined. In turn this leads to one of Crane's finest scenes, in Chapter Eleven, where Jimmy, doing the only thing he can think of, picks up a friend and goes to the saloon where Pete tends bar to beat up Pete. They have a bar-fight the like of which we never see on television; it is too realistic.

In Chapter Twelve appear Pete and Maggie together, Pete lording it with infinite condescension over a Maggie utterly humble and dependent. Simultaneously, Mary Johnson, puffing with self-righteousness, talks with a Jimmy trying dimly to think his way through the situation. Shouldn't they, he wonders, get Maggie home? Shouldn't they understand and take her back? But the mother forbids such wicked thoughts: she's a beast, that Maggie, not entitled to human consideration. Finally, three weeks after Maggie's ruin, she loses Pete in a saloon to a smart, hard, polished, resourceful little whore named Nelly. Pete just walks out, leaving Maggie bewildered.

Next chapter, in a very interesting scene, suddenly interjected, Jimmy finds himself accosted on the street by a girl named Hatty whom he has earlier seduced and abandoned. To her appeal Jimmy says, "Oh, go teh hell!" Thus, when Maggie has to come home, her appearance simply gives the mother opportunity to stage a melodrama, tauntingly vicious; and when Maggie turns to Jimmy, he takes the same moral line. There is nothing to do but turn and leave. And so in the next chapter she goes to Pete in the saloon, which upsets and worries him. He has already been in a fight over her in his own saloon, and he fears that the owner will see Maggie. When she asks, "But where can I go?" we know what he will answer: "Oh, go teh hell!" At the very end of the chapter, wandering around town, wondering what to do, where to go, she tries to speak to a most respectable, clerical gentleman. Taking one look at Maggie, the bishop saves his respectability by leaping wonderfully away. How, asks the narrator, was he to know that here was a soul that needed saving?

Then comes one of the most marvelous scenes, which isn't quite a scene because it is a process, in Chapter Seventeen. Crane shows us a sweeping, cinematic view of a woman of the street, not identified as Maggie, who begins, smartly dressed, tapping along on her high heels in the most glittering part of New York. Seductively she passes through and then, in what is apparently a single action but might symbolize several years, she walks down and down and down through levels of the city life which are also in a sense levels of hell. Downward level by level she accosts increasingly repulsive customers and is rejected until her path ends at the river.

In the final chapter Jimmy comes home and finds his mother sitting there, stuffing herself with bread. He says, "Well, Mag's dead." And his mother says, "What?" He says, "Mag's dead." When her coffee is finished, Mary begins to weep. She plays out a violent scene of sentimentality about Maggie as a baby and the little knitted boots she wore. Neighbors come in to help with the melodrama until finally, in the last terrible irony, Mary says, "Oh, yes, I'll fergive her! I'll fergive her!" as if somehow she were doing dead Maggie a sacrificial favor.

Now, what do we really know about this book? So many interesting things that it is a shame we don't know more. If we want to synthesize all the testimony and not question any of it, we can suppose that there were four stages of composition of *Maggie*. Frank Noxon said that Crane began it when he was a student at Syracuse University in the spring of 1891. After he left college, perhaps he tried to rewrite it. In 1892 he made a new version, as he told a friend, in a few days before Christmas; and finally he took a manuscript to a cheating printer and had it privately printed. The title was *Maggie, A Girl of the Streets,* and the author appears as "Johnston Smith." Crane applied for a copyright on the 19th of January 1893, which date is almost the only fact about which we can feel sure.

The history of *Maggie* is heartbreaking. Crane wrote a landmark book, a work of art; and nobody would publish it. He had a family friend, Richard Watson Gilder, editor of a famous magazine, the *Century.* He took the manuscript of *Maggie* to Gilder, who read it and said, "I'm sorry, I can't publish it." When Crane asked, "Why not, Mr. Gilder?" Gilder said, "It's too cruel." Crane said, "You mean, it's too honest, don't you?" And Gilder said, "Yes, perhaps I do."

Crane had made another friend while throwing a baseball back and forth at Asbury Park one summer. Hamlin Garland had come to lecture about the new realistic movement, and Crane wrote a newspaper report so understanding that Garland was impressed. When *Maggie* came out, of course nobody paid any attention. Crane confessed later that he thought that if he just got his book printed it would become famous like the Waverley Novels before it was known that Scott had written them. Then, said Crane, like an acrobat swinging down from the trapeze, he meant to appear and say, "Behold, I am Johnston Smith." But the public paid no attention. Garland, however, was willing to send a copy to his friend Howells. Howells was intrigued and as the most influential critic of the time began to make Stephen Crane known. Eventually, though, Crane's fame was taken out of Howells' hands by the overnight international sensation of *The Red Badge of Courage.* Then, but after it had been suitably revised, Appleton's was happy to publish *Maggie, A Girl of the Streets* in regular form.

That history points to the question of which *Maggie* text to read. One ought to know about two books, a facsimile edition of the first edition, the 1893 *Maggie,* edited by Professor Joseph Katz, and a volume which is called *Stephen Crane's "Maggie," Text and Context,* edited by Professor Maurice Bassan, which provides a number of relevant and useful documents. Both Katz and Bassan are committed to the notion that the *Maggie* for us to read is *not* the one generally known, which is the text of the 1896 edition. They think that we should read *Maggie* as Crane first wrote it, out of his own sense of the way it ought to be. The text is fortunately being edited, in what should be the definitive edition, by Professor Fredson Bowers. In the first volumes of the Virginia edition we shall have an established text to go by. It will be based fundamentally on the 1893 edition, so that on the whole the 1896 edition will simply disappear: and good riddance, too.

Concerning the 1893 *Maggie,* it becomes essential to talk about the language. When Howells was trying to make Crane famous, he kept saying: Mr. Crane has written a magnificent book about common life, slum life, and low life in America. It is better than anything ever written, but the subject matter may be too grim to be popular; and the language probably bars it from the cultivated home. To see the language objected to in Crane's book by Howells and the people of Crane's own generation, we may count, "what deh hell" thirty-two times; "where deh hell," twice; "go teh hell," fifteen times. There are some fifty other uses of "hell," sixty-four "damns," seven or so uses of the name for the deity dialectically spelled "Gawd." And that's about it. There are a good many abstract references to oaths, curses, swearing. One could now (as then) easily hear in any American town much more colorful profanity than that. Not that Crane didn't use it well; no sensitive reading can escape the terribly ironic reverberations built up in *Maggie* by the phrase, "Go teh hell!"

What was Stephen Crane's point of view? A point of view is not exactly an opinion but something which may lead to an opinion. Our point of view is the place where we stand to see something, and it determines the way we see. Crane's point of view was of fundamental importance.

A fragment survives of a letter Crane wrote to a Miss Catherine Harris after publication of the 1896 *Maggie.* She must have written him a letter about *Maggie,* for which he thanks her. Then he says:

Mrs. Howells was right in telling you that I have spent a good deal of time on the East side and that I have no opinion on missions. That— to you—may not be a valid answer since perhaps you have been informed that I am not very friendly to Christianity as seen around town. I do not think that much can be done with the Bowery so long as the poor [?] are in their present state of conceit. The person who thinks himself superior to the rest of us because he has no job and no pride and no clean clothes is as badly conceited as Lillian Russell. In a story of mine called "An Experiment in Misery" I tried to make plain that the root of Bowery life is a sort of cowardice. Perhaps I mean a lack of ambition or to willingly be knocked flat and accept the licking. The missions for children are another thing and if you will have Mr. Rockefeller give me a hundred street cars and some money I will load all the babes off to some pink world where the cows can lick their noses and they will never see their families any more. My good friend Edward Townsend—have you read his "Daughter of the Tenements"?—has another opinion of the Bowery and it is certain to be better than mine. I had no other purpose in writing *Maggie* than to show people to people as they seem to me. If that be evil, make the most of it.

Central to Crane was his defiance, and one of the reasons for the defiance was that he was what used to be called in the colleges "a preacher's kid." To be the child of a Methodist minister was a peculiar fate. Such people were often very gifted; but at least in their college years they had a lot of trouble, and one reason for that trouble was that they were often in profound revolt against childhood years of repression, not only within the family but from congregations and communities, all the world. One can see in Stephen Crane a deep concern for ideas in which he did not pretend to be a believer, toward certain of the ideas of original Christianity. But that was of course radically different from Christianity as seen around town. The pretentiousness, hypocrisy, stupidity, the anti-Christianity of institutional Christianity, revolted Stephen Crane.

On the other hand, Crane held a point of view which conflicts sharply with Christianity in his letter to Catherine Harris. It was the point of view of an athlete, a man who believed in ultimate and fundamental effort and suffering, in paying the price, in standing up for a value, in developing an ideal and going for it straight even if he knew he was going to lose. But there was still another thing people noticed in Stephen Crane, and that was his compassion—for children, for women, for animals, for working people. Look sometime at a sample of Crane's handwriting. It is perfectly beautiful, and it is so because young reporter Crane discovered that printers did piecework; they got paid by the number of lines they could set by hand. If they had to read bad manuscript it held them up, but if they had good clean manuscript they could make money. Crane developed the discipline of being unmistakable. That sense of going all out for an ideal, for what one thought right, for what one perceived to be true even though it might prove ultimately not true, was fundamental to Crane. In a sense his total lack of compassion for the egotistical self matched his antipuritanical, almost total compassion for the suffering of others.

A great advantage of teaching is that one keeps learning, especially from students. And I have come to change one opinion about *Maggie* since I wrote a little book on Stephen Crane. What I said there was that the next to last chapter in which we see Maggie going down to death is a classic example of experimentalism because it shows Crane doing a virtuoso job of compressing a time sequence into a symbolic drama. I argued, however, that this became a flaw in the novel because it is too quick and too short. My assumption was that the subject of the novel is Maggie, but I have since perceived that I was wrong. It is not a novel about Maggie as a person. She is in fact the character least studied. She seldom speaks or acts; her activities, ideas, and feelings are summarized, foreshortened, compacted and described to us while the dramatic action goes on all around. The carefully characterized people are Mary, an ogre; then Jimmy, and then Pete. In the way Pete talks and acts he is a perfect Bowery tough, the essence of whose life is cowardice.

Crane studied the ecology for us so that we must see that it is impossible to imagine that Maggie has really gone to hell. The right phrase for Maggie was the one Robert Frost picked up from Christopher Marlowe: the life around her would have given Maggie, had she the wit, the right to say, "Why this is hell, nor am I out of it." To get out of hell was to get out of that life.

Thus the novel lends an ironic, effective point to the famous inscription Crane wrote across the paper cover of the 1893 edition of *Maggie* which he presented to Hamlin Garland:

> It is inevitable that you be greatly shocked by this book but continue, please, with all possible courage to the end. For it tries to show that environment is a tremendous thing in the world and frequently shapes lives regardless. If one proves that theory one makes room in Heaven for all sorts of souls (notably an occasional street girl) who are not confidently expected to be there by many excellent people... .

The present importance of the book, as distinct from its historical or technical importance, what makes *Maggie* alive and vital right now, is its moral significance. There was a moment in American life when we thought there would be no more slums, and while we were looking the other way something dreadful happened. That may sound silly, but it describes the way many people achieved what consciousness they have of what has been called "the other America." While we were looking the other way, suddenly (of course it *wasn't* sudden, that's a lie we tell ourselves) here were the slums again, more dreadful for the people in them than before. And what ought our attitude to be toward those people? Stephen Crane meant us to discover compassion for those people by showing us how intolerable were the ironies of the pretense and hypocrisy, and the stupidity and egotistical indulgence of men and women who would not see, who will not see the truth of the human experience involved. That is why *Maggie* is a great book, perhaps now a greater book than it ever was before, which is one of the things that happen to great books.

16 HENRY JAMES: THE AMBASSADORS

Leon Edel

The Ambassadors was written by Henry James between the middle of 1900 and the early months of 1901 although it was not published until 1903. It inaugurated the new fiction of the new century. In retrospect we can recognize its importance as an experimental novel, for it made many innovations in the art of storytelling. It anticipated the reflective novel of Proust; it used a scenic method akin to the drama; it foreshadowed the camera-visuality of Robbe-Grillet; it opened the way for the inner monologues of Joyce, Virginia Woolf, Faulkner. Deliberate, measured, highly "structured," it is the record of an adventure of the spirit rather than a tale of physical adventure. The only violent character in the novel is an opinionated lady from a provincial American town, with a sharp temper and a closed mind. It is a story of civilized manners and civilized society told with remarkable technical virtuosity.

André Gide long ago remarked that Henry James "lets only just enough steam escape to run his engine ahead, from page to page; and I do not believe [said Gide] that economy, that reserve, has ever sagaciously been carried further." James himself was aware of this deliberateness. To a literary-minded English duchess, who had difficulty reading this novel, he wrote: "Take, meanwhile pray, *The Ambassadors*, very easily and gently: read five pages a day—be even as deliberate as that—but *don't break the thread.* The thread is really stretched quite scientifically tight. Keep along with it step by step—and then the full charm will come out."

This charm resides not only in James's human comedy; it is to be found in the pattern or shape of the book, in its symmetries and its calculated scenes as well as in its richly worked style. There are thousands of writers in every generation, but only those survive who say memorable things in a memorable way. James's style, which he achieved after many years, is intricate and difficult, but it is characteristic and it is memorable. It was designed to catch the nuances and the subtleties of reflective man. To capture subtlety language must be used with subtlety. And we must make our peace with James's style, as readers learned to read the river-like sentences of Proust and mastered the intricacies of Joyce.

James always regarded style as a writer's passport to posterity. His own style to be sure grew increasingly elaborate and ornate; there are times when it is baroque or "mandarin" to excess; its expanding metaphors and large similes contain many frills and decorations. This is often the first problem for readers of *The Ambassadors*. They must accustom themselves to James's accuracy of language, and the demands this makes on their attention. The opening sentence illustrates the difficulty, "Strether's first question, when he reached the hotel, was about his friend; yet on his learning that Waymarsh was apparently not to arrive till evening he was not wholly disconcerted." *Not wholly disconcerted.* A sentence later we discover that Strether is prompted "not absolutely to desire." These negatives seem at first like willful mannerisms. They can soon be recognized as having a distinct intention. James could have said that Strether was "not wholly disturbed," or that he was "untroubled." We must however allow an author his language. We must not substitute banalities for his way of saying things. What we come to recognize is that from the first James is attempting to put us into the way of thinking of his principal character. Strether seems a hesitant sort of man. He qualifies, he thinks in negatives. This then is James's way of giving the language a descriptive function when he is not actually engaged in description. Strether, we discern, is not having very positive, very sharp feelings. Moreover at this stage we know nothing about Strether; and we are told nothing. He has simply arrived at his hotel and we see him acting himself out, inquiring about his friend or acquaintance Waymarsh. We discover soon enough that James tells us his story in what we might call a very "modern" way.

It is modern in that unlike the old novelists, unlike Dickens or Thackeray, James has done no old-fashioned narrating; we're not told everything we need to know; we're not fully informed of the facial appearances, the personae, the motives, the goals. We discover little bits and pieces of our story; we are given many glimpses. This is the way we discover things in life, of course. And James's narrative is highly visual. Before the era of the camera he seems to be aware of the existence of the lens—he moves, shifts, goes from close-up to distance, gives us only as much information as Strether himself has. It's a curious way of telling a story—that of withholding information rather than giving it, sometimes withholding it altogether. The notable instance in this novel is the question of what the Newsome family manufactures in Woollett, Massachusetts. The family fortune is founded on it. It's a common household article. Strether mentions it early in the book. But he doesn't name it. Is it combs? watches? bobby pins? E. M. Forster thinks it might be buttonhooks or, as he puts it, "if you choose to be coarse and daring and visualize it for yourself, as, say, a buttonhook, you can, but you do so at your own risk; the author remains uninvolved."

There's really no risk, for it doesn't matter. James is up to one of his favorite tricks, which is to let the reader think what he will. The Newsomes are rich; they have a son who has lingered in Paris; and it is the drama of his lingering and of the ambassador, Strether, sent to bring him home, that is important: not the incidental fact of the source of their wealth. In a larger sense James is perhaps suggesting that when one meets men of great wealth, one doesn't always know from what particular fount the gold flows. *The Ambassadors* was written in the era when the first great American fortunes were being made; and James had always been interested—for his grandfather had amassed an enormous fortune in New York State—not in how the money is made, but in how it is used, what its effect is on the lives of individuals and families. In an early novel, James's American hero has made a pile in washtubs; doubtless some similar mundane article served to endow the Newsomes. This, then, is a novel in which many of the usual things are omitted. James's search was always for a strict relevance. What is relevant in *The Ambassadors* is the sentience of his hero, Lewis Lambert Strether. The lady, Maria Gostrey, whom Strether meets at Chester, remarks that his name reminds her of a novel by Balzac. Strether agrees. He was named after *Louis Lambert*. A bad novel, the lady remarks. Strether also agrees, but the literary footnote has been placed. *Louis Lambert* is one of Balzac's philosophical novels. We shall see that *The Ambassadors* might be called a philosophical novel as well.

The reading of *The Ambassadors* is first and foremost a matter of our becoming familiar with its style and grasping its method. Once we realize that we, as readers, are gatherers of information, along with Strether, and not merely persons being given vast amounts of "story," we can take hold of those tight threads, and follow them into the heart of the comedy. On the surface it seems trivial enough. Mrs. Newsome, the grand and powerful lady of Woollett (a town-name James invented, but it might be Worcester or Waltham), has decided to send her friend the middle-aged Lambert Strether to Paris to see why her son Chad has remained there for so long. She wants Chad home and in the family business. Somewhat delicate in health herself, she remains in Woollett, like any foreign office or state department. Strether is her "ambassador." We will never see Mrs. Newsome, for she has all the remote power of a foreign office. It exists; it is felt; it acts through envoys, dispatches, orders, counter-orders, public relations; it issues instructions; it practices stratagems. In Sardou's five-act play *La Famille Benoîton* Madame Benoîton never appears, but we get to know her very well before the play is ended. So Mrs. Newsome is always offstage. But her power animates *The Ambassadors*.

Like all good diplomats, Strether has an open mind. He will gather his information; only then will he reach his conclusions. Woollett however has made up its mind long ago. There must be a woman somewhere in young Chadwick Newsome's life. That is Mrs. Newsome's theory. *Cherchez la femme.* Strether however keeps an open mind. A true diplomat, if not a professional one, he is a man of delicacy; he knows that he must be discreet, for Chad Newsome is full grown. It is not Strether's intention to meddle in his life. That may be Chad's mother's intention, but it cannot be his. He will simply use his eyes, keep his ears open, seek "psychological" evidence. This kind of evidence, James remarked in an earlier novel, is the only kind of evidence that is honorable. Any other belongs, he said, to the detective and the keyhole.

As a story this genial comedy is comparatively simple. Strether finds Chad much changed—the young rude provincial has been converted into a suave man of the world; he has an apartment, beautifully furnished, and in good taste, in the Boulevard Malesherbes. He has a charming circle of American expatriate and French friends. He seems the happy heir of the new America, and he lives with considerable refinement and without vulgar ostentation. Looking about him, to see who has worked this miracle, who has disprovincialized Chad, Strether decides the young man has had the guidance of a Frenchwoman of distinction, Madame de Vionnet. She is part English, part French, separated from her husband, and with a grown and marriageable daughter. One of Strether's first theories is that Madame de Vionnet would like to marry her daughter to Chad. The central irony of the story is soon established. The ambassador who has come to Paris to take Chad home is converted to Chad's side. He has not been abroad since his youth; in middle age he falls anew under the spell of the *ville lumière*—and we might add of Chad's entourage. He not only disqualifies himself for his mission by his own conduct; he comes to the "wrong" decision. He believes Chad should continue his stay abroad: this is not the conclusion he was supposed to reach.

With the careful symmetry James used in his late novels, this is the midpoint of the book. The story has been moving forward steadily. At the point where the ambassador reverses himself, Mrs. Newsome, from her "foreign office" in Woollett, disturbed by his letters, recalls Strether. She promptly dispatches a new set of envoys, including Chad's aggressive sister. The second half of the book deals with the continuing "education" of Strether and the work of the new ambassadors.

James spoke of each part of this novel as being "like a rounded medallion, in a series of a dozen, hung with effect of high relief, on a wall." Whether we think of the medallions, or of a row of columns, the effect is classical. The book is divided into twelve parts. In the fifth book and the eleventh, that is, in the all but last book of each half, James reaches a climactic scene. The two climaxes represent the highest points in Strether's middle-aged education. The first climax occurs in a garden on the Left Bank on a beautiful day of late spring. It is the garden of Gloriani, the artist, and in these surroundings, Strether suddenly feels release from the compulsions and rigidities of Woollett. The actual garden James had in mind was that of the American painter Whistler, in the Rue de l'Université. Some remark, by a young artist, acts as the stimulus for a long speech Strether makes; this contains within it the philosophy of the book. Strether delivers himself of a deeply felt monologue. "Live all you can," he says; "it's a mistake not to. It doesn't so much matter what you do, in particular, so long as you have your life. If you haven't had that what *have* you had?" This has the quality of a profound *cri de coeur*—it comes straight from the heart. At middle life, Strether feels that somehow he has missed his train, that it has left without him; and he looks back upon his lost opportunities. Of course, living all one can is not a matter for James of epicureanism; *carpe diem* is banal enough. It is a question of living in terms of perception, awareness, clarity of vision, attention to one's surroundings, to one's relations with others. Late in the book the phrase "live all you can" will be echoed as *"see* all you can." Thus living and seeing are equated. Life exists, says James, only when we perceive. Without perception we are only vehicles of instinct and impulse.

This however is a mere preamble to the significant statement of this novel. One might almost say that it was for this that James wrote the book, and it is at this point that *The Ambassadors* becomes not simply an agreeable comedy of international manners, a weighing of Woollett's provinciality against the cosmopolitanism of Paris. It's here that we find the "philosophical" nature of the book. Strether goes on to say, after his exclamation that we must live all we can, that life is like a mold, used by a cook to shape a jelly or a pudding; that each human being's consciousness is shaped—shaped early in life—*conditioned,* as we might put it in our time, and that then, once the jelly has jelled, or the pudding taken its form, there is no altering it. We are what we are. One must, says Strether, "live in fine as one can"; and within this, there seems to be an early foreshadowing of Sartrian existentialism half a century before Sartre. One's jelly has taken its form; one exists; the question then is what one does with that existence. The answer James provides may seem curious. If man is not free, if he lives in a predetermined world, and has a predetermined existence he still has, says Strether, "the illusion of freedom." This makes life bearable: this makes life interesting, makes it possible for us to open ourselves to experience, to the world.

The refined existentialism of Henry James is stated in these positive terms. Strether may be unhappy that he has not lived by this illusion; that he has in reality led a constricted life in an American provincial town; but his Parisian adventure has shown him that a man can be as free as he feels; that it is possible to have this feeling of freedom, even though it might, in terms of reality, be characterized as illusory.

James uses all the resources of style and charm of imagery to make us aware of the expanding consciousness of Strether; of the way in which, during that spring and summer of the new century in Paris, the American shakes off the constraints of his past. He does not altogether succeed. He knows that his change is not fundamental; but it is also not superficial, for there is a new state of sentience and an understanding of the kind of liberty he possesses. He has also, in a sense, changed his relationship to Mrs. Newsome. He has struck for freedom. He can truly allow his own conscience to be his guide. In the early stretches of the book Strether looks constantly at his watch, pats his coat pocket to make sure his wallet is in its place; he has been always aware of counting the hours, of ticking off life according to clock-time. He has talked in his great speech in Gloriani's garden of having missed the train. Late in the book he literally takes a train, going to a Paris station and boarding a suburban local picked at random. He isn't going anywhere in particular. His new journey will not be measured, planned, calculated. He simply moves into the French countryside. Once in Boston, in an art gallery in Tremont Street, he had seen a painting by a minor French landscapist, Lambinet. He liked the metallic green in the picture; and he now takes this train into the French rural scene in quest of nothing more than the same shade of green.

This is, for Strether, a show of spontaneity of which he would have been incapable in the first part of the book. And James tells the story as if he had a premonition that the television camera would be invented. His visual sense gives us the picture of the Lambinet; and when the camera moves toward the picture Strether is seeking, it picks up a stream, the greenery, the church spire. Descending from the train, Strether walks right *into* the picture he has sought:

> the oblong gilt frame disposed its enclosing lines; the poplars and willows, the reeds and river—a river of which he didn't know, and didn't want to know, the name—fell into composition, full of felicity, within them; the sky was silver and turquoise and varnish; the village on the left was white and the church on the right was grey; it was all there, in short—it was what he wanted; it was Tremont Street, it was France, it was Lambinet. Moreover he was freely walking about in it.

Strether has discovered an interesting kind of freedom, one that disengages him in the first instance from the timetable, the set journey, the designated place, even from the names of places: "a river of which he didn't know, and didn't want to know, the name." He has sought the freedom to *be*, to *feel*, to *see*—silver and turquoise, poplars and willows. He has escaped from the rigidity of Woollett and cultivated his illusion of freedom which contained within it a very true sense of actual freedom. We assist at this personal adventure of the innocent middle-aged American, an innocent in search of himself.

Strether's day in the country has its particular climax. The day begins more happily than it ends. The American walks for some hours in the rural landscape. Late in the afternoon he finds a rustic inn. He orders his dinner still in his mood of carefree and almost cultivated irresponsibility. While it is being prepared he makes his way to the edge of the river on which the inn is perched. He looks out upon the calm gathering of twilight. Manet might have painted the scene; a boat rounding the bend, in it a young man, and a lady with a pink parasol. But the art changes to reality: the young man is Chad in shirtsleeves; the lady is Madame de Vionnet informally attired. They see Strether; they join him for dinner, but it is now clear to him that he has simply refused to see what everyone could have told him: that Madame de Vionnet is Chad's mistress. In its own crude way Woollett has been right. Strether recognizes that he has been innocent beyond belief; living in a world of delicate relations and high nuances, he has failed to pay attention to physical fact. But we presently see that he has understood human values better than Woollett. He feels particularly unhappy at his failure to see Chad as he really is. He has endowed the young man with finer qualities than he really possesses. When he examines all his evidence he understands that Chad is, after all, a true son of Mrs. Newsome. He is weary of Madame de Vionnet; he has a way of dodging responsibilities; he is perfectly willing to return to Woollett—in fact he is ready to embrace the brave new world of advertising, to advance the family business. Strether has to tell himself that he has endowed Chad with more romance than the situation warranted. He now sees Madame de Vionnet's anguish.

Ultimately we discern what James is saying about the European experience of his sentient Americans. There is the appeal of art, of culture, of the visual world, of human types and foreign manners. There is the cultivation of personal relations. There is the question of enjoyment and responsibility. And there is the appeal of civilization: the established ways of life, the rituals which civilized society creates and codifies. They are designed to allow individuals their individuality. This Woollett refuses to do. Strether has his problem, however. He cannot be wholly Europeanized. He takes his Europe "hard." He is not in complete harmony with its ease, its *laisser-aller*. There remains something strenuous in his make-up. So it has always been. Somehow Americans either have taken their Europe strenuously or, like Jim Pocock in this novel, simply as a playground. Even James himself in a certain sense had an active, strenuous, obsessive view of Europe. It remained for him his great life-myth—the question of two worlds, their engagement, their conflict, their differing values. *The Ambassadors* is a tale of both sides of the sea, a moral com-

edy about provincials and cosmopolitans. It is also in its perceptions one of the first great psychological novels of our century.

What remains with us when we set this novel down? Above all
we see Strether on his relaxed strolls through Paris, relaxed yet
somehow a bit stiff, enjoying the beauties of the city at first
within the limitations of his New England conscience and later
in a more expansive way; we are aware of his memories of his
youth, the lemon-colored novels he had bought long ago; and
now he indulges himself by buying eighty volumes bound in red
and gold, a set of Victor Hugo. Or we remember his encounter
with Madame de Vionnet in the quiet coolness of Notre Dame,
Strether loitering there in a secular fashion, she sitting in meditation and prayer; and then his experience of taking her to lunch
on the quays, a memorable lunch. There is a quaint legend that
James's characters never do anything so physical as to eat. But
one remembers the *omelette aux tomates* which Strether and
Madame de Vionnet order in the restaurant by the Seine, and
the bottle of straw-colored Chablis with which they wash it down,
and the way in which Madame de Vionnet's eyes move in and
out of their talk. But perhaps we remember most Strether, at the
end of his free day in the country. He has found his Lambinet.
He has walked through its enclosing frame; he has found his
metallic green. He discovers freedom, and he discovers also
anguish—the anguish of Madame de Vionnet, no longer the
grand lady, simply a woman in love like any other, facing separation from her lover. To the modern sophisticated world the innocence of Strether is difficult to understand. Some of us have to
take it on faith that there were such innocents and James seemed
to think not only of Emerson, but also of his friend William
Dean Howells, the novelist, whose remark "Live all you can" to a
young writer one day in Whistler's garden had been the original
spark that touched James's imagination and led him to write this
novel.

To say this of *The Ambassadors,* to speak of Strether's deep
innocence and wonderment and he a man of middle age, is not
to exhaust the interest of this novel. There is the *ficelle*-character,
the "string" character, James creates as if she were a puppet,

Maria Gostrey, who becomes Strether's confidante: she talks with him and helps him out in his adventure of seeing, his attempt to see *through* his experience. She is a kind of chorus; she asks the right questions, elicits the right information. She is a characteristic Jamesian device designed to aid him in giving data to the reader that might not otherwise be available. Maria provides an extra "point of view," a further angle of vision. In the end James was pleased with her; he called her "the reader's friend"; but he had also turned her, he boasted, from a device into a living and "functional" character.

The other characters represent polarities of American and European experience. Madame de Vionnet and Mrs. Newsome, the French mother and the American: Madame de Vionnet has brought up her daughter as a *jeune fille,* has prepared her in a traditional way for the world. Mrs. Newsome's children are less prepared; Chad is a rough personage until Madame de Vionnet refines him; and his sister Sarah is crude, and devoid of sensibility and finesse. Mrs. Newsome in Woollett occupies herself with good works and "culture." Madame de Vionnet in Paris is concerned with personal relations. Gloriani, the European artist, is a picture of success and the enjoyment of it; Waymarsh, the successful American, is dyspeptic and has a sour view of the world. Strether is deeply changed by Europe; Chad has been superficially changed. For James it is Europe that is the touchstone, and the novel is clearly weighted in favor of the Old World. Thus there is no European character in the book like Sarah Pocock, indeed no other person as unpleasant and disagreeable.

James's Europeanized Americans are all interesting, all figures alive and matured by expatriation. There are however no Americanized Europeans, for that was yet to come. We may be sure that if the novel were written today James would indeed have to take into account the American influence in Europe. He wrote when the exchange was still in one direction; and in raising the questions between America and Europe he was asking himself questions which we in our time are trying to answer. What European values must be preserved? What American values? What has been the effect of the cross-fertilization? The end of this large chapter of history is yet to be written.

Long ago E. M. Forster described *The Ambassadors* as a book that was created as a "pattern," into which life is fitted. We have seen how James told his story in two sections, each divided into six parts, twelve in all. Forster argued that novels as a rule are not capable "of as much artistic development as the drama." He said that the novel's "humanity, or the grossness of its material hinder it. To most readers the sensation from a pattern is not intense enough to justify the sacrifice that made it, and their verdict is 'beautifully done, but not worth doing.'" This was the judgment of the author of *A Passage to India:* and it was later echoed by F. R. Leavis. But in the same chapter, in his *Aspects of the Novel,* Mr. Forster discussed the idea of "rhythm" in the novel and showed how in Proust the "little phrase," the stray bit of music written by Vinteuil, does more than anything else "to make us feel that we are in a homogeneous world." The function of rhythm, in fiction, he said, was "not to be there all the time like a pattern but by its lovely waxing and waning to fill us with surprise and freshness and hope."

It is fascinating to discover how a great artist can see one thing in a novel to the exclusion of the other. I agree that *The Ambassadors* is a pattern, that its scenes are "set" like a play of Racine. But James was craftsman enough to realize what in effect Forster is saying, that these patterns can take on life only if infused with rhythm, with recurring images and symbols. The homogeneity of James's novel resides in the singular unity of its simple symbolic devices—the recurrent time signals, the trains, the boats—Strether who has missed his train and Madame de Vionnet who is in a rocking boat, and would like Strether to climb into it and help her to steady it; or the realized rhythm of Strether's standing early in the book in the Boulevard Malesherbes looking up at Chad's balcony and wondering what lies ahead; and his returning to the same position at the end of the book, to remember how expectant and innocent he had been, how unaware of his adventure to come. And now it is over, in the way in which things end in life, and he has "lived," and seen, and learned. To reread *The Ambassadors* is to discover its art and its benign humanity and to understand why many regard it as an authentic masterpiece of the civilized American imagination.

17 JOHN WESLEY POWELL: EXPLORATION OF THE COLORADO RIVER

Murray G. Murphey

John Wesley Powell is not usually regarded as a great scientist. In the current histories of science in America, Powell is rated far below such men as Benjamin Franklin and Willard Gibbs, Joseph Henry and Albert Michaelson. Yet Powell was in many ways far more typical of science in America before 1900 than these more famous men. During the colonial period and until late in the nineteenth century, the United States lacked the educational and research centers necessary to create and maintain a first-rate scientific community. American scientists therefore were not able to compete with those of Europe on equal terms; only a few men such as Franklin or Henry made contributions which would have been considered outstanding in Europe. But American scientists were able to make important contributions to science by the collection of data to which their unique geographical position gave them exclusive access. Accordingly, the primary form of scientific activity in this country became the survey or collecting trip which brought together new data which could then be classified and interpreted by specialists in Europe. By the middle nineteenth century there were a few American scientists, and educational centers, sufficiently advanced to take over the functions previously performed in Europe, but survey and collection remained the dominant type of scientific work, and the men engaged in it remained relatively unspecialized and often self-taught. Much of this survey work was carried on by the United States government though the exploring activities of the army and navy, through the United States Coast and Geodetic Survey, and through the variety of geological surveys which it supported. Indeed, in the middle and later nineteenth century, these government agencies provided a critically important institutional basis for the development of the sciences, and the heads of these bureaus and surveys were among the most influential and important scientific personnel in the nation. Among these, perhaps the most powerful—at least for a time—was John Wesley Powell.

Powell was born in 1834 in Mount Morris, New York, the son of an immigrant farmer and Methodist circuit rider. His family soon moved west to Ohio and then to Wisconsin, where the boy grew up. His education was spotty at best, but from a neighbor, George Crookham, who was an amateur naturalist, Powell acquired an early love of natural science, and began making collections of his own. Though he had little money, Powell managed to attend the Illinois Institute briefly and to spend a year at Illinois College and some time at Oberlin, but he never received a degree and was fundamentally self-educated. After leaving Oberlin he taught school in Illinois and continued his collections, particularly of mollusks. When the Civil War began he enlisted in the army as a private, rose to captain of artillery, and lost his right arm at Shiloh, but he continued in service even after that and was mustered out a major. In 1865 he became professor of geology at Illinois Wesleyan University at Bloomington, and in 1866 took a similar post at Illinois State Normal University. In 1867 he led his first expedition to the Rockies, and two years later he and nine others began their famous trip down the Colorado River.

At the time of Powell's Colorado venture, the canyons of the Colorado River were one of the last major unexplored areas in America. No one knew the precise course of the river, or what lay in those canyons, but most were convinced that no one could go through them by boat alive. Powell thought otherwise: he had done a fair amount of river exploration, had made careful plans for the expedition, and had ordered boats built to his specifications. Yet by any standard, Powell's exploring party was a set of rank amateurs. All were volunteers, for he had no money to hire professionals; some were mountain men, some were Powell's relatives, and some were adventurers who went for excitement. None but Powell was a scientist, and he was but self-taught. For so motley a group to undertake so perilous a venture seems fool-hardy to most people, and the dismal forecasts of the party's future appeared to be confirmed when a man named Risdon appeared claiming to be the sole survivor of the expedition. Thus when Powell and six of his men emerged from the canyons alive after a successful passage, Powell found himself a popular hero—the last of the romantic explorers of the West. Powell was delighted with his new-found fame, and when he wrote an account of the trip which appeared in *Scribner's Magazine* in 1874–1875 and was later published as Part One of his book, *Exploration of the Colorado River,* it is hardly surprising that his narrative should read like what it was: a tale of derring-do.

Powell's narrative is written in the form of a journal. It is not identical with the original journal of the trip, although it is based upon that journal—the published account is a much more elaborate story, and includes material from other exploring trips. The story begins on May 24, 1869, when the party set out in four boats from Green River City, carrying provisions for ten months in the canyons, and a variety of scientific instruments with which they hoped to plot the river's course, determine the rate of its fall, and measure the depth of the canyons. Traveling south down the Green River toward its junction with the Grand and Colorado rivers, they entered the first of the canyons, which they named Flaming Gorge, on May 30th. They were soon faced with rapids which even their specially built boats could not navigate, and they were forced either to make portages, or, where the terrain made that impossible, to lower the boats over the rapids by ropes. Powell was extremely cautious, fortunately, and preferred safe but laborious methods to risking life and limb. Nevertheless, on June 9th, one of the boats went over a fall and, although the three men aboard escaped alive, the boat was wrecked and most of its cargo lost. The other boats were repeatedly overturned, but since they were constructed with watertight compartments which made them unsinkable, they could be quickly righted again—nonetheless, the loss of provisions and instruments from such accidents was heavy. Despite these delays and difficulties, the party reached the Grand River by July 17th, the Little Colorado by August 10th, and soon after entered the Grand Canyon. Powell gave daily descriptions of the ever-changing river and the gradually deepening canyons as they proceeded, and included accounts of some hazardous adventures while climbing the canyon walls. He was also a close observer of the geology of the canyons, and was particularly fascinated by the ruins of Indian dwellings which they found in the depths of the canyons, dwellings which showed a higher culture than that of the Indians then living in the surrounding areas. By the time they had passed through the Grand Canyon, three of the men had had enough, and on August 28th, these three left the party, convinced that further progress by boat was impossible. Powell and the others went on, and two days later reached the Rio Virgen, having made the first successful passage through the canyons.

The remainder of the book is a journal of events in the fall of 1870. By that time it was known that the three men who had deserted Powell's party the year before had been killed by Indians, and Powell was determined to find out how and why they had died. With the aid of the Mormon missionary, Jacob Hamblin, Powell found the Indians who had killed his men, and learned that they had done so under the mistaken impression that the three deserters had been responsible for the killing of an Indian woman. Powell sought neither revenge nor punishment; he accepted the Indians' explanation as an adequate justification for their action with the terms of their culture rather than a proof of criminality. "That night," he remarks, "I slept in peace, although these murderers of my men . . . were sleeping not five hundred yards away."

The *Exploration* cannot be regarded as a purely factual account: it is rather a literary work and must be interpreted as such. Powell was seeking to capitalize on his fame as explorer and he worked for dramatic effects rather than for scientific objectivity, even modifying certain factual matters, such as the date of his trip into what is now Zion National Park, to fit literary needs. Indeed, the account is anything but objective. Powell lays great emphasis throughout upon the emotions which the adventures in the canyons aroused in himself and his men. And his subject was one which lent itself very easily to this type of romantic treatment. The canyons themselves presented a scene of vast distances, great heights, and magnificent color, while the river, with its natural alternation of rapids and calm, danger and safety, gave him a

perfect vehicle around which to structure his account. Throughout the book, Powell weaves around the account of daily adventures a continual sense of foreboding over the perils ahead which
makes every terror a titillating hors d'oeuvre for those terrors yet
to come. Thus on August 13, 1869, he writes:

> We are now ready to start on our way down the Great Unknown.
> Our boats, tied to a common stake, are chafing each other, as they are
> tossed by the fretful river. They ride high and buoyant, for their
> loads are lighter than we could desire. We have but a month's rations
> remaining. . . .
>
> We are three quarters of a mile in the depths of the earth, and the
> great river shrinks into insignificance, as it dashes its angry waves
> against the walls and cliffs, that rise to the world above; they are but
> puny ripples, and we but pigmies, running up and down the sands,
> or lost among the boulders.
>
> We have an unknown distance yet to run; an unknown river yet
> to explore. What falls there are, we know not: what rocks beset the
> channel, we know not; what walls rise over the river, we know not.
> Ah, well! we may conjecture many things. The men talk as cheerfully
> as ever; jests are bandied about freely this morning; but to me the
> cheer is somber and the jests are ghastly.[1]

One can see here the blending of the sensation of awe aroused
by the depth of the canyon with those of fear and foreboding
over the unknown danger yet to be which typifies the book.
Moreover, by presenting his account in the form of a journal,
Powell is able to build the suspense day by day as the party
moves on through the ever-deepening canyons, until the climax
when the three men desert and Powell, after an agonizing decision to press on, nevertheless brings the remainder of the party
safely through to the Rio Virgen. The final section describing
Powell's search to determine how his men died is no less dramatic
and is necessary to round out the story of the expedition. It, too,
has its own special setting of strangeness provided by the Indians, and its own suspense, and it also carries the implicit moral
that had not the three men lost their courage and deserted they
would have come out safely. All in all, the *Exploration* is a
splendid adventure story in a highly romantic vein, complete
with wild scenery, Indians, murder, endless perils, and brave and

gallant hearts. Powell was the last of the romantic western explorers, and he quite deliberately played the part to the hilt. It was the fame which his exploits as an explorer won him which enabled Powell—a self-taught unknown with no scientific publications to his name—to persuade Congress to convert his amateur expedition into the Geographical and Geological Survey of the Rocky Mountains and to give him the money to continue his work.

Powell was not merely a dashing explorer. The expedition of 1869 was but the first of several, and the later ones involved far more thorough and detailed scientific study of the canyons. This soberer side of Powell's work found its expression in the second part of the *Exploration* entitled "The Physical Features of the Valley of the Colorado," and in his work on the Unita Mountains. If the first part of the *Exploration* reminds one too strongly of the "delicious sensations" of fear and awe, danger and grandeur, cultivated by nineteenth-century romantics, the second part is remarkable for its clear and sober analysis of the geological nature and causes of the canyons. For amid the boiling rapids and towering canyon walls, what Powell saw first and foremost was erosion—erosion on a staggering scale. Powell also saw that the river's course was not simply a function of topography: the river cut straight through mountains where it might have flowed around them. This led Powell to the realization that the river antedated the mountains, that the river had preserved its level while the mountains were lifted up, and, as a circular saw on a fixed pivot remains stationary while the log through which it cuts is moved, so the river had cut through the rising land mass to produce the canyons. Based on this insight, Powell defined three classes of drainage systems, of which two were new classes: he called a valley *antecedent* if the river was established prior to the rising of the land and had maintained its course by cutting through the land, *consequent* if the corrugation of the bed altered the course of the river, and *superimposed* if, after the drainage course had been established by peculiar topographical conditions, subsequent erosion eliminated those conditions, so that the water course appeared as superimposed upon an earlier topography. Powell also noted that since the degradation of the land has a lower limit in the level of the standing water which receives the drainage, the type of degradation in a particular area will depend upon this limiting surface, or "base level of erosion" as he called it. And, in one of those shifts of perspective which are the mark of a fine scientific mind, Powell pointed out that however staggering the evidence of erosion presented by the Colorado canyons might be, the area was one of lesser rather than greater erosion: had the rainfall in the area been that of the Appalachians, the entire region would have been reduced to a base level which would be that of the sea. These concepts and insights were new when Powell introduced them, and have since become the basis for physiographic geology, but they were extensions and developments of the general uniformitarian theory of which Powell was an adherent. Thus Powell's early work in geology lies within the tradition of survey and data collection, but it produced more than simply fresh data to support an old theory; it also produced elaborations and refinements of that theory to deal with new aspects of the data, an achievement which was indeed remarkable for a self-taught man.

However important his contributions to geology, Powell still belonged to the tradition of the unspecialized natural history collectors. The brilliant insights he gleaned from the Colorado canyons were not rigorously developed by him—instead, he left their systematic elaboration to his assistants, G. K. Gilbert and Clarence E. Dutton. Meanwhile, his own interests turned toward ethnology. Even in 1869 he had been careful to observe and record Indian customs and language, and he devoted himself increasingly to these subjects as the 1870's wore on. With the encouragement of Joseph Henry and the Smithsonian Institution, Powell began a thorough study of Indian languages, which led in 1877 to the publication of his *Introduction to the Study of Indian Languages.* In 1879 he became the director of the Smithsonian's new Bureau of Ethnology, which he continued to head until his death, and the president of the newly formed Anthropological Society of Washington. In ethnology, as in geology, Powell worked within the framework of established theories. His views were, of course, those of an evolutionist, but not a social Darwinist; he was a follower of Lewis Henry Morgan, not of Herbert Spencer. He regarded social evolution as linear and progressive, and he accepted Morgan's description of the stages of evolution as savagery, barbarism, and civilization. But Powell agreed with Thomas Huxley and with Lester Ward, who worked under him in the Bureau of Ethnology for many years, that social evolution was not governed by the survival of the fittest, and that human ethics were not a transcription of nature's Malthusian horrors. As Huxley put it, "the ethical progress of society depends, not on imitating the cosmic process, still less in running away from it, but in combatting it." [2] That ethical progress was possible through the increasing mastery of man over himself and his environment, and that science was the road to such mastery, Powell devoutly believed. Thus he was a meliorist who believed that social progress through intelligent planning was both possible and practical.

This broad evolutionary conceptual scheme formed the framework of Powell's ethnological work. He regarded the Indians as belonging to the high savage or low barbarian stage of social evolution, and made elaborate and detailed collections of Indian languages and customs. Powell's special interest was in developing an orderly classification of the Indians—something which was totally lacking in 1879—and he believed that such a classification could only be made on the basis of Indian languages. Accordingly, he and his assistants at the Bureau began the immense task of collecting, analyzing, and codifying the Indian languages, and tracing relations among groups on the basis of language. The work was still unfinished at Powell's death, but it marked the beginning of the systematic ethnological study of the American Indians.

By the late 1870's no less than four major geological surveys were in the field: Clarence King's survey of the fortieth parallel under the War Department, Ferdinand Hayden's survey under the Department of Interior, Lieutenant George Wheeler's survey under the Army topographical engineers, and Powell's. In 1879 Congress consolidated these into the United States Geological Survey with Clarence King as director, but King resigned in 1881 and Powell was named his successor. Powell became administrative head of one of the major scientific bureaus of the United States government, and for ten years he was brilliantly successful. Under Powell, the Geological Survey was extended to the entire country and its appropriation rose from one hundred fifty-six thousand dollars to over half a million dollars—an extraordinary sum for that period. Although his main endeavor was the topographical and geological mapping of the country, he brought into the Survey a number of first-rate scientists from fields as varied as paleontology and sociology, and his men worked on basic theoretical problems as well as on problems of immediate practical importance. During the 1880's Powell became the most successful scientific administrator the United States had seen. The catholicity of his own interests, his immense energy and drive, his political skill in dealing with Congress, and his complete honesty made the Survey the strongest scientific agency in the government.

The Geological Survey was a data-gathering agency, not a policy-making one, but for a man like Powell, who believed in rational planning as the road to future progress, this was a hard distinction to make, particularly when his interpretation of the data he was gathering pointed unmistakably to the need for a drastic change in federal land policy. Accordingly, in 1879 Powell published a document entitled *Report on the Lands of the Arid Region of the United States* in which he proposed a radically new concept of settlement for the West. Federal land policy prior to this time had been designed to transfer public land to private hands as rapidly and efficiently as possible. In the early days of the Republic, it had been expected that the sale of the public lands would be a major source of revenue for the government, but the demands of prospective settlers and the adequacy of other sources of revenue soon led to the use of the public lands to underwrite migration. This policy reached its crowning expression in the Homestead Act of 1862 under which a migrant might acquire a quarter-section free merely for settling and farming it. But whether used for revenue or as an inducement to settle, the land had to be cut into manageable blocks with easily identifiable boundaries, and the system of doing this, which became universal, was the rectangular survey. Since straight lines and right angles were the easiest boundaries for a surveyor to mark, the land was cut into rectangular blocks for sale or claim, and this settlement pattern, once established, became invariable and permanent.

Even today, the pattern of the rectangular grid is obvious

throughout the Midwest. But the rectangular pattern and the choice of one hundred and sixty acres as the homestead unit were predicated upon certain climatic conditions—notably, upon adequate rainfall. The sacred straight line of the surveyor paid no heed to topography because it was assumed that topography was irrelevant: any one hundred and sixty acres made an adequate farm. Nothing in the federal land policy gave special attention to access to water: the prevailing doctrine was that of riparian rights, according to which a man could make any use he wished of the water on his property, provided it was returned to its channel when he was through with it. However, the condition of adequate rainfall did not obtain west of the one hundredth meridian—from that line on the rainfall was below twenty inches per year and in many areas far below it. In such subhumid and arid lands, as Powell pointed out, land was worthless unless there was water for irrigation. To lay out farms in such a way that each would have access to irrigation meant abandoning the rectangular survey; it meant division of land based on topography. Moreover, the figure of one hundred and sixty acres became impractical under these new conditions: if the land were irrigated and farmed, the greater productivity of such land meant that one hundred and sixty acres was at least twice as large as a man could handle; if it was used for pasturage, one hundred and sixty acres was far too small and twenty-five hundred and sixty acres was barely adequate. Most important of all, in arid land the doctrine of riparian rights became a permit for monopoly, for land without water was useless, and he who controlled the water had all lands downstream at his mercy. The right to water, Powell therefore asserted, must inhere in the land, so that a man who takes his neighbor's water is as much a thief as one who takes his land. Thus Powell's report on the arid lands called for a thorough revision of land and water laws in the United States to fit the climatic conditions of the West.

But Powell went even further than this: not only did he ask for a change in the laws, he asked for a change in the customs as well. It was obvious that to irrigate an area required resources beyond those of an individual. Powell, therefore, proposed that any nine farmers settling on adjacent irrigable lands could organize themselves into a self-governing irrigation district and jointly construct the necessary irrigation works. After three years of demonstrated irrigation of the lands, they would acquire title to their farms, and the titles would include water rights. Thus Powell proposed a complete break with the tradition of extreme individualism and absolute private control over property, and urged instead local cooperative institutions as a basis for a rationally planned method of settlement. The report on the arid lands was indeed an astounding document, but even more astounding is the fact that the plan came very near actually going into effect.

The period of the early 1880's had been one of exceptionally heavy rainfall in the western plains, and lured by the rain, by ignorance of the cyclical character of western droughts, and by popular beliefs that cultivation of land would somehow increase the rainfall in the area, thousands of settlers had homesteaded on the arid plains. In 1886 their luck ran out and the drought returned. Facing financial ruin, they demanded action by the government, and their chosen representatives began seeking something to do about their plight. In February of 1888 a Senate resolution asked the Secretary of the Interior whether the Geological Survey should be asked to make an irrigation survey for the purpose of determining which lands were irrigable, and what reservoirs and canal sites were possible. To Powell, this request suddenly opened the possibility that the plan for the arid lands he had proposed a decade before might in fact be put into effect, and he leaped at the chance. With Powell's enthusiastic support, the Congress authorized such a survey, and on October 2, 1888, passed a bill withdrawing from sale all lands susceptible of irrigation by the reservoirs which the Survey would locate. In effect, this act closed the entire public domain west of the hundredth meridian, and so gave Powell his golden chance to redesign the whole pattern of western settlement. His plan for the arid lands now seemed virtually enacted, not indeed with its local cooperative features intact, but with the federal government assuming the duty to construct irrigation works and regulate settlement for the welfare of all. Powell at once threw his organization into the project of making the topographical map necessary for designing the reservoir sites and laying out the irrigable lands.

But Powell had overreached himself. To carry out his plan required closing the public domain until the mapping was done and the designations of sites and lands completed. Such a map could not be made immediately, and Powell would take no shortcuts; meanwhile, demands for access to the public domain piled up and congressional patience wore thin. Congress had not intended to enact Powell's plan of 1879; few congressmen intended to close the entire public domain until Powell's survey was finished, and fewer yet favored such an expansion of federal power as Powell's plan involved. Nor was Powell more successful in winning public support. Too many interests in the West depended upon population expansion to tolerate any extended interference with settlement, and few in the East understood the issues involved. By hindsight, one can see that Powell's plan had much in its favor: it was based upon a realistic appraisal of the conditions of agriculture in the West and it proposed a method of dealing with those problems which was scientifically sound. It was even, from a technical point of view, a practical plan, but not politically practical. It abridged too many basic beliefs of the culture, it conflicted with major economic and political interests, and it demanded a role for science in policy-making which might be acceptable today but which was unheard of then. In 1890 Congress eliminated the irrigation survey and reopened the public domain, and four years later Powell resigned as director of the Geological Survey.

The career of John Wesley Powell is in many ways a summation of the scientific tradition of nineteenth-century America. Chiefly self-taught, Powell was and always remained far more akin to the unspecialized collectors of an earlier day than to the new breed of academically trained professional specialists even then emerging. His own scientific work, despite some fine contributions to geological theory, was primarily that of a collector and administrator. Beyond question, his greatest service was in the latter field—not only was his performance on the Geological Survey outstanding, but the Bureau of Ethnology was virtually his creation. Many outstanding scientists made their careers in the institutions Powell built, and they owed much of their success to him. But Powell's career also illustrates the emerging problem of the scientific administrator. Possessing the knowledge necessary to see what the consequences of current land policies would be, and the imagination to devise a scientifically feasible alternative which he considered more just and equitable, Powell, like many of his successors, felt impelled to use his position to implement his own plan. Recent scholars who share Powell's values have regarded his fight for his new land policy as the crusade of the people's champion against the forces of vested interest. The people did not so regard Powell in 1890, as their failure to rally to his banner shows, nor is it at all clear that Powell was justified in the course he pursued. His was the problem that many a scientific administrator has faced since: what should be the role of such an officer in the making of public policy? What is the line between technical advice and policy-making, and how far may a government scientist go in urging a policy which involves more than merely technical considerations? If the fight over the arid lands was one of the first events to raise that issue in dramatic form, that in itself is a tribute to the influence which Powell commanded within government, science, and the nation.

Notes

1. John Wesley Powell, *Exploration of the Colorado River* (Chicago, 1957), p. 83.
2. Thomas Huxley, *Evolution and Ethics and other Essays* (New York, n.d.), p. 83.

18 EDWARD BELLAMY:
LOOKING BACKWARD, 2000–1887

Arthur P. Dudden

The concept of utopia, that is the idea that there could be created a bright and wonderful new world or community somewhere, has fascinated people repeatedly. Any new society must almost inevitably seem much more appealing to its beholders than their own everyday reality, however fantastic its imaginary design happens to be or whatever the circumstances of their ordinary condition.

The longings of men and women for some brave new social order of spaciousness, abundance, health, happiness, and hope might well express themselves, for example, out of their own congestion, hunger, squalor, futility, and despair. War or domestic turmoil could summon up prescriptions for more peaceful ways of life founded upon communal and fraternal harmony. It is not surprising, therefore, that the writing of fiction which portrays utopia as a possibility capable of realization has often been a popular enterprise because of the optimistic contrasts offered by its author to the drearier circumstances normally characteristic of the here and the now.

One of the greatest successes of utopian fiction, perhaps indeed the greatest ever for Americans, has been *Looking Backward, 2000–1887*, a novel of modest dimensions by Edward Bellamy (1850–1898).[1] Bellamy was a struggling writer in chronically poor health, who came from an industrial district of western New England. Published in 1888, this book became an instant phenomenon, its author a celebrity overnight. Translated into a dozen languages, Bellamy's novel quickly attracted the notice of the western world, while its idealized portrayal of a virtually perfect social order, as having been brought about peacefully through a rational accommodation with the evolutionary processes of human history, touched off a reformist movement within the United States itself. For the cultural development of the American people during their recent past, it is an important document to study, its own inherent artistic limitations notwithstanding.

Looking Backward is not a great book by a great writer, but it is a strange and awesome product of naive genius. And like modern primitive art in general, Edward Bellamy's most famous work is highly personal in nature. Any man inhabiting an earthly paradise would not, it seems certain, have wished to create a better world. A sensitive man who found himself recoiling in horror from his environment, as Bellamy did from the pervasive savageries of industrialization, might very well have imagined that somehow a society could be induced to flourish free of hardship and cleansed of inequity. For such a man of the late nineteenth century, it was reasonable to expect that the unfulfilled promises of machinery would in fact be made good someday soon. Thereupon an entirely novel human environment could be created, a utopian society itself even more dazzling to contemplate than the new technology.

Bellamy's achievement depended upon his demonstrating exactly how this socialistic utopia, for socialist he destined it to be, could emerge triumphantly out of the worsening conditions of industrial society. His simple didactic tale provided the method for him, as much as it provided an attractive futuristic vision for its readers. In *Looking Backward,* by a familiar kind of deterministic dialectic, the colossal defects of American society at the close of the nineteenth century, in 1887 to be precise, have transformed themselves into the glorious achievements of the twentieth century at its termination one hundred and thirteen years later. Today's readers, however, will know poignantly in advance that the twentieth century supplies terrible dilemmas of its own, and they will know all too well that utopia is as remote as ever despite the technological fulfillment of a large portion of Bellamy's dream.

Edward Bellamy delineated his utopia by means of a number of tricky, flashforwards to the year 2000 to reveal the future in contrast to the present moment—the year 1887 when his story opens and to which it returns occasionally by means of flashbacks. He invites his readers to look ahead with him to a glittering prospect of universal well-being. Then he has them look backward from their futuristic vantage-point newly won, in order that they might be reminded of the harrowing circumstances of their own lives. At the same time he invites one and all to join him in preparing the way for a splendid century of progress.

Julian West, an embodiment of Boston's old-style aristocracy, is the transplanted character in the novel who writes retrospectively of his experiences. "I cannot do better than to compare society as it then was to a prodigious coach," Bellamy's famous metaphor begins, "which the masses of humanity were harnessed to and dragged toilsomely along a very hilly and sandy road." Seated atop this awful vehicle and safely aloof from life's filth and misery, the leisured classes of society were carried along in idle luxury by the labor of men and women less fortunate than themselves. Such lofty places were in great demand. They were extremely insecure as a result. "It was naturally regarded as a terrible misfortune to lose one's seat, and the apprehension that this might happen to them or their friends was a constant cloud upon the happiness of those who rode."

"But did they think only of themselves?" Julian West asked rhetorically. "Had they no compassion for their fellow beings from whom fortune only distinguished them?"

"Oh yes, commiseration was frequently expressed by those who rode for those who had to pull the coach, especially when the vehicle came to a bad place in the road, as it was constantly doing, or to a particularly steep hill," Julian West answered his own question. "At such times the passengers would call down encouragingly to the toilers of the rope, exhorting them to patience, and holding out hopes of possible compensation in another world for the hardness of their lot, while others contributed to buy salves and liniments for the crippled and injured," Julian West explained. "It was agreed that it was a great pity that the coach should be so hard to pull, and there was a sense of general relief when the specially bad piece of road was gotten over. This relief was not indeed wholly on account of the team, for there was always some danger at these bad places of a general overturn in which all would lose their seats."

What appeared to be a deliberate sadism was in truth the impersonal fault of the system of industrial capitalism and private property, Bellamy explains through West. "In the first place," West recognized,

> it was firmly and sincerely believed that there was no other way in which society could get along, except the many pulled at the rope and the few rode, and not only this, but that no very radical improvement even was possible, either in the harness, the coach, the roadway, or the distribution of the toil. It had always been as it was, and it would always be so. It was a pity, but it could not be helped, and philosophy forbade wasting compassion on what was beyond remedy.

And, in the second place, there prevailed a singularly curious hallucination, which atop the coach the riders shared, that "they were not like their brothers and sisters who pulled at the rope, but of finer clay, in some way belonging to a higher order of beings who might justly expect to be drawn," as West stated. "The effect of such a delusion in moderating fellow feeling for the sufferings of the mass of men into a distant and philosophical compassion is obvious," he observed caustically.

Meanwhile the absorption of small holdings of capital and private businesses into ever larger corporations and monopolies had continued unabated, or so developments are described by Dr. Leete, who serves as West's guide to the year 2000 and is himself the utopian counterpart of Julian West. The social gap widened irretrievably between the fortunate few and the hapless majority. "In the United States there was not, after the beginning of the last quarter of the [nineteenth] century, any opportunity whatever for individual enterprise in any important field of industry, unless backed by a great capital," Dr. Leete recalled. This process of concentration was soon complete. Small enterprisers yielded the field to great aggregations of capital and industry. There seemed to be no way to restore that equality of conditions, which for a long time had been revered as exemplifying an earlier and better order of things, without sacrificing the material progress demanded by the age of iron and steam and telegraphs and rapid locomotion.

"The records of the period show that the outcry against the concentration of capital was furious," Dr. Leete observed, continuing his historical explanation for Julian West. "Men believed," he went on, "that it threatened society with a form of tyranny more abhorrent than it had ever endured. They believed that the great corporations were preparing for the yoke of a baser servitude than had ever been imposed on the race, servitude not to men but to soulless machines incapable of any motive but insatiable greed."

Was there no way out? Surprisingly there was. More surprising, as developments followed, it had merely required that the true significance of historical evolution be understood, in order that men should cease fighting futilely against the discipline of machine technology and its natural proclivity for industrial consolidation. Instead of persisting to base society upon irresponsible individual selfishness, a cooperative commonwealth had to be instituted without delay.

"At last," Dr. Leete concluded triumphantly, "strangely late in the world's history, the obvious fact was perceived that no business is so essentially the public business as the industry and commerce on which the people's livelihood depends, and that to entrust it to private persons to be managed for private profit is a folly similar in kind, though vastly greater in magnitude, to that of surrendering the functions of political government to kings and nobles to be conducted for their personal glorification."

Still most surprising of all, this stupendous change was enabled to take place without great bloodshed or violent convulsions, because public sentiment recognized the consolidating process as a transitional phase in history's evolution toward an equitable industrial system. The epoch of monopolies had ended in the great national trust under popular control. "In a word," Dr. Leete recapitulated, "the people of the United States concluded to assume the conduct of their own business, just as one hundred years before they had assumed the conduct of their own government, organizing now for industrial purposes on precisely the same grounds that they had then organized for political purposes."

It was the harshness of industrial society that tortured Edward Bellamy. Mere sight of the "children of misery," as he characterized the workers as well as the unemployed, "so old and miserable to look at, yet so young," was proof enough for him that a great wrong existed somewhere in the scheme of things. Neither rationality nor justice could be discovered in the society sprawling around him. Hence he invented an ideal world to provide a framework for his hopes for social reform. His utopia lay neither far away in distance nor even very remote in time, but it was located enticingly within the familiar precincts of Boston and little more than a century henceforward. If his neighbors could comprehend their dilemma, they could contrive their own salvation, if not for themselves then at least for their great-grandchildren or certainly for their great-great-grandchildren.

Thus the glorious promise of utopia could be fulfilled by the year 2000, while for the sake of Bellamy's plot Boston would be reborn as a heavenly city of the future. Bellamy's messages were imparted fictionally through his two spokesmen, Julian West and Dr. Leete. The way *it was* in 1887 is recounted by Julian West; the way *it comes to be* in 2000 is described and explained by Dr. Leete. By means of romances, which are unbelievably insipid even by Victorian standards, two young ladies coincidentally named Edith (Edith Bartlett and Edith Leete, the daughter of the good doctor) keep Mr. West from suffering the derangements threatening him as the result of the identity crisis induced by his extraordinary sleep.

Today's reader will find it difficult to measure the importance of Edward Bellamy's *Looking Backward,* or even to explain its one-time popularity. Yet for fifty years or so, *Looking Backward* appeared on lists of the great books of all time compiled by American publishers and critics, and it was read enthusiastically by a generation of reformers hopeful of social change without bloody upheaval. Such readers did not mistake *Looking Backward* for a precise guide to the future. It was not Bellamy's model of utopia but his indictment of capitalism, as the philosopher John Dewey realized, that inspired reformers to imagine the

possibility of better social systems before devising ways to introduce them. Despite the radicalism of the utopian device itself,
Looking Backward reflects the underlying conservatism of American society and was constructed to reinforce its native values and
traditions.

Thus the secret of *Looking Backward*'s popularity emerges. No
great impassable gulf separates the good people of today from
their descendants of tomorrow. Between the troubled Bostonians
of 1887 and the happy citizens of the year 2000 there stretched a
broad continuum of hopeful direction. Professor John L.
Thomas of Brown University has aptly classified *Looking Backward* as a statement of American conservatism. "It reaffirmed belief in a specifically American doctrine of progress which it
strengthened with a new organicism and historicism," he observes. "The book reasserted even as it modified the primacy of
moral reform as the American Way and helped to connect the
evangelical perfectionism of the pre-Civil War reformers with the
moralistic prospect of the progressives. As a central text in the social gospel movement, it underscored in a peculiarly forceful way
the Christian content of American social thought and more particularly the notion of reform as a moral enterprise directed toward conversion and regeneration." Bellamy's novel helped to
create a renewed sense of national mission, yet for readers abroad
as well as at home *Looking Backward* was a moral restorative for
the vision of a promised land—a vision which had been sorely
qualified in America by slavery and more recently by industrial-
ism's inequities. Like the patent medicines and advertisements of
his day, Bellamy's panacea promised hope for everything and
salvation for everybody.

Edward Bellamy had struck responsive chords among his countrymen. His portrayal of an ideal world undoubtedly reflected his
own private imperatives for a well-ordered life free of anguish
and pain, as his biographers have suggested—a life full of hope
and satisfaction instead of sickness, invalidism, disgust, and despair. But *Looking Backward* embodied more than its author's
fantasy. Bellamy combined the apprehensions of his fellow Americans that the gates of their opportunistic democracy were being
closed by corporate capitalism with their longings for spiritual
rebirth, moral improvement, and material progress.

He and his readers wanted wealth for themselves and well-being for all mankind, but they did not want to abandon any cherished values and traditions in the begetting. They wanted to augment their precious heritage of liberty and democracy rather than to permit it to be still further diminished. They needed assurance of spiritual regeneration against the danger of a descent into the hell of industrial barbarism. Their salvation hinged more upon the machine than the cross, their paradise would be born on earth instead of in heaven. Their method would be entirely pragmatic, in keeping with historical evolution and industrial discipline. If they failed to comprehend the danger of their willful escape from freedom into a comfortable totalitarianism, it was owing to the bitterness of their present circumstances and the intensity of their longings for a revival of prospects.

Essentially Bellamy agreed with the leading criticisms being voiced against American society, that the central problem of the age was social rather than political and that its characteristic was the growing tendency toward inequality. The symptoms were defined by Henry George, the single-taxer, as parallel proclivities toward progress and poverty, and by Henry Demarest Lloyd, the antimonopolistic accuser of the Standard Oil Company, as the conflict between wealth and commonwealth. For Bellamy, as we know from his metaphor of the coach, the contradictory principles of aristocracy and democracy were manifesting themselves. All such critics agreed with Bellamy that a "deep disease" was present in American civilization.

Such analyses, including Bellamy's own, agreed superficially with the so-called "scientific" insights of the Marxists. Industrialization itself had initiated an apparently irresistible trend toward the centralization of wealth in the hands of the owners of the means of production. Instead of healthily regulating the marketplace, competition raged like private warfare among the giants of finance. Economic power begat political power in turn. Capitalists hired the government to protect their property and safeguard them in their exploitation of the wage slaves and tillers of the soil. "The very rich," Bellamy had written, "can make their own terms with the agents of their work, and they do it, as a rule, so as to realize excessive profits." If the great capitalists should ever gain complete control, then American democracy would be extinguished and a plutocratic tyranny instituted by the privileged holders of wealth.

Edward Bellamy and his fellow social philosophers rejected the economic predeterminant of Marxism, however. Unlike the Marxists, Bellamy, George, Lloyd, and others of their kind could never dismiss ethical factors as mere bourgeois illusions. Indeed their preoccupation with capitalism's ethics provided their thought with a predilection for catastrophe and a moral urgency for their argument. Neither did Bellamy favor any trade-union theory of socialism. To obtain permanent employment for all, both capital and labor would have to be organized, and only his "Nationalism," which he called his system, could accomplish this.

Bellamy's Nationalism, as it emerges from *Looking Backward* and his subsequent works, resembles a transcendent cooperative state-capitalism more than any of the familiar forms of socialism, though it shares a number of socialistic premises and has itself generally been described as socialism and even as communism in the pre-Bolshevik sense. Bellamy agreed with socialists that class antagonism would end only with the consolidation of the means of production and distribution by the state, that for the state to possess political power alone would prolong its subservience to the interests of money and private monopoly, and that in the meantime the middle class was being proletarianized and the working class driven to the verge of starvation. He came to hold that the distribution of the fruits of labor must be absolutely equal. Equality became a moral imperative for him and an ideal to inspire and guide all Americans. It went far beyond Tocqueville's classic description of life in the United States as characterized by a substantial equality of condition.

Nationalism in Bellamy's terms means a society which cleverly extracts performances from each person according to his ability and rewards each not simply according to his needs but according to his desires. A life spent richly in producing and consuming was guaranteed by the equalitarian principles of the state. The accumulation of goods for the sake of accumulation itself would be most unlikely to occur, since anyone could always obtain whatever he really wanted merely by requisitioning it at the public warehouses or commissary stores. Nationalism, Bellamy asserted, was a form of religion in fact. It demanded a sense of consecration from its followers. Nationalism rested on economic law and on the Christian principles of cooperation. Cooperation stood in complete opposition to the principle of competition, another name for warfare in Bellamy's opinion, and it went much farther than the principle of brotherhood. Cooperation for Bellamy was so much the most important consideration that, if it could be obtained only by a sacrifice of material considerations, the true Nationalist would seek it above all else.

In truth Edward Bellamy's *Looking Backward* is a religious fable.

Looking Backward seems to be composed of a pair of separate and almost unrelated stories—the miraculous resurrection of Julian West in the year 2000 and the accounting furnished him by his spiritual guide, Dr. Leete, for the creation and operation of the future paradise. Bellamy employed the device of fantasy to win recognition of the need for a social reformation. He used sugarcoated arguments to stress his belief that material and cultural delights lie within reach, but at the same time he sought to prepare his readers for the psychological drama of conversion as the price demanded for entry into the New Jerusalem.

Julian West is revealed to be a prisoner of himself in the supposedly real society of upper-class Boston in 1887. It is made clear at the outset that the industrial and social crisis of the day results from the blind oppressiveness of Julian's class of aristocrats. The last evening before he falls into his trance is spent at the home of his fiancée in general denunciation of the laboring class. Upon returning to his own house, he retires to a sealed sleeping room underground, a retreat from his self-enclosed personality and an escape from his insomnia. Julian is spiritually and symbolically dead, interred in a tomb of his own contriving. Only the offices of hypnotism and suspended animation preserve any shadow of life.

One hundred and thirteen years later Julian West awakens to discover the splendor of the brave new Boston at his feet. The view of utopia and the exhilaration induced by the city's spaciousness make him feel freer and more alert than ever before.

Intoxicated, he experiences heartfelt sympathy for the people for the first time.

Quickly, however, the ecstasy of his escape from bondage yields to a gathering terror as Julian West begins to comprehend his fate. Isolated in an alien world, his personality dissolves before his very eyes into a terrifying duality of psychic division. "There are no words for the mental torture I endured during this help-less, eyeless grasping for myself in a boundless void," he cries out of his anguish. "No other experience of the mind gives probably anything like the sense of absolute intellectual arrest from the loss of a mental fulcrum, a starting point of thought, which comes during such momentary obscuration of the sense of one's identity."

Thereupon Bellamy reminds us that Julian West—and each one of us also for that matter—is actually two persons, a remem-bered self and an impersonal superego standing outside and above experience. *Looking Backward*'s central point comes in a section on "The Religion of Solidarity," wherein Bellamy re-duces the problem of society to the quest for solidarity through the cultivation of impersonality. Julian West is enabled to make this leap of consciousness, from his former selfishness to a free-dom from his guilty past, by the love of Dr. Leete's daughter for him. Under her tender care, he savors the impersonal mood with-out despair and recalls his old life with equanimity. By then he is ready for his education in solidarity or "Nationalism," as it is known in utopia, and he absorbs Dr. Leete's gentle indoctrina-tion gratefully. The climax of his initiation comes through a radio sermon in which the speaker extols the coming transforma-tion of all mankind as having begun already by the American nation's regeneration.

This millennial prophecy is carried back by Julian West to Boston in 1887 in a nightmare of hallucinatory proportions. He tries in vain to convince his old friends of his utopian truth. "Still I strove with them," he related. "Tears poured from my eyes. In my vehemence I became inarticulate. I panted, I sobbed, I groaned, and immediately afterward *found myself* sitting up-right in bed in my room in Dr. Leete's house, and the morning sun shining through the open window into my eyes." The miracle of conversion, Bellamy's chosen instrument, had brought salvation to the repentant sinner by restoring him to paradise once more.

Utopia, explains Bellamy through Dr. Leete, could come to the late twentieth century just as it did to Julian West, through conversion by means of a change of heart. So long as most Americans remained unseeing like Julian himself, their industrial civilization would continue to lurch violently toward collapse, crushing innocent people along the way. So long as class exploited class oblivious to the message of brotherhood, new machines and inventions would only intensify the problems of society. To save themselves Americans first had to be converted to the principle of solidarity. This was the singular truth upon which utopia could be built. A small band of evangelists would emerge to lead the way. Their truth would become social doctrine. The triumph of solidarity would make all other things simple thereafter.

In *Looking Backward,* the vision was more important for Edward Bellamy than either the social philosophy or the mechanism by which utopia shall be achieved. Just as life had evolved slowly to its present condition, it would continue to aspire upward in all ways. Bellamy anticipated that human society would move away from individualism toward socialistic consciousness. Beyond that he believed the human race will return to God, and "the divine secret hidden in the germ shall be perfectly unfolded." Utopia is a palace in the clouds after all. Yet, just for a moment in *Looking Backward,* it had appeared through the outlines of a perfect society to be a cozy cottage for ordinary men and women.

Note

1. Reissued exactly as it first appeared together with changes noted for the second edition and a highly original introduction by John L. Thomas, the best available version of *Looking Backward* is a John Harvard Library book published at Cambridge, Massachusetts, 1967. See also Walter Teller's "Looking Back at *Looking Backward,*" *The New York Times Book Review,* December 31, 1967.

19 THORSTEIN VEBLEN: *THE THEORY OF THE LEISURE CLASS*

Stow Persons

The Theory of the Leisure Class, An Economic Study of Institutions, published in 1899, was the first book of an obscure instructor in economics at the University of Chicago. It was not the kind of book calculated to win academic status and security for its author, who in fact never did achieve those conventional objectives, and who probably did not prize them. Nevertheless, the book was a masterpiece of its kind; and far from being an isolated peak in the intellectual landscape it would soon be seen as part of a vast upthrust of social criticism which would transform American scholarship in the twentieth century.

In the history of American economic thought Thorstein Veblen takes his place with the large number of economists and social critics who at the end of the nineteenth century were busily undermining the foundations of the established classical economic theory. The historical school of economists insisted upon a positive role for the state in shaping economic conditions in terms of the general welfare. The institutional school produced empirical studies of the actual functioning of economic institutions without regard for the pieties of classical theory. Henry George had vigorously and effectively focused public attention on the paradoxical persistence of poverty amidst a rising standard of living. Socialists, both utopian and Marxist, gained a wider hearing among immigrant groups and humanitarian reformers. Veblen was touched by all of these currents. Edward Bellamy's utopian romance, *Looking Backward,* published a decade earlier, had moved him deeply, and had in fact turned his interest from philosophy to social theory. His own view of the

evolution of social institutions had so many similarities to Marxism that for years to come the scholars would debate whether he
might not properly be considered a Marxist.

Veblen also was involved in the social transformation of the
academic community which occurred during his lifetime.
Throughout the nineteenth century, college and university professors had been an integral part of the gentry elite which
perpetuated a traditional gentry culture. Gentility furnished a
convenient common ground for the alliance of religion and commerce which supported American higher education. But a cluster
of scholars, of whom Veblen was one, all born in the decade
1854–1864, would challenge these traditional affiliations and
play prominent roles in destroying them. Richard T. Ely, John
R. Commons, and Veblen in economics, John Dewey in education and philosophy, Edward A. Ross in sociology, and J. Allen
Smith in political science were controversial figures who declined
to wear the traditional robes of academic detachment, and who
began the process of recasting the universities in their twentieth-
century role as service institutions. The influence of these reformers was felt outside the scholarly community as well as
within it; they appealed to journalists and publicists, and often
wrote for popular magazines. Veblen's sardonic temperament
prevented him from participating in many of these activities, but
it did not discourage the small but devoted group of disciples,
mostly outside the academic community, who gathered around
the master to mitigate the rigors of a deepening social isolation.

The Theory of the Leisure Class must have been an awkward
book for readers to take hold of because it did not resemble the
usual forms of economic analysis. Veblen's ultimate purpose was
to show that economic behavior was not governed by carefully
calculated considerations of self-interest. Although men do
possess "economic" instincts, notably the instinct of workmanship, they also have a range of selfish, antisocial instincts. Economic behavior is said to result from the interaction of these
instincts with institutional determinants. Leisure-class behavior
was likewise institutionalized behavior, backed by the sanctions
of tradition, and gratifying the instincts of mastery and ag-
grandizement. Drawing upon the currently fashionable Darwin-
ian notion of the struggle for existence, Veblen undertook to

trace the social evolution of the leisure class from its origins in earlier cultural epochs. The result was a work which bore a closer resemblance to an anthropological than to an economic treatise.

The central thesis of the book is that the leisure class was a product of the barbarian stage of human culture. When productivity had increased to the point where a surplus was available, the earlier peaceable state of savagery gave way to predatory barbarism with its characteristic institution of private property. Possession of women was the earliest form of property; and the basic barbarian distinctions between leisure and labor, drudgery and exploit, honor and disrepute all traced back to the domination of women by men. Coming as it did after a century of feminist agitation *The Theory of the Leisure Class* could readily have served as a textbook on the origins of the exploitation of women.

The leisure class was the property-owning and ruling class. As economist, Veblen was less concerned with its governing and managerial functions than with the ways in which it manifested its power and prestige through the conspicuously wasteful consumption of time and goods. As critic, his object was to puncture the self-righteous pretensions of the rich by showing that far from serving a useful economic function, as their apologists often claimed, their behavior was wholly wasteful and stultifying. The leisure class, together with its retinue of servants, women, scholars, clergymen, gamblers, and sporting types, was diverting a significant portion of the productivity of the community to wasteful purposes. Veblen's book was a study in social pathology. It showed how leisure-class behavior undermined the constructive expression of the instinct of workmanship, and thus thwarted the progress through productive enterprise which that healthy instinct would assure were it allowed unimpeded expression.

For more than two centuries American moralists had solemnly preached the dignity of labor. Veblen availed himself of this tradition when he planted labor in human nature in the guise of the instinct of workmanship. So far as the history of mankind formed a progressive sequence—and Veblen believed that in a qualified way it did—it was due to the constructive expression of this instinct in social cooperation and a higher standard of living. Darwin, William James, and others had made theories of instinct fashionable in the 1890's, and Veblen built his theory of social change around the interaction of instincts with institutionalized habits. In a later work he would develop more systematically the conception of instinct which is only casually mentioned in the *Leisure Class*. In fact, all the themes of his life's work are anticipated in his first book.

Although Veblen drew his evolutionary anthropology from Sir Edward Tylor, Lewis H. Morgan, and William G. Sumner he gave the anthropological past a relevance to the present that even Sumner had not achieved. The earlier anthropologists had equated the cultural stage of civilization with the invention of writing, thus separating modern civilized man from his primitive past by some thousands of years. They had shared with their readers complacent assumptions of the secure triumph of civilization over primitivism. One studied social evolution as through a glass at the museum, but Veblen found the full development of the barbarian leisure-class institution in feudal Europe, thus bringing barbarism to the very doorstep of the reader, so to speak. The modern leisure class was itself a barbarian survival. There are many passages in the book where it is difficult to tell whether Veblen is describing past or present usages. One may read of a familiar practice only to be casually informed that it is identified with the previous stage of quasi-peaceable barbarism. Because of the impulse of the lower classes to emulate the leisure class powerful forces were at work to perpetuate barbarism.

Veblen heightened his dramatic effects by the deliberately contrived contrast between a bland professorial style and the exaggerated oscillations in the pattern of social evolutionary development. The earliest stage of peaceable savagery was a highly constructive epoch in which the most essential institutions and habits were established. Yet this age was characterized as "proto-anthropoid," a cultural stage which Veblen declared "possibly sub-human." At the other extreme, the later stage of predatory barbarism was dominated by a temper of pugnacity, with masterful aggressiveness and cringing subservience. The survival of these attitudes in the latter-day leisure class greatly foreshortened the social evolutionary scale and brought contemporary civilized man much closer to his simian ancestors. In the complacent Edwardian era such notions must have been more shocking than they are to our own benighted age.

The book closes on a cautiously hopeful note. Veblen professed to see in the working class the reemergence of peaceable and purposeful industrial habits which could eventually outmode the predatory and parasitic leisure-class outlook. This would be a spontaneous development of the industrial order resulting in a recovery of the peaceable savage traits of the earliest stage of social evolution. Only for brief moments would the sardonic Veblen indulge himself in such fantasies, but the few glimpses permitted the reader show that under his detached, analytical exterior Veblen harbored Edward Bellamy's utopian vision of a cooperative industrial society.

Far from being a mere academic exercise in institutional economics *The Theory of the Leisure Class* was a deeply felt tract for the times. Its central concerns: work, leisure, power, pride, and condescension, were all themes with which Americans were at the moment more than usually preoccupied. Leisure may have been a mere side effect of power, but in the 1890's leisure was being conspicuously consumed with a flamboyance hitherto unknown to Americans. The great financiers and industrialists were now highly visible, and the mass media assured them a national notoriety. Architects led by Richard Morris Hunt and Henry Hobson Richardson built them stately mansions in which servants and dependents celebrated their masters' power by vicarious consumption. The rapid development of trusts and holding companies in which manufacturing and transportation systems passed under the control of financiers indicated ominous concentrations of power. Veblen's conception of the basic conflict between industrial production for use and business enterprise for profit was directly relevant to this situation. His purposefully casual remarks on the common traits shared by businessmen and delinquents must have delighted all of those readers who shared the general resentment of the rich.

The new generation of scholars, of whom Veblen was one, no longer felt the restraints which the tradition of gentility had imposed upon the critical faculties. Ever since his undergraduate days at Carleton College, Veblen had contemptuously rejected gentility as a prime example of conspicuously wasteful display of privilege. At the University of Chicago, where the scholar worked on his book, President William Rainey Harper mediated uneasily between an all-powerful sponsor, John D. Rockefeller, and a restless faculty often resentful of Harper's timidity. Under such circumstances sensitive scholars felt themselves to be the kind of decorative embellishment that Veblen described in his concluding chapter. Like the traditional court jester who was obliged to cloak his sage advice to the monarch in whimsy, Veblen fired his blast at Rockefeller in the guise of an anthropological treatise.

Persuasive though it might appear at first glance, Veblen's analysis of the leisure class and its motives left certain unresolved questions. The leisure class, he said, "are not in the full sense an organic part of the industrial community"; they are not exposed to the exigencies of industrial life which would compel them to accommodate themselves to its imperious demands. This explains their conservatism, and particularly the survival in them of archaic, preindustrial traits of character. And yet by definition the leisure class is the owning and managing class. Here was Veblen's basic paradox. He asked his readers to believe that industrial institutions had evolved in the face of an owning and managing class which had played a purely passive, parasitic role, a class which held innovation to be vulgar and conservatism the only respectable point of view. What was the source of technological innovation and industrial development? Veblen never tells us. He seems to have regarded industrial evolution as an impersonal process in which initiative and decision need not be identified beyond bland references to a vague instinct of workmanship. It was enough to know that the leisure class exploited the industrial process for its own enjoyment. Veblen's preoccupation with leisure to the exclusion of management led to his famous distinction between business and industry. Business, the proper province of the leisure class, was a matter of exploitation, fraud, and chicane. Industry, on the other hand, was a wholesome concern with production for use and serviceability. What Veblen lightly put asunder a whole generation of entrepreneurial historians have subsequently labored to join together.

That Veblen was aware of this problem is apparent from the

fact that his definition of the leisure class fluctuates, depending on the purpose of the moment. At times it is the governing class, at others the parasitic leisure class. In order to bridge the gap he explained that leisure often takes the form of conspicuous consumption practiced vicariously by a hanger-on for the honor of a powerful personage too busy to perform the function himself. Wives do this while their husbands attend to their business at the countinghouse; or, on a grander scale, the professors at the University of Chicago carry on their arcane pursuits for the greater glory and honor of Rockefeller. The fact was, however, that the evolution of economic institutions was rapidly moving beyond the point where leisure-class behavior and attitudes had the importance in American society that Veblen wanted his readers to believe they had.

In the twentieth century the social significance of leisure has rapidly changed as a large measure of it has been achieved by the laboring class. While it is certainly true that this newly won leisure is often displayed by a blatantly conspicuous consumption that would have delighted Veblen, his thesis would nevertheless be strained by the attempt to show that leisure and labor still represent antithetic instincts. As leisure has become more readily available, its honorific value as evidence of prowess has quickly withered. Veblen sensed this also, and suggested that as the more vulgar manifestations of leisure became commonplace, subtle and refined forms of conspicuous consumption, such as the refinements of gentility, had to be developed. But gentility of course has suffered the same fate of diffusion and attenuation as leisure itself.

When one turns to the relationship between leisure and power Veblen's treatment seems similarly dated. When he wrote in 1899, the high visibility of the rich and powerful was undoubtedly a function of conspicuous consumption, sharpened and focused by a generation of social criticism. But progressive taxation and the austerities of war and depression have subsequently brought about a revolutionary homogenization of spending habits. Wealth and power may be as narrowly concentrated as they ever were, but their display by conspicuous leisure has been swamped out in the general waste of a consumer-oriented mass society.

Veblen's doctrines of hereditary traits and of racial differences, fashionable though such theories were at the turn of the century, are of dubious value today. He declared the leisure class to be composed principally of long-headed blond Nordics whose mastery had been established during the stage of predatory barbarism. The domineering, aggressive traits of the class are said to be perpetuated by heredity, as is the easy-going attitude of serviceability displayed by the servile class, generally composed of Alpine and Mediterranean types. However, even though Veblen extended the later quasi-peaceable stage of barbarism into modern times it was impossible for him to demonstrate historically the ethnic continuity of the American leisure class required by his theory. He was forced to admit that the American leisure class was of very recent formation, its members being recruited largely from lower-middle-class sources. By what mechanism then did it inherit the proper attitudes of the leisure class when its own hereditary traits were those of servile craftsmanship? Veblen could only say that its emulation of the true hereditary leisure class was a matter of "protective mimicry," a weak explanation. He had earlier characterized American colonial settlement by Europeans, who thus escaped the rigors of the emerging industrial discipline, as a reversion to barbarism on a continental scale. It was all the more paradoxical, therefore, that the social composition of the American leisure class should have proved to be so unstable. Veblen's theory of racial heredity could not stand the test of facts. One suspects that it has escaped censure largely because he inverted it in order to reflect invidiously on the Nordic race of which he himself was so splendid an exemplar. Had he ventured to predict the extinction of, say, the black race he would have precipitated a scandal of continental proportions.

The Theory of the Leisure Class is not in fact a work of scholarship primarily, but a work of art; not an objective study of a social institution, but a deeply felt and cunningly constructed portrayal of a social type. As an alienated critic of his society, Veblen made a heavy emotional investment in his analysis of the masterful ways of the "captain of industry" in whose honor so many camp followers passed their days in performing irksome leisure-class functions. The author's frequent ironic protestations of scholarly impartiality merely underscored these effects. The ponderous mock-heroic circumlocutions in which the book abounds invite the reader to share the author's condescending contempt for the genteel pieties which masked the naked realities of power and privilege. When the entire course of social evolution is found to swing in a vast arc between "serviceability" and "wastefulness" who could refrain from condemning the leisure-class practices which exalted conspicuous waste and despised mere labor as menial? On the whole, however, these devices were employed with too heavy a hand for the durable effect Veblen intended. While his book achieved a measure of fame that may well have surprised him, it remained a period piece. Its richly ornamented facade recalled the elaborate mansions being built at that moment for the American leisure class. Both suffered a rapid obsolescence decreed by changing social conditions.

W. E. B. DU BOIS:

THE SOULS OF BLACK FOLK

Everett S. Lee

It is hard to be fair to W. E. B. Du Bois. He was a man of talent and of passion, of deep humanity and of bitter intolerance. Arrogant and impatient, he condemned all who did not agree with him, and he was often more of a trial to his friends than to his enemies. A sound scholar at the beginning of his career, he came to value propaganda over scholarship, and he filled many pages with vituperation and patent exaggeration. Yet he was one of the great men of his times, one of a handful of important Negro leaders, and he produced a book, *The Souls of Black Folk*,[1] that ranks among the few to signal the turning point of a social movement.

It was recognized as such from the beginning. As perceptive an observer as James Weldon Johnson, the Negro author, musician, and diplomat, described it as having "a greater effect upon and within the Negro race than any single book published in this country since *Uncle Tom's Cabin*."[2] It was hailed as the "political bible" of the educated Negro, and Du Bois was cast as the "long looked for political Messiah."[3] First appearing in the spring of 1903, *The Souls of Black Folk* has gone through more than twenty editions and is still in print. No other book written by a Negro has had the impact in America that this book has had.

Curiously, Du Bois pays scant attention to it in his autobiography, *Dusk of Dawn*.[4] There he simply notes that after forty years he was gratified that it was still selling and that he was satisfied with it. In the same volume he remarks that his favorite among his own books was *Dark Princess*,[5] a stilted novel, now read only because Du Bois was its author. He also remarks that one of the best things he had done was a biography of John Brown, the abolitionist and, to Du Bois, the martyr of Harper's Ferry.[6] Little more than a pastiche of quotations from other writers, to which Du Bois added a peculiar and biased interpretation, it was soundly condemned, and in the first seven years after publication it sold only six hundred sixty-five copies.[7] This Du Bois attributed to the malevolence of a reviewer, upon whose chosen field he had encroached and who, in control of the scholarly press, would allow him no chance of rejoinder.

Writers, however, are seldom the best judges of their own works, and an attack upon a bad book can arouse the kind of uncritical defense that meets the evaluation of a poorly performing child. And Du Bois, far more than most men, was unable to admit deficiencies in himself or in his work. He was a man who had to stand alone; he had to lead because he could not follow; the enormity of his ego was matched by his contempt for ordinary men. Preoccupied with self and obsessed with the racial question, he permitted autobiographical statements to stray into his work in the most unexpected places, and he mingled observations from Olympus with outright polemicism. A hero to thousands, but without a single disciple, he was a man of enormous successes and egregious failures, and he did not clearly distinguish the one from the other.

Du Bois' work is so much an extension of his personality that we must study the man and his times in order to understand his work. He was born just three years after the Civil War had ended, and it was nearly a hundred years later, in 1963, that he died. His first book appeared when he was twenty-eight, and he did not stop writing until his death, two-thirds of a century later. His bibliography would fill many pages, and he was editor and historian as well as sociologist, essayist, novelist, and poet. His early work was painstaking and scholarly, but in mid-life he became careless with facts, sometimes ignoring them and sometimes twisting them to suit his purpose. *The Souls of Black Folk* comes near the point of transition, and it is written with restraint and clarity. Here the occasional introduction of loose symbolism and intellectual posturing is not without charm. From the literary point of view everything Du Bois had done before was prologue; what he wrote later adds little to his reputation as a scholar or a writer, though much to his stature as a racial leader.

Du Bois was born in Great Barrington, Massachusetts, a little town "up in the hills of New England, where the dark Housatonic winds between Hoosac and Taghkanic to the sea." [8] He was a mulatto, the descendant on the paternal side of a French Huguenot and his mulatto slave mistress. On the other side there was a mingling so that Du Bois was born with "a flood of Negro blood, a strain of French, a bit of Dutch, but, thank God! no Anglo-Saxon." [9] Some of his relatives passed themselves off as white and their children grew up ignorant of their black ancestry. He lived with his mother in her father's house since his own father had left them to try his luck as barber and preacher in distant towns, finally to disappear altogether.

In Great Barrington race prejudice was minimal, and Du Bois was not fully aware of the gulf between the races until a girl newcomer refused to take the visiting card that Du Bois, along with the other youths of the town, was affecting. From that time on he knew that "he was different from the others; or like mayhap, in heart and life and longing, but shut out from their world by a vast veil." [10] The realization of that veil was to stir the deepest emotions in Du Bois for the rest of his life, but he declares: "I had thereafter no desire to tear down that veil, to creep through; I held all beyond it in great contempt, and lived above it in a region of blue sky and great wandering shadows. The sky was bluest when I could beat my mates at examination-time, or beat them at a foot-race, or even beat their stringy heads." [11]

Du Bois did well in high school and he was encouraged by his principal to prepare for college. He aimed at Harvard but his townsmen raised funds to send him to Fisk where, for the first time, he found himself in a colored world and one in which there were beautiful black girls. The theme of black beauty was one he returned to frequently; in *Dusk of Dawn* he noted that there could be no "question that as colors, bronze, mahogany, coffee, and gold are far lovelier than pink, gray, or marble." Hair, he added, was a matter of taste, but he preferred "the crinkly kind, almost wavy, in black, brown, and glistening gold." [12] He hated "straight features; needles and razors may be sharp, but beautiful never." As a "child of twilight and night . . . [he chose] intricately curly hair, black eyes, full and luscious features; and that air of humility and wonder that streams from moonlight. Add to this voices that caress instead of rasp, glances that appeal rather than repel, and a sinuous litheness of movement to replace Anglo-Saxon stalking—there you have my ideal." [13]

He graduated from Fisk and went to Harvard where he repeated the junior and senior years and was awarded a fellowship for graduate study. At Harvard he studied with William James and read Kant with George Santayana. James advised him away from philosophy, but Albert Bushnell Hart took him into his seminar in history. Led by Hart to seek an understanding of the present through the study of institutions and their development, he combed the statutes, the Congressional Record, executive documents, and contemporary records for materials on the African slave trade. In time this led to his doctoral thesis, *The Suppression of the African Slave Trade to the United States of America, 1638–1870,* which was published as the initial volume of the Harvard Historical Series.[14] First appearing in 1896, this book was reissued in 1965. It is a careful, workmanlike, and altogether admirable piece of work.

At the end of the second year of graduate study, Du Bois badgered the Slater Fund into allowing him money, part grant and part loan, for study in Germany. He landed in Holland, which he described as an "extremely neat and well-ordered mud puddle, situated at the confluence of the English, French, and German languages." [15] In Europe he learned something of beauty and elegance, he came to know the symphonies of Beethoven and the colors of Titian, and he flirted with white girls. One of these he felt it necessary to warn of the difficulties she would encounter if he married her and took her to America.

At the University of Berlin he entered the seminars of Gustav Schmoller and Adolph Wagner, from both of whom he obtained pleasing testimonials to his work. He also studied with Heinrich von Trietschke and heard him thunder, "Mulattoes are inferior." [16] At the end of two years he returned to the United States and though he was one of the most educated Negroes in the country, he had some difficulty in finding a job. When he was offered the Chair of Classics at Wilberforce University in Ohio, a small Negro school, he accepted immediately, and was thus unable to consider Booker T. Washington's later offer to teach mathematics at Tuskegee.

Du Bois arrived at Wilberforce wearing a Vandyke beard and affecting the high silk hat, gloves, and cane of the German scholar. He taught Latin, Greek, English, and German, and would have added sociology had he been permitted. Almost happy at first, he soon grew disillusioned with Wilberforce where moral and religious tone was as highly valued as intellectual performance. He nearly lost his job for refusing to pray at a student meeting and he noted in his diary that, during a week in which classes were canceled for a religious revival, he was "driven almost to distraction by the wild screams, groans and shrieks that rise from the chapel below me." [17]

At Wilberforce he met his wife, a dark-eyed girl with an Alsatian mother, and after two years he found release from his professional unhappiness in an offer from the University of Pennylvania to study the Negro community in Philadelphia. He went at a cut in salary and produced a book, *The Philadelphia Negro*,[18] which was acclaimed by Gunnar Myrdal nearly half a century later as a model study of a Negro community.[19] As a pure scholar Du Bois reached his zenith with this book; his later scholarly attempts were numerous but nothing else of research value attained the same level of conciseness and conclusiveness.

From Philadelphia Du Bois went to Atlanta University to take charge of the work in sociology. As a condition of employment he had to agree to engage in public prayers, of which he wrote: "I am not sure that they were orthodox or reached heaven, but they certainly reached my audience." [20] Seeking to discover the laws of human behavior, he mapped out an ambitious program of studies of the American Negro, the results of which appeared in the Atlanta University *Publications*. He had little support for these efforts, financial or otherwise, and the *Publications* were of varying quality, sometimes quite good, more often mediocre. There was, however, nothing else of equal value, and they became basic to contemporary studies of the Negro.

He had been in Atlanta six years when he was asked by Mc-Clurg and Company if he did not have some material for a book. Du Bois suggested a summary of the Atlanta Conferences he had been conducting, but the publisher wanted something immediately and mentioned articles that had appeared in the *Atlantic Monthly* and elsewhere. Du Bois agreed to assemble some of his essays and other fugitive pieces. To these he added a chapter, "Of Mr. Booker T. Washington and Others" and called the assemblage *The Souls of Black Folk*. It was this added chapter that gave to the book an instant and lasting importance, that elevated Du Bois to the front rank of Negro leaders, and that plunged him into years of bitter controversy.

Booker T. Washington was the most powerful Negro American of his day and none other has ever achieved such eminence. Du Bois himself said that "the most striking thing in the history of the American Negro since 1876 is the ascendancy of Mr. Booker T. Washington," [21] and called him "the most distinguished Southerner since Jefferson Davis, and the one with the largest personal following." [22] Presidents depended upon him for advice; Andrew Carnegie and John D. Rockefeller bowed to his judgment. Funds for Negro education were funneled through his hands; careers of Negro professors and intellectuals were made and unmade by him. In all things Washington was a remarkable man. Born in a slave cabin, the son of a white father, Washington obtained an education against great odds and established Tuskegee Institute almost single-handed. He was, furthermore, so personable and so unassuming that he was accepted in places no other Negro could go. He visited Theodore Roosevelt in the White House and had tea at Windsor Castle with Queen Victoria. But what endeared him to the white community was his program for Negro advancement, summed up in a famous speech at the Cotton States Exposition at Atlanta in 1893. In effect he renounced immediate demands for social equality and suggested that Negroes should earn privileges through hard and constant effort in agriculture, mechanics, domestic service, and in the professions, and not through artificial forcing. Referring to the races, he raised his hand, spread apart the fingers, and announced: "In all things that are purely social we can be as separate as the fingers, yet one as the hand in all things essential to mutual progress." [23]

Du Bois was no man to accept a policy of gradualism, or to counsel patience while Negroes acquired the skills of agriculturists and craftsmen or assembled a little capital to start independent enterprises. Not that Du Bois was against the training of artisans. He recognized its importance for the mass of Negroes, but above all Du Bois pinned his hopes upon the "talented tenth," his term for the gifted few who could be trained in universities and colleges to become teachers, professional men, and leaders. An aristocrat at heart, Du Bois had little faith in the masses. Moreover he felt personally threatened by Washington and his "Tuskegee Machine," and he despised Washington's submissiveness and moralizing.

Nevertheless, Du Bois was fair to Washington in his essay, crediting him for two great achievements. First, Washington had accomplished the almost impossible task of gaining the sympathy and cooperation of the white South, some elements of which interpreted his program as a basis for mutual understanding while others saw it as the complete surrender of the demands for civil and political equality. At the same time Washington had gained the consideration of the North by appealing to the spirit of industry and commerce that animated that section of the country. From these accomplishments flowed gains to the American Negro but, according to Du Bois, at great expense.

Little attention had been paid to the debit side of the ledger, however, because criticism had been stilled while only Washington spoke for the Negro people. As Du Bois saw it, Washington had asked the Negro to give up three precious things—political power, the insistence on civil rights, and higher education for Negro youth—and had asked him to concentrate on industrial education, the accumulation of wealth, and the conciliation of the South. In return the Negro had received disenfranchisement, a legally certified status of civil inferiority, and the withdrawal of aid from institutions of higher learning for Negroes. These led to the paradoxes of Washington's program.

Though Washington had tried valiantly to turn Negroes into businessmen and property owners, it was impossible for them to protect their rights if they could not vote. And though Washington had emphasized thrift and self-respect, his counsel of submission had sapped away the manhood of the race. Finally, the advocacy of industrial training over higher education was self-defeating because of the need for teachers trained in Negro colleges. In opposition to Washington it was therefore necessary to demand three things: the right to vote, civil equality, and the education of youth according to ability. Insofar as Washington stood for thrift, patience, and industrial training for the masses he was to be applauded, but to the degree that he apologized for injustice, failed to appreciate the value of the vote, and failed to understand the emasculating effect of caste distinction and lack of higher education, he was to be opposed.

Du Bois was roundly denounced by the Negro, as well as the white, press for his attack on Washington. The *Colored American* saw it as an attempt to sell a book that would otherwise have attracted little attention.[24] While it is possible that without the chapter on Washington the book would have been met with the indifference that was the fate of most of Du Bois' books, it is not true that there is little merit in the other sections of *The Souls of Black Folk*. Quite to the contrary several of the chapters are of considerable value as sensitive contemporary accounts of conditions in the South and several portray in compelling fashion the agony of a sensitive but arrogant soul forced into a position of official inferiority.

Admittedly, the organization of the essays into a book is forced, though Du Bois does attempt a short justification in the Preface. The book is, he says, an attempt to show the meaning of being black in the twentieth century. First, he tries to show the meaning of emancipation to intelligent Negroes; from there he proceeds to an examination of the rise of Negro leadership, the famous essay on Washington. Thereafter he sketches the world within and the world without the Veil, and then he raises the Veil to expose the intensity and passion of the struggle of the black folk.

Each section of the book is preceded by a phrase from one of the "Sorrow Songs," the great spirituals of the American Negro, and Du Bois closes the book with an essay on this music through which the slave spoke to the world. The book begins with a bar from "Nobody knows the trouble I've seen," and other chapters are headed by strains from "Swing low, sweet chariot," "Roll, Jordan, roll," and "My way's cloudy." These songs, "the sifting of centuries," are to Du Bois "the music of an unhappy people, of the children of disappointment. They tell of death, and suffering and unvoiced longing toward a truer world, of misty wanderings and hidden ways." [25] But through them there breathes hope and a faith in ultimate justice, and it is upon this note that Du Bois closes the book.

The Souls of Black Folk is dedicated to Burghardt and Yolande, his two children—Yolande, who delighted him with grandchildren, and Burghardt, the son who died in early childhood. These he calls the lost and the found, and in a poignant essay he sketches his joy in his son and the grief in his death. He says that he did not love the child at first, because it seemed a ludicrous thing to love, tiny and formless, "all head and all voice." But he learned to love the child through the girl-mother to whom the arrival of a child brought "an unfolding like the glory of the morning."

Yet the child was born within the Veil and within the Veil he had to live, a Negro and a Negro's son, a Negro in a world where to Du Bois freedom was a mockery and liberty a lie. When he died the parents carried him into the North because they would not bury him in Georgia. On the day of the funeral an awful gladness came to Du Bois and his soul whispered to him, "Not dead, not dead but escaped; not bound, but free." And Du Bois consoled himself by saying, "Well sped, my boy, before the world had dubbed your ambition insolence, had held your ideals unattainable, and taught you to cringe and bow." [26]

None of the other chapters of the book have the importance of the essay on Washington or the impact of the essay on the death of the first-born. Nevertheless, they sometimes attain a remarkable intensity of feeling and of foresight. In one Du Bois gives his version of the work of the Freedmen's Bureau, the agency set up to deal with the problems of the ex-slaves but abolished before its work was done. Several essays deal with the living conditions of the Negro in the South at the turn of the century, and there is even a short story, "Of the Coming of John," that portrays the efforts of a young Negro man to obtain education and then to bring it to Negro children. An essay, "Of the Training of Black Men," sketches the efforts that had been made to educate the southern Negro and argues that the Negro is capable of higher education, at that time still a debatable matter.

In *The Souls of Black Folk* Du Bois was the disciplined writer, still reflecting the careful objectivity and restraint that he had been taught at Harvard and to which he had schooled himself in his books on the slave trade and the Philadelphia Negro. Only occasionally do we find the diffuseness and labored metaphor that mars his later work and against which he had been warned by his English instructor at Harvard. At this point in his career, Du Bois still thought it possible to achieve a rapprochement between the races, he still had faith in a science of man, and he still had the capacity of detaching himself from his surroundings and of viewing the most distressing situation without exploding in anger or lashing out with sarcasm. He was still a sensitive observer, receptive to beauty, and far from the position he later took when he declared, "I do not give a damn for any art that is not used for propaganda." [27]

A few years after the publication of *The Souls of Black Folk*, Du Bois left Atlanta to become editor of *Crisis*, the organ of the National Association for the Advancement of Colored People. His powerful editorials and his surveys of the current scene were important factors in promoting the cause of the American Negro. Moving beyond national concerns, Du Bois allied himself with the Pan-African Movement and eventually he embraced Marxism, the tenets of which he never fully grasped, but which he interpreted to suit his own version of history and the racial struggle.

He became more and more estranged from the white world. In the end he no longer sought integration and success through cooperation with whites. Instead he urged the setting up of an independent Negro society within America, one complete with black businesses, black schools, black officials, and a whole range of separate institutions. He approved the setting up of Negro colleges and he protested against the idea that segregated institutions were by necessity inferior. He attempted to work out a comprehensive plan for Negro self-sufficiency and succeeded in alienating a considerable number of young Negro leaders. Du Bois was moving against the tide in his own race and, as his friend Francis J. Grimké remarked, if Du Bois thought he could lead the Negro back into segregation his leadership was at an end.[28]

Unlike Washington, Du Bois had little support among whites, and as the outstanding spokesman for his race he came under fire from both conservatives and radicals. Conservatives saw him as overly aggressive while Negro radicals of the 1920's judged him to be the captive of the white establishment, and he was described by the editors of *Messenger,* a radical journal edited by A. Philip Randolph and Chandler Owen, as one of the "hand-picked, me-too-boss, hat-in-hand, sycophant, lick spittling" Negroes.[29] Du Bois had never expected much from whites, but to be assailed by Negroes, and particularly those of the left, was a cruel blow.

Forced out of his editorship of *Crisis* because of his disagreements with its board, his unwillingness to brook any interference with his conduct of the magazine, Du Bois returned to Atlanta University where he founded *Phylon,* Atlanta University's "review of race and culture." Here he began again his program of research on the American Negro and he undertook the development of an "Encyclopedia of the Negro." His attention was drawn away from the American scene, however, by his increasing interest in colonialism and Pan-Africanism. When he was seventy-seven years old, he published a book, *Color and Democracy: Colonies and Peace,*[30] that dealt with racism and imperialism and denounced the failure of the Dumbarton Oaks Conference to emphasize the rights of colonial peoples. When he was ninety-three he joined the Communist Party, noting that "he had been long and slow in coming to this conclusion," and when he was ninety-four he became a citizen of Ghana where he spent the last years of his life. His death on August 27, 1963, came at the time of the Great March on Washington and the quarter of a million people gathered there paused to pay tribute to him.

His was a long life full of conflict and contradiction but of enormous achievement. Perhaps in characterizing the American Negro in a memorable passage in *The Souls of Black Folk* Du Bois really described himself as

a sort of seventh son, born with a veil, and gifted with second sight in this American world,—a world which yields . . . [the Negro] no true self consciousness, but only lets him see himself through the revelation of the other world. It is a peculiar sensation, this double-consciousness, this sense of always looking at one's self through the eyes of others, of measuring one's soul by the tape of a world that looks on in amused contempt and pity. One ever feels his two-ness,—

an American, a Negro; two souls, two thoughts, two unreconciled strivings; two warring ideals in one dark body, whose dogged strength keeps it from being torn asunder.[31]

Notes

1. Chicago, 1903. Page references are to a reprinting in *Three Negro Classics* (New York, 1966), with an introduction by John Hope Franklin.

2. *Along This Way* (New York, 1933), p. 203.

3. Elliott M. Rudwick, *W. E. B. Du Bois: Propagandist of the Negro Protest* (New York, 1968), p. 68.

4. New York, 1940. Strictly speaking, this is more a statement of Du Bois' concept of race than it is an autobiography. There is yet no adequate biography since his papers have not been released to scholars. See, however, the books by Rudwick and Broderick listed in notes 3 and 7.

5. New York, 1928.

6. *John Brown* (Philadelphia, 1909).

7. Francis L. Broderick, *W. E. B. Du Bois: Negro Leader in a Time of Crisis* (Stanford, California, 1959), p. 82.

8. *Three Negro Classics*, p. 214.

9. *Darkwater: Voices from Within the Veil* (New York, 1920), p. 9.

10. *Three Negro Classics*, p. 214.

11. *Ibid.*

12. *Dusk of Dawn*, p. 142.

13. *Ibid.*

14. New York, 1896.

15. *Dusk of Dawn*, p. 45.

16. *Ibid.*, p. 99.

17. Broderick, p. 33.

18. Philadelphia, 1899.

19. *An American Dilemma* (New York, 1944), pp. 1, 132.

20. *Dusk of Dawn*, p. 63.

21. *Three Negro Classics*, p. 240.

22. *Ibid.*, p. 241.

23. *Ibid.*, p. 148.

24. Broderick, p. 70.

25. *Three Negro Classics*, p. 380.

26. *Ibid.*, p. 353.

27. Broderick, p. 157.

28. *Ibid.*, p. 177.

29. Rudwick, p. 241.

30. New York, 1945.

31. *Three Negro Classics*, pp. 214–215.

21 WILLIAM JAMES: *PRAGMATISM, A NEW NAME FOR SOME OLD WAYS OF THINKING*

Gay Wilson Allen

A great European scholar and critic of American literature, Professor Heinrich Straumann of the University of Zürich, begins his history of *American Literature in the Twentieth Century* with this observation:

> To the foreign observer of the growth of American thought it will always remain an enigma that the one aspect of American conduct generally accepted as outstanding found its philosophical interpretation at such a late date. The pragmatic view of life more commonly and also more honestly adopted in the United States than anywhere else in the Western world had its firm grip on the majority of Americans long before anyone attempted to describe it in terms of abstract thought. Perhaps the very naturalness of that outlook prevented its theoretical discussion, but once this was started it did not stop and has led to a number of most decisive trends in modern thought.[1]

William James published his *Pragmatism,* subtitled *A New Name for Some Old Ways of Thinking,* in 1907,[2] though he had delivered a lecture on "Philosophical Conceptions and Practical Results" at the University of California in 1898, and during 1906 and 1907 he had used chapters of his forthcoming book for lectures in Boston and New York. But the philosophical movement called Pragmatism is usually dated from the publication of James's book in 1907, though John Dewey had been developing a similar theory at the University of Chicago, and a professor of philosophy at Oxford University in England had published a book in 1903 called *Humanism* which both he and James recognized as another name for Pragmatism.

"The term," James said in his chapter on the meaning of the word,

is derived from the same Greek word πράγμα, meaning action, from which our word "practice" and "practical" come. It was first introduced into philosophy by Mr. Charles Peirce in 1878. In an article entitled "How to Make our Ideas Clear," in the "Popular Science Monthly" for January of that year Mr. Peirce, after pointing out that our beliefs are really rules for action, said that, to develop a thought's meaning, we need only determine what conduct it is fitted to produce: that conduct is for us its sole significance. And the tangible fact of the root of all thought-distinctions, however subtle, is that there is no one of them so fine as to consist in anything but a possible difference of practice. To attain perfect clearness in our thoughts of an object, then, we need only consider what conceivable effects of a practical kind the object may involve—what sensations we are to expect from it, and what reactions we must prepare. Our conception of these effects, whether immediate or remote, is then for us the whole of our conception of the object, so far as that conception has positive significance at all (p. 46).

Later Peirce thought that James had distorted his theory and changed his term to "pragmaticism" to distinguish it from James's Pragmatism. Suffice it to say that whereas John Dewey emphasized a pragmatic—or practical—method of solving problems, and Peirce a method for avoiding ambiguity and imprecision, James was concerned with establishing a *theory of truth*. This theory was actually, as James also stressed, a *method* for determining what in a specific situation can be regarded as sufficiently useful and reliable to be acted upon with successful results. Stating it this way, James was simply saying that only the test of experience can prove the reliability of assumptions. This is why he insisted that "There is absolutely nothing new in the pragmatic method. Socrates was an adept at it. Aristotle used it methodically. Locke, Berkeley, and Hume made momentous contributions to truth by its means" (p. 50). And he dedicated his book "To The Memory Of John Stuart Mill From Whom I First Learned The Pragmatic Openness Of Mind And Whom My

Fancy Likes To Picture As Our Leader Were He Alive To-Day."
James insisted, however, that "these forerunners of pragmatism
used it in fragments; they were preludes only" (p. 50).

William James became a philosopher after a long apprenticeship in science (chemistry, biology, anthropology, anatomy,
physiological-psychology), and he was thoroughly trained in the
so-called "scientific method," which consists of collecting all the
facts possible with a completely open mind, then after close observation and analysis of the facts, final arrival inductively at a
tentative conclusion, to be tested by further observations and
hypotheses. Belief in this empirical method was the one faith all
scientists shared. All progress in science had been made by em-
ploying this method; it obviously worked. Now James wanted to
employ this method in the pursuit of *all truth*—or, as he preferred, *truths*—and to maintain that only the test of experience
can separate truth from falsehood. For *true* he would substitute
workable: what works, solves problems, proves most practicable
in a given situation is true for us, though possibly only in that
particular situation or one very similar to it, and we must always
be on guard against seeming or misleading similarities.

The aspect of this doctrine which stirred up the most opposition, in fact the denunciation of all people who loved abstractions more than concrete facts, was James's disdain of universal
truths. Plato regarded *truth* as eternal, *fact* as temporal, therefore
impermanent and illusory. In the western world the very word
truth had long been clothed with divinity. Now James challenged its sacredness.

In all his philosophical writings James maintained that most,
if not all, metaphysical assumptions can never be absolutely settled by objective proof one way or the other. Take the doctrine
of determinism: whether man has free will or whether all his
actions are determined either by God or blind physical forces we
can never actually know. But by believing that he has at least
some control over his destiny, an individual can effect practical
results in the realm of his daily life. Since this assumption, or
strategic belief, is useful, it has pragmatic value, or in James's
terms, "truth." The only test of its truth is the degree of its
usefulness. Critics said that this view of truth was psychological,
not philosophical. They might grant its psychological value yet

deny its contribution to truth. Some said James simply abandoned, or at least bypassed, metaphysics altogether, and to a certain extent he did.

For example, a central doctrine dear to metaphysicians for centuries was the doctrine of *substance*. In the Middle Ages scholastic philosophy had perfected distinctions between *substance* and *attribute,* and this distinction had become "enshrined," as James said, "in the very structure of human language." As an example he cited a piece of chalk. Its attributes are whiteness, friability, insolubility in water, and so on. "But the bearer of these attributes is so much *chalk,* which thereupon is called the substance in which they inhere" (p. 85). But all we can ever know by experience about a piece of chalk is that it has these attributes. These we experience through our senses and can manipulate in practical ways, such as using the friability to make marks on a blackboard; we never experience the unseen *substance,* which is a pure abstraction, taken on faith.

In the same way we may say that climate determines our weather, though actually it is only the average of a great many days of different kinds of weather that gives us the concept of climate. Perhaps it is obvious that "climate" is a statistical concept instead of a substance, but James argued that objects which occupy space, such as a piece of chalk or a piece of wood—that is, chunks of "matter"—have no more experienceable substance than "climate."

Here James was in agreement with Berkeley, whose criticism of *physical matter* James called "absolutely pragmatistic." And he also claimed Locke as a pragmatist for his criticism of *spiritual substance.* For example, in his treatment of "personal identity" Locke "immediately reduces this notion to its pragmatic value in terms of experience. It means, he says, so much 'consciousness,' namely the fact that at one moment of life we remember other moments, and feel them all as parts of one and the same personal history. Rationalism had explained this practical continuity in our life by the unity of our soul-substance" (p. 90).

So long as theology regarded human conduct as something to be rewarded or punished in a future existence in heaven or hell, soul-substance had its use. But for all practical purposes here on earth in the twentieth century James found it purely speculative and of no practical use. Of course, "Locke, compromiser that he was, passively tolerated the belief in a substantial soul behind our consciousness. But his successor Hume, and most empirical psychologists after him, have denied the soul, save as the name for verifiable cohesions in our inner life. They redescend into the stream of experience with it, and cash it into so much small-change value in the way of 'ideas' and their peculiar connexions with each other" (p. 92). Although James does not say so, for "verifiable cohesions in our inner life" psychologists had already begun to use the term *psyche* instead of *soul*. Etymologically *psyche* means *soul*, but in empirical psychology it came to mean something like a controlling center of personal identity (or consciousness of a *self*) rather than an immaterial soul or spirit.

For rejecting *soul-substance* as a useful concept James was accused of being a materialist. However, he was neither a materialist nor a spiritualist but a thoroughgoing empiricist. Thus he adopted the argument of Berkeley, an idealist, against *material substance* as giving cohesion to the attributes of physical objects; and of Locke, an anti-idealist (though not consistently materialistic) against *spiritual substance*. The argument between materialists and spiritualists James regarded as largely aesthetic. The spiritualist looks upon matter as "gross, coarse, crass, muddy," and spirit as "pure, elevated, noble" (p. 94). The materialist says that the "laws of physical nature are what run things," and that all knowledge of the universe consists of "acquaintance with the facts, out of their physiological conditions, regardless whether nature be there only for our minds, as idealists contend, or not. Our minds in any case would have to record the kind of nature it is, and write it down as operating through blind laws of physics" (p. 93). James was not sure that these laws were blind, but the whole argument seemed to him useless anyway. "What practical difference can it make *now* that the world should be run by matter or by spirit?" he asks (p. 96). If we observe what operations work best in the realm of our actual experience, we can discover how to increase our successes and reduce our failures in achieving our objectives. This is all that matters, and this is the pragmatic method.

James had long ago decided that every philosophy is highly subjective, although most philosophers have deluded themselves

with the belief that their thinking is strictly objective and impersonal. And not only philosophers, but most human beings choose
their beliefs to satisfy their temperaments. The two basic classifi-
cations are the "tender-minded" and the "tough-minded," the
former inclined to be spiritual, idealistic in the everyday sense of
the term, thinking in terms of general principles, "laws," creeds,
comfortable abstractions; the latter inclined to be materialistic,
skeptical, more interested in facts and concrete situations than
generalizations. "The tough think of the tender as sentimentalists
and soft-heads. The tender feel the tough to be unrefined,
callous, or brutal" (p. 13). From this characterization of the two
types we might suppose James, the Pragmatist, to classify himself
as "tough-minded," the mind temperamentally inclined toward
pragmatic thinking and conduct. But actually he had in his temperament something of both groups. Though he favored facts
over abstractions, he too wanted to hold on to some abstractions
and he did not regard all religious faiths as delusions, or as
useless: "spiritualistic faith in all its forms deals with a world of
promise, while materialism's sun sets in a sea of disappointment,"
and it is much easier to live in a world of promise than in one of
inevitable disappointment. "I myself believe that the evidence
for God lies primarily in inner personal experiences" (p. 109).

What James objected to were attempts to prove the existence
of God by logic, such as design in nature as evidence of a benevolent Creator. He stated:

> The first step in these arguments was to prove that the design *existed.*
> Nature was ransacked for results obtained through separate things
> being co-adapted. Our eyes, for instance, originate in intra-uterine
> darkness, and the light originates in the sun, yet see how they fit each
> other. Vision is the end designed, light and eyes the separate means
> devised for its attainment.
>
> It is strange, considering how unanimously our ancestors felt the
> force of this argument, to see how little it counts for since the tri-
> umph of the darwinian theory. Darwin opened our minds to the
> power of chance-happenings to bring forth "fit" results if only they
> have time to add themselves together. He showed the enormous waste
> in nature in producing results that get destroyed because of their un-
> fitness. He also emphasized the number of adaptations which, if de-
> signed, would argue an evil rather than a good designer. *Here,* all

depends upon the point of view. To the grub under the bark the exquisite fitness of the woodpecker's organism to extract him would certainly argue a diabolical designer (p. 111).

All metaphysical assumptions can be attacked in the same way. Whether they are accepted or rejected depends upon the point of view of the beholder and what he, perhaps unconsciously, is looking for—whether he sees from the point of view of the woodpecker or the grub. So it is with that major rational abstraction in the history of human thought, the unity of the universe— notice that it is called a *uni-* not a *multi-*verse, another presupposition built into the language. "Loosely speaking," says James,

> and in general, it may be said that all things cohere and adhere to each other *somehow,* and that the universe exists practically in reticulated or concatenated forms which make of it a continuous or "integrated" affair. Any kind of influence whatever helps to make the world one, so far as you can follow it from next to next. You may then say that "the world *is* One,"—meaning in these respects, namely, and just so far as they obtain. But just as definitely is it *not* One, so far as they do not obtain; and there is no species of connexion which will not fail, if, instead of choosing conductors for it you choose non-conductors. You are then arrested at your very first step and have to write the world down as a pure *many* from that particular point of view. If our intellect had been as much interested in disjunctive as it is in conjunctive relations, philosophy would have equally successfully celebrated the world's *disunion* (pp. 137–138).

Consequently:

> "The world is One," therefore, just as far as we experience it to be concatenated, One by as many definite conjunctions as appear. But then also *not* One by just as many definite *dis*-junctions as we find. The oneness and the manyness of it thus obtain in respects which can be separately named. It is neither a universe pure and simple nor a multiverse pure and simple. And its various manners of being One suggest, for their accurate ascertainment, so many distinct programs of scientific work. Thus the pragmatic question, "What is the oneness known as? What practical difference will it make?" saves us from all feverish excitement over it as a principle of sublimity and carries us forward into the stream of experience with a cool head. The stream may indeed reveal far more connexion and union than we now sus-

pect, but we are not entitled on pragmatic principles to claim absolute oneness in any respect in advance (pp. 148–149).

The not claiming of "absolute oneness" in advance is the very
heart of James's pragmatic theory of truth. Rationalists regard
truth as static, inert, unchanging. As James summarizes this view,
"When you've got your true idea of anything [that is, what the
believer in absolutes regards as true], there is an end to the
matter. You're in possession; you *know;* you have fulfilled your
thinking destiny." But:

> Pragmatism, on the other hand, asks the usual question. "Grant an
> idea or a belief to be true," it says, "what concrete difference will its
> being true make in any one's actual life? How will the truth be
> realized? What experiences will be different from those which would
> obtain if the belief were false? What, in short, is the truth's cash-value
> in experiential terms?"
>
> The moment pragmatism asks this question, it sees the answer:
> *True ideas are those that we can assimilate, validate, corroborate and
> verify. False ideas are those that we can not.* That is the practical
> difference it makes to us to have true ideas; that, therefore, is the
> meaning of truth, for it is all that truth is known-as.
>
> This thesis is what I have to defend. The truth of an idea is not a
> stagnant property inherent in it. Truth *happens* to an idea. It *be-
> comes* true, is *made* true by events. Its verity *is* in fact an event, a
> process: the process namely of its verifying itself, its veri-*fication.* Its
> validity is the process of its valid-*ation* (pp. 200–201).

Ideas which have thus been tested and found operationally
dependable become "invaluable instruments of action" (p. 202).
(This is very similar to John Dewey's "instrumental theory of
truth.") The value of such intellectual instruments as workable
ideas is demonstrated every day of our lives. As James says, "We
live in a world of realities that can be infinitely useful or infinitely harmful. Ideas that tell us which of them to expect count as
the true in all this primary sphere of verification, and the pursuit
of such ideas is a primary human duty" (pp. 202–203).

To drive home the meaning of his theory of truth as evolving,
or being evolved by trial and error, James often used words with
unpopular connotations, such as the "cash-value" of truth. He
also spoke of "expediency," which has the connotation of lazy,
cowardly, or greedy compromise, unwillingness to fight for moral

principles, and the like: *" 'The true,' to put it very briefly, is only the expedient in the way of our thinking, just as 'the right' is only the expedient in the way of our behaving.* Expedient in almost any fashion; and expedient in the long run and on the whole, of course; for what meets expediently all the experience in sight won't necessarily meet all further experiences equally satisfactorily. Experience, as we know, has ways of boiling over, and making us correct our present formulas" (p. 222).

Thus all James means by "expediency" is that nothing we at one time have sufficient grounds for believing to be true is necessarily going to remain true in other situations and at other times:

> . . . we have to live to-day by what truth we can get to-day, and be ready to-morrow to call it falsehood. Ptolemaic astronomy, euclidean space, aristotelian logic, scholastic metaphysics, were expedient for centuries, but human experience has boiled over those limits, and we now call these things only relatively true, or true within those borders of experience. "Absolutely" they are false; for we know that those limits were casual, and might have been transcended by past theorists just as they are by present thinkers (p. 222).

A Danish thinker has remarked that we live forward but understand backward. Pragmatism reminds us that not only our scientific ideas but quite literally all our ideas may in the future become as untrue as Ptolemy's doctrine that the sun revolves around the earth and that our small planet is the center of the universe.

In a chapter on "Pragmatism and Humanism" James shows how much he and F. C. S. Schiller, the British humanist, agree. The term gives a useful emphasis to James's contention that *all truths* are man-made, and hence finite, imperfect, anthropomorphically biased. In our courts interpretations of our laws change as the social environment changes. In fact, any language if still spoken, a "living" language, changes in form, meaning, and pronunciation. "Mr. Schiller applied the analogy [of laws and language] to beliefs, and proposes the name 'Humanism' for the doctrine that to an unascertainable extent our truths are man-made products too. Human motives sharpen all our questions, human satisfactions lurk in all our answers, all our formulas have a human twist" (p. 242).

This doctrine, both for James and Schiller, also implies a philosophical conception of reality as pluralistic. The only *reality* we can ever experience comes to us through the flux of our sensations. They simply come to us, and we have little control over their coming, but we have, James says, "a certain freedom in our dealing with them . . . but *which* we attend to, note, and make emphatic in our conclusions depends on our own interests; and, according as we lay the emphasis here or there, quite different formulations of truth result. . . . We receive in short the block of marble, but we carve the statue ourselves" (pp. 246–247).

Thus, "We *add,* both to the subject and to the predicate part of reality. The world stands really malleable, waiting to receive its final touches at our hands. Like the kingdom of heaven, it suffers human violence willingly. Man *engenders* truths upon it." The great difference between the rationalist and pragmatist is, finally, *"that for rationalism reality is ready-made and complete from all eternity, while for pragmatism it is still in the making, and awaits part of its complexion from the future.* On the one side the universe is absolutely secure, on the other it is still pursuing its adventures" (p. 257).

James called his *Pragmatism* "a philosophy with *no* humbug in it . . . ," [3] and the phrase is both typical and significant, typical of his untechnical, pungent, informal literary style, and significant of his desire to live without pretense. It takes courage, integrity, a sense of humor, and a youthful spirit to live in a universe in which nothing is certain except change and pragmatic adaptation to it, but James's prose, sparkling and crackling with the novelty and surprise of his kinetic imagery and supple idiom, conveys the excitement of living in a world which is, James assures us, "really malleable, waiting to receive its final touches at our hands."

Yet in spite of James's belief in a pluralistic universe and man-made truths, he grants in his final chapter that there may be a reality unknown to human senses—not only may be but probably is. Therefore, he does not scorn hypotheses about God or a spiritual world, and if they give comfort or courage to human beings he does not object to them as hypotheses, but cautions that no one hypothesis about God is pragmatically useful to all men. "I firmly disbelieve, myself," he confesses, "that our human experience is the highest form of experience extant in the universe." However, this is frankly an "overbelief," held to satisfy an inner need. All that Pragmatism insists upon is that no one has a right to dogmatize on an overbelief. Let him make use of it, but let every man remain free to choose his own overbeliefs. For this tolerance James was accused of sanctioning wishful thinking and confusing it with "truth," but of course he intended that even an overbelief must be subjected to the same pragmatic tests which he had advocated for all truths.

The pragmatic theory of truth no longer stirs up heated argument; not that everyone accepts it, but the conception of truth as relative, as an hypothesis to be tested by experience, is at least not shocking today as it was half a century ago. Yet the theory is just as pertinent as it was at the beginning of this century. In spite of the fact that Americans are famous the world over as pragmatists, they still show a tendency to rationalize the larger issues in religion or government such as foreign policy or economics, rather than adopt hypotheses which they can test, modify, and reshape to fit changing political, social, or economic reality. Nor are Americans unique in this inherited way of thinking and acting. If they are inclined to think of communism as an absolute evil, and have difficulty in distinguishing varieties of socialism, so also do the adherents of Marxist "truths." Many nations, in fact, still interpret American capitalism in terms of its nineteenth-century reality. Application of James's pragmatic approach to truth could bring about much greater understanding and tolerance between nations, making it possible to compromise their differences and ease tensions. Perhaps there has never been a time in human history when Pragmatism, William James's "new name for some old ways of thinking," was so much needed as now.

Notes

1. Heinrich Straumann, *American Literature in the Twentieth Century* (3rd rev. ed.; New York, 1965), p. 1.

2. William James, *Pragmatism, A New Name for Some Old Ways of Thinking: Popular Lectures on Philosophy* (New York, 1907). Throughout the chapter page numbers are given in parentheses after each quotation.

3. William James to Théodore Flournoy, March 26, 1907, *The Letters of William James and Théodore Flournoy,* ed. Robert C. Le Clair (Madison, Wisconsin, 1966), p. 187.

22 THE EDUCATION OF HENRY ADAMS

Allen Guttmann

In the *Edinburgh Review* for October 1840 John Stuart Mill published a lengthy analysis of the second volume of the English translation of Alexis de Tocqueville's classic study, *Democracy in America.* Mill discussed the optimistic bent of most Americans, their tendency to believe in progress, to assume that change is synonymous with improvement. Mill's explanation for this faith in progress pointed to ideal and material factors. He wrote,

> Respect for old opinions must diminish wherever science and knowledge are rapidly progressive. As the people in general become aware of the recent date of the most important physical discoveries, they are liable to form a rather contemptuous opinion of their ancestors. The mere visible fruits of scientific progress in a wealthy society, the mechanical improvements, the steam-engines, the railroads, carry the feeling of admiration for modern and disrespect for ancient times, down even to the wholly uneducated classes.

In short, there was in America a widespread assumption that technological innovations are evidence of moral and political progress. It was an easy assumption, one that Darwin's theory of evolution seemed to support. It was an assumption that Henry Adams struggled to refute.

His autobiography, *The Education of Henry Adams,* turns backward to a time that was, if not golden, at least better than the Gilded Age in which he lived. He looked at the corruption of the United States in the 1870's and wrote, with Olympian disgust, "The progress of evolution from President Washington to President Grant, was alone enough to upset Darwin." Because of his contempt for what most Americans meant by "success," he was proud to call himself a failure.

He was sly as well as proud. His detractors have always been quick to point to the contrast between his career and the careers of his father, his grandfather, and his great-grandfather, but Adams anticipated his critics. He made that very contrast one of the themes of his autobiography. He tells us, in the first chapter of *The Education,* that he sat, when attending church as a child, directly behind his grandfather, John Quincy Adams, sixth President of the United States, and directly beneath a tablet in memory of his great-grandfather, John Adams, second President of the United States. The church was a fixed point in his early life; his own eventual succession to the presidency was another. As he tells it, in the third person, "The Irish gardener once said to the child, 'You'll be thinkin' you'll be President too!' The casualty of the remark made so strong an impression on his mind," Adams continues, "that he never forgot it. He could not remember ever to have thought on the subject; to him, that there should be a doubt of his being President was a new idea. What had been would continue to be."

Like any child, he assumed *his* situation was quite ordinary. Presidential grandparents can be taken for granted. Looking back, in old age, he realized how extraordinary his own childhood had been. The first paragraph of *The Education* sets the scene with characteristic artfulness. Place seems prior to time, and time takes precedence over individual identity. The book begins, "Under the shadow of Boston State House, turning its back on the house of John Hancock, the little passage called Hancock Avenue runs, or ran, from Beacon Street, skirting the State House grounds, to Mount Vernon Street, on the summit of Beacon Hill; and there, in the third house below Mount Vernon Place, February 16, 1838, a child was born, and christened later by his uncle, the minister of the First Church after the tenets of Boston Unitarianism, as Henry Brooks Adams." He goes on to discuss associations, which he calls both "colonial" and "troglodytic," and to pair his birth with that of a hypothetical Israel Cohen, "born in Jerusalem under the shadow of the Temple and circumcised in the Synagogue by his uncle the high priest. . . ."

Boston is, however, part of a slightly larger context. In the summer, young Henry Adams lived with his grandparents in nearby Quincy. The first two chapters of *The Education* turn upon the antithesis of Boston and Quincy. The places symbolized concerns that ran the length of Adams' life. "Town," he wrote, "was winter confinement, school, rule, discipline. . . . Town was restraint, law, unity. Country, only seven miles away, was liberty, diversity, outlawry, the endless delight of mere sense impressions given by nature for nothing, and breathed by boys without knowing it. . . . Summer was the multiplicity of nature; winter was school." Unity and multiplicity—the terms are central to his thought.

Although town and country were different places associated with different seasons, they were part of a greater unity of time. As he perceived Boston and Quincy, both were part of the eighteenth century. Then, with dramatic suddenness, came the technological facts that John Stuart Mill rightly pointed to. On the third page of his book Adams repeats the word "troglodytic" and sounds the theme of alienation:

> He and his eighteenth-century troglodytic Boston were suddenly cut apart—separated forever—in act if not in sentiment—by the opening of the Boston and Albany Railroad; the appearance of the first Cunard steamers in the bay; and the telegraphic messages which carried from Baltimore to Washington the news that Henry Clay and James K. Polk were nominated for the Presidency. This was in May, 1844; he was six years old; his new world was ready for use, and only fragments of the old met his eyes.

Nurtured in the eighteenth century, he faced the nineteenth. As he repeatedly asserts in his autobiography, his education had been amiss. Not for thirty years, however, not until the administration of Ulysses S. Grant, was he to realize the extent of his estrangement from the general tenor of American life.

In 1844, he was too young to understand the significance of the industrial age. In 1850, when his father, Charles Francis Adams, took him to Washington, he had his first glimpses of political corruption, his first awareness that Bostonians had not, in his phrase, "solved the universe." The compromises over slavery disturbed him. More disturbing still was the fact that slavery seemed inseparable from American history. George Washington himself had owned Negro slaves. The road to Mount Vernon, which Adams visited, was poor and to a New Englander poor roads meant poor morals. "Slavery," he writes, "was wicked, and slavery was the cause of this road's badness. . . . and yet, at the end of the road and product of the crime stood Mount Vernon and George Washington. . . . [He] never thought to ask himself or his father how to deal with the moral problem that deduced George Washington from the sum of all wickedness."

The purpose of eduation is, after all, to answer just such questions as young Henry Adams asked, but his education provided no answers. He went to Harvard College in 1854 and to Berlin in 1858. Ironically, he learned the most when least a student, when, for instance, he sat in a beer garden in Berlin and listened to the music of Beethoven, and realized how deprived he had been of sensual experience.

In Italy, in 1859, Adams discovered more paradoxes, more data incompatible with the dogma of progress. "Rome could not be fitted into an orderly, middle-class, Bostonian, systematic scheme of evolution. No law of progress applied to it. Not even time sequences—the last refuge of helpless historians—had value for it. The Forum no more led to the Vatican than the Vatican to the Forum." Adams quotes Edward Gibbon, who tells us in *his* autobiography of the moment when, sitting on the steps of a Roman church and listening to vespers, he determined to write a history of the decline and fall of the Roman empire. But no such inspiration came to Adams.

He returned, briefly, to America, to events which seemed to threaten the decline and fall of the United States. Abraham Lincoln had been elected to the presidency; the South was about to secede from the Union. Lincoln selected Charles Francis Adams, Henry's father, as minister to England. Henry accompanied his father to London, as his private secretary. Chapters Eight through Fifteen of the autobiography are largely devoted to the diplomatic efforts of the father and the social and intellectual adventures of the son. It is best to admit that they are, with one exception, the least satisfactory chapters of *The Education.*

The exception is Chapter Fifteen, entitled "Darwinism." In this chapter, Adams introduces one of his most important symbols, the fish *pteraspis,* a cousin, Adams tells us, of the sturgeon. Looking for an approach to the doctrines of Darwin, Adams had taken up the study of geology under Sir Charles Lyell. With typical irony, Adams indicates the contemporary view of evolution: "Unbroken Evolution under uniform conditions pleased every-one—except curates and bishops; it was the very best substitute for religion; a safe, conservative, practical, thoroughly Common-Law deity." Evolution was a pleasant doctrine but one with intellectual difficulties. Adams soon discovered forms, like *terebratula,* which had not changed throughout the whole span of geological time. *Pteraspis* was still more of a puzzle. It was the first vertebrate and before it was, in a phrase that Adams surely intends to have Biblical overtones, the "eternal void." Like the children who are told that God made the world, and who then ask who made God, Adams learns that man evolved from *pteraspis.* But no one can tell him where *pteraspis* came from. That twentieth-century biology can provide answers is beside the point. Adams seized his symbols and employed them to argue that, in his words, "Evolution . . . did not evolve; Uniformity . . . was not uniform; and Selection . . . did not select." *Pteraspis* and *terebratula* reappear in subsequent chapters, to haunt Adams with their presence, to provide him with metaphors.

The Adams family returned to the United States in 1868. The nation had changed and Adams was bewildered. He chose an exotic metaphor to describe his family's bewilderment. "Had they been Tyrian traders of the year B.C. 1000, landing from a galley fresh from Gibraltar, they could hardly have been stranger on the shore of a world, so changed from what it had been ten years before." The nation which John Adams had helped to found was now in the hands of Robber Barons, industrialists who looted a continent with barbaric enthusiasm. The nation was mortgaged to the railroads. Congress was hopelessly corrupt. When Adams asked a cabinet officer to be patient with Congress, the officer shouted, "You can't use tact with a Congressman! A Congressman is a hog! You must take a stick and hit him on the snout!" And Ulysses S. Grant was President. Adams pondered the mysteries of this fact: "America had no use for Adams because he was eighteenth-century, and yet it worshipped Grant because he was archaic and should have lived in a cave and worn skins." In the face of evidence like Ulysses S. Grant, the theory of evolution was ludicrous.

In 1870, bewilderment and frustration turned to anguish. His brother-in-law summoned him by telegram to Italy, where his sister Louisa was dying of tetanus. Outside her room was the softness of an Italian summer. Inside was horror. "The last lesson," writes Adams, "the sum and term of education—began then. He had passed through thirty years of rather varied experience without having once felt the shell of custom broken. He had never seen Nature—only her surface—the sugar-coating that she shows to youth. Flung suddenly in his face, with the harsh brutality of chance, the terror of the blow stayed by him henceforth for life, until repetition made it more than the will could struggle with; more than he could call on himself to bear." He saw nature now as "a chaos of anarchic and purposeless forces." Later in the autobiography he summed up the lesson in his most famous epigram: "Chaos was the law of Nature; Order was the dream of Man."

The rest of the book describes his quest for that dream. He became a historian. He taught briefly at Harvard and published a number of books in American history, the most important of which was his nine-volume *History of the United States during the Administrations of Thomas Jefferson and James Madison.* The history was an ironic meditation on national failure. Adams saw Jefferson as the archetypal liberal, the believer in progress, the man whose intent was to institutionalize his faith in reason. Madison, equally a figure of the Enlightenment, was Jefferson's disciple as well as his successor in the White House. They meant well and all their plans went awry. The war with England that they endeavored to avoid broke out despite them. The city of Washington was burned by the British, and the ruined capitol seemed, to Adams, a fit symbol for the fate of naive aspiration. In this and in other works Adams proved that he possessed a historical imagination of the highest order, but the autobiography, written to dramatize its author's failures, scarcely mentions his scholarly achievements.

The quest for order led him to Chicago's Columbian Exposition, in 1893, where he found only "breach of continuity—a rupture in historical sequence." At that exposition Frederick Jackson Turner read a paper which set forth his thesis on the importance of the frontier in American history, but Adams was more impressed by technological changes, by the energies unleashed by industrial capitalism. *The Education* chronicles the rise to political power of his friends, John Hay and Theodore Roosevelt, but the *political* decisions of the day struck Adams as inconsequential when set against the changes in technology and in scientific theory. He began to study mathematics and physics. In the theoretical physics of Karl Pearson he found confirmation of his own sense of chaos. He quotes Pearson: "Order and reason, beauty and benevolence, are characteristics and conceptions which we find solely associated with the mind of man." Adams took the work of Pearson to mean that the scientist imposes order upon the whirl of atoms. He set about with renewed determination to emulate the physicist, to impose an order on the apparently chaotic facts of history.

In Paris, at the Great Exposition of 1900, he found another pair of symbols, the Virgin and the Dynamo. In his own words, "to Adams the dynamo became a symbol of infinity. As he grew accustomed to the great gallery of machines, he began to feel the forty-foot dynamos as a moral force, much as the early Christians felt the Cross." Beyond the dynamo lay the mysteries of radiation, so that Adams could speak of himself, figuratively, as lying on the floor of the Gallery of Machines, "his historical neck broken by the sudden irruption of forces totally new."

Against these new forces Adams set the symbol of the Virgin. The Virgin, Mary of Nazareth, represented the force of love. "Symbol or energy," he comments, "the Virgin had acted as the greatest force the Western world ever felt, and had drawn man's activities to herself more strongly than any other power, natural or supernatural, had ever done." But how had this force given way to the forces symbolized by the dynamo? To answer that question, Adams studied the era when the Virgin was preeminent in men's minds, the century that stretched from 1150 to 1250 A.D. This was the moment from which he might "measure motion down to his own time." Writing of this period in his life, he says, "Setting himself to the task, he began a volume which he mentally knew as 'Mont-Saint-Michel and Chartres; a Study of Thirteenth-Century Unity.' From that point he proposed to fix a position for himself, which he could label: 'The Education of Henry Adams: a Study in Twentieth-Century Multiplicity.' With the help of these two points of relation, he hoped to project his lines forward and backward indefinitely, subject to correction from any one who should know better." In other words, he established his coordinates and began to plot his graph.

He studied Newton and Leibnitz and attempted to work out a calculus of historical forces to parallel their mathematical descriptions of velocity and acceleration. In the autobiography, and in other essays as well, he traced the curve of historical change and asserted that the movement from unity into multiplicity, from 1200 to 1900, was so rapid in acceleration that another generation might require what he called "a new social mind." Anticipating the consequences of the discovery of nuclear energy, he saw—once again—change rather than progress, the threat of cataclysm rather than the promise of utopia. He made no predictions about the final outcome of historical development, and he allowed himself to hope that the future might contain, in his words, "a world that sensitive and timid natures could regard without a shudder." But hope seems as out of place in *The Education* as in Pandora's box.

We must, however, be careful not to take his predictions more seriously than he himself did. For all his use of scientific theories, he remained essentially an artist, perhaps even a romantic one. The dynamic theory of history which he propounded was, after all, one of many possible theories. The important point is that he had utilized it to create his own order out of the chaos around him. In *The Education* he wrote, "Every man with self-respect enough to become effective, if only as a machine, has had to account to himself for himself somehow, and to invent a formula of his own for his universe, if the standard formulas failed." In his own metaphor, his theory was no absolute truth; it was merely "a spool on which to wind the thread of history without breaking it." The thread, by which Adams meant the historical data, was real enough, but the spool was made to order and the design he wove was uniquely his. Adams asserts that "any schoolboy could work out the problem if he were given the right to state it in his own terms," but this is but another example of his irony.

We are, therefore, fairly warned. *The Education of Henry Adams* is an eccentric book because it is the order that a strange and wonderful man made out of his own life and times. It leaves out a great deal, as Ernest Samuels has shown us in the three volumes of his biography of Henry Adams. To seize upon a single example, we learn from Samuels that the allegorical statue of Grief which Adams described in *The Education* had a significance far beyond that given it in the autobiography. Adams refers to the bronze figure by Augustus St. Gaudens and dwells on the various people who came to Rock Creek Cemetery to wonder what the statue meant. He deliberately fails to state that it was a memorial to his wife, who committed suicide in 1885, shortly after the death of her father. We know, from letters and other documents, that this loss was as tragic as that of Adams' sister, and yet he chose to omit any mention of it from his autobiography.

There is no reason to be surprised or disappointed by this or other omissions. What we have in any autobiography is a work of art based on a man's life. Henry Adams was as sensitive and intelligent a man as his presidential ancestors. If his life was, nonetheless, a failure, his autobiography—his work of art—is not. Fifty years after his death it seems all to prophetic.

23
H. L. MENCKEN:
THE AMERICAN LANGUAGE

Raven I. McDavid, Jr.

For half a century H. L. Mencken's *The American Language* has delighted and instructed those who are interested in the history, the vitality, and the abundant variety of American English. Beginning in 1919 as a modest work of some three hundred pages, it grew to nearly seven hundred by the fourth edition of 1936; each of its two supplements, of 1945 and 1948, was still larger. The abridgment of 1961 is a drastic reduction of the bulk of material the author left behind, but it still comes to seven hundred seventy-seven pages, and that without prefatory matter, the list of words and phrases, or the general index. As *particeps criminis* in this latest version I can point to a second ulcer as evidence of the grinding toil and the agonizing choices experienced by an editor of an enduring work of art that aims at presenting the linguistic experience of an energetic, sometimes wise, and almost always amusing people.

It is true of *The American Language,* as of many other great books, that it is often misrepresented by those who know it only at secondhand. As late as the fall of 1967 an observer in *The New York Times Book Review* referred patronizingly to Mencken's erroneous belief that American and British English were drifting apart so rapidly that they would soon become mutually unintelligible languages. True, Mencken suggested this possibility in the first edition and in its successors of 1921 and 1923; but by 1936, in the Preface to the fourth edition, he had observed that the pressure of events was inexorably bringing the English-speaking peoples ever closer together, so that differences in language, as in other forms of behavior, could be expected to diminish in intensity. What is even more amusing is that many of those who denigrate Mencken's 1919 statement on the growing mutual unintelligibility of "English" and "American" fail to recognize that it was at least partially derived from a well-known lecture by Mark Twain, whom Mencken regarded as one of the greatest of American writers.

Misinterpreted or not, *The American Language* is still read and enjoyed, often to the despair of the stuffy literary professoriat that dominate university departments of English. Given to the self-fulfilling prophecy that no student of English will take any more work in language than he is compelled to, and to the disparagement of mechanistic science and of the writing of social scientists, the literary lamas cannot conceive that a sound and serious book on language could be written well enough to attract a popular audience.

Yet this has happened. The first edition, of fifteen hundred copies, was sold out almost overnight; the fourth edition and the two supplements have been reprinted several times, and the new abridged version has had steady sales since its appearance. The early versions attracted to linguistics such scholars as Einar Haugen, the preeminent authority on bilingualism and linguistic borrowing, and David Maurer, the indefatigable student of the language and the other behavior of the American criminal subcultures. In 1945 the late A. G. Kennedy noted that there had been more studies of American English published since the first edition of *The American Language* than in the three preceding centuries; the bulk of such studies has probably trebled in the past quarter-century. Furthermore, much of the new scholarship of significance is markedly indebted to Mencken for either the original suggestion, serious encouragement, or financial assistance; a partial list includes the American Name Society, the journal *American Speech,* the Linguistic Atlas project, Mitford Mathews's *Dictionary of Americanisms,* George R. Stewart's *Names on the Land,* Frederic G. Cassidy's *Dictionary of American Regional English,* Allen Walker Read's *The English of England: A Dictionary of Briticisms,* and the recent intense interest in social dialects, aimed at providing more effective programs for teaching English in the schools.

The reasons for this paradoxical influence are relatively simple. First, Mencken had an inexhaustible delight in the antics of *homo boobensis Americanensis*. Second, he tried to keep up with research in the field; not only did he read widely himself and belong to most relevant professional organizations, but he often found his perspective corrected and enlarged by his readers, and his mass of data from lay sources was heavily augmented by the vacuum-cleaner operations of a clipping service. And finally, Mencken's habit of wide reading and his decades of experience in meeting newspaper deadlines developed in him a clear and astringent style which titillated even those who did not agree with his point of view. As a matter of fact—and this has been noted by almost everyone familiar with Mencken—these qualities, of gusto and knowledge and astringent style, distinguish Mencken's writing on all subjects. The delights in the language as a mirror of the activities of the people who use it, and the ability to turn a pungent and irreverent phrase when occasion called for it, make *The American Language* a far better written book than any of the revelations of the structuralists, transformationalists, stratificationalists, or other competing sects—in the same way that Mencken's comments on Veblen and Dreiser are far more perceptive than the prissy pontifications of the major prophets of present-day literary criticism.[1]

The organization of *The American Language* varies a little from one edition to another; even in the abridgment of 1963 there have been several minor changes. There has been a steady increase in the amount of scholarly apparatus, as both scholars and laymen paid increasing attention to the ways in which Americans use their language. By the 1936 edition there were so many footnotes to so many sources of various kinds that Mencken abandoned the formal bibliography of the earlier versions. The survey of non-English immigrant dialects in the United States, with indications of the effects of English on these languages, was omitted beginning with the 1948 supplement. On the other hand, the number of references to such projects as the *Dictionary of American English* and the Linguistic Atlas grew as more evidence from these enterprises became available.

But the basic structure of the book has remained more or less the same, especially since 1936. The first two chapters are a sort of prologue. "The Two Streams of English" deals with the earliest attention to peculiarities of American usage (it seems strange today that the inoffensive *bluff,* denoting a feature of the terrain, should have been the first word assailed as an American barbarism, in 1735, by one Francis Moore, an early settler of Georgia); the history of British objections to American linguistic practices and of American reactions to such criticisms; and the struggle for the acceptance of these usages among American men of letters, the learned professions, politicians, and scholars of other nations. "The Materials of Inquiry" examines the essential characteristics of American innovations and analyzes the various ways in which observers have tried to define and classify Americanisms; it is not surprising that no two observers agree in detail. Then come three historical summaries: "The Beginnings of American" (the colonial period), "The Period of Growth" (The Revolution to the Civil War), and "The Language Today." In each of these chapters there is an overview, delightfully irreverent, of the country and its people during this period, with examples of loan words, changes of meaning, new derivatives and compounds, and outright coinages. The sixth chapter, "American and English," describes the present-day intermingling of the two varieties of the language and compares usage, both in general and in such particular semantic fields as honorifics, euphemisms, taboo words, and profanity. Then come three chapters on structural aspects of the language—pronunciation, spelling, and grammar (this last provocatively labeled "The Common Speech" and designated as The Vulgate). There are two long, discursive, and entertaining chapters on "Proper Names in America" and "American Slang," and a brief coda on "The Future of the Language."

Within this framework there have been numerous changes, in response to the increasing knowledge of the last half-century. In the earliest editions the ubiquitous *O.K.* was described as of uncertain lineage, with some attention to Woodrow Wilson's private theory of a Choctaw derivation. In the 1945 supplement Mencken retained the discussion of the more or less fantastic hypotheses of its origin, but accepted the more plausible suggestion of Allen Walker Read that it sprang into popular view as a Democratic war cry in the 1840 presidential campaign, being an abbreviation for *Old Kinderhook,* a nickname for the incumbent

President, Martin Van Buren. In 1963, thanks to further research by Read (and a private feud with Woodford Heflin of the *Dictionary of American English*), it was traced, and it now seems definitively, to a vogue for alphabetical slang in the Boston newspapers of 1838. Similarly, the early lists of principal parts of verbs in the American Vulgate—lists derived partly from popular fiction, partly from imagination—were replaced in 1963 by evidence from the field records of the Linguistic Atlas, as surveyed by Virginia McDavid and the late E. Bagby Atwood. Without losing any of its sparkle or other value as entertainment, the chapter on slang has become an impressively documented comment on American society, thanks to such investigations as David Maurer's of the criminal professions. The status of Canadian English and American social dialects, especially the dialects of Negro Americans, is more clearly and accurately presented, in the light of the findings of Walter S. Avis and Lorenzo Turner.

This summary, of course, gives only a dim adumbration of the riches in *The American Language*. Not a section lacks its entertaining digressions: on the origin of the American institution of the Christmas tree (almost certainly introduced by colonists of German ancestry); on the fantastic suggestions for the etymology of Yankee (probably from *Jan Kees,* a diminutive of *Jan Cornelius,* used among the Dutch as *John Doe* or *Richard Roe* is used in the United States, to designate a male of indefinite identity); on the putative origins of the inevitable *cocktail* (likely in New Orleans, from the French *coquetier,* "egg cup") with formulae for various interesting if sometimes lethal decoctions; on the history of the verb *to goose;* on the reception of Mencken's coinage *ecdysiast* to denote a strip-tease artist (a profession facing obsolescence with the introduction of the bikini and the topless gown and the unchecked rise of the miniskirt); on the proliferation of titles in an allegedly democratic society; and on the gaudy extravagance of the mortical profession (anticipating Jessica Mitford's *The American Way of Death*). There are hundreds of indications of Mencken's literary and social attitudes: his enthusiasm for the vigor of Mark Twain and Ring Lardner, his disdain for the thin-bloodedness of Fenimore Cooper and Henry James, his contempt for the pretensions of literary critics and schools of education, his amusement at the perennial antics of American politicians of whatever party or faction (and in his accumulated wisdom as a veteran political reporter, he was properly most suspicious of the eager reformer and the man of self-assertive virtue).

Nor should one overlook the footnotes. These are not merely generous acknowledgments of the contributions of professional scholars and amateur observers (many of whom went on to serious investigations of their own, thanks to Mencken's recognition and encouragement), but in their own right perhaps the most enjoyable reading of their kind since the footnotes in Gibbon's *Decline and Fall of the Roman Empire* or Sir Richard Burton's translation of the *Arabian Nights*. Typical is one following his comment on the proliferation of American verbs in *-ize:*

> I had hardly got this paragraph on paper when someone sent me a copy of the *Literary Supplement* of the London *Times* for June 7, 1934, with the ghastly verb *to obituarize* marked with a red circle. Worse, I discovered that it was in the OED, credited to the London *Saturday Review* for Oct. 17, 1891. If I may intrude my private feelings into a learned work I venture to add that seeing a monster so suggestive of American barbarism in the *Times* affected me like seeing an archbishop wink at a loose woman (p. 243).

In the same spirit is the comment on early southern reactions to *jazz* as a kind of music: "According to Raven I. McDavid, Sr., of Greenville, S.C., the announcement, in 1919, of the first jazz band to play in Columbia [the state capital], where he was then serving in the state legislature, inspired feelings of terror among the local Baptists, such as might have been aroused by a personal appearance of Yahweh. Until that time *jazz* had never been heard in the Palmetto State except as a verb meaning to copulate" (p. 743).

With linguistics only now beginning to assume full-blown academic respectability, many of the more caste-conscious brethren tend to disparage what they consider Mencken's amateurishness, and to deplore his lack of interest in systematic phonology and explicit grammatical theory. But as one who tried hard to help present a systematic account of American pronunciation, only to be spattered with transformational billingsgate, I remain unimpressed with any approach to language, the most characteristic human activity, that considers data orientation a dirty word. To the person who feels that the greatest significance of American English is the way in which it mirrors the social and cultural experience of the American people, the elegant Cartesianism of the Lower Charles is as trivial and sterile as the scholasticism of Duns Scotus to the cattle breeder. Granted that the making of theoretical models has its place, it is no substitute for the painstaking examination of ways living people have actually spoken and written to other living people, in a variety of situations and with a variety of purposes and results. By shunning commitment to any single theoretical approach, Mencken saved his work from becoming dated when, as inevitably happens, one revelation gives way to another. He was well aware that the taste of the American public, including that of the scholarly professions, is transient and volatile:

> The American is not, of course, lacking in a capacity for discipline; he submits to leadership readily, and even to tyranny. But, curiously, it is not the leadership that is old and decorous that commonly fetches him, but the leadership that is new and extravagant [—even when, as in the demagogue-infested South, it purports to defend tradition]. He will resist dictation out of the past, but he will follow a new messiah with almost Russian willingness, and into the wildest vagaries of economics, religion, morals and speech. A new fallacy in politics spreads faster in the United States than anywhere else on earth, and so does a new revelation of God, or a new shibboleth, or metaphor, or piece of slang (p. 99).

Actually, Mencken's grasp of linguistics was far from elementary. He was particularly knowledgeable about the historical branch of the science; his summary of the history of noun inflection is as terse and elegant as anything professional scholars have written: "The primordial Indo-European language had eight cases of the noun; in Old English they fell to four, with a moribund instrumental, largely identical with the dative, hanging in the air; in Middle English the dative and accusative began to decay; in Modern English the dative and accusative have disappeared altogether, save as ghosts to haunt grammarians" (p. 526). One is tempted to speculate on the way Mencken might have reacted to the events of the twenty years since his first stroke made him cease writing. He would certainly have acid words for the Veblenian waste of television, superhighways, and jet travel to nowhere. For the efflorescent bureaucracy, from Pentagon protocol to the vested interest of welfare workers in perpetuating the dependency of their clients, he would have had few kind words. He would probably have shown wry amusement at the new militancy of some ethnic groups; having noted the past reluctance of middle-class Negroes to confess a liking for watermelon or fried chicken, he would not have missed the complaint of black militants at Northwestern University that the dining halls failed to serve such "soul food" as chittlings, collard greens, or sweet potatoes.

Having documented the past insistence on *Negro* /nigro/ instead of other designations, he would observe sardonically that this term is now considered derogatory, and that *black,* once the most despised of all epithets, is now proudly acclaimed—at least by the self-appointed fuglemen and haruspices of the group. No friend of the professional do-gooders, but a nineteenth-century liberal with a firm belief in the rights of law-abiding citizens to be unmolested by hoodlums, he would be less than sympathetic with recent court decisions that hamper the police, and he would probably complain that the relaxation of restrictions on pornography and obscenity have not only afflicted the reader with a good deal of tedious tenth-rate writing, but have taken a good deal of the fun out of life. He would have had one of his finest hours in the banality of the Eisenhower sultanate, with Eisenhese as splendidly vulnerable to parody as the Gamalielese of the earlier guide to normalcy, Warren G. Harding.

In short, he would find no dearth of antics and affectations to portray, along with the more sober phenomena of American life. He would have had a field day with the reception of the *Merriam Webster's Third New International Dictionary;* he would have given as short shrift to the inept company publicity as to the inane belletristic pietism of such pundits-at-large as Wilson Follett, Dwight MacDonald, and Jacques Barzun—to say nothing of the drearily repetitive assaults by newspaper columnists and literary critics too ignorant of the history of lexicography to know what dictionaries are designed to do, and too lazy to examine the *Third* for themselves. I can imagine him chuckling over the fact that most of the adverse criticisms were directly based on the company handout and that the writers for the *Atlantic* showed less knowledge of dictionary-making than their predecessors of 1890.

He would have stern reproof for "intellectuals," like our college New Leftists, who abandon the use of their intellect, refuse to examine the evidence, and squawk monotonously the parroted slogans of their self-styled leaders; he would show equal scorn for the "humanists" who sneer at those disciplines like anthropology and sociology that are concerned with the activities of human beings, and for the precious aesthetes who swarm into graduate departments of literature and turn their backs on the language problems of the public schools. And he would present his case so well that he would subvert even some of the most pious among the literary gentry into appreciating the richness of the ways in which Americans develop new uses of their language.[2] As he once said to me, "The whole purpose of the infernal labor was to convince 200% Americans that the study of the national tongue could be interesting—and more than interesting, important." He succeeded so well in what he attempted that *The American Language* is justly appraised as the work by which Mencken will be longest remembered.

Notes

1. "Among humanistic technicians, the jargon of the social scientist is a favorite straw man for verbal clobbering, but the literary critics —New, Aristotelian, and Freudulent—are at least as good at obfuscation. American linguists also have an elaborate trade jargon. Much of its complexity comes from their practice, like that of their prototype, Leonard Bloomfield, of insisting on rigorous scientific method and precise terminology; but some of it simply comes from bad writing and probably muddled thinking" (pp. 336–337). References are to pages of the 1963 one-volume abridgment.

2. And in whatever Valhalla he now graces, he must be uproarious on learning that the editor of the 1963 abridgment has been rewarded with an honorary degree from an institution supported by the Southern Baptists.

24 CHARLES IVES:
ESSAYS BEFORE A SONATA

Alfred V. Frankenstein

There is a great Man living in this country—a composer.
He has solved the problem how to preserve one's self and to learn.
He responds to negligence by contempt.
He is not forced to accept praise or blame.
His name is Ives.

These lines are famous now and have appeared as epigraph on many a record jacket and concert program of recent years. But *only* of recent years. They are a private jotting of the composer Arnold Schoenberg, and they were found among his papers after his death. During his lifetime, which coincided almost precisely with that of Ives himself, Schoenberg said nothing about his American colleague, nor did anyone else during that period, except at its very end.

The history of Ives's third symphony is a microcosm of his career: Begun in 1901, finished in 1904, first performed in 1946, awarded the Pulitzer Prize in 1947, published in 1948, recorded in 1950. The Pulitzer Prize seldom goes to works in any medium forty-three years after they have been completed, but Ives has been getting the equivalent of the Pulitzer Prize and all other prizes imaginable in wildly heaping measure since that time, and especially since his death in 1954.

I can remember the day when Nicolas Slonimsky presented, in the most gingerly and cautious fashion, "The Housatonic at Stockbridge," from Ives's *Three Places in New England;* that was the first performance of any orchestral work by this composer in New York; it was thirty years ago and the piece was then thirty years old, but Ives had such a frightening reputation as a musical wild man that even so daring and iconoclastic a conductor as Slonimsky attempted only one of the three movements in the suite and hedged it about with all manner of apology. Today practically all the music of Ives is recorded. Most of his major works have been recorded several times, and the issuance of large boxes of Ives records, containing all four of his symphonies, all of his piano music, all of his short orchestral pieces, and so on, is a commonplace.

When Schoenberg said Ives had "solved the problem how to preserve one's self and to learn," he referred, of course, to the fact that Ives retired from the ratrace of musical professionalism almost before he got into it, went into the insurance business, built up an agency which was the largest in the world at the time of his death, and composed in private—one is tempted to say in secret—for about twenty years. He ceased to compose around 1918, although he lived another thirty-six years. All his literary activity, including his book called *Essays Before a Sonata*, took place after he had given up the creation of music.

Why Ives stopped composing is one of the great psychological mysteries of the twentieth century. No one has the answer, but in the twenty years of his activity he wrote as much as any full-time composer could be expected to write—and he was a weekend composer with a huge, growing business on his hands. He made very little effort to put his music forward and, indeed, repeatedly placed obstacles in the way of those who took an interest in it. But his second piano sonata is one of the very few things of his own that he did put forward, and with it he put out the essays which are the springboard for this discussion.

The second of Ives's two numbered piano sonatas bears a title: "Concord, Massachusetts, 1840–1860." Each of its four movements has a title of its own: "Emerson," "Hawthorne," "The Alcotts," and "Thoreau." The music was written between 1909 and 1915; both the sonata and the essays—a slim book filling a hundred pages in the collected edition of Ives's prose—were published, at the composer's expense, in 1920.

For a composer to accompany a sonata with a series of essays is, to say the least, unusual, but the reason for it comes clear when one compares the notes which Ives jotted on the manuscript of his first piano sonata with the book he wrote to go with the second. Concerning the first sonata, completed in 1909, Ives inscribed on the manuscript itself:

> What is it all about—Dan S asks. Mostly about the outdoor life in Conn. villages in '80s and 90s. Impressions, Remembrances & Reflections, of Country Farmers in Conn Farmland. On pg 14 Fred's Daddy got so excited that he shouted when Fred hit a Home Run & the school won the baseball game but Aunt Sarah was always humming— Where is my wandering Boy—after Fred and John left for a job in Bridgeport—there was usually a sadness—but not at the Barn Dances with its jigs, foot jumping and reels mostly on winter nights. In the summer times, the Hymns were sung outdoors, Folks sang—as ole Black Joe—& the Bethel Band—Quickstep Street Marches & The people like things as they wanted to say and to do things as they wanted to in their own way—and many old times. . . . there were feelings, and of spiritual Fervency!

This is the standard Charles Ives program note. He wrote dozens of versions of it, but they are all very much the same. This program note has a most extraordinary quality, one which is responsible for the enormous Ives boom of the present moment. Its imagery is of the most commonplace, ordinary, and stereotyped kind; it is entirely of a piece with the myth of small-town America which Norman Rockwell painted for all those *Saturday Evening Post* covers; it is associated, however, with some of the most wildly iconoclastic, rugged, uncompromising, and modern-sounding music ever set down; and one can recognize just enough of the stereotypes of the literary "program" in the imagery of the music to create an extraordinarily unexpected and stimulating shock of recognition. Hence the enormous contemporary delight in Ives.

The *Concord Sonata* is something quite different. There are no baseball games in it. Here Ives turns from image to idea, from childhood reminiscence to mature inward thought. It is, as the composer says in his Preface to the *Essays,* "an attempt to present one person's impression of the spirit of transcendentalism that is associated in the minds of many with Concord, Massachusetts, of over a half century ago." (So far as the dates are concerned, remember that this was written in 1920, and that the title of the sonata is *Concord, Massachusetts, 1840–1860.*)

There are, all told, six essays before the *Concord Sonata*—one about each of the four authors after whom a movement of the sonata is named, plus a prologue and an epilogue.

In the prologue, Ives plunges into the following questions:

How far is anyone justified, be he an authority or a layman, in expressing or trying to express in terms of music (in sounds, if you like) the value of anything, material, moral, intellectual, or spiritual, which is usually expressed in terms other than music? How far afield can music go and keep honest as well as artistic? . . . Can a tune literally represent a stone wall with vines on it or even with nothing on it, though it be made by a genius whose power of objective contemplation is in the highest state of development? Can it be done by anything short of an act of mesmerism on the part of the composer or an act of kindness on the part of the listener?

These questions never bother Ives in writing his innumerable compositions about ball games, camp meetings, Fourth of July celebrations, and all such, but they bother him enormously when he turns to writing music about the spirit of Transcendentalism. Ives wrestles with this problem for several pages and ultimately finds an answer in an essay by the English philosopher, Henry Sturt, who held that "civilization is mainly founded on those kinds of unselfish human interest which we call knowledge and morality"; hence "it is easily intelligible that we should have a parallel interest, which we call art, closely akin and lending powerful support to the other two."

This [says Ives] reduces, or rather, brings the problem back to a tangible basis; namely the translation of an artistic intuition into musical sounds, approving and reflecting, or endeavouring to approve and reflect, a "moral goodness," a "high vitality," etc., or any other human attribute, mental, moral, or spiritual. Can music do *more* than this? Can it *do* this? And if so, who and what is to determine the degree of its failure or success?

Ives finds no satisfactory answers to these last questions, and, like many who are faced with intellectual dilemmas they cannot solve, he shoves it all onto the shoulders of the future: "We . . . believe that music is beyond any analogy to word language and that the time is coming, but not in our lifetime, when it will develop possibilities inconceivable now—a language so transcendent that its heights and depths will be common to all mankind."

So ends the first of the essays before the *Concord Sonata.*

Ives's essay on Emerson is the longest and most densely written of the six, as the Emerson movement is the longest and most densely written part of the sonata. It is obvious that Ives adored Emerson, whom he calls

America's deepest explorer of the spiritual immensities—a seer painting his discoveries in masses and with any color that may lie at hand —cosmic, religious, human, even sensuous; a recorder freely describing the inevitable struggle in the soul's uprise, perceiving from this inward source alone that "every ultimate fact is only the first of a new series," a discoverer whose heart knows, with Voltaire, that man seriously reflects when left alone and who would then discover, if he can, that wondrous chain which links heaven with earth—the world of beings subjected to one law. In *his* reflections, Emerson, unlike Plato, is not afraid to ride Arion's dolphin and to go wherever he is carried —to Parnassus or to Musketaquid.

"Musketaquid," one should add, was the old Indian name for the Concord River.

The essay then proceeds to examine Emerson's thought from numerous points of view. And it makes the following oblique reference to the Emerson movement of the sonata:

There is an "oracle" at the beginning of the *Fifth Symphony;* in those four notes lies one of Beethoven's greatest messages. We would place its translation above the relentlessness of fate knocking at the door, above the greater human message of destiny, and strive to bring it towards the spiritual message of Emerson's revelations, even to the common heart of Concord—the soul of humanity knocking at the door of the divine mysteries, radiant in the faith that it *will* be opened—and the human become the divine!

That famous four-note motif with which Beethoven opens his Fifth Symphony is also the principal theme of the Emerson movement in the sonata, and it recurs repeatedly in other movements as well. This use of thematic material derived from other composers was habitual with Ives, not because he was incapable of inventing his own but because the quoted themes had, for him and for his audience, whole clusters of associations which their citation out of context was bound to invoke. The composer George Rochberg likens Ives's quotations to the stream of consciousness technique of James Joyce, and the analogy is very apt and revealing.

Verbally, Ives summarizes Emerson as follows:

> A working woman after coming from one of his lectures said: "I love to go to hear Emerson not because I understand him but because he looks as though he thought everybody was as good as he was." Is it not the courage, the spiritual hopefulness in his humility, that makes this story true? Is it not this trait in his character that sets him above all creeds—that gives him inspired belief in the common mind and soul? Is it not this courageous universalism that gives conviction to his prophecy, and that makes his symphonies of revelation begin and end with nothing but the strength and beauty of innate goodness in man, in Nature, and in God—the greatest and most inspiring theme of Concord Transcendental philosophy, as we hear it?

The "Hawthorne" movement of the *Concord Sonata* is a scherzo, and the Hawthorne essay is short. It barely fills three pages, but it ends with one of the most remarkable passages of descriptive prose in all the literature on music. Ives tells us first that:

> Any comprehensive conception of Hawthorne, either in words or in music, must have for its basic theme something which has to do with the influence of sin upon the conscience—something more than the Puritan conscience, but something which is permeated by it. . . . Hawthorne would try to spiritualize a guilty conscience. He would sing of the relentlessness of guilt, the inheritance of guilt, the shadow of guilt darkening innocent posterity.

Then, at the end of the essay, Ives describes the Hawthorne movement in the sonata:

> [The] fundamental part of Hawthorne is not attempted in our music (the 2d movement of the series) which is but an "extended fragment" trying to suggest some of his wilder, fantastical adventures into

275

the half-childlike, half-fairylike phantasmal realms. It may have something to do with the children's excitement on that "frosty Berkshire morning, and the frost imagery on the enchanted hall window"; or something to do with "Feathertop," the scarecrow, and his "Looking Glass" and "the little demons dancing around his pipe bowl"; or something to do with the old hymn-tune that haunts the church and sings only to those in the churchyard to protect them from secular noises, as when the circus parade comes down Main Street; or something to do with the concert at the Stamford camp meeting or the "Slave's Shuffle"; or something to do with the Concord he-nymph, or "The Seven Vagabonds," or "Circe's Palace," or something else in *The Wonder-Book*—not something that happens, but the way something happens; or something to do with "The Celestial Railroad," or "Phoebe's Garden," or something personal, which tries to be "national" suddenly at twilight, and universal suddenly at midnight; or something about the ghost of a man who never lived, or about something that never will happen, or something else that is not.

Everything about this paragraph is perfect, down to the very verbal rhythms with which the scurry of the music is suggested. The paragraph is a little masterpiece of impressionistic criticism, however much Ives might have protested its being described as such.

The essay on the Alcotts is even shorter than the one on Hawthorne, and the Alcott movement of the sonata is closer to the early-American-antimacassar-Currier-and-Ives-antique-shop aspect of the composer than the others. He describes it as follows:

> We won't try to reconcile the music sketch of the Alcotts with much beside the memory of that home under the elms—the Scotch songs and the family hymns that were sung at the end of each day—though there may be an attempt to catch something of that . . . strength of hope that never gives way to despair—a conviction in the power of the common soul which, when all is said and done, may be as typical as any theme of Concord and its Transcendentalists.

Ives's essay on Thoreau has several main themes and sub-themes, but its main line is what Beethoven—whom Ives several times likens to the recluse of Walden Pond—called "the worship of God in Nature." And the *Concord* is, without much question, the only piano sonata in existence which, on the sixty-seventh of sixty-eight pages, suddenly introduces a flute solo for a few bars. The flute alludes to the one Thoreau played at Walden. The flute also brings back the motif from Beethoven's Fifth Symphony, which has run throughout the sonata.

In the sixth and last of his *Essays Before a Sonata*, "The Epilogue," Charles Ives confronts the age-old problem of style versus substance in art, and he comes up with the following conclusion:

> At any rate, we are going to be arbitrary enough to claim, with no definite qualification, that substance can be expressed in music, and that it is the only valuable thing in it, and, moreover, that in two separate pieces of music in which the notes are almost identical, one can be of substance with little manner, and the other can be of manner with little substance. Substance has something to do with character. Manner has nothing to do with it. The substance of a tune comes from somewhere near the soul, and the manner comes from—God knows where.

Ives then devotes thirty closely packed pages to arguing this antithesis between manner and substance, drawing his examples from every kind of human activity and experience, but principally from music. We have time for only one paragraph out of these thirty pages, but one which is very typical of Ives and explains why it took so long for his music to find its way into general acceptance:

> A MS. score is brought to a concertmaster—he may be a violinist—he is kindly disposed, he looks it over, and casually fastens on a passage: "That's bad for the fiddles—it doesn't hang just right—write it like this, they will play it better." But that one phrase is the germ of the whole thing. "Never mind, it will fit the hand better this way—it will sound better." My God! What has sound got to do with music! The waiter brings the only fresh egg he has, but the man at breakfast sends it back because it doesn't fit his eggcup. Why can't music go out in the same way it comes into a man, without having to crawl over a fence of sounds, thoraxes, catguts, wire, wood, and brass? Consecutive fifths are as harmless as blue laws compared with the relentless tyranny of the "media." The instrument!—there is the perennial difficulty—there is music's limitation. Why must the scarecrow of the keyboard—the tyrant in terms of the mechanism (be it Caruso or a Jew's-harp)—stare into every measure? Is it the composer's fault that

man has only ten fingers? Why can't a musical thought be presented as it is born—perchance "a bastard of the slums," or a "daughter of a bishop"—and if it happens to go better later on a bass-drum than upon a harp, get a good bass-drummer. That music must be heard is not essential—what it *sounds* like may not be what it *is*. Perhaps the day is coming when music-believers will learn "that silence is a solvent . . . that gives us leave to be universal" rather than personal.

At length, of course, the whole argument of the essays before the *Concord Sonata* comes back to Concord itself and what it stands for, intellectually and spiritually. These are the last lines of the epilogue:

There are communities—now partly vanished, but cherished and sacred—scattered throughout this world of ours, in which freedom of thought and soul, and even of body, have been fought for. And we believe that there ever lives in that part of the over-soul native to them the thoughts which these freedom-struggles have inspired. America is not too young to have its divinities, and its place-legends. Many of those "Transcendent Thoughts" and "Visions" which had their birth beneath our Concord elms—messages that have brought salvation to many listening souls throughout the world—are still growing day by day to greater and greater beauty—are still showing clearer and clearer man's way to God!

No true composer will take his substance from another finite being —but there are times when he feels that his self-expression needs some liberation from at least a part of his own soul. At such times, shall he not better turn to those greater souls, rather than to the external, the immediate, and the "Garish Day"?

The strains of one man may fall far below the course of those Phaetons of Concord, or of the Aegean Sea, or of Westmoreland—but the greater the distance his music falls away, the more reason that some greater man shall bring his nearer those higher spheres.

25 *THE AUTOBIOGRAPHY OF AN IDEA*

Wayne Andrews

In 1924, when the great American architect Louis Sullivan published his autobiography, it was obvious that he was a spokesman
for a lost cause. Although he and his partner Dankmar Adler had
given Chicago the greatest opera house in the world, and although he had proved he was a peerless designer of skyscrapers,
he was an all but forgotten man in the 1920's. On April 14, 1924,
he died in a Chicago hotel that had no pretensions to comfort or
elegance. He was then sixty-seven. For twenty years no major
commission had come into his office.

The cause of modern architecture, to which Sullivan made so
distinguished a contribution, was everywhere overlooked in the
America of the 1920's. This was the decade in which Frank Lloyd
Wright, Sullivan's most brilliant disciple, managed to complete
no more than seven commissions. And this was the decade when
the once successful modernists of California were finding the intellectual climate less and less congenial. Bernard Maybeck was
neglected; so were the brothers Greene and Greene; so was Irving
Gill, who like Wright was a graduate of the Sullivan office. There
was no hope on the West Coast until 1928 when Richard Schind-
ler from Vienna designed an astonishingly charming house for C.
H. Wolfe on Catalina Island.

To review *The Autobiography of an Idea* in 1924 is one thing.
To mention it now is another. For experimentation is condoned
in our time, if not exactly encouraged, and modern architecture
—good, bad, or indifferent—is everywhere to be seen. Now may
be the perfect moment to consider this book. An objective glance,

279

that would have been both tasteless and graceless in the year of Sullivan's death, may be welcome.

The Autobiography of an Idea is the autobiography of a failure, admittedly a failure who will never cease charming ambitious architects. Like many failures, Sullivan was the prisoner of his childhood. It was not something to be lived *once,* and then to be destroyed by the victories of later years. It was something to be lived *with* forever. He made this plain when he dedicated two-thirds of the book to the period before he began studying architecture at the Massachusetts Institute of Technology.

He was born in Boston on September 3, 1856, the son of an Irish dancing master and a pianist, half French-Swiss, half German, who had come to America from Geneva. This meant that he was to be an outsider in a New England that had only contempt for Irish immigrants. Automatically excluded from the world that spelled success in Boston, he dreamed of imposing his will nonetheless. "One day on Commonwealth Avenue," he tells us, "he saw a large man of dignified bearing, with beard, top hat, frock coat, come out of a nearby building, enter his carriage and signal the coachman to drive off." He wondered what lay behind this dignity, and asked a workman. "Why, he's the archeetec [*sic*] of this building," came the answer. "He lays out rooms on paper, then makes a picture of the front, and we do the work under our own boss, but the archeetec's the boss of everybody."

Such was Sullivan's ambition that he could not be satisfied with the teaching at the Massachusetts Institute of Technology, even though his professor William R. Ware was to acquire a considerable reputation. With Henry Van Brunt, a devoted Ruskinian who translated Viollet-le-Duc into English, Ware was responsible in 1875 for Memorial Hall at Harvard.

In search of advice and a job, Sullivan descended on New York City. "Richard M. Hunt was the architectural lion there, and the dean of the profession. Louis called upon him in his den, told him his plans and was patted on the back and encouraged as an enterprising youngster." Hunt was the first American to graduate from the École des Beaux Arts, and it is obvious that it was in the Hunt office that the young man learned that the best instruction in the world was to be had in Paris.

Sullivan was to get his first job in Philadelphia in the office of

Furness and Hewitt, who are remembered even today and occasionally admired for the fearsome brutality of their bank buildings. But he was fired when the Panic of 1873 put an end for a time to the practice of architecture, and on the day before Thanksgiving, 1873, found himself in Chicago, a city being rebuilt in the wake of the Great Fire of 1871. "Louis tramped the platform," we are told, "stopped, looked toward the city, ruins around him; looked at the sky; and as one alone, stamped his foot, raised his hand and cried in full voice: THIS IS THE PLACE FOR ME!"

This was the greatest mistake Louis Sullivan ever made. For Chicago was a tough town, far too tough for an idealist. Like Ralph Waldo Emerson, who argued that "the intellectual life may be kept clean and healthful if man will live the life of nature and not import into his mind difficulties which are none of his," Sullivan could close his eyes to reality, if reality proved to be ugly.

"Never in man's time has there been such sound warrant for an attitude of Optimism as in our own, the very present day," he declared in *The Autobiography*. "The beauty, the passion, the glory of the past shall merge into a new beauty, a new passion, a new glory as man approaches man, and recognizing him, rejoices in him and with him, as born in power."

The truth is that men were dealing with men every day in the week on the streets of Chicago, and the results were not always edifying. Sullivan was to live through the Haymarket Riot of 1885 and the mistrial of the anarchists for their part in the killing of six persons and the wounding of seventy-two, and above all the hounding of Governor John Peter Altgeld for having the courage to pardon three of the anarchists who had not been hanged. He was also to live through the Pullman Strike of 1894, which was to illuminate so brilliantly the character of George Mortimer Pullman. "A man who won't meet his own men half-way is a God-damn fool!" commented Mark Hanna on the intransigeance of the industrialist and master of the model town of Pullman, Illinois.

The Chicago that Sullivan idealized would never have been recognized by Marshall Field, P. D. Armour, or Gustavus F. Swift, to name three of the great businessmen. Field, who accumulated one hundred twenty million dollars, the greatest fortune in the history of the city, was never sorry he missed a college education. "For most young men," he decided, "a college education means that just at the time when they should be having business principles instilled into them, and be getting themselves energetically pulled together for their life's work, they are sent to college. Then intervenes what many a young man looks back on as the jolliest time of his life. . . . Often when he comes out of college the young man is unfitted by this good time to buckle down to hard work, and the result is a failure to grasp opportunities that would have opened the way for a successful career." Armour, whose packing plant was as essential to the city as Field's department store, would have heartily endorsed the merchant's sentiments. He liked to get down to work, he made plain, "before the boys with the polished nails show up." As for Armour's rival Swift, he too stood for no nonsense. "No young man," Swift pointed out, "is rich enough to smoke a twenty-five cent cigar."

So much for the philosophy of the lords of Chicago. The fact that it was next to impossible to live up to their strenuous ideals did not in the least discourage architects who bid for commissions from these titans. Sullivan met jovial Major William Le Baron Jenney, who in 1883 was to design the Home Insurance Building, usually considered to be the first skyscraper, or tall steel-frame building. He also met Marvin Roche who with his partner William A. Holabird was to build the Tacoma Building in 1885, a far more graceful creation, and sometimes judged the first skyscraper in which the frame carried all the weight traditionally borne by the walls.

Sullivan labored in Jenney's office until July 1874 when he sailed to France and the École des Beaux Arts. Like Henry Hobson Richardson, like C. F. McKim, and many another important American architect of the nineteenth century, Sullivan was to receive the benefit of French training, and it is interesting that nowhere in *The Autobiography* does he disparage the École. "There came," he admits, "the hovering conviction that this Great School, in its perfect flower of technique, lacked the profound animus of primal inspiration." Which is another way of saying that he felt he could teach himself all that was to be learned.

The only unfortunate experience of Sullivan in Paris was his meeting with a Monsieur Clopet, who tutored him in mathematics and boasted that *"here our demonstrations shall be so broad as to admit of* NO EXCEPTION." Clopet was taken seriously by his student. All too seriously. "Instantly the words had flashed, there arose a vision and a fixed resolve; an instantaneous inquiry and an instant answer. The inquiry: If this can be done in Mathematics why not in Architecture? The instant answer: It can, and it shall be! *no one has—I will!"* Out of his preoccupation with Monsieur Clopet's statement came Sullivan's most unfortunate formula: *Form follows function.* This "would mean, in practice," he argued, "that architecture might again become a living art, if this formula were but adhered to."

It is safe to say that this silly oversimplification has done architecture untold harm. *Form follows function* has turned up in innumerable books written by critics who have never glanced at a building designed by Sullivan, and this slogan has led many simple souls to believe that Sullivan himself designed according to this rule. Nothing can be further from the truth. Although this is not the place to discuss his career as an architect, it is obvious that in practice he had the courage to seek a new solution for every problem that came into his office, especially after he and his partner Dankmar Adler received the commission for the Auditorium.

Not too long after his return from Paris, Sullivan joined the firm of D. Adler and Company in Chicago. By May 1, 1881, the firm had become Adler and Sullivan: at the age of twenty-five, he "became a full-fledged architect before the world." The earliest work of the firm was undistinguished, but on December 9, 1889, the Auditorium, a complex including an opera house and a hotel, was opened to the public, and his reputation was assured. With Adler at his side to watch over the difficulties of engineering, he seemed unassailable.

Adler, Sullivan writes, "was a heavy-set, short-nosed Jew, well-bearded, with a magnificent domed forehead which stopped suddenly at a solid mass of black hair. He was a picture of sturdy strength, physical and mental." This was not all. Adler was a profoundly practical man, apparently never given to the flights of idealism which his partner could not resist. When the firm fell upon hard times, as did many others, in the depression of 1893, Adler resigned to become sales manager of the Crane Elevator Company. Sullivan was alone, and alone he was an unhappy man. Without Adler he was at a loss in handling important clients, and he did his last major work in 1900 when he created the magnificent store of Schlesinger and Mayer on State Street, now occupied by Carson, Pirie Scott and Company. In his last years he was reduced to designing banks for country towns in the Middle West. These were occasionally masterpieces, but we shall always regret that he was not given greater opportunities.

Sullivan, of course, has his own explanation to offer for his defeat, and it should be carefully considered. By the time he wrote his autobiography he decided that one thing was to blame, the World's Fair of 1893.

The Fair, the most successful in American history—four hundred thousand people poured through the gates on opening day —had been placed in the hands of the Chicago firm of Burnham and Root, internationally recognized for the massive skyscrapers they had been erecting in the Loop. Like Adler and Sullivan's Auditorium, these owed much to the example of Henry Hobson Richardson, whose marvelous massing of granite could be seen in the Marshall Field wholesale store. It so happened that neither John Root, who died two years before the Fair was opened, nor Daniel Hudson Burnham designed a single building for the Fair. Instead they invited easterners, headed by Richard Morris Hunt and the firm of McKim, Mead and White, to collaborate on the enterprise. Sullivan himself was not neglected. He was given the chance to design the Transportation Building, whose dazzling golden doorway was an incredible specimen of his genius for decoration. And at the time he had, apparently, no complaint to offer.

But listen to *The Autobiography* on the subject of the Fair:

These crowds [of visitors] were astonished. They beheld what was for them an amazing revelation of the architectural art, of which previously they in comparison had known nothing. To them it was a veritable Apocalypse, a message inspired from on high. Upon it their imagination shaped new ideals. They went away, spreading again over the land, returning to their homes, each one of them carrying in their soul the shadow of the white cloud, each of them permeated by the most subtle and slow-acting of poisons; an imperceptible miasm within the white shadow of a higher culture. . . .

The damage wrought by the World's Fair will last for half a century from its date, if not longer. It has penetrated deep into the constitution of the American mind, effecting there lesions significant of dementia.

To make matters very simple, Sullivan was objecting in 1924 to the great advertisement the Fair gave to architects working in what might be called the Renaissance revival. Back in 1881 Richard Morris Hunt had the happy idea that a palace in the style of the early French Renaissance might be just the thing for W. K. Vanderbilt's new house on Fifth Avenue, New York City. This palace was a highly functional building; it impressed New Yorkers with the importance of the Vanderbilts, and here, on March 26, 1883, Mrs. Vanderbilt gave the celebrated ball which brought the family the social recognition that had long been denied them. Messrs. McKim, Mead and White did not need to be told that Hunt had found an ideal solution for the problem of a millionaire's palace. Forsaking their quite original and "modern" work in the shingle style, they too turned to the Renaissance for inspiration. The formal planning of the Renaissance, they reasoned, was ideally suited to the formal life of the wealthy.

So the World's Fair of 1893, with its classical buildings and its idyllic lagoons, was simply a reflection in Chicago of what had been attempted so successfully in New York. Was such a reflection not to be tolerated? Sullivan's indignation suggests that he considered Hunt and McKim, Mead and White and their followers to be no better than criminals.

It must be admitted that Sullivan was only one in a long line of modern critics who have abused the Renaissance. Pugin, we must remember, did not despair of seeing St. Peter's "rebuilt in a better style." As for Ruskin, he decided that the architecture of the Renaissance "had in it . . . no mercy. The proud princes and the lords rejoiced in it. It was full of insult to the poor in every line." Taking his cue from Ruskin, William Morris went on to speak of "the death or cataleptic sleep of the Renaissance."

And finally, there was the verdict of Viollet-le-Duc on the Renaissance as interpreted for the seventeenth century in France: "Louis XIV succeeded, as regards art, in completely crushing the natural and original genius of the French people."

From these quotations we may infer, quite correctly, that what we call modern architecture grew out of the Gothic Revival, whose apostles were ready to believe the worst of the Italian masters of the sixteenth century and those who carried on their tradition in France and England. Sullivan, unfortunately, seems to have been the most virulent of all in his denunciation of what he likened to an Italian disease. If he had had his way, every vestige of the Renaissance in America would have been erased from the map. We should be deprived of a colonial masterpiece like Miles Brewton's town house in Charleston; we should miss Jefferson's Rotunda at the University of Virginia; even the Capitol at Washington would have to be pulled down.

Sullivan seems to have assumed, so bitter was his invective, that modern architecture was at best a pale flower that might wither away if set in the shade of a Renaissance-inspired structure. In fact, the exact opposite was the case.

In the twenty-five years following the Fair, while Sullivan's own practice dwindled, his former draftsman Frank Lloyd Wright was gloriously successful, building not only the great Larkin factory at Buffalo but dozens of distinguished houses throughout the Middle West. And Wright was not alone. No historian can afford to neglect the work of the other members of the Chicago School, all of whom may be said to have followed Sullivan's precedent. Men like Barry Byrne, Hugh Garden, Walter Burley Griffin, Guenzel and Drummond, George W. Maher, Dwight H. Perkins, and Purcell and Elmslie all made a distinct contribution despite the Fair. True, architecture may be said to have declined in the 1920's, but it is difficult to see how the Fair was responsible.

So *The Autobiography of an Idea* is a book to be consulted with caution. It is the testament of a very great architect who could never quite cope with the spirit of Chicago. Today, when modern architecture has come into its own, we may be more tolerant than Sullivan of non-modern architecture. Perhaps the most tolerant people of all are certain leading modern architects.

When McKim's Pennsylvania Station in New York was recently destroyed, there was a parade to protest the leveling of that classical structure. Leading the procession were Philip Johnson and the widow of Eero Saarinen.

26 E. E. CUMMINGS: *THE ENORMOUS ROOM*

James P. Dougherty

In the early fall of 1917, two young Americans serving with a Red Cross ambulance unit in the northern French sector of the Western Front were arrested by the civil police on charges of treason, a censor having detected in their correspondence some descriptions of widespread low morale in the French army. While the charges were being investigated, they spent three months in a prison in the Normandy hills—a detention camp for suspicious aliens and prostitutes found in the war zone. One of them, William Slater Brown, who had in fact written the objectionable letters to friends in America, was sentenced to prison; the other, Edward Estlin Cummings, who had written no letters but who had twice refused to dissociate himself from his friend, was released and returned to America.

Cummings took sketchbooks and notebooks with him into the prison, and after the war transformed these impressions into a book, *The Enormous Room,* which for several reasons remains an important imaginative record of that violent time when the "modern" spirit was in birth.

One reason for this importance is that Cummings' subsequent career established him as at least a major minor poet of the modernist movement, best known for his typographic arrangements and experiments in syntax, extending the spirit of cubism into verbal media to render the simultaneity and immediacy of unreflective experience. *The Enormous Room* does not use these techniques, but it explains why Cummings later felt them necessary for poetry in the twentieth century.

The inherent importance of *The Enormous Room* will be considered as a part of the literature of that well-known disillusion which followed the Great War; as a modern extension of the American radical tradition of Emerson, Thoreau, and Whitman; and as an anticipation of the post-modern world of the 1960's.

The Enormous Room is best known as a narrative of disillusion, taking its place between the memoirs of Siegfried Sassoon and Robert Graves, and the imaginative fictions of Hemingway, Dos Passos, Barbusse, and Remarque. Today that postwar mood must seem an historical curiosity, the product of a sentimental faith in liberal statecraft and military valor, alien to our time. But the myth of the 1920's was the myth of a Lost Generation, born just before the turn of the century, who found their inherited political, social, and philosophical pieties evaporated in the crucible of war, and who spent their later lives in search of new faiths.[1]

It cannot be said that *The Enormous Room* is organized to make the disillusion of its protagonist a climactic plot event, as are Hemingway's *A Farewell to Arms* and Dos Passos' *Three Soldiers*. Yet a major concern of Cummings is to expose the stupidity, injustice, and cruelty of which a government is capable in times of national hysteria. Though he occasionally alludes to the barbarity of warfare itself, he concentrates on the brutalizing effect war has on civilians and civil authority. To his own experience he adds two chapters of anecdotes, Chapters Five and Seven, which illustrate the paranoia of *le gouvernement français* by cataloging the pretexts on which Cummings' fellow prisoners were jailed. He writes:

> For who was eligible to La Ferté? Anyone whom the police could find in the lovely country of France (*a*) who was not guilty of treason, (*b*) who could not prove that he was not guilty of treason. By treason I refer to any little annoying habits of independent thought or action which *en temps de guerre* are put in a hole and covered over, with the somewhat naïve idea that from their cadavers violets will grow whereof the perfume will delight all good men and true and make such worthy citizens forget their sorrows. Fort Leavenworth, for instance, emanates even now a perfume which is utterly delightful to certain Americans.[2]

Later he explains that he is thinking of the imprisonment of conscientious objectors and the harassing of anyone "cursed with a talent for thinking during the warlike moments recently passed" (p. 139).[3]

Cummings' real disillusionment is not just an initiation into the ugly realities of war. It is a loss of faith in the systems and categories taught him by the experiences of his first twenty-three years of life. Immediately after his arrest he undergoes an interrogation in which three kindly old men dissolve his identity, by altering its terms to fit their own categories. They mispronounce his name; they are sure he is Irish, and when he proffers a story of his Scottish ancestor, The Red Comyn, they record that he denies his Irish parentage; when he says his father is a Unitarian minister, they hesitate between "Free Thinker" and "Protestant," finally choosing the latter; and he was educated at a school they have never heard of, called Harvard. There is grotesque comedy in all this, but its impact on Cummings is considerable. His old, inherited credentials are destroyed. In prison he finds a world of men whom the authorities have found "puzzling, or . . . insusceptible of analysis" (p. 114), men without public identities, establishing themselves rather on their appearance, their temperament and activities, and the sum of their relationships with fellow prisoners, whom they encounter with "a gentility accessible to no measure of taste or custom previously established." [4]

Among them he learns a direct, personal understanding of himself; he is given new names—"Jean" or *"l'américain"*—and builds a new identity as an artist. At the end of his book, as he leaves the Room, he announces the sum of his experience there: "For an educated gent or lady, to create is first of all to destroy— . . . there is and can be no such thing as authentic art until the *bons trucs* (whereby we are taught to see and imitate on canvas and in stone and by words this so-called world) are entirely and thoroughly and perfectly annihilated by that vast and painful process of Unthinking which may result in a minute bit of purely personal Feeling. Which minute bit is Art" (p. 307). In choosing the role of artist as a new identity, he makes a typically "modern" decision, comparable to those of Yeats, Pound, Joyce, Hemingway, and Stevens.

The book itself is a product of this unlearning process. The *bons trucs* of art, language, and social contact are conventions mediating between our minds and the imperious chaos of reality, establishing categories and hierarchies through which we can conduct our lives. But these conventions also betray the immediacy of experience, and are accessible to manipulations through which we can be morally betrayed as well. At every stage of his imprisonment Cummings has been so betrayed. His first interrogation culminates in the question "Do you hate the Germans?"; his response "No, I love the French" is taken as a confession of guilt. This use of language is so bizarre that Cummings can only respond silently *"C'est rigolo"*—this is a joke. He soon discovers what acts of personal cruelty men in power can justify by invoking the right public convention. In the name of *le gouvernement français* or *le patriotisme,* men may be accused of thought crimes, held without trial, beaten, and starved, machine-gunned if necessary; one of the most persistent and least funny jokes of *The Enormous Room* is Cummings' satiric invocation of *le gouvernement français* to explain every absurdity and outrage. The camp itself is a verbal trick: nominally a *porte de triage,* a detention center where suspects are held pending trial, it has become in fact a concentration camp from which some are sent to a more secure prison, many found innocent are detained indefinitely after trial, and some are held by the expedient of trying them over and over again. The authorities at La Ferté Macé are very insistent that their center is not a prison. Today we are familiar with "resettlement camps," "labor camps," "relocation centers," and other benevolent enclosures.

This manipulation of language makes it difficult for Cummings to assess the gravity of what he experiences and to react with an appropriate level of diction. There is complete discontinuity between the style of Cummings' father, in the Foreword, and the style of the book itself. Cummings senior, in describing his son's imprisonment, maintains a tone of righteous indignation, the product of liberal certainties, Victorian-Edwardian gentlemanliness, and American national vanity. He invokes the classics and the Scriptures, and appeals to international law, national honor, and motherhood. "My boy's mother and all American mothers have a right to be protected against all needless anxiety and sorrow" (p. xiii). This is not just a difference between formal and informal writing; no doubt the elder Cummings had an informal style too. *The Enormous Room* is a mélange of many levels of diction: mannered, formal, informal, vulgar, technical. What has been lost is the sense of occasion, the capacity to establish a tone that is correlated to the situation. Early in his adventure he jokes to a guard about being guillotined, and is chilled by the answer "Oh, hardly guillotined I should say" (p. 7). There is no moment during his arrest and captivity when he is sure how serious things are. Even in retrospect, he is unsure whether his experience was a season in hell (cf. Chapter Six) or a time when he was "happier . . . than the very keenest words can express" (p. 313). Hence, perhaps, the diction of the famous description of the crucifix in a Norman roadside shrine, in which the agony of Christ becomes "funny," "jocular," and "droll." Cummings' father knew that indignation was the proper response to injustice. His son is no longer sure. The style of *The Enormous Room,* its events, and its hero's decision to unlearn the social and artistic conventions in which he was educated, all display Cummings' loss of confidence in the certainties of his past. And in this he is part of the Lost Generation.

"In prison one learns several million things," writes Cummings, "—if one is *l'américain* from *Mass-a-chu-setts*" (p. 110). Many years later, discussing *The Enormous Room* with a correspondent for *Figaro Littéraire,* Cummings quoted enthusiastically from another American from Massachusetts who had learned a great deal in prison, Henry David Thoreau.[5] It is with the American radicals, Thoreau, Emerson, and Whitman, that *The Enormous Room* should be placed, rather than just with the Lost Generation.

Three Soldiers and *A Farewell to Arms* shows heroes whose exposure to official stupidity and the absurdities of war converts them from loyal discharge of duty to withdrawal, disgusted, into private commitments: art for John Andrews, romantic love for Frederick Henry. But Cummings is always in opposition. First he is seen chafing under the authority of Mr. A., the chauvinistic head of his ambulance section; throughout most of the narrative he is set against the director and guards of La Ferté Macé; and in a parenthetical comment toward the story's end, he presents himself, in the moment of writing, as the prophet of a new aesthetics disregarded by "The Great American Public." [6] Society, by arresting him or releasing him, can only change the name of the power he resists. The shape of this book is not linear, a dramatic fall from innocence, but rather cyclic, the hero thrust into a situation where he must create an identity by resistance, and from which he is eventually delivered into something new. In a later book, *i: Six Nonlectures,* Cummings called this endless metamorphic process "self-transcendence." [7] It is to an earlier self-transcender and resister of unjust authority, Henry Thoreau, that we can turn for many of the patterns of *The Enormous Room.*

The American tradition of prison epistles, which Roger Williams began [8] and to which Martin Luther King, Jr., contributed his "Letter from Birmingham Jail," [9] has in Thoreau's "Civil Disobedience" its central principle: "Under a government which imprisons any unjustly, the true place for a just man is also in prison. The proper place today, the only place which Massachusetts has provided for her freer and less desponding spirits, is in her prisons." [10] Cummings, surveying the inhumanity of his jailors and the humanity of his fellow prisoners, declares that "in finding us unworthy of helping to carry forward the banner of progress, alias the tricolour, the inimitable and excellent French Government was conferring upon B. and myself—albeit with other intent—the ultimate compliment" (p. 167).[11]

In destroying his identity, Cummings' interrogators leave him just one thing: his guilt by association with Brown. He seizes this straw. Knowing that they have already condemned his friend, he maneuvers them into assigning him also the honorific title of "criminal," a title which he repeatedly applies to himself, perhaps with a certain self-sustaining bravado, during his journey to prison. His identification with Brown is so complete that once he describes the cumbersome baggage he carries to prison as a *"sac full of suspicious letters"* (p. 52), though he has in fact written no such letters.[12] "We are comrades" he explains to a prison official (p. 58)—a term Walt Whitman would have understood but which, in those days just before the October Revolution, may have conveyed something else to the official.

Cummings' captors however seldom refer to him as a criminal. Rather, in contexts in which the appropriate word would be "traitor," "défaitiste," or at least "suspect," they regularly call him "the American." Whenever his guards are asked "What you got there? they answer, "An American" (pp. 10, 28, 46). In prison, each interview begins with the item "You are an American?" (pp. 57, 105). The word soon comes to mean "rebel," "anarchist," or "dangerous person." When at last he is set free through the efforts of the American embassy, his journey ends with the vision of New York harbor, his symbol of freedom. America as the symbol of individual liberty recurs in his works, as it did in his predecessors'—Whitman in *Leaves of Grass* and *Democratic Vistas,* Emerson in "Self-Reliance," and Thoreau in *Walden:* [13] "The only true America is that country where you are at liberty to pursue such a mode of life as may enable you to do without [luxuries], and where the state does not endeavor to compel you to sustain the slavery and war and other superfluous expenses which directly or indirectly result from the use of [luxuries]." [14]

That such an America was a country of the mind rather than of the map, Cummings knew as well as Emerson and Thoreau. He begins his book with a satiric portrait of his commander, Mr. A., who would like the world remade in the image of America; and his poetry is as critical of the real America as were the writings of Emerson and Thoreau, and as full of exhortations to improvement. One finds today also, in that strand of civil dissent which stems from the native radicalism of the last century, the same invocation of America as symbol, as unattained ideal. [15]

Like some of today's dissenters, Cummings finds in jail a purification, a recovery of innocence. Of entering a cell for the first time, he writes "I was myself. An uncontrollable joy gutted me after three months of humiliation, of being bossed and herded and bullied and insulted. I was myself and my own master" (p. 23). It is like the purification Thoreau found in Concord jail, or even more in the cabin at Walden Pond. For each man, moral cleanliness comes both from the act of dissociation and from new enlightening contacts: for Cummings the simple men he calls Delectable Mountains, and for Thoreau such noble savages as the French-Canadian woodcutter. [16]

One fruit of that purificatory isolation is the cleansing of the eye and tongue. Long before the Lost Generation, Thoreau anticipated Cummings' disillusionment and his wish to abolish the *bons trucs*, the conventions of artistic perception:

> I have lived some thirty years on this planet, and I have yet to hear the first syllable of valuable or even earnest advice from my seniors. They have told me nothing, and probably cannot tell me anything.[17]

> I perceive that we . . . live this mean life that we do because our vision does not penetrate the surface of things. We think that that *is* which *appears* to be. . . . Look at a meeting-house, or a court-house, or a jail, or a shop, or a dwelling-house, and say what that thing really is before a true gaze, and they would all go to pieces in your account of them.[18]

Cummings' poetic style, a product of the unlearning process he underwent in prison and afterward, does just that: it makes things go to pieces. In its espousal of self-purification through resistance to society's conspiracy against individual manhood, *The Enormous Room* is a part of the tradition of American radical thought, a *Walden* for the twentieth century.

But it is a *Walden* for the *twentieth* century. The conspiracy is now a great, ubiquitous machine, the mass society, which one cannot escape, as Thoreau did, by physical flight or rapport with nature. There is nowhere to go. Almost no one escapes from the Room or even considers escape. Nature is hostile, its season an autumn dying away from Cummings' nostalgic memories of high summer and an outdoor feast among his French comrades (pp. 174–175, 297), to a lonely psychological collapse during the first fall of snow (pp. 317 ff.). That American invention, the mass society, is the common enemy of Thoreau and Cummings, but Cummings meets it not with silence and isolate individualism, but with voice and a universe of personal relationships.[19] In both books, essays crowd out the narrative; but while Thoreau's are on the mysteries of Walden Pond, Cummings' are sketches of the men he knew in prison.

Gypsies, Negroes, Jews; Polish peasants, Dutch sailors, Belgian artisans; Russians, Turks, Austrians; socialists, anarchists, madmen; salesmen, musicians, millionaires. All they have in common is being not French. But in their cramped barracks there is no space for partitions. Endless conversation fills the Room, dissolving all such distinctions, or reducing them to a mere source of new personal names—as Cummings is dubbed *l'américain,* and others known as The Wanderer, the Machine-Fixer, Garibaldi, and so on.

It is not its size, twelve meters by twenty-four, that makes the Room enormous. It is voice, and physical proximity. Cummings first enters at night; in the silent dark he cannot judge its size. At the guard's departure, "There rose a sea of most extraordinary sound . . . the hitherto empty and minute room became suddenly enormous: weird cries, oaths, laughter, pulling it sideways and backward, extending it to inconceivable depth and width, telescoping it to frightful nearness. From all directions [came] at least thirty voices in eleven languages" (p. 60). Later there will be nearly eighty voices in this cell. En route to La Ferté he had always been jailed alone. Alone he could say "I was myself and my own master." But now he must find himself in relation to a mass of human persons.[20] Much later Cummings said of his life as a poet, "Poetry is being, not doing. If you wish to follow . . . the poet's calling . . . you've got to come out of the measurable doing universe into the immeasurable house of being." [21] "The immeasurable house of being" is the same as *The Enormous Room:* freedom found not in a void, but in limits, in necessary contact with other men. This is not an orthodox American point of view; Americans have tended to think of freedom as disengagement, spiritual cleanliness. Cummings' experience confirms the disengagement of man from state, but not man from man.

In his book for America, *Man Against Mass Society,* Gabriel Marcel urges those who wish to survive as humans in the mass state to create a small circle of intimates among whom one can work and live with a sense of personal reality.[22] Beyond that circle, one can only resist dehumanization. No politics can mediate man with mass society. Cummings' prison likewise is a world of personal encounters, surrounded by the inhumane machine of state. Nothing mediates between them. Nothing can, for the Room contains just those people whom a nation geared for war cannot tolerate: the human dirt who clog the machine and confuse its systems. Naturally they set up no infra-government: they are the puzzling ones, the disorderly, the chaotic. They combine only for ad hoc purposes: to smuggle in a bucket of water, torment a guard, invade the women's barracks. Otherwise there are only individual men, face to face in relationships ranging from the hatred they all feel toward informers to the sentimental hankering Cummings betrays for the Negro Jean.

From the moment of his arrival, Cummings is overwhelmed by the intensity with which the prisoners respond to even the most insignificant events. Any movement in the Room at night brings a storm of abuse; four men fight for the privilege of arranging an arrival's bedroll; the supper call transforms everyone into a slavering animal. The overcrowding produces two contrary effects: though the prisoners have developed strategies of civility and passivity to smother belligerence—they are too close together to tolerate much fighting—nevertheless their very number keeps the Room in a continual tumult of practical jokes, bullyings, thefts, games, attempts to outwit the guards, and in the tribal society of the Room there is no refusing to be part of that tumult. A climate of monotonous hysteria uses men up very quickly, especially men like Cummings, accustomed to the measured responses and the degrees of involvement or detachment which he had learned from turn-of-the-century America. These are the cultural assumptions underlying the *bons trucs* he seeks to repudiate as a result of his imprisonment.

Most of the men in the Room are analphabets (p. 116). Voice is their first means of encounter. They have nothing to do but talk, endlessly, about anything, speculating, exaggerating, lying—no matter, so long as a current of words is kept in circulation. To resist their guards they shout, curse, make animal noises. Literacy is irrelevant: no one seems more futile than the men who spend their days writing petitions to their governments. When Cummings' heroes hold prayer book or newspaper upside down, pretending to read (pp. 257, 271), the joke is on the book, not on the heroes, whose vitality and endurance seem a function of their illiteracy.

Cummings' own literacy is eventually borne under by the Room; when he secures some books, he finds "reading Shakespeare did not appeal to my disordered mind" (p. 323). This disorder is the analphabetic vision, without equitone, without perspective: the permanence of Cummings' derangement can be measured in the mélange of styles in *The Enormous Room,* in the frequent refusal of his poems to take a perspective that pretends sensations happen one by one, and in his tendency to treat language in his poems as a kind of tribal magic. In a voice culture, art loses the specialness that made it a supreme value to the Lost Generation, and becomes dependent on interpersonal needs.

Cummings stresses that his illiterate heroes communicate with each other not only by voice, but also by gesture and physical attitude. Perhaps this is responsible for the tactile imagery and the synaesthesia so frequent in this book. Cummings speaks of friends "whom I see and hear and smell and touch and even taste, and whom I do not know" (p. 255), describing them in tactile or kinetic images; his narrative is dense with synaesthesia redistributing the sensorium: "ponderous reek of bodies," "clear, hardish eyes," "gnarled voice," "loudly stinking mound." For these men, the whole body talks.

In the Room, of course, bodies can never be forgotten. The call to the two daily meals of bread and soup transforms the men into "a sole chaos of desire; a fluent and numerous cluster of vital inhumanity. . . . I felt that the last vestige of individualism was about utterly to disappear, wholly abolished in a gambolling and wallowing throb" (pp. 90–91). If jails are where societies put their dirt, keeping jails clean would plainly be both gratuitous and self-contradictory. The overwhelming impression of *The Enormous Room* is of the massing of dirty bodies and of the body's products: hair, spittle, urine, excrement. Cummings spends his initiatory night in the Room sleeping in the latrine area. In the weeks that follow, his growing uncouthness becomes a badge of identification with these men whom tribunals have declared dirt in the gears of the engine of state, filth, that must be excluded from the pure temples of *le gouvernement français.* Cummings begins a steep regression into coprophilia: "I wallowed in a perfect luxury of dirt. . . . By being dirtier than usual I was protesting . . . against all that was neat and tidy and bigoted and solemn and founded upon the anguish of my fine friends" (pp. 323–324).

If the Room is a microcosm, as Cummings suggests in his Introduction (p. vii), it is one disquieting to the liberal mind, offering an alien notion of freedom, repudiating many of the symbols of cultural and psychological development, and its effects on Cummings are both creative and destructive. It does give him a new and authentic foundation for his art. But the pressures of the Room are finally too intense for him, and when he is delivered from it he is on the point of psychic death.

His collapse begins when a judiciary commission comes to interrogate all the detainees and pass on their cases. From the personalist viewpoint of the Room, the commission's legalist judgments seem totally haphazard. It condemns equally the brutal, the demented, the simple, the gentle, and the brave. The same incongruity occurs among those acquitted and those held for reexamination. The commission sentences Brown to prison, but reaches no decision on Cummings. In so distinguishing between them, this commission completes the demolition of Cummings' identity that began on the day of his arrest. Deprived of name, family, religion, and social class, he chose then to be a "friend of Brown," and therefore "criminal." The commission determines he is not a criminal, and dissolves the intimate association with Brown which sustained him through their months in prison.[23] The very process of interrogation, with its canons of relevance, its lack of reciprocity, and its obsession with facts, shatters a sensibility accustomed to the conversation of the Room. Cummings describes another man leaving his interrogation "looking as if he had submitted to several strenuous fittings of a wooden leg upon a stump not quite healed" (p. 296); Cummings in turn emerges trembling and exhausted (p. 300). "The judgment of the Three Wise Men," he writes, ". . . knocked me for a loop. . . . When I finally made my exit, the part of me popularly referred to as 'mind' was still in a slightly bent if not twisted condition" (p. 314).

He has, of course, his role as an artist. But once the personal commitments, on which art depends, have been shaken by Brown's departure, art alone can no longer sustain him. He remarked earlier that his fellow prisoners could not write or draw (p. 116); and as he drowns in the illiterate tribalism of the Room, his art identity perishes too. He lies in bed seeing nothing, or walks mechanically in the prison yard—"once I was sitting alone on [a] long beam of silent iron and suddenly had the gradual complete unique experience of death" (p. 308). At the end of this season of decomposition, it begins to snow: "I lay down, closing my eyes, feeling the snow's minute and crisp touch falling gently and exquisitely, falling perfectly and suddenly, through the thick, soundless autumn of my imagination" (p. 317).

Then, suddenly, on this brink of psychological death there is deliverance! The machinery of the state has inscrutably manufactured his innocence. The date is December 21st, solstice, when sunlight begins to return. In seven pell-mell pages he is rehabilitated—equipped with his name, which he hasn't used since arrest, given a passport, discharged from his ambulance corps, cleared by the French police, transported across the Atlantic. All is changed: his goodbyes in the Room are to people whom he can scarcely recognize; to an American official he admits that Brown's letters *were* "a little foolish"; he is ashamed of his prison filthiness and conscious of his strange clothes, and of whether he is traveling first, second, or third class; he is, finally, *self*-conscious, an experience almost impossible within the Enormous Room. But he cannot be rehabilitated exactly as he was before arrest; the book itself demonstrates the profound effect his captivity had on him. In the last paragraph he describes his new vision of the Manhattan skyline as he lands there on January 1st, the first day of a new year:

> The tall, impossibly tall, incomparably tall, city shoulderingly upward into hard sunlight leaned a little through the octaves of its parallel edges, leaningly strode upward into firm, hard, snowy sunlight; the noises of America nearingly throbbed with smokes and hurrying dots which are men and which are women and which are things new and curious and hard and strange and vibrant and immense, lifting with a great ondulous stride firmly into immortal sunlight (pp. 331–332).

As a writer of the Lost Generation, he reaffirms in this energetic description his commitment to art. To the American radical, descendant of Thoreau, the skyline symbolizes the life of personal integrity and freedom for which he went to prison; it is the Celestial City, completing the image pattern he has taken from *The Pilgrim's Progress*. As a prophecy of the post-modern mass society, this is the revelation of another enormous room, from which there is no escape, a great engine full of "hurrying dots which are men and which are women," within whose limits he must continue to create the relationships which are his only identity.

Notes

1. The book has so been treated by F. J. Hoffman, *The Twenties: American Writing in the Postwar Decade* (New York, 1955); John Aldridge, *After the Lost Generation* (New York, 1958); Marilyn Gaull, "Language and Identity: E. E. Cummings' *The Enormous Room*," *American Quarterly*, XIX (Winter 1967), 645–662; Stanley Cooperman, *World War I and the American Novel* (Baltimore, 1967).

2. *The Enormous Room* (New York, 1934), pp. 115–116. (Subsequent references will be incorporated in the text.) Another irony, not quite external to this book since Cummings' father alludes to it (p. xvii), is that the delay in handling Cummings' case may have been due to confusion within the Ministry of the Interior following the removal of the minister, M. Louis Jean Malvy, who had himself been charged with treason.

3. See "i sing of Olaf glad and big," *W*, xxx (*Poems 1923–1954* [New York, 1954], pp. 244–245). About four hundred and fifty American conscientious objectors who refused even noncombatant service were imprisoned during the First World War.

4. Hoffman, p. 85.

5. Mario Maurin, "E. E. Cummings, le poète 'maudit' de Greenwich Village nous parle d'Apollinaire et de lui-même," *Figaro Littéraire,* XIII (July 5, 1958), 12.

6. "Had I, at this moment and in the city of New York, the complete confidence of one-twentieth as many human beings I should not be so inclined to consider The Great American Public as the most aesthetically incapable organization ever created for the purpose of perpetuating defunct ideals and ideas. But of course The Great American Public has a handicap which my friends at La Ferté did not as a rule have—education" (pp. 306–307). This is the introduction to his remarks on *bons trucs*.

7. Cambridge, 1953, Chapter Three.

8. "Letter to John Cotton of Plymouth, March 25, 1671," *Roger Williams: His Contribution to the American Tradition,* ed. Perry Miller (New York, 1965), pp. 237–240. A letter from exile rather than a letter from prison.

9. *Why We Can't Wait* (New York, 1964), pp. 77–100.

10. Boston, 1960, p. 245.

11. Throughout the book Cummings denominates Brown as "B.,"

inadvertently revealing his name only once (pp. 308–309). Though Brown should be an important character, he remains both nameless and faceless. See note 23.

12. The overwhelming load which Cummings takes to prison—and leaves there, returning light—works into the image pattern he borrows from *The Pilgrim's Progress*—the Slough of Despond, Apollyon, the Delectable Mountains, and so on; Cummings shares with Thoreau a serendipitous gift for making fact symbolic. Note, later, the dates of his release from prison, and of his arrival in America.

13. In *Eimi* (New York, 1958), pp. 47–48, 181, 262, 376; and ["Is Something Wrong?"], "War and the Poets (A Symposium)," ed. Oscar Williams, *Harper's Magazine*, CXC (April 1945), 464–465; see Paul Rosenfeld, "The Enormous Cummings," *Twice a Year*, 3–4 (1939), 276, for a discussion of this symbol. Such poems as "o to be in finland" (*XAIPE*, 43 [*Poems 1923–1954*, p. 452] and "THANKSGIVING(1956)" (*95 Poems*, 39 [New York, 1961], imply this symbolic identification of America and liberty by criticizing the United States for not coming to the aid of Finland in 1940 and of Hungary in 1956.

14. P. 141 (Chapter Ten, "Baker Farm").

15. For example, Dr. King's "The goal of America is freedom. Abused and scorned though we may be, our destiny is tied up with America's destiny" ("Letter from Birmingham Jail," p. 97); or James Baldwin's meditations on the connection between being free and being American, in "The Discovery of What It Means To Be An American," *Nobody Knows My Name* (New York, 1961), p. 9.

16. Pp. 99–104 (Chapter Six, "Visitors"). These contacts mean more to Cummings than to Thoreau.

17. P. 5 (Chapter One, "Economy").

18. P. 66 (Chapter Two, "Where I Lived and What I Lived For").

19. The "helluva good universe" to which he directs us in "pity this busy monster,manunkind," *1 x 1*, xiv (*Poems 1923–1954*, p. 397). Cummings is valuable to our time for suggesting that the Good Place is not remote in time or space, but available to all who dare the dooms of love.

20. "i am through you so i," "i am so glad and very," *50 Poems*, 49 (*Poems 1923–1954*, p. 386).

21. *i: Six Nonlectures*, p.24.

22. Chicago, 1952. I am also indebted to Terry Eagleton's "Politics and the Sacred," *Commonweal*, LXXXVII (December 29, 1967), 402–406. Mr. Eagleton's discussion of socio-political "dirt," however, is oriented toward the possibility of justice and the assimilation of outcasts: British, Catholic, and Marxist, he is the pole opposite to Cummings' anarchism.

23. One of the severest weaknesses of *The Enormous Room* as a "so called novel" is Cummings' failure to develop Brown as an identified person. He exists only as a reinforcement of the narrator's own persona, his reality confined to reduplicative phrases like "B. and I."

27 ERNEST HEMINGWAY: *THE SUN ALSO RISES*

Earl H. Rovit

Within the entire canon of Hemingway's works—some seven novels, fifty-odd short stories, a play, and several volumes of nonfiction—*The Sun Also Rises* is something of a curious exception. Published in 1926 while Hemingway was still in his twenties and relatively unknown, it was his first serious attempt at a novel; [1] yet, in spite of the fact that it was to be followed by such overwhelming commercial successes as *A Farewell to Arms* (1929), *For Whom the Bell Tolls* (1940), and *The Old Man and The Sea* (1952), most critics agree that *The Sun Also Rises* is his one most wholly satisfying book. Here Hemingway indelibly fixed the narrative tone for his famous understated ironic prose style. And here he also made his first marked forays into an exploration of those themes that were to become his brand-mark as a writer and which were to occupy him throughout his career. The pragmatic ideal of "grace under pressure," the working out of the Hemingway "code," the concept of "style" as a moral and ethical virtue, and the blunt belief or determination that some form of individual heroism was still possible in the increasingly mechanized and bureaucratic world of the twentieth century: these characteristic Hemingway notions deeply inform the structure of *The Sun Also Rises*. And while Hemingway was to develop these ideas at much greater length and with perhaps more drama in his subsequent work, they achieve a balance and a cogency in *The Sun Also Rises* which, it seems to me, he never really equaled again except in some of his short stories.

At the same time, while *The Sun Also Rises* is characteristically Hemingway, it is radically different from Hemingway's typical fictions. Indeed, it may be precisely in the area of its differences that it attains its special quality and pertinence as a major American novel. For there are subtleties of tone and meaning in *The Sun Also Rises* which suggest a profounder confrontation with the ambiguities of the modern "experience" than Hemingway was ever to sustain again. Hemingway himself regarded this work not as "a hollow or bitter satire, but a damn tragedy with the earth abiding forever as the hero." [2] Without worrying about Hemingway's use of the academically sacred word, "tragedy," I think he may be correctly pointing his reader to the general area where the complexities of the novel come into focus. *The Sun Also Rises* is a novel about loss. Most of Hemingway's work is about loss; the loss of one's desires, one's loves, one's life. But *The Sun Also Rises,* alone among Hemingway's novels, begins with the loss as a "given," as a fatal limitation on open possibilities and opportunities. As in the best of the Nick Adams stories, *The Sun Also Rises* is concerned with that moral space which remains for man's occupancy after necessity has effected its inexorable curtailment on his freedom. And the concentrated passion which gives this novel its tautness of structure and its authority of statement is its exploration of that diminished measure of dignity and endurance which a man may still strive for even while he is a captive in the nets of bleak fatality.

When one considers the gallery of the popular Hemingway heroes—and how difficult it is to refrain from imposing Hemingway's own photogenic features on those of his heroic characters—the composite image can almost be stereotyped in Hollywood terms. The Hemingway "hero" is first and foremost a vigorously athletic figure. He is a man who eats and drinks with natural gusto, a generally successful womanizer who, paradoxically, is innocent of lust, a man professionally dedicated to a physically oriented métier, a hunter-fisherman-soldier who battles against fate with the native resources of his own skill, endurance, and courage in order to wrest a small victory in a long war which he knows he cannot possibly win. As Sean O'Faolain has pointed out, Hemingway's concept of heroism is almost unique in serious modern literature in the mere fact that, as it is presented, it is a convincing possibility.[3] Far from being a passive pawn, the Hemingway hero succeeds in maintaining his own initiative and

momentum in those isolated pockets of endeavor such as sports
and war, which he carves out for himself in a dehumanized
world. At the end, of course, he loses; the winner is allowed to
take nothing, nothing except a sense of moral success in knowing
that he has lost on his own and not on the world's terms.[4] The
typical background for the hero's exploits is a technicolor adventure world, a world of armies clashing and retreating, of wild
animals charging from the tall grasses, of great fish lurking beneath the opaline surfaces of mighty seas. The snow-topped
mountain peak, the massive motion of the great Gulf Stream, the
abiding earth, which, on occasion, may move in intimate response to the hero's ardor, are appropriately epic as both foil for
and projection of the hero's ritual gestures in his dramatic dance
with fate. Nor were the critics slow to attack the validity of
Hemingway's fictional world. Dazzled by the exotic color and the
Horatio Alger bravura with which Hemingway painted his version of moral struggle, they accused him of a variety of artistic
and philosophical sins, ranging from the venial sin of romantic
primitivism to the mortal sin of arrant commercialism.[5] But this
is to read Hemingway with a malicious premeditated selectivity.
It is to ignore the marvelous classic restraint of his prose style. It
is to fail to measure the qualitative difference between his heroic
"heroes" and his typical narrator-protagonists.[6] And it is almost
wholly to disregard *The Sun Also Rises* as a work of art in itself,
as well as a radical metaphor in terms of which Hemingway
fashioned the most effective and influential elements of his work.

To be sure, *The Sun Also Rises* has been the most variously
interpreted of all Hemingway's fiction.[7] Critics have failed to
agree on where, if at all, the base of values resides in the novel.
They have argued the importance of Pedro Romero as a "code-
hero"; they have disagreed on the goodness or badness of Lady
Brett; and they are far from unanimous on the meaning of Jake's
role or experience. The causes of these confusions would seem to
be inherent in the novel itself and not in the subjective predilec-
tions of the critics; but in this case, at least, the confusions attest
to the vitality rather than the incoherence of the work of art. On
its most accessible level, *The Sun Also Rises* is a novel of deceptively casual surfaces, a seemingly realistic *roman à cléf*, narrated
by Jake Barnes-Hemingway, which sketches several months in the

lives of a not particularly prepossessing band of expatriated Bohemians in Paris in 1925.[8] Nothing happens of much moment in the novel as the merrymakers drink, dance, arrange abortive liaisons, backbite, and generally fritter away their time in an empty irresponsible pursuit of joyless pleasure. The narration begins in the spring, builds up a small tension when Robert Cohn goes off to San Sebastian with Lady Brett, and comes to a climax at the final gathering and dispersion of the band in Pamplona for the July 6th Festival of San Fermin.

The critics who stress what Hemingway referred to as "the hollow or bitter satire" of the novel have had two options open to them. They can see the force of the novel's anger as directed against the characters in the novel who, for the most part, assume mawkish postures of self-pity and self-indulgence, while they excuse themselves from responsibility because they are all "a lost generation." From this viewpoint, *The Sun Also Rises* is a fictional extension of Hemingway's lifelong disgust with Bohemianism, tourism, amateurism, and lack of self-discipline.[9] And certainly, narrated as it is by a character who stands off on the margins of the group, the novel supports this effect. The other option open to the critic of this persuasion is to view the satire in a larger, even a cosmic, dimension. The "dirty war" is the immediate historical antecedent behind the bombed-out lives of the expatriates. Jake Barnes has been rendered sexually impotent by his wound in the war. Brett Ashley's "true love" died of dysentery. The sustaining values of western civilization—religious, ethical, philosophical—have been exploded. The frenetic hedonism of the Bohemian group is only a desperate and hopeless complement to the futility and nihilism which the First World War has revealed as the essential element within which human beings have always lived when, for one reason or another, illusions are denied them. This critical view can treat the satire as historically contained—a condemnation of the shallow bourgeois Protestant ethic when it is tested by the absurd degradation of modern war; [10] or, more ambitiously, as Hemingway's attempt to universalize the stark lessons of stoicism and philosophical resignation which have always ruled against man's attempts to impose transcendent meanings upon life. And again, the rhetorical resonance of the novel, as well as its ruthless, if muted, rejection of illusions, will offer a good deal to substanti-ate this position.

Probably, no interpretation will adequately capture the shift-ing nuances of meaning which generate the deeper energies in *The Sun Also Rises*. Satire, tragedy, even some variation of "ro-mance" can find a supporting configuration in the novel, but only at the cost of deflecting the main thrust of the novel in an effort to make it amenable to the understanding. And the ulti-mate inconclusiveness of any interpretation will be almost en-tirely due to the ambiguous status of Jake Barnes. As the first-person narrator, he and only he is responsible for what the reader knows and what the reader can never know. But his reliability as a reporter is seriously affected by two factors: first, his inevi-table physical and psychological passivity (unlike the popular Hemingway "hero," Jake is pre-eminently a man to whom things happen); and, second, his intense emotional involvement in the events that he describes, precisely because he is fighting as hard as he can to keep from succumbing to hysteria or despair. More than anything else, the novel is Jake's story, a blow-by-blow de-scription, told from the inside, by a man struggling to catch his balance as he teeters on the edge of spiritual suicide. For Jake has already suffered his irreparable loss when the novel begins. Unusually responsive to physical sensation as are all Heming-way's heroes, Jake is continually beset by stimuli which mix a witches' brew of memory and desire in him. But he is not free to act upon his desires; the option of love is forever foreclosed in his life. *The Sun Also Rises* is a chronicle of Jake's attempt to live in a centerless world as a personality lacking a vital center. His dislocation is not single, but double, and it pervades his entire existence. Since Hemingway has chosen to locate the novel's viewing-point within a focus of such radical dislocation, we ought not to be surprised at the resultant confusion of interpre-tation because it is inherent in the internal dissociation of the narrative voice itself.

The point is that Jake cannot trust himself, nor can he even believe that he possesses or will ever possess a stable core of being which is potentially trustworthy. He must ignore his desires be-cause they can only cause him anguish. He must try to bury his memories because they are only desires in a concealed guise. Even as he tries to maintain himself as a careful spectator in life, nurturing his epicurean satisfactions in the pleasures of trout fishing and watching bullfights, he finds himself acting the pander between Brett and Pedro Romero, and hence he betrays both his desired love and his hard-won *aficion*. He cannot trust himself because his grotesque wound has denuded him of man's most cherished illusion—the illusion that there is a center to one's life. It is in this context that Jake's often-quoted reflections during the fiesta should be interpreted:

> I thought I had paid for everything. Not like the woman pays and pays and pays. No idea of retribution or punishment. Just exchange of values. You gave up something and got something else. Or you worked for something. You paid some way for everything that was any good. . . . Either you paid by learning about them, or by experience, or by taking chances, or by money. Enjoying living was learning to get your money's worth. The world was a good place to buy in. It seemed like a fine philosophy. In five years, I thought, it will seem just as silly as all the other fine philosophies I've had.
>
> Perhaps that wasn't true though. Perhaps as you went along you did learn something. I did not care what it was all about. All I wanted to know was how to live in it. Maybe if you found out how to live in it you learned from that what it was all about.[11]

This famous "exchange of values" philosophy is a movement from a concern with "essence" (*"what* it was all about") to a focus on "existence" (*"how* to live in it"). It is a movement which candidly rejects "centers" and transfers its interest to the peripheries of one's sensations. It suggests that life can be dealt with only as a system of transactions, a volatile sequence of energy-exchanges where the difference between life and death, value and worthlessness, being and nothingness, is dependent only on the capital reserve that is left in the credit column. And thus the structure of *The Sun Also Rises,* symmetrically but deceptively patterned in terms of the three acts of the classic bullfight, rests on a dynamically askew and radically dislocated, shifting basis.

This, it would seem, is the main source of the novel's strength and the root reason for Jake's moral success in achieving "a way to be" in the world. Without this eccentric focus, the novel would be little more than a banal variation of another "identity-quest," trite and pompous in its acquisition of platitudinous "truths." But Jake finds a different way out, or at least a viable technique of living within a world of inexorable loss. *Style* is what Jake resorts to after alcohol, religion, and philosophy have proved ineffectual in keeping him from crying at night in his room. Style of whatever kind is no more nor less than a manner, a system of rhythmic interrelationships, an achieved harmony of disparate movements, intentions, and effects. A "good" style is one which gives the impression of being inevitable and one which works; which, that is, accomplishes the job that it is set to do. And Hemingway's style in *The Sun Also Rises,* a style which is synonymous with Jake's voice, is the best documentation that we possess of Jake's success in working out for himself a psychological and spiritual balance without a center of gravity. Of all the characters in the novel, only he (and possibly Count Mippipopolous) achieve this order of style. Pedro Romero has an admirable style, of course, but it works only when he is fighting his bulls or Robert Cohn, and, at any rate, it is a "received," traditional style which is his by initiation and apprenticeship. Bill Gorton, Mike Campbell, and Brett also possess a style of sorts; but it doesn't work particularly well for them, nor does it seem inevitable and natural.

The general life-style of the rootless expatriate world, as Hemingway presents it, is like that of an endless costume party where the drunks get drunker and the cheap finery gets shabbier and shabbier under the harsh lights. And Robert Cohn, of course, is the horrible example in the novel of precisely "the way *not* to be." In some sense Jake's alter ego,[12] Cohn is sensitive, intelligent, and desperately eager to discover meaning and value in experience. However he is basically dishonest in his keeping of the accounts of his energy-transactions—the cardinal sin of an exchange-of-values philosophy is falsification—and his various styles (the romantic artist, the unrequited lover, the self-pitying martyr) are a succession of ill-fitting, secondhand gestures and responses which fool no one and fail to work at all. Only Jake has the self-discipline, the honesty, and the driving need to achieve a thin sleeve of freedom in recognizing and accepting the limitations of his condition. The prose style of *The Sun Also*

Rises and the moral style which Jake successfully strives for are what give this book its power and continued relevance.

Hemingway was not to follow up this direction in his later work. Probably such an effort would have required an expense of psychic energy which no human being could have long sustained. Instead, he held on to the prose style which was Jake Barnes's achievement of a *moral* style, but he employed it to narrate the stories of men in the process of suffering loss. Thus, Frederick Henry's loss of Catherine, Jordan's and Cantwell's loss of their lives, and Santiago's loss of the big fish are superbly crafted and genuinely moving stories of their kind, but their effects are qualitatively different from the more somber tonalities which *The Sun Also Rises* almost effortlessly evokes. Occasionally in these other novels, the prose style dips into the sentimental and the melodramatic and becomes susceptible to the charges that Hemingway was parodying his own best work. If a successful style should appear inevitable and do its work well, such criticism in certain instances is justified. Jake Barnes's style was developed in order for him to arrive at an equilibrium of which he had been deprived by an unredeemable, spirit-shattering loss. The same style is hardly consonant with a narrative structure that displays a psychically centered protagonist losing something—even if it is something as dear to him as his own life. Only in some of the magnificent short stories like "Big Two-Hearted River" (1925), "In Another Country" (1927), "The Clean Well-Lighted Place" (1933), and "The Snows of Kilimanjaro" (1936), stories, incidentally, in which the loss has occurred *before* the narrative begins, do we find that conjunction of prose style and moral style which Hemingway forged in *The Sun Also Rises,* seemingly as a last-ditch strategy to cope with a world stripped of illusions where *nada* is omnipresent and well-nigh omnipotent.[13]

It would be well to remember here that as significant as the novel may have been in the development of Hemingway's work, *The Sun Also Rises* has enjoyed an importance of its own apart from Hemingway. What fortuitous conjunction of events it is that transforms a novel into a cultural document—what makes some works of art take on an additional life as expressions of an historical period or, indeed, a national life-style, we do not at all know. Yet it cannot be denied that such metamorphoses do take place and it sometimes even seems that this may be one of the more valuable and mysterious functions that a literature performs for its culture. At any rate, it is surely provocative to note that *The Sun Also Rises* was published within four years of such major American statements as Eliot's *The Waste Land,* Dreiser's *An American Tragedy,* and Faulkner's *The Sound and the Fury.* Certainly these four books are vividly independent, each pursuing its own content and creating its own form in terms of each individual author's unfathomable needs and artistic gifts. And yet there are curious similarities and parallels between these titles. If not one of them is a tragedy, still they all of them traffic surprisingly close to that mood of grotesque poignancy which may be the nearest our age can come to the spirit of the tragic. In Hemingway's and Eliot's works there is literal sexual impotence; in Dreiser's and Faulkner's books, a symbolic impotence is a major factor in the development of both plots. Further, all four books are, in their various ways, equally zealous at unmasking the social and metaphysical illusions which impose palpably false meanings on human experience.

Jake Barnes had suggested that "you paid some way for everything that was any good." "After such knowledge, what forgiveness?" asks Eliot's Gerontion, and, in a sense, all four of these books, foundering on the jagged intransigencies of payment and retribution, brood over the dark implications in those two statements: implications which challenge the very existence of moral impetus, responsibility, and the primal integrity of the human consciousness. The four authors differ greatly in the degree of intensity with which they suggest an ultimately nihilistic reality as the sole reality in the universe, and each, perhaps, offers his own tentative saving graces, but the void is frighteningly near to the surfaces of all of these texts. Most coincidentally of all, each of these books is fundamentally *uncentered* in a manner similar or analogous to the way *The Sun Also Rises* is uncentered. Eliot's poem and Faulkner's novel possess no obvious protagonist and both structures are deliberately fragmented. Dreiser's novel has a protagonist, to be sure, but he is a protagonist without a personality, without a core of moral being; in fact, Clyde Griffiths is so much a product of his landscape as to be part of it and hardly human at all.[14] But this is not the place to investigate the deeper levels of the literary climate of opinion of the 1920's. It is enough to suggest that this congruence of metaphor and structure in what are probably the four outstanding books of that great decade may indicate one reason why *The Sun Also Rises* has had a singular position among the scores of very good books that are part of the post-First World War disillusionment. These four works not only *reflect* the whirling frenzy of a culture in the midst of historical upheaval, but they also *project* metaphorical patterns of thought (specifically, those concerned with the most basic metaphor of all—the metaphor of man himself) that we are only now beginning to recognize and investigate with care.

Purely as a result of a geographical and a series of historical accidents, American culture has always been a "modern" culture; and its most basic and constant experience has been that of radical dislocation. Obviously this fact has been a source of both cultural strength and weakness. But one of the strengths has been the peculiar position accorded to the American writer within, as well as on the margins of, the western world. The American artist has enjoyed (or been burdened by) a special prescience, an almost preternatural and prophetic sensitivity to the major movements in modern life. Since his equilibrium has never come from traditionally supported bases of gravity, like a seismograph he has been inordinately receptive to the slightest of vibrations. Modern existentialism, nihilism, and absurdism are cleanly prefigured in the major works of the nineteenth-century American romantics. While Hemingway can be seen as at least a partial heir to that tradition,[15] *The Sun Also Rises* is informed by an uncanny intuition of a new metaphor. As the Newtonian world-machine image of the eighteenth century gave way to the organic metaphor of the nineteenth century, so it is possible that the organic metaphor has already been supplanted by a new world-view, a view for which the most adequate metaphorical image may be that of explosion. If this is so, then it is likely that radically dislocated structures that are capable of functioning well, and personalities without a vital center that can maintain viable lives should have a special meaning for us today. And it is, finally, for this reason that *The Sun Also Rises* ought to continue to command our attention and provoke our thought.

Notes

1. Although *The Torrents of Spring* was published some months earlier, it seems to have been written between the drafts of *The Sun Also Rises*. See Carlos Baker, *Hemingway: The Writer as Artist* (3rd. ed.; Princeton, 1963), p. 76. Baker also reports that an earlier novel was among the baggage of manuscripts that Hemingway lost.

2. In a letter to Maxwell Perkins, November 19, 1926. Quoted in Baker, p. 81.

3. *The Vanishing Hero* (Boston, 1956), p. 164.

4. Hemingway's attitude toward his own death may be pertinent here: "Who the hell should care about saving his soul when it's a man's duty to lose it intelligently, the way you would sell a position you were defending, if you could not hold it, as expensively as possible, trying to make it the most expensive position that was ever sold." Lillian Ross, *Portrait of Hemingway* (New York, 1961), p. 48. One inevitably wonders how to balance the expensiveness and the responsibility of suicide and how Hemingway balanced them on July 2, 1961.

5. Sufficient representative material can be found in Wyndham Lewis, "The Dumb Ox: A Study of Ernest Hemingway," *The American Review,* III (June 1934), 289–312; and Otto Friedrich, "Ernest Hemingway: Joy Through Strength," *American Scholar,* XXVI (Autumn 1957), 410, 518–530.

6. It should be clear that I am following the distinction which Philip Young brilliantly crystallized in his *Ernest Hemingway* (New York, 1952) on the difference between the "code-hero" and the Nick Adams-autobiographical hero. In my own study, *Ernest Hemingway* (New York, 1963), I make a further development of his thesis, using my own terms, the "tutor" and the "tyro."

7. Two interesting studies of the novel are Mark Spilka, "The Death of Love in *The Sun Also Rises,*" *Twelve Original Essays on Great American Novels,* ed. Charles Shapiro (Detroit, 1958), pp. 238–256; and Robert O. Stephens, "Hemingway's Don Quixote in Pamplona," *College English,* XXIII (December 1961), 216–218.

8. Some of the autobiographical bases of the novel, as well as a superficial identification of most of the characters, can be guessed at from Morley Callaghan's *That Summer in Paris* (New York, 1964) and Harold Loeb's *The Way It Was* (New York, 1959). Hemingway himself contributes some additional obscurity on the matter in his posthumous *A Moveable Feast* (New York, 1964). I am rather strongly convinced, however, that bringing in superfluous fictions of reality ("the way it *really* was") to "explain" or account for a novel can serve only to

muddle and degrade the much more interesting and valid reality of the fiction. Hemingway's autobiographical intrusions into his stories are such a labyrinthine intermixture of public posturing and private inaccessibility that the critic who tries to track him by his spoor is likely to find only himself at every turning.

9. See, for example, Hemingway's amused disgust in his feature article, "American bohemians in Paris," Toronto *Star Weekly*, March 25, 1922.

10. A comprehensive view of the decade's response to the First World War can be gathered from Frederick J. Hoffman's *The Twenties* (New York, 1955). A more detailed summary is available in Stanley Cooperman's *World War I and the American Novel* (Baltimore, 1967).

11. *The Sun Also Rises* (New York, 1926), p. 153.

12. Poor Cohn is doubtless more sinned against than sinning, but Hemingway is not noted for his justice or compassion in dealing with the temporary targets of his vituperation. Cohn occupies the role of Jake's "double"–a double that must be destroyed. Like Jake, Cohn plays tennis and boxes, is a writer, falls in love with Brett, and is concerned to find "meaning" in life.

13. Here it is probably pertinent to note Hemingway's intense fascination with the bullfight which produced, among other things, that strange masterpiece, *Death in the Afternoon* (New York, 1932). Critics are quick to remark Hemingway's professional expertise and sympathy with the matador, but it is at least equally true that he identified as strongly with the "brave bulls." If a bullfight has something of the structure of a classical tragedy, it is the bull and not the matador that is doomed when the fight begins.

14. The supporting argument for this interpretation would require far more detail than can be provided here. For an exposition, see Frederick J. Hoffman's comparison of Dostoevsky's *Crime and Punishment* with Dreiser's *An American Tragedy* in his *The Mortal No* (Princeton, 1964), pp. 179–201.

15. See my *Ernest Hemingway, op. cit.,* especially pp. 167–169.

28 SINCLAIR LEWIS: *BABBITT*

Mark Schorer

It has been fashionable since some time before his death in 1951 to say that Sinclair Lewis' fiction has nothing now to say to Americans, and nothing to say any longer that is centrally relevant to American life. Americans no longer talk like Lewis' characters, it is asserted, if indeed they ever did. Sinclair Lewis is dead! To the bulk of his twenty-one novels and to almost the entire mass of his shorter fiction, the charge is probably applicable enough, but to three or four or possibly even five novels, above all, to *Babbitt*, it is not. That *Babbitt*, at least, retains much of its original relevance, hence much of its original force, is suggested by two illustrations that have recently come to my attention.

About a year ago a young English instructor in one of the state colleges in southern California, while teaching *Babbitt* in his course in the American novel, was discussing the hero's oration at the dinner of the Zenith Real Estate Board (end of Section Three of Chapter Fourteen), and he suggested that several paragraphs of that speech could be sent to the editor of a considerably conservative local newspaper as a reader's letter, and that it would probably be published. The suggestion caused a ripple of appreciative laughter and the instructor thought no more of the matter until the next week, when, to his astonishment, he came across the following in the "Letters to the Editor" section of the newspaper in question:

> Irresponsible Professors Considered "Menace"
> Editor: I would like to call attention to a problem that is confronting the citizens of the United States.

As I read of the University of California and the riots over everything and anything, I cannot help but think that the worst menace to sound government is not the avowed socialists but those who work undercover—the long-haired gentry who call themselves "liberals" and "radicals" and "non-partisan" and intelligentsia.

Irresponsible teachers and professors constitute the worst of the lot and I am ashamed that several of them give a bad impression of the faculty of our great state university. There are certain instructors who seem to think that we ought to turn the conduct of the nation over to a group of hoboes and roustabouts.

I think that this sort of thing must be stopped as soon as possible.

—LEWIS SINCLAIR

A comparison of this letter with Babbitt's declamation demonstrates that the student who took up his instructor's whimsical suggestion made only the slightest changes in the language of the original in order to suit the words of 1922 to a local situation in 1967. Below his assumed name the student gave his own address, and within two days he received a letter "in complete agreement," urging his support for a particular rightist candidate in an impending election.

Gratified by his success, the student at once followed up his first letter with a second, this one a parody of the Lewis-Babbitt style which, on behalf of the city's taxpayers, attacked "Bearded philosophers, poets and others who are interested in teaching extremism and pacifism! Leftist political scientists bent on the destruction of our democratic society! And English professors who find a 'new morality' in the works of Salinger, Miller and the like." This letter, again signed Lewis Sinclair, was also duly printed in all seriousness. In San Diego, California, at least, George F. Babbitt lives, and with him, Sinclair Lewis!

They live, in fact, throughout this country, as the second illustration shows. In April 1968 the Columbia Broadcasting System initiated a television series called "The Great American Novel" in which dramatized sections of novels are juxtaposed with shots of comparable situations in real life, and the performers themselves are both professional actors and ordinary citizens. This series opened with *Babbitt,* and this production was, like the novel itself, both hilarious and pathetic. "Taking his camera to a Lions Club meeting in Duluth," the *New York Times* television reviewer reported next day, the director "brought George F. Babbitt gloriously to life. In the bargain, he reminded the viewer that there is a little bit of Babbitt in most of us":

> One of the most amusing sequences had Pat Hingle [the professional actor who played Babbitt] delivering Babbitt's famous "booster" speech to the assembled Lions [Duluth citizens], with the camera observing the members' reactions. Many approved of the sentiments expressed. One member was overheard to say that it sounded like a Goldwater speech of a few years ago.
>   "Just as dynamic, too," observed another member.
>   The Duluth businessmen were great boosters of their town's virtues, and all agreed that they were in a boom era.
>   Most admitted that they were conformists, and said that even having a mistress was ruled out more by social or business pressure than by morality. The Lions play hard and work hard, and can't imagine themselves doing anything else. A few had some doubts, but the consensus was voiced by one dour-faced man during a wild party when he asked: "Who has more fun than we do?"
>   It was very sad. . . .

That a novel like *Babbitt* should continue to have relevance in our lives is perhaps surprising when we remember that one of Sinclair Lewis' most striking qualities in his successful novels was to anticipate by just a moment what would in the next become a prevailing national mood. With the passing of such moods, one might well expect the passing of such books.

Main Street was published in 1920. This story about the sluggish backwaters of American village life was published in the year that officially announced American village life to have become a backwater. The 1920 census showed that at some point between 1915 and that year American society had crossed a line from what had been a rural to what had become an urban society. Sometime between those years, the old majority of farmers and villagers had become the minority, and the residents of cities comprised the new majority. *Babbitt* opens in April 1920. It is concerned not only with the new urban society but also with certain new urban attitudes that attach to American commercial culture: the idea of "boosting," for example, that aggressive promotion of special civic interests that finally finds its apotheosis in our enormous system of Public Relations; and that idea of business "service" to the community, which bears the same relationship to the actual practices of commercialism as the idea of "the white man's burden" bears to the actualities of imperialism and colonialism. Yet it shows us, too, how the residents of Zenith, booming the city, profess still much of the rural faith of their fathers, and how from this conflict between old and newer attitudes proceed frustration, guilt, despair of a watered kind, at last emptiness.

Before Sinclair Lewis finished *Main Street,* he was already contemplating the materials of the next novel, "the story of the Tired Business Man, of the man in the Pullman smoker, of our American ruler, of the man playing golf at the country club at Minneapolis, Omaha, Atlanta, Rochester," a man to be called G. T. Pumphrey, of Monarch City; the book to be called *Pumphrey.* And toward the end of *Main Street,* Gopher Prairie is indeed reaching toward Zenith. The town launches a "campaign of boosting" under the auspices of the Commercial Club, and a newcomer, "Honest Jim" Blauser, a "Hustler," is its director. The banquet given in his honor is the occasion for

> . . . oratorical references to Pep, Punch, Go, Vigor, Enterprise, Red Blood, He-Men, Fair Women, God's Country, James J. Hill, the Blue Sky, the Green Fields, the Bountiful Harvest, Increasing Population, Fair Return on Investments, Alien Agitators Who Threaten the Security of Our Institutions, the Hearthstone the Foundation of the State, Senator Knute Nelson, One Hundred Per Cent. Americanism, and Pointing with Pride—

all the clichés of our commercial culture delivered in the braying public voice that speaks for that milieu, the *blat* and *clak* and *zing* and *wowie* that characterize the rasping rhetoric of American business enterprise at its crudest middle-class level. The campaign of boosting for new enterprises in Gopher Prairie came to nothing. This is the world of George F. Babbitt, and we must move on to the middle-sized, midwestern city of Zenith. *Babbitt* is a satiric prelude to a decade of dizzying and often mindless economic expansion, the epic of our "boom" years, and it remains today the major documentation in literature of American business culture in general. We can no longer say, as Woodrow Wilson said in 1900, that "The history of a nation is only the history of its villages written large." By 1920, we substitute for *village* the name of *Zenith*.

As we see Zenith looming beyond Gopher Prairie, so we see Gopher Prairie still in the process of receding in Zenith. On the first page "the mist took pity on the fretted structures of earlier generations: the Post Office with its shingle-tortured mansard, the red brick minarets of hulking old houses. . . ." There is the explicit contrast between Babbitt and his father-in-law, Henry Thompson, between "the old-fashioned, lean Yankee, rugged, traditional stage type of American business man, and Babbitt, the plump, smooth, efficient, up-to-the-minute and otherwise perfected modern." The ironic limitations of this contrast are underlined in the discussion of small towns at the Babbitts' first dinner party in the novel, when the talk of the whole company, consisting of the emptiest banalities and comprising a pure parody of any interchange that could be called conversation, laments the absence of meaningful conversation and "culture" in the "hick towns" that Chum Frink, "a Famous Poet and a distinguished advertising agent," has just been touring.

Physically, the culture has become predominantly urban; but psychologically it is in large part still stubbornly rural, perhaps even more profoundly provincial than before. This is curious, because late in 1920, when he was already at work on *Babbitt*, Sinclair Lewis himself seemed to believe that because of the difference in size, a city might offer its residents a kind of spiritual grace that a village denied them. He was writing to Floyd Dell, who had suggested that perhaps he, in his novel *Moon-Calf*, through his character Felix Fay, had said the same thing that Lewis, through Carol Kennicott in *Main Street*, had said at about the same time. Lewis wrote:

> Don't you think that the difs between M-C and M St are 2, both important. One, Felix is young, unbound, a male—*free to go*; while Carol is (since she *thinks* she is) not free. Second, your Davenport is just enough bigger than G.P.—to be worlds bigger. Give Carol just one Felix Fay (who isn't silly & you know it!) and she would be contented enough to begin to create life about her.

But the whole aim of the documentation of *Babbitt* is to demonstrate that with the cultural shift, the slavery of the individual has become even more rigid, that freedom exists only in impossibly infantile, whimpering dreams.

I have twice used the word *documentation,* and quite intentionally. *Babbitt* is the first of Lewis' novels that rests on what was henceforth to be his characteristic method of "research." His preceding five novels had shown traces of similar "research," but now it becomes nearly systematic. He established a *pied-à-terre* at the Queen City Club in Cincinnati, Ohio, and if Zenith is modeled on any one city, it is this one. Here he consolidated his researches, and his gray notebooks were already fat with his notation.

The method involved a series of steps. First, he chose a subject and a "field" within it to be mastered—not, as for most novelists, a character situation or a mere theme, but a social area (a subclass within the middle class) that could be studied and "worked up"—in this instance, the world of the small businessman and within that, real estate. Then, armed with his notebooks, he mingled with the kind of people that the fiction would mainly concern. In Pullman cars and smokers, in the lobbies of side-street hotels, in athletic clubs, in a hundred junky streets he watched and listened, and then meticulously copied into his notebooks whole catalogs of expressions drawn from the American lingo, elaborate lists of proper names, every kind of physical detail. Once his story was determined, he drew intricately detailed maps, and maps not only of the city in which the story was set but of the houses in which his actions would take place, floor plans with furniture precisely located, streets and the kind and color of dogs that walked on them. Once his chief characters were settled upon, he wrote out full biographies of all of them. From this body of material, he would then write out a summary of his story, and from this, a much more extended "plan," as he called it, with every scene sketched in, the whole sometimes nearly as long as the book that would come from it. A first draft would then follow, usually much longer than the final version, and then a long process of revision and cutting, and at last the publishable text. For *Babbitt,* he traveled the length and breadth of the United States in 1920 and 1921, always listening and looking with nothing but that novel in mind, and Cincinnati was the center of these efforts.

The immediate result is not surprising even though the ultimate effect may be. The immediate result is a fictional approximation of the social anthropologist's field report. A year after the publication of *Babbitt,* when asked about its origins, Lewis said that all he could remember was that the original name of the protagonist was Pumphrey and that "I planned to make the whole novel 24 hours in his life, from alarm clock to alarm clock. The rest came more or less unconsciously." In fact, so late as July 1921, Lewis had not found his title or his hero's name. In that month he wrote to his editor with various suggestions for a title: *Population, 300,000; Good Business; A Good Practical Man; A He-Man; The Booster; A Solid Citizen; Zenith.* But the name of the protagonist, Pumphrey, had changed to Fitch, and Fitch had changed to Babbitt, "commonplace yet will be remembered." Once thought of, *Babbitt* seemed inevitable, "and two years from now we'll have them talking of Babbittry." As they indeed did. The name *Pumphrey* remained as that of a minor character— "Professor Joseph K. Pumphrey, owner of the Riteway Business College and instructor in Public Speaking, Business English, Scenario Writing, and Commercial Law"—and the original structural conception remained in the first seven chapters, in which we do indeed follow George Babbitt from dreaming sleep to dreaming sleep. But that is only one-fourth of the whole novel.

The remainder, twenty-seven chapters, did not come about "unconsciously," as their obviously planned substance makes very clear. They are, rather than "unconscious," a quite highly conscious, indeed systematic series of set pieces, each with its own topic, and all together giving us an almost punctilious analysis of the sociology of American commercial culture and middle-class life. Over halfway through the novel, mingling with these set pieces, the first of three "plots" begins.

These twenty-seven chapters could well have carried, in the convention of earlier fiction, subject titles. Chapters Eight and Nine, in which the Babbitts entertain at dinner in their Floral Heights house, could have been called Domestic Manners of the Americans. The next two chapters might have been headed

Marital Relations and Pullman Car Customs. Chapter Twelve is about Leisure: baseball, golf, the movies, bridge, motoring. Chapter Thirteen takes up the phenomenon of the annual Trade Association Convention and, since it ends with some adult but immature louts in a brothel, Juvenile Delinquency. Chapter Fourteen has to do with Political and Professional Oratory, and Fifteen, with Class Structure. The next two chapters devote themselves to Religion, and Eighteen, to Family Relations. The first of the three separate "plots" begins in the next chapter, Nineteen, and delaying discussion of these for a moment, we may observe that the general topics remaining are the weekly Service Club Lunch, the Bachelor, the Barber Shop, Labor Relations, the Speakeasy, and "Crank" Religion. It is a very thorough canvassing of an entire milieu, and its nearly anthropological intention is made evident in such a sentence as "Now this was the manner of obtaining alcohol under the reign of righteousness and prohibition," the sentence that introduces Babbitt's visit to a bootlegger.

If the canvas that these pieces comprise is surprisingly complete, their ordering is nevertheless quite haphazard. They might have been presented in almost any other sequence, and that is because there is no genuine plot or coherent, causative march of dramatic events from beginning to end that would necessarily have determined their order. Their fragmentariness is in part overcome by the fact that it is the single figure of Babbitt who moves through all of them in the course of his mounting discontent, revolt, his retreat and relapse into resignation. Each of these three stages centers in a narrative more or less separate from the others. The first develops after Babbitt's one real friend, Paul Riesling, shoots his wife and is given a three-year prison sentence. It is this event that suddenly makes Babbitt feel that his life is empty and that all his bustling activities are meaningless. It is in this mood that he decides to be "liberal" (although he hardly knows what the word means) and thus declare his independence from the clan of his business associates. Paul Riesling pretty nearly disappears from the novel, but now Babbitt meets a new friend, Mrs. Tanis Judique, a silly adventuress with whom, in the absence of Mrs. Babbitt, he begins a love affair of sorts.

This open break with the professed moral code of the middle

class is the dramatization of his revolt from the values of his business culture. He tries to forget the discontent and insecurity and fear from which he is immediately suffering by drink and debauchery with "the Bunch," a miscellaneous group of trivial and tawdry persons who are Tanis Judique's friends. These pleasures pall, and presently he breaks off his friendship with Tanis, who now disappears from the novel. In the meantime, Virgil Gunch and other of Babbitt's associates are forming the Good Citizens' League, an anti-labor vigilante organization, and they attempt to coerce Babbitt into joining them. In his mood of stubborn discontent, he resists their efforts; as a result, he suffers alarming social and economic injuries, and it is only his wife's happily coincidental emergency operation that enables him to scuttle into the League and thus back into the old security of the Boosters' Club and the stolid business order of Zenith. Perfectly safe again, he recognizes at the end of the novel that he has never in his life really done anything that he wanted to, and he hopes for a fuller, more independent life for his not very promising son, Theodore Roosevelt Babbitt. But he cannot define for himself anything real that he ever did want to do except what in fact he had always done.

It is Babbitt's tragedy that he can never be anything but Babbitt, even though he has a glimmering recognition of what it is about being Babbitt that he does not always like:

> He was conscious of life, and a little sad. With no Virgil Gunches before whom to set his face in resolute optimism, he beheld, and half admitted that he beheld, his way of life as incredibly mechanical. Mechanical business—a brisk selling of badly built houses. Mechanical religion—a dry, hard church, shut off from the real life of the streets, inhumanly respectable as a top-hat. Mechanical golf and dinner-parties and bridge and conversations. Save with Paul Riesling, mechanical friendships—back-slapping and jocular, never daring to essay the test of quietness.

The terror and loneliness that he feels in his brief taste of freedom (and that freedom itself consists largely of a very "mechanical" bit of adultery) arise from the fact that when he is free he is nothing at all. His only self is the self that exists solely within the circle of conformity.

Since the publication of *Babbitt*, everyone has learned that conformity is the great price that our predominantly commercial culture exacts of American life. But when *Babbitt* was published, this was its revelation to Americans, and this was likewise how the novel differed from all novels about business that had been published before it.

American literature had a rich if brief tradition of the business novel. Henry James, William Dean Howells, Charles and Frank Norris, Jack London, David Graham Phillips, Robert Herrick, Upton Sinclair, Edith Wharton, Theodore Dreiser, Ernest Poole, Booth Tarkington—all these writers and others as well had been concerned with the businessman, and after James and Howells, only Tarkington was to find in him any of the old, perdurable American virtues. Business was synonymous with ethical corruption; the world of business was savagely competitive, brutally aggressive, murderous. The motivation of the businessman was power, money, social prestige, in that order. But the businessman in all this fiction was the tycoon, the powerful manufacturer, the vast speculator, the fabulous financier, the monarch of enormous enterprises, the arch-individual responsible only to himself. He was the equivalent in the developing industrial world of the old, aggressively independent frontiersman. And his concern was with production, if only of more money from money.

After the First World War and our shift to an urban culture, the tycoon may still have been the most colorful and dramatic figure in the business myth, but he was no longer by any means the characteristic figure, and *Babbitt* discovers that difference. If George F. Babbitt has vague hankerings after the old frontier independence, his incompetence in that role is made plain enough by his ridiculous vacation excursions into Maine. His is the shriveled office world of the small businessman, and more particularly, of the small middleman. If his morals are no better, his defections are anything but spectacular: a little cheating in a deal, a little lie to one's wife, a little stealthy fornication that one pretends did not occur. Not in the least resembling the autocratic individualist, he is always the compromising conformist. No producer himself, his success depends on public relations. He does not rule; he "joins" to be safe. He boosts and boasts with his fellows, sings and cheers and prays with the throng, derides all difference, denounces all dissent—and all to climb with the crowd. With the supremacy of public relations, he abolishes human relations. And finally, therefore, without at all knowing it, he abolishes all but a wretched remnant of his own humanity.

All this Sinclair Lewis' novel gave back to a culture that was just becoming aware that it would not be able to tolerate what it was in the process of making itself. And his novel did it with a difference. The older novels, generally speaking, were solemn or grandly melodramatic denunciations of monstrous figures of aggressive evil. *Babbitt* was raucously satirical of a crowd of ninnies and buffoons who, if they were vindictive and petty, were also absurd. Yet, along with all that, Babbitt himself was pathetic. How could the novel possibly have failed? It did not. It was one of the greatest international successes in all publishing history.

The European response was unadulterated delight: this was the way—crass, materialistic, complacent, chauvinistic—that Europe had always known America to be, and now an American had made the confession to the world. In the United States the response was, understandably, more diluted. Among those who were either unimpressed or outraged, there was, however, small complaint on the score of the deficiencies of *Babbitt* as a novel. No one, for example, observed the slack structure, or the repetitiousness of point in the long series of sociological demonstrations. Edith Wharton, in her letter of congratulation to Lewis, did recognize that he seemed to depend on an excess of slang, on nearly endless imitation of midwestern garrulity; but this did not bother others. Had anyone complained, for example, that in his use of public addresses of one sort or another, Lewis' pleasure in mimicry threatened to carry him far beyond the demands of his fiction, it could have been pointed out that here is a very integral part of his satire. Elocution is an old American institution, and a windy, mindless rhetoric has been of its essence, as the oratory at the conventions of either of our chief political parties still painfully reminds us. Lewis' use of elocution adds a swelling note to the already loud *blat-blat* of the public voice that roars and rattles through the novel, and if Lewis lets Babbitt admire Chan Mott because he "can make a good talk even when he hasn't got a doggone thing to say," he is also making an observation on the empty and noisy restlessness of American life.

It was not generally the writing, nor even Lewis' satiric exposure of American commercial culture in itself that disturbed those readers who were disturbed, but rather their failure to find in the novel anything beyond this grossness. With George Santayana, who was otherwise impressed by the novel, they saw "no suggestion of the direction . . . in which salvation may come." The complaint was to say of Lewis, in effect, what Lewis had himself said of Babbitt, that he was "without a canon [of value] which would enable him to speak with authority." If Babbitt, with his faint sense that the values of excellence, joy, passion, wisdom, do indeed exist somewhere, but had not the slightest notion of how to pursue them, did Sinclair Lewis?

It became a commonplace to say of Lewis that he was himself too much a George F. Babbitt to lift his sights to values beyond Babbitt's own. In many ways the charge is just. But Lewis is different from Babbitt in one supreme way: he *observed* him, and Babbitt had not been observed before; thus he *created* him; and Babbitt endures in our literature as in our life, where Sinclair Lewis enabled all of us to see him for the first and for an enduring time.

He endures with a special kind of solidity and vitality. He is so inexhaustibly *there*. This achievement obviously derives from Lewis' technique. That mass of social notation that we have remarked, notation that Lewis pursued with all the naturalist's compulsiveness, is yet, in the end, not at all a naturalistic performance. It shares rather in the realm of what today we call Pop Art. Take any very mundane item from our daily lives—a Campbell's Soup can, for example; observe it in the most exact and even microscopic detail; then enlarge it; then repeat it over and over in the monotonous design; and at last something *not* naturalistic but rather grotesque and even monstrous emerges, and something in the end much more substantial than the absurdity from which it is constructed.

It was this quality that Constance Rourke had in mind in 1931 when she singled Lewis out among his contemporaries: "With one exception none of those definitive novelists have appeared who make an aspect of contemporary life their own and leave it with the color of their imagination upon it forever afterward. The exception of course is Sinclair Lewis. . . ." The term *novelist* in the usual sense was not quite right for him. She gave him, and we do still, the larger title: *fabulist*.

29 JAMES AGEE: *LET US NOW PRAISE FAMOUS MEN*

Samuel Hynes

> I care mainly about just 2 things. Sometimes they seem identical or at
> least like binary stars, & sometimes they seem like a split which can
> completely destroy. They would be (1) getting as near truth and
> whole truth as is humanly possible, which means several sorts of
> "Truth" maybe, but on the whole means spiritual life, integrity and
> growth; and (2) setting this (near-) truth out in the clearest and
> cleanest possible terms.[1]

In the library of a small college where I once taught, James
Agee's *Let Us Now Praise Famous Men* is shelved with books
on the history of Alabama. This is rather like classifying *Moby
Dick* as a book about whales, but one can understand the librari-
an's dilemma, for Agee's book is fundamentally unclassifiable. It
is neither fiction nor poetry, though it is full of sensitive poetic
writing; it is factual and descriptive, but it is not documentary;
it has no imaginary characters or situations, but it is a work of
the imagination. Though it is longer than most novels, it is unfinished as it stands: Agee said that it was only the "dissonant
prologue" to a vast work to be called *Three Tenant Families.*
What that complete work would have been like we cannot say,
for Agee never wrote it; we can only say that the fragment that
exists belongs to no genre, resembles nothing but itself, and defies
definition, unless one accepts the author's own definition: "it is
an effort," he wrote, "in human actuality." [2]

An effort in human actuality is what the book became, but it
began as something altogether less original and ambitious. In
1936 Agee was commissioned by *Fortune,* the business magazine on which he was a staff writer, to write an article; it was to

be, as he described it, "a story on: a sharecropper family (daily and yearly life): and also a study of Farm Economics in the South . . . : and also on the several efforts to help the situation: i.e. Government and state work; theories and wishes of Southern liberals; whole story of the 2 Southern Unions." [3] That summer he drove to Alabama with his friend, the photographer Walker Evans, to gather material for the article.

The fact that the book began in this way is important, because the original intention affected the final tone. Agee knew from the start that the task was an impossible one for him. For one thing, the economic aspect of the subject was beyond his range of knowledge; he was a poet, not a statistician. But more important, the assignment seemed to him immoral: he saw himself as a spy sent by an indifferent, profit-making organization to invade the lives of innocent, vulnerable people for profit. Feeling that he could not perform his mission, either technically or morally, he nevertheless proceeded with it, and his sense of guilt and betrayal as he did so is tangible in the book that he finally wrote.

The intensity of Agee's feelings for this task may be more understandable if we recall some facts about the occasion and the author. The United States in 1936 was deep in the Great Depression,. and farmers had been hit badly by it, and southern farmers worst of all. Agee was by birth a southerner, and by conviction a somewhat heterodox member of the political left (sometimes he called himself a communist, sometimes an anarchist, but he was not a formal member of either group). He was also, emotionally if not always intellectually, a Christian. His feelings for the condition of the southern poor drew upon all these sources: they were partly regional, partly political, and perhaps most of all religious. He thought of the subject of his study as his own people, and he could not turn them into commercial magazine copy; he chose instead to treat them with meticulous delicacy and reverence, and to turn his assignment into "an independent inquiry into certain normal predicaments of human divinity." Not surprisingly, *Fortune* rejected the product of this inquiry; a commercial publisher subsidized Agee in further writing, and then also refused it; finally, five years after that visit to Alabama, the book was published. But by then the war had begun, and the suffering of a few tenant families was diminished by the suffering of nations. The book appeared too late to succeed. It sold only five hundred copies during its first year, and a decade later one could still buy copies of the first edition in New York for a dollar.

To state the time, the place, and the occasion of *Let Us Now Praise Famous Men* is to see at once the inadequacy of such modes of description. The book has a place in time; it is a product of the 1930's, but it is not topical: or at least what is most valuable in it is not. Agee chose to write about three white tenant families living in rural Alabama, but he wrote about them, not as typical examples of a social and economic problem, but as human beings, as a "portion of unimagined existence." His book is above all a book about *knowing,* about how one human being may realize the existence of another, and of the obstacles to such knowledge. The obstacles are moral and psychological, and, in the expression, aesthetic, and Agee wrote about them all. It is this effort at knowing human actuality that gives the book its peculiar form—the form of a series of new approaches to an insoluble central problem—and its tone of painstaking tenderness and love.

Let me try to describe some of these approaches. There are, first of all, Walker Evans' photographs—thirty-one of them in the first edition, placed together at the beginning of the book. Agee put them there because he wanted them to be seen, not as illustrations to his text, but as "Book One," a unit equivalent in importance to the five hundred pages of prose which are "Book Two." "One reason I so deeply care for the camera," he wrote, "is just this. So far as it goes . . . and handled cleanly and literally in its own terms, as an ice-cold, some ways limited, some ways more capable, eye, it is, like the phonograph record and like scientific instruments and unlike any other leverage of art, incapable of recording anything but absolute, dry truth." [4] Evans' photographs are not ice-cold, but they are very clean, honest-looking pictures of the people and places that Agee writes about; they show without artfulness the grain in the unpainted boards of the houses, the seams in the weathered faces, and the naked poverty of the life. They demonstrate the first principle of the book—that knowing depends on seeing, really seeing things and people as they exist.

Agee's prose text embodies three approaches, each in its way a correlative of the photographs. First, the descriptive approach: Agee's attempt to realize in words the thoroughness of the camera's record. Second, the personal approach: the equivalent of the human sensitivity that chose these poses, these faces, these scenes, and made them seem significant and true. Third, the aesthetic: the artist's meditations on the problems of reality, truth, and art that the occasion poses. The book sets these approaches, each with its characteristic style, in a pattern of repetitions, so that one comments on another, and each alone is seen to be inadequate to the whole truth of the subject. There is nothing that could be described as movement or development in this structure; the effect is rather of hovering, failing, and trying again to express the whole of this human actuality in words.

The descriptive matter is gathered into one section titled simply "Some Findings and Comments," and divided into "Money," "Shelter," "Clothing," "Education," and "Work." Each part is an effort to describe, objectively and without judgment, the subject as it touched the lives of the three tenant families. Agee did this by including everything he observed, and by treating each object, however trivial, with the same scrupulous care. The description of a tenant house, for example, includes this careful catalog of the objects at the bottom of a dresser drawer:

> The two parts of a broken button.
> A small black hook, lying in its eye.
> Another small black hook.
> In the corners of the pale inward wood, fine gray dust and a sharp-grained unidentifiable brown dust.
> In a split in the bottom of the drawer, a small bright needle, pointed north. . . . [5]

The central section of the book, some two hundred pages, is devoted to this kind of detailed writing, and it is one of the poignancies of the experience that the entire contents of the tenants' lives, every scrap of paper, every broken toy or abandoned garment, *could* be recorded—that these lives were so bare that they *could* be contained within the limits of a few pages in a book.

Yet paradoxically, though this book is full of particulars the particulars in themselves are not important. What *is* important is the attitude implied in the details. Consider this passage, from Agee's description of one of the houses:

> The Gudgers' house, being young, only eight years old, smells a little dryer and cleaner, and more distinctly of its wood, than an average white tenant house, and it has also a certain odor I have never found in other such houses: aside from these sharp yet slight subtleties, it has the odor or odors which are classical in every thoroughly poor white southern country house, and by which such a house could be identified blindfold in any part of the world, among no matter what other odors. It is compacted of many odors and made into one, which is very thin and light on the air, and more subtle than it can seem in analysis, yet very sharply and constantly noticeable. These are its ingredients. The odor of pine lumber, wide thin cards of it, heated in the sun, in no way doubled or insulated, in closed and darkened air. The odor of woodsmoke, the fuel being again mainly pine, but in part also, hickory, oak, and cedar. The odors of cooking. Among these, most strongly, the odors of fried salt pork and of fried and boiled pork lard, and second, the odor of cooked corn. The odors of sweat in many stages of age and freshness, this sweat being a distillation of pork, lard, corn, woodsmoke, pine, and ammonia. The odors of sleep, of bedding and of breathing, for the ventilation is poor. The odors of all the dirt that in the course of time can accumulate in a quilt and mattress. Odors of staleness from clothes hung or stored away, not washed.[6]

This rendering of the odors that identify the house identifies also the quality of the life lived there—the meager materials of the building itself, the poor and monotonous food, the smell of labor and of sleep. And it describes that life without repugnance or indignation, which are removed, superior emotions, but with careful and reverent precision. Agee's respect for the actual was great, but it did not lead him to literary realism or to mere documentation: "description," he wrote, "is a word to suspect." His subject, as he said, was "certain normal predicaments of human divinity"; so that I suppose he might properly be described as a Christian realist. He strove to realize in his writing the divinity in each individual, by treating each person as he was; no one in this book is mythologized, not even the author, and no one becomes a representative case; Agee leaves his people alone, as separate and unique souls.

One can see the consequences of Agee's feelings about individualism in his accounts of the clothing that his people wear. He is careful to note that ill-fitting shoes are commonly cut out for comfort, but that the cutting is done in individual ways, and may be beautifully patterned; and that the styles of the homemade dresses vary, and express the characters of the makers. Here is a description of the Ricketts family's hats:

> All symbolisms in clothing are complex and corrupt in this country; they are so specially so in the matter of hats, and the variety of personal choice is so wide, it can easily seem pure casual chance and carelessness, which I am sure it is not. In any case an absolutely minimum social and egoistic requirement of a man's hat in this class and country is that it be ready-made and store bought. And so the fact that Ricketts is willing to work and to appear in public in a home made hat is significant of his abandonment "beneath" the requirements of these symbologies, both toward himself and toward his world. A hat could be bought for fifteen cents. But he, and his family, all wear identical hats, which they casually exchange among themselves. They are made of cornshucks. These are plaited into a long ribbon; the ribbon is then sewn against its own edges from center outward in concentric spirals. Margaret or Paralee can make one in a day. They are the shape of very shallow cones, about eight inches in diameter, light enough in the crown that they do not stay easily on the head. They are not only unmistakably home made, and betraying of the most deeply rural class; they suggest also the orient or what is named the "savage." The shucks are of a metal-silk brilliance I have never seen in other straw, and in this, its painstaking but unachieved symmetries, and the cone and outward spiral, each hat is an extraordinary and beautiful object: but this is irrelevant to its social meanings, as are nearly all products of honesty, intelligence, and full innocence.[7]

This passage, with its careful recognition of the social meaning, the making, and the beauty of these hats, and its awareness of the people who wear them, and why, is characteristic of Agee's attitude toward his subject. His conviction, manifested here and everywhere in his work, that it is demeaning to a man to treat him as a representative case, makes his writing more than either mere documentary or mere propaganda.

Agee shared with many people of his time a deep concern for the miseries of the poor, but he knew that such concern had no political or historical limits, and he reminded his readers of this truth by placing at the head of his text two very different but related epigraphs. One is from the *Communist Manifesto*: "Workers of the world, unite and fight. You have nothing to lose but your chains, and a world to win." The other is from *King Lear*:

> Poor naked wretches, whereso'er you are,
> That bide the pelting of this pitiless storm,
> How shall your houseless heads and unfed sides,
> Your loop'd and window'd raggedness, defend you
> From seasons such as these? O! I have ta'en
> Too little care of this! Take physick, pomp;
> Expose thyself to feel what wretches feel,
> That thou may'st shake the superflux to them,
> And show the heavens more just.

Agee said of these two quotations that they were the first and second themes of a sonata: politics and poetry, action and compassion, woven together into a complex musical form. But one's final impression is of a book nearer in tone to Lear than to Marx. Compassion means "feeling with," and Agee's book is a work of fellow-feeling, a sensitive man's careful efforts to enter into the beings of other men.

This fellow-feeling made the second of Agee's approaches, the personal method, a necessary complement to the descriptive matter. Agee had what many religious men have: the need to testify. This is probably almost the opposite of the will to reform; it places the testifier in a relation of sympathetic equality to the subject, whereas reform implies a degree of elevation, a point of view. Agee's testimony is an agonized account of his love for, and separateness from, the people he met, his awareness of each person, but also of the distance between them, which even love cannot bridge. Early in the book a white landlord summons three Negroes to sing for Agee and Walker, and Agee writes of the experience:

Meanwhile, and during all this singing, I had been sick in the knowledge that they felt they were here at our demand, mine and Walker's,
and that I could communicate nothing otherwise; and now, in a
perversion of self-torture, I played my part through. I gave their
leader fifty cents, trying at the same time, through my eyes, to
communicate much more, and said I was sorry we had held them up
and that I hoped they would not be late; and he thanked me for
them in a dead voice, not looking me in the eye, and they went away,
putting their white hats on their heads as they walked into the
sunlight.[8]

And there are similar tender accounts of meetings with the members of the white tenant families, of their shy good manners, and
of his inarticulate affection for them.

Beyond this kind of testimony there is another, more private
kind—those passages in the book in which Agee writes of his
personal sense of the realities around him. If we take from his
statements of his intentions two key words, *actuality* and *divinity,* then these passages are meditations on the divinities of
things. Here is the beginning of such a meditation, titled "On
the Porch: 1":

The house and all that was in it had now descended deep beneath
the gradual spiral it had sunk through; it lay formal under the order
of entire silence. In the square pine room at the back the bodies of
the man of thirty and of his wife and of their children lay on shallow
mattresses on their iron beds and on the rigid floor, and they were
sleeping, and the dog lay asleep in the hallway. Most human beings,
most animals and birds who live in the sheltering ring of human influence, and a great portion of all the branched tribes of living in
earth and air and water upon a half of the world, were stunned with
sleep. That region of the earth on which we were at this time
transient was some hours fallen beneath the fascination of the stone,
steady shadow of the planet, and lay now listing toward the last
depth; and now by a blockade of the sun were clearly disclosed those
discharges of light which teach us what little we can learn of the stars
and of the true nature of our surroundings. There was no longer any
sound of the settling or ticking of any part of the structure of the
house; the bone pine hung on its nails like an abandoned Christ.[9]

If, as Agee said, there are several sorts of truth, this is the kind that comes with night and an open sky; it sets the human subject in a huge, cosmic perspective. But the passage also has its roots in literature, and uses self-consciously the cadences and metaphors of poetry. It is in such passages that one is most conscious of Agee's youth, and of his young naiveté, his taste for large and lyrical statements about art and life. The most highly colored prose is here, and Agee's critics have taken from these sections their examples of what they have called his over-written, inflated style. Certainly the book *is* written, some of it, in a high rhetorical style. So is *Moby Dick.* So is much of Faulkner. So is *King Lear,* for that matter. Twentieth-century America is embarrassed by the emotive use of powerful language; we are the heirs of Hemingway's Frederick Henry, who mistrusted words like *honor,* and only believed in the numbers of regiments and the names of battles. Agee uses that austere style at times, but he has also the high style that Hemingway was afraid of. This style is sometimes described as "poetic," but that term seems to be the wrong one for this kind of writing; it is not prose trying to be something else, but simply prose reaching to its rhetorical limits. Sometimes when Agee wrote in this style he failed, but those passages are *badly* written rather than *over*-written. Like most writers of high style, Agee loved words, and sometimes his love of words got in the way of his love of truth, but this will happen to any writer who tries to be true both to experience and to his medium at its richest.

Agee's two approaches to the problem of knowing, the descriptive and the personal methods, complement and extend each other. But we must also recognize a third approach, of a rather different sort: the *aesthetic.* Almost at the exact center of the book is a passage of some thirty pages titled "On the Porch: 2," in which Agee considers the aesthetic aspects of his work. This section, essential to an understanding of what Agee was trying to do, says

> I believe, that works of the imagination . . . advance and assist the human race, and make an opening in the darkness around it, as nothing else can. But art and the imagination are capable of being harmful, and it is probably neither healthy for them nor, which is more to the point, anywhere near true even to the plainest facts, to rate them

so singly high. It seems to me there is quite as considerable value (to say nothing of joy) in the attempt to see or to convey even some single thing as nearly as possible as that thing is.[10]

And he goes on to argue that "everything in Nature, every most casual thing, has an inevitability and perfection which art as such can only approach, and shares in fact, not as art, but as the part of Nature that it is." [11] This proposition—that the actual is not only different from, but superior to, the forms that man makes of the actual—is the basic aesthetic principle of the book. It underlies the use of the photographs as "Book One," and the meticulous descriptions of seemingly trivial details of decoration, clothing, and the like. It sets aside art and all aesthetic intentions: the writer's aim is simply to render experience in words and pictures, so that it approaches as nearly as possible the mode of existence of the people and things that are the subject of the book.

This is a radical idea of what a literary work should be, and surely in the end an unworkable and self-defeating one (as perhaps Agee's inability to finish his book shows). But one can understand the instincts that brought him to such a position. In the presence of extreme, dignified human suffering, one might well feel that no words could express the quality of the actual. In the presence of such human experience, words can easily come to seem *mere* words, and art an idle and indulgent activity. Since not everyone can witness the actual lives of these people, the writer must put his testimony into words as best he can, but he will do so with a sense of inadequacy, and even of betrayal. Thus Agee writes:

It is important that you should so far as possible forget that this is a book. That you should know, in other words, that it has no part in that realm where disbelief is habitually suspended. It is much simpler than that. It is simply an effort to use words in such a way that they will tell as much as I want to and can make them tell of a thing which happened and which, of course, you have no other way of knowing. It is in some degree worth your knowing what you can of it not because you have any interest in me but simply as the small part it is of human experience in general.[12]

But though the book is anti-art, it is also artful; that is, it is composed in intricate ways, on patterns that have analogies to works of art, and not actuality. There is, for example, the remark that the epigraphs are the themes of a sonata form. In a letter to his friend, Father Flye, Agee wrote that he wanted to "write symphonies," and the musical element in his work was always strong. *Let Us Now Praise Famous Men* was written to be read continuously, he said, "as music is listened to or a film watched," and these two forms of music and film with their variations, modulations, and repetitions are central to Agee's conception of the book's shape. And perhaps one should add that music had one further attraction for Agee, that a sonata cannot, by its nature, be imperative; musical form protected him from the pull toward propaganda. Agee's book has no argument, no narrative line, and no evident logic; it is one enormous *now,* a feeling, symphonically orchestrated, but conceptually undeveloped and unresolved, beginning with the immediacy of the photographs, and ending with a sentence that mixes the past and future tenses. In the body of the book the observations stand like a series of photographs, or like film clips, each one a few feet of sharply recorded motion—a car rolls through a small town, a storm comes up, and the images are recorded to stand, each separate and clear and isolated in space.

Time is not a significant dimension in this book. And so, though musical form is one suggestive analogy to its arrangement, the idea of *spatial* form is perhaps more important. The book resembles a collage, an arrangement of many diverse materials to make an integrated whole. In addition to Evans' photographs, it contains verse by Agee, a page from a third-grade geography textbook, Agee's answer to a *Partisan Review* questionnaire on "some questions which face American writers today," the 43rd Psalm, an article on Margaret Bourke-White from the *New York Post,* the Beatitudes, and a selection from Blake's "Proverbs of Hell." Agee regretted that he could not also include "fragments of cloth, bits of cotton, lumps of earth, records of speech, pieces of wood and iron, phials of odors, plates of food and of excrement." [13]

One can see how Agee's actualizing aesthetic would lead to such a desire for *things.* But we must also recognize that *Let Us*

Now Praise Famous Men is also a book of words. Whatever his assertions about the superiority of things, Agee was a writer in love with words and fascinated by the problems arising from the use of words. His heroes were the great word users, and James Joyce in particular appears in the book as an exemplary artist, one who took seven years to record nineteen hours. Agee took one of his goals to be "the cleansing and rectification of language," and this concern linked him to another line of modern writers, the poets from Mallarmé to Eliot who were the purifiers of the dialect of the tribe.

The book also shows the influence of Joyce, and of other moderns like Faulkner and Dos Passos, in its formal complexity, in its discontinuities, its variations of style and tone. But perhaps its most modern quality of all is that it is about itself; it is a work of art concerned with the problems of creating a work of art; like Gide's *Counterfeiters,* Joyce's *A Portrait of the Artist as a Young Man,* Yeats's *Tower,* and Eliot's *Four Quartets,* it offers, as a primary experience, the experience of creating the work itself.

Agee called his book a failure, and did so with a kind of pride; failure, he said, was an obligation in such work. And his critics have accepted this judgment. But what does failure mean in such a book? Perhaps only that the book did not become the vast and complete record that Agee imagined. Or perhaps that it was written in words, and not in fragments of cloth and lumps of earth that he imagined to be truer to reality. But to fail in these terms is simply to fall short, in achievement, of the splendor of the conception, and in this sense every effort of the human mind fails.

The book was left unfinished, and it is hard to see what prodigy of human creation could have finished it. The unfinished state is, in fact, a significant part of its meaning—a symbol of the impossibility of adequately and completely expressing the predicaments of human divinity. I have not mentioned the ways in which *Let Us Now Praise Famous Men* is peculiarly American, and I am somewhat reluctant to, because I would not wish to suggest that it will not speak with an equal voice to all feeling men, but perhaps it *is* American in this: that it is naively and vastly ambitious in its goals. But I think it is American also in the eccentricity of its form, and in certain powerful feelings that it evokes—of human separateness and loneliness, and of distance and space. It is most a product of its origin in the way it celebrates whatever exists. One might return to the musical analogy, and say that Agee wrote, not a description, but a great Psalm, a hymn to actuality, on the theme that "everything that is is holy."

Notes

1. *Letters of James Agee to Father Flye* (New York, 1962), p. 85.
2. James Agee and Walker Evans, *Let Us Now Praise Famous Men* (Boston, 1941), p. x.
3. *Letters to Father Flye*, p. 92.
4. *Let Us Now Praise Famous Men*, p. 234.
5. *Ibid.*, p. 169.
6. *Ibid.*, p. 154.
7. *Ibid.*, p. 272.
8. *Ibid.*, p. 31.
9. *Ibid.*, p. 19.
10. *Ibid.*, p. 232.
11. *Ibid.*, p. 233.
12. *Ibid.*, p. 246.
13. *Ibid.*, p. 13.

WILLIAM FAULKNER:
"THE BEAR"

Daniel Hoffman

William Faulkner's story, "The Bear," has come to occupy a
place in his work similar to that held by "Billy Budd" in Herman Melville's and by *The Old Man and the Sea* in Ernest
Hemingway's. All three tales are relatively brief, and were written after the major novels by these authors, works of which these
stories seem to be epitomes. Faulkner's tale comes after most of
the books in his Yoknapatawpha saga, following *The Sound and
the Fury* (1929), *As I Lay Dying* (1930), *Light in August* (1932),
Absalom, Absalom! (1936), and *The Hamlet* (1940). "The
Bear" in its present form appeared in 1942, as one of the seven
interrelated stories in his book *Go Down, Moses*. These tales
comprise the chronicle of one of the families in Yoknapatawpha
County, that fictive domain in Mississippi which Faulkner created out of his own knowledge of his native region. The family
in *Go Down, Moses* are the McCaslins, the descendants in both
the white race and the black of an early settler of the place. This
version of "The Bear" is the successor, however, to an earlier,
shorter, and simpler story, written a few years earlier. Faulkner
has said of his intricate novel *The Sound and the Fury* that
he had to write the story of the same events four times, each
from the viewpoint of a different character. In his revisions of
"The Bear" we see a similar determination of the tale to haunt
its author until the full complexity of the truth that is in it
struggles toward expression.

The outline of the action in the tale is easily summarized. The
bear of the title is a huge beast, whose pursuit on a remote tract
of wilderness land owned by Major de Spain is the object of a

hunting party each November. We follow this annual hunt through the adventures of its youngest member, Isaac McCaslin, who is only sixteen years old in 1883 when the story begins. The bear, nicknamed Old Ben, is a wily and formidable adversary, who easily outwits the most skillful hunters and their most tenacious dogs. Isaac, or Ike, as he is called, is schooled in hunting by Sam Fathers, a strange and noble huntsman who is the son of a Chickasaw Indian chief and a Negro slave. After several years Sam finds in the woods the dog who will be able to track down Old Ben, and he succeeds in training this fierce dog, called Lion, without breaking its wild spirit. At last, with the help of Lion, Old Ben is indeed cornered, but when the two beasts are locked in a death struggle, another part-Indian member of the hunting party, named Boon Hogganbeck, leaps into the fight and stabs Old Ben in the heart with his knife. This much of the action occupies the first three of the five chapters in the tale.

To continue the consecutive summary of the action we must pass over Part Four for the moment. In Part Five, Ike McCaslin returns to the hunting ground two years after Old Ben's death. Everything is changed now, for Major de Spain has sold his hunting lands to a lumber company, and civilization—the railroad, the loggers, the exploitative destruction of the wilderness—are already encroaching upon the virgin land. It is evident that Old Ben was more than merely a beast to be hunted, he was somehow the embodiment of the spirit of the wilderness. With the bear's death, the wilderness itself is doomed. This fact is prefigured in the passing of Sam Fathers, the last speaker of the aboriginal language and the last priest of its sacred totem. At the moment when Old Ben is slain Sam falls to the ground in a seizure from which he does not recover. Ike and Boon stay behind to care for Sam when the rest of the party return to town, and at his death they inter him as he had desired, in the fashion of his Indian ancestors.

In the fifth section of the tale Ike is aware, on his return, that the locomotive is now the dominant image of energy and motion in the woods. Why does Ike come back? He returns to make a pilgrimage to the hallowed places where the wilderness spirit had enfolded him, where Lion is buried, where Sam Fathers lies. At the graveside of the tutelary master of his boyhood Isaac has an epiphany of the immortality of all life. The tokens he had left on Sam's grave—the twist of tobacco, the bandanna, the peppermint candies—these things, Ike knows, are gone,

> not vanished but merely translated into the myriad life which printed the dark mold of these secret and sunless places with delicate fairy tracks, which, breathing and biding and immobile, watched him from beyond every twig and leaf until he moved, moving again, walking on . . . quitting the knoll which was no abode of the dead because there was no death, not Lion and not Sam: not held fast in earth but free in earth and not in earth but of earth, myriad yet undifferentiated of every myriad part, leaf, twig, and particle. . . .

This vision of Isaac's makes him aware of the eternity of the processes of nature, the energy of life encompassing death and translating it, restoring the vigor of their spirit to all perished things. Such a consolatory view of nature as the mother of life, such a view of immortality beyond good and evil, is more like the pantheism of Walt Whitman than it is like the immortality proposed by Christianity. Although Isaac McCaslin is the truest Christian in Faulkner's tale, as will be seen in Part Four, he is at the same time the one true acolyte of Sam Fathers, the Chickasaw shaman. In the midst of this reverie on the immortality of all that is mortal, Ike is awakened by an intuitive fear; at his feet a rattlesnake is slithering across the forest floor, pausing to raise its head by his knee. Confronted by this creature, "the old one, the ancient and accursed about the earth, fatal and solitary . . . evocative of all knowledge and an old weariness and of pariah-hood and of death," Isaac, without premeditation, raises one hand, as Sam had done when the boy had shot his first buck, and, "speaking the old tongue which Sam had spoken that day without premeditation either: 'Chief,' he said, 'Grandfather.'"

This is surely one of the most touching, the most nearly unbearable moments in American fiction, so beautifully has Faulkner embodied the mystical realization of nature which runs through our literature from Thoreau and Emily Dickinson to Robert Frost. The serpent in "The Bear" is only residually the Christian emblem of man's temptation and the Fall. This snake appears to Isaac primarily as Sam would have seen it, indeed it comes as the temporary vessel embodying the spirit of Sam Fathers, his ancestor and his immortality. In both the mythology of the American Indian and the folklore of the Negro, the snake is a figure of kingly stature and mysterious supernatural power. Faulkner is being profoundly true to the mingled strains in Sam Fathers' blood in giving his spirit this mortal form.

There is only another page or two to the story. Ike pushes further into the woods until he comes upon Boon, frantically hammering his gun-barrel with one of its dismembered parts. Boon is screaming, "Get out of here! Don't touch them! They're mine!" as a maelstrom of squirrels leap from branch to branch in the tree above him. The mighty slayer of the bear is reduced to this hysterical claimant of ownership over squirrels. On this note of moral diminution and pathos ends the greatest American hunting story of the twentieth century.

I have omitted from my summary the entire fourth part of the tale, for this section breaks up the time sequence and introduces a totally different style to recount a different order of experience. Part Four begins when Ike McCaslin is twenty-one years old. If Parts One through Three were Ike's coming-of-age in the wilderness, Part Four is his coming of age into society. With the help of his older cousin, McCaslin Edmonds, Ike retraces the history of the family from the arrival of their grandfather Carothers McCaslin in Mississippi. This Scotsman had purchased the family plantation from an Indian chief, had begotten twin sons by his wife, and also was progenitor of an illegitimate line of descendants by his Negro slave-women. Ike and McCaslin Edmonds have a family of black cousins living on the place, and it is with the guilt and responsibilities of this inheritance that Ike has to come to terms.

The style of the hunting story is on the whole straightforward narrative, but Part Four is told through quite a different fictional method. This is stream-of-consciousness writing, the movement of the prose evoking and corresponding to the tortuous processes of self-examination and self-knowledge which Isaac McCaslin undergoes in his search for the meaning of his heritage. Some readers are confused by a single sentence five pages long, or a parentheses enclosing a thousand words; but these devices are not as difficult as they may at first seem. Indeed, once one is caught up in Isaac's search, the dazzling ingenuity of Faulkner's style seems absolutely necessary to guarantee the truth of the experience. Part Four is enveloped by the hunting story, but in temporal terms it envelops them, since this chronicle within the tale goes back three generations to the founding of the Mc-Caslin domain and extends beyond the end of the hunt to tell us of Ike's later life. The implications of this chronicle juxtapose to the wilderness ethic of the hunt the Christian ethic of society. But before attempting to trace this conflict, it is necessary to go over the narrative once again, this time with themes rather than the action of the plot primarily in mind.

"The Bear" is at once so simple and so complex that it surrenders its meanings to the conscious mind only after repeated readings and much brooding. Yet it communicates its significances instantaneously, although we may not at once be able to restate those meanings. As T. S. Eliot has said of poetry, it can be appreciated before it is consciously understood. One reason why this is true of "The Bear" is that the events of the plot correspond to several of those patterns of human behavior which are intrinsic to all our cultural experience; indeed these patterns seem to be a part of the biological inheritance of man. The Hunt in this tale is at once a Pursuit and a Quest. The Hunt of the Sacred Beast, a Divine Totem, is perhaps the most ancient action in the repertoire of human stories. In whatever form, whether in an epic poem like *Gilgamesh,* an allegory like the hunting of the unicorn, a saint's legend like that of St. George and the Dragon, a novel like *Moby Dick,* or a tall tale like Thomas Bangs Thorpe's "The Big Bear of Arkansas," the pursuit of the supernatural beast defines the world of nature and of man. The huntsman who succeeds in this pursuit is marked for life and immortality as a culture hero, a deliverer of his people. Faulkner's "The Bear" conforms to this general and universal pattern, but only up to a point. The differences as well as the affinities of Isaac McCaslin with the kind of hero we expect from such a preternatural hunting tale are very important to our comprehension of his role and of Faulkner's achievement.

The Hunt, however, is only one of the archetypal patterns in the story. This hunt is a Quest, a quest for a more spiritual way of life than the common lot of our ordinary days. Isaac is the designated hero of this quest, seeking, in the first three parts of the tale, to discover the ultimate truth according to the guidance of Sam Fathers, in an unmediated relationship with Old Ben, the spirit of the wilderness. In Part Four he must seek his truth in the world of men, his familial inheritance of guilt and attempted expiation. We must not forget that this hero is named for the Isaac in the Old Testament who was a sacrificial offering to the Lord.

If we consider the themes of Hunt and Quest together we find that they comprise still another fundamental human pattern: that of Initiation. In a very primitive sense this story is a coming-of-age ceremony for Ike McCaslin. The Hunt is the first stage of his initiation; his realization that the Hunt is in fact a Quest is what we may call the second stage. The third stage in Ike's initiation is played out in Chapter Four, where he is initiated into knowledge of evil. The final stage is his attempted expiation of the guilt of his fathers.

These patterns of the Hunt, the Quest, and the Initiation give "The Bear" much of its intuitive power. Whether such patterns are, as Carl Jung maintains, inherent archetypes of the human psyche, or whether they are the structures of myth to which our culture gives a reflexive response, they operate upon the reader to make the actions of the tale seem larger than the events and lives in which they take place. Further, these basic patterns are fused in the tale with other conflicts and tensions characteristic of American life. Indeed, the mythic and ritualistic actions are deeply imbedded in conflicts which define the great crises of American history—the tensions between wilderness and civilization, between the red man's ethic and the white man's exploitative way of life; the conflict between freedom and slavery; and between instinctual, pagan values and Christian obligations, between unfallen freedom and knowledge of sin.

Parts One and Two, we recall, presented Ike's initiation into the mystery of the wilderness through his taking part in the "yearly pageant-rite" of the "bear's furious immortality." In Part Three we find that although the initiation into these values has already been performed, the hunt inexorably continues. At last, Ben is slain by Lion and by Boon, the part-savage with the mind of a child. Reflecting upon the symbolic correspondences among the participants in the final, fatal hunt, we recognize that Lion, the untamable dog, can approach Ben only because his wild spirit is akin to the bear's; and further, that Boon can approach Lion, can feed the beast from his hand and sleep with Lion in his bed, only because Lion recognizes in Boon a nature savage like his own. The euphony of Boon's name with Ben's—we think of a famous bearhunter of olden times, Daniel Boone—links the totem beast with his slayer. These similarities are on the animal, instinctual levels. The hunt as performed in this tale is of course a white man's codification of a "yearly pageant-rite" as old as human experience, an activity of which Sam Fathers was the rightful High Priest and Grand Master.

But Sam, like Isaac, has had opportunities to slay Old Ben, yet had always, in reverence and humility, declined to raise his gun against his sacred, tutelary spirit. Ike had even dropped his gun and rushed between the bear's hind legs to save his little dog, an act of charity which Old Ben acknowledged by not harming either when so completely in his power. It remains for the near-imbecile Boon, who lives a life of only animal perceptions and creature satisfactions, to fulfill with his brute strength and brute courage the behest of his white superiors. Only dimly are General Compson and Major de Spain aware that the end of the bear is the end of the old times, of the wilderness. They do not know why Sam Fathers falls to the ground as Ben and Lion are dying; only Isaac knows that Sam is dying too.

Thus the Hunt, for all its urgency, must pursue contradictory ends. The Hunt initiates its worthy participants into the grace that comes with true knowledge of the wilderness. Yet it pursues its proximate object to destruction. The latter end annihilates the former, and changes the world.

We move now from the red man-white man world of the hunting party into the tangled self-examination of the fourth section. Here is the white man-black man world of the plantation. But the plantation was founded in the wilderness, originally the home of the red man, and we discover that the aboriginal red man had already learned from his white neighbors to enslave his black ones. The Chickasaw chieftain Ikkemotubbe (he is in fact the one who fathered Sam upon his Negro woman, and sold the plantation to Isaac's grandfather, Carothers McCaslin) Faulkner might have presented as a Noble Savage, but he appears instead

347

as the perpetrator of a double original sin: he enslaves his fellow-man and he sells his birthright.

The rest of Isaac's and his cousin's contemplation of the old plantation ledgers which record the family history reveal the continuation of these two sins through the bloodline of Carothers McCaslin. He in his turn inherits the Indian's sins, as codicils to the property deed. Grandfather McCaslin bought more slaves and, in the most culpable denial of another person's liberty, he seduced his Negro servant Eunice. This sin he compounded twenty years later by seducing the daughter Eunice had borne him. With such guilt Carothers McCaslin, the recusant Scots-Presbyterian, could live, but the double shame of her own seduction by her master and his incest with their daughter is too terrible for Eunice to bear. On Christmas Day, 1832, she commits suicide by drowning herself in the river.

To Ikkemotubbe's sins of greed and lust, the first McCaslin adds the sin of pride. Pride is further expressed, comically, in the pretensions of Isaac's mother, who before her marriage to Buck McCaslin, who *had* to marry her, for she was the stake in a poker game he lost to her brother, was Miss Sophonsiba Beauchamp. The absurdities of Miss Sophonsiba and her brother Hubert, briefly recounted in Part Four of "The Bear," are more fully told in the opening story in *Go Down, Moses*. In that story, "Was," we get the full account of how Miss Sophonsiba had a barefoot Negro boy blow a trumpet at the gate of their house, which she insisted on calling "Warwick," as though setting up an earldom in the midst of the wilderness. This theme, which Faulkner may well have borrowed, comic touches and all, from Hawthorne's *The House of the Seven Gables,* is stitched into the fabric of the McCaslin family's graver sins. For Hubert Beauchamp in his time commits these sins too. He is discovered to have had sexual affairs with a freed Negro girl on his place, and his greed is revealed when Isaac, aged twenty-one, opens the burlap bag in which Hubert had sealed a silver cup filled with gold pieces as a bequest at his nephew's birth. The uncle had borrowed back his own bequest to cover his losses at poker, and he had substituted for it a tin coffeepot filled with copper pennies and (now that he is dead) unredeemable promissory notes.

But if the McCaslin sins prove graver than those of Hubert or

Ikkemotubbe, there are signs of a latent capacity in the family—in the blood, perhaps Faulkner would say, to attempt to make expiation. Old McCaslin was too proud to admit his offenses to his contemporaries; which is another way of saying he lacked moral courage. Yet he made a partial, posthumous gesture of responsibility, for in his will he left a thousand dollars to each of his three Negro grandchildren, to be given them on their coming of age. Not a very satisfactory expiation, this, since it cost him nothing and deprived his white grandchildren of money that would otherwise be theirs. Further, he left the humiliating delivery of the guilt-money to those who had nothing to do with the incurring of the debt. In Part Four, Isaac takes it upon himself to deliver these payments to his black cousins. With great tenacity and unselfishness he finds the girl Fonsiba, married to a freedman on a barren farm in Arkansas. Another cousin has disappeared, but the third, Lucas Beauchamp, whom readers of *Intruder in the Dust* will know as a proud and intransigent man, comes to demand the money himself on his twenty-first birthday.

In the second generation of McCaslins the expiatory gesture was much more personal than a money deed. Before his marriage to Miss Sophonsiba, Ike's father had lived with his twin brother on the old McCaslin place. The brothers, Uncle Buck and Uncle Buddy, had manumitted their slaves and, taking upon themselves something like vows of partial poverty, they lived in a log cabin built with their own hands, turning the great house over to the blacks as a dormitory. This was taken as a foolish eccentricity by their neighbors in pre-Civil War Mississippi. It was the brothers who kept the scrawled ledgers over which Ike pores. They recorded the evidence of their father's debauchery, but it was for his grandson Isaac fully to understand the family guilt, and most fully to try to expiate it.

Isaac goes much further than his uncle and father in renouncing his inheritance from Carothers McCaslin. Not only does he make good his grandfather's bequests to his black cousins, but he gives up all his property—his lands, farm, house, everything. Like Christ, he takes up the craft of carpentering; and when his wife demands that he reclaim his abandoned property and beget children to whom this property would be passed on, Isaac renounces marriage. He becomes "Uncle to a country and father to none." The intuitive wisdom of Sam Fathers recognized in Ike a fitting candidate for spiritual revelation, and Ike passed all the Indian's tests to become a witness of truth from the Other World. But after the death of the bear, of Sam Fathers, and the end of the wilderness, Isaac must bring his gifts to his own inheritance. He is not only a shaman, he is a Christian with full knowledge of original sin—and a Calvinist conscience.

We have noticed that Ike's renunciations differ more in degree than in kind from the expiatory gestures of his forebears. We may observe, too, that such gestures of selflessness and generosity are a part of the ethical code of the very class responsible for the burden of history: the southern aristocracy, as Faulkner presents it. We see lesser instances of this spirit of *noblesse oblige* in the aristocracy in Major de Spain's invitation to the squatters, who have farmed and trespassed on his property, to take part in the hunt and share in the game. We see it again in McCaslin Edmonds' assumption of the debt to Isaac of the birthright cup of gold coins which his uncle Hubert Beauchamp had bequeathed and then denied him. This spirit of *noblesse* appears in the camaraderie of the hunting camp, where the strict hierarchy of classes in town is suspended for the fortnight in the woods. There General Compson and Major de Spain acknowledge that the pride of Uncle Ash, the old Negro cook, requires that he, too, be permitted to hunt with the white men after Isaac, a mere boy, had killed a buck. It is evident in their dealings with all their kith, kin, and servants, whether white, black, Indian, or mixed in blood, that these men, in Faulkner's view, are like the knights of the Round Table in their unfailing courtesy. The hunting party with its male camaraderie and earned distinction is associated in their minds with their service in the Confederate Army, another Quest, another romantic lost cause.

Such generosity, such nobility of spirit, is found among the leaders and is the reason they are respected by the plebeian members of their society. In Faulkner's work, when a man who has assumed the moral prerogatives of leadership proves not to possess the true leader's nobility of spirit, he has betrayed a sacred trust. It is such a betrayal which makes fitting the death of Thomas Sutpen in *Absalom, Absalom!* at the hands of Wash, the poor white farmer whose daughter Sutpen had seduced in hopes of begetting a male heir and abandoned when the baby was born a girl. In "The Bear" there are no such ignoble leaders. But none of the aristocrats makes such renunciatory and expiatory gestures as does Isaac. If they are the princes of this world, their generosity flawed by their unacknowledged implication in our common fallen state, Isaac McCaslin is clearly the nearest among them to a higher principality.

What, however, does Isaac accomplish by his giving up of property, marriage, fatherhood, all the goods of this world? His imitation of Christ is surely incomplete, for he cannot—indeed, as we see in the sequel story in *Go Down, Moses,* he does not wish to—assume the burden of suffering for all of his kind. His renunciation is personal, his possible salvation is therefore also personal. He is neither Christ nor a saint; he bears his own sins and his family's, but not the world's, and nobody else imitates his example. Trained to be a priest of the wilderness by his Indian mentor, he acknowledges the power and the authority of the God whose creations man should receive in stewardship, not in covetousness. But Isaac is born into the death of one order, the wilderness, whose spiritual qualities cannot be transferred to, or enacted in, the world of history which follows after.

The wilderness is a primeval, unfallen world, a timeless expanse, an experience of eternity. It is peopled with mythic creatures, the only kinds of action possible within it are ceremonies and rituals. The casual and accidental becomes subsumed in the larger meaning of the "annual pageant-rite." When Ike makes his shamanistic journey of initiation into the heart of the wilderness to *see* the bear (not to slay him), he must divest himself not only of his gun but of his watch and compass. These renunciations have ceremonial significance. Ike has cut himself off from what is man-made—the metallic objects, the implements that impose our measurements upon time and our directions upon space. Without these artifacts of intellectual pride Ike can become Man as a part of nature. Only then is he worthy of the vision vouchsafed him by the bear. Then, having seen Old Ben, he finds that without his watch and compass he is lost. Isaac has lived out the Biblical injunction that "ye must lose yourself to find yourself." This renunciation, in the great woods, of man-made values in order to become worthy of revelation is clearly a foreshadowing of Isaac's later abnegations. But the world of history, of time, of exploitation and selfhood has no spiritual vision to vouchsafe to Isaac McCaslin, save the grim satisfaction that he, at least, does not partake of its sins. Like Santiago, the fisherman in Hemingway's *The Old Man and the Sea,* who returned from *his* heroic quest with only the bare bones of the great fish, Isaac wins a victory, but it is Pyrrhic.

If "The Bear" reminds us of an epic in the scale and resonance of its action, the consequences of that action point toward tragedy. Isaac can be a spiritual hero but not, as was true of Gilgamesh, St. George, Perseus, or the Grail Knight, a culture hero. He does not lead his nation; he can but show his heedless fellow-men how difficult it is to live by the dictates of the soul.

31 EUGENE O'NEILL: *THE ICEMAN COMETH*

Gerald Weales

In the summer of 1940, in a letter to Lawrence Langner of the Theatre Guild, Eugene O'Neill said of *The Iceman Cometh,* "I have a confident hunch that this play, as drama, is one of the best things I've ever done." His confidence was justified. During the 1920's, with plays as varied as *The Emperor Jones, Desire Under the Elms,* and *Strange Interlude,* O'Neill established himself as America's most important and most ambitious playwright. His struggle to wed a natural theater talent to grandiose poetic and philosophic longings created a series of theatrical experiments— huge in intention, at least—which gave him an impressive international reputation, crowned in 1936 with the Nobel Prize. Today, however, his attempts at high tragedy, by Freud out of the Greeks, like *Mourning Becomes Electra;* his manipulation of masks and obvious symbolism, as in *The Great God Brown;* his concept-bound exercises, like *Lazarus Laughed,* are fallen giants. They have been overthrown by time and, more important, by the excellence of his own last plays of which *The Iceman Cometh* and *Long Day's Journey into Night* are the finest examples.

The plays of the late 1930's and early 1940's, many of them using and transforming the material of O'Neill's own life, marked a return to the modified realism of the early sea plays. Having freed himself from the over-elaborate literary and theatrical devices with which he tried to bring universality to the plays of his middle years, O'Neill was able in his last plays to speak more directly. He was concerned, as he always had been, with man's place in an apparently uncongenial universe, but in the more nearly realistic context in which he was working toward

353

the end of his life, the larger problem became the backdrop against which particular men could act out their particular dramas, and it is the force of the drama rather than the attaching of the labels that gives the plays their heightened significance.

Not that a play like *The Iceman Cometh* is realistic in the narrow sense of the word. It is not a documentary on Skid Row bums, as Mary McCarthy seemed to imply it should be, when, in her review of the original production,[1] she went on and on about the playwright's presumed inadequacy in depicting alcoholics. Eric Bentley, in "Trying to Like O'Neill,"[2] his famous condescending attack on the playwright, insisted that there were two plays in *Iceman,* one realistic, one expressionistic. There is a truth of sorts in that division if we doctor Bentley's assertion in three ways: substitute "nonrealistic" for "expressionistic," since the latter word conjures up a play like *The Emperor Jones,* suggests a subjective rather than an objective scene; discard his assumption that the realistic play is "genuine" and the other one "nongenuine"; recognize that the two plays are, in fact, one. As with the best of the presumably realistic dramatists—think of Ibsen in *The Master Builder,* or Shakespeare in *Hamlet,* for that matter—O'Neill tells a story that is at once a meticulously motivated psychological drama and a generalized statement about the nature of man. His setting is both a recognizable bar and a workable stage metaphor. His secondary characters are simple stereotypes, chosen to illustrate aspects of his theme, but there is verisimilitude in that device, too; after all, most of the people we know, particularly those we meet in bars, insist on showing only one face. Doris Alexander has argued[3] that O'Neill's Hugo is an accurate portrait of Hippolyte Havel, an anarchist whom O'Neill knew in Provincetown and Greenwich Village, but neither a real source nor a realistic description needs keep the character from being a stereotype, as O'Neill indicates in his stage directions when he says that Hugo has "a strong resemblance to the type Anarchist as portrayed, bomb in hand, in newspaper cartoons."

O'Neill's conscious use of stock stage types is only one example of the way in which he has qualified his realism. It can be seen, too, in his manipulation of the set; in his use of the secondary characters as a single dramatic unit, a chorus in effect; in his careful and obviously artificial balancing of one character against another. Yet, none of these are contradictions of the play's realistic surface; they are simply extensions of it. The strength of *The Iceman Cometh* is that one's intellectual response to the non-realistic devices and the thematic thrust of the work need not interfere with emotional identification or sympathy with the characters. Larry Slade's separation from the other characters at the end of the play is presented visually and orally; he is isolated at the table at the front left and he is silent in the face of the cacophonous singing of the chorus. Yet, the final irony of the play is not so much perceived as felt, for the audience has been waiting with Larry for the sound of Parritt's body falling outside the window.

Perhaps this double nature of the play can best be seen in O'Neill's use of language—and so much of it, since the play runs four hours. "Stammering is the native eloquence of us fog people," says Edmund in *Long Day's Journey into Night,* commenting on the "faithful realism" that was to be "the best I'll ever do." Since Edmund is O'Neill himself, the playwright has put into his own mouth one of the harshest criticisms that can be made against him as a writer: "The *makings* of a poet. No, I'm afraid I'm like the guy who is always panhandling for a smoke. He hasn't even got the makings. He's got only the habit." No one is likely to put together an evening of O'Neill readings, for the sake of the words themselves, as they have with Shakespeare and Shaw, and O'Neill was aware of that. A line of his, out of dramatic context, is usually awkward, frequently ludicrous. Yet back in the 1930's, when nice girls still took elocution lessons to improve themselves, one of the popular set pieces was a long monologue constructed of the heroine's speeches from the big scene in Act III of *Anna Christie.* Hang an O'Neill speech to a character and the verbal inelegancies seem unimportant; the dated slang, the stage dialect, the clumsy locutions become an integral part of the total dramatic experience.

The stammering eloquence of *The Iceman Cometh* can be heard not simply in a character like Hickey, whose verbal pattern suggests both his evangelical background and his occupation as salesman, but in the voices that provide the background. Yet the "faithful realism" of that milieu is only apparent. The weight of

355

the words alone, the relentless repetition, makes clear that O'Neill is building an artificial pattern out of the presumably verisimilar language. When the play first opened, a number of critics [4] howled at its excessive length, dead certain that what O'Neill needed was an editor with a heavy hand. His producer shared that conviction. In his account of the *Iceman* rehearsals,[5] Lawrence Langner tells how Paul Crabtree, who played Parritt, counted the number of times he was expected to repeat a particular point; when, at Crabtree's urging, Langner took the count to O'Neill, the playwright's response was, "I *intended* it to be repeated eighteen times!" When José Quintero came to direct the off-Broadway revival in 1956, he worked within O'Neill's intentions. "It resembles a complex musical form," he said later of the play,

> with themes repeating themselves with slight variation, as melodies do in a symphony. It is a valid device, though O'Neill has often been criticized for it by those who do not see the strength and depth of meaning the repetition achieves.[6]

It would be a mistake to suppose that the word "meaning" in the Quintero quotation referred simply to a reiteration of theme. It is true that O'Neill establishes, for each of the characters, an illusion based on the doubtful past, the unidentifiable present, or the unlikely future, and lets the characters parade their "pipe dreams" so often that the audience can anticipate the lines before they are spoken. What O'Neill *is* doing, as the Quintero production showed, is providing the texture of life in Harry Hope's bar. "What kind of joint is it, anyway?" Parritt asks, and Larry Slade answers:

> It's the No Chance Saloon. It's Bedrock Bar, The End of the Line Café, The Bottom of the Sea Rathskeller! Don't you notice the beautiful calm in the atmosphere? That's because it's the last harbor. No one has to worry about where they're going next, because there is no farther they can go.

Without Larry's rhetoric, it is a combination bar and hotel, a high-class flophouse, where a number of derelicts live on the charity of the owner, who shares their dependence on whiskey and dreams. At first glance, it may seem to be "de Morgue wid all de stiffs on deck," as Margie calls it when she makes her first entrance in Act I, but Margie is part of it and she knows better. There is life at the bottom of the sea. "The lie of a pipe dream is what gives life to the whole misbegotten mad lot of us, drunk or sober," says Larry, as the play opens, and later, identifying the inhabitants for Parritt, he defines the variety of illusions. Most of the denizens, such as James Cameron, whose nickname is Jimmy Tomorrow, insist that they are going to pull themselves together, clean themselves up, and go out and find again their lost places in the large world. This "tomorrow" dream depends, in most cases, on a falsely remembered past, as in Harry Hope's re-creation of his dead wife that turns her from a nag into a saint; and on a motivating lie, as in his insistence that it is grief for the dead Bessie that has kept him from putting a foot outside the door for twenty years. If all that O'Neill intended were to present the illusionary setting of the play, Larry's long exposition would have done the job. It is the feel of the place and not a description of it that the playwright is after.

As, one by one, the bums awaken and join the drifting conversation, we see that they form a self-protective community, feeding one another's illusions, listening to one another's endlessly familiar speeches, amiably insulting one another, cuing one another into bad jokes or set pieces. Since the central action of the play does not begin until Hickey arrives toward the end of Act I, the bulk of that long act is used to establish an atmosphere. It is essentially comic. Some critics—George Jean Nathan and Eric Bentley,[7] for instance—actually find it funny, but O'Neill's comedy has never made me laugh; think of the story about pigs and the oil millionaire's pond in *A Moon for the Misbegotten*. Laughable or not, the first act of *Iceman* provides an affectionate portrait of a family of sorts, a stable environment ripe for disruption.

Because of its setting and a possible equation of characters, *The Iceman Cometh* has been compared to Maxim Gorki's *The Lower Depths*. Because Hickey, like Gregers Werle, is supposedly an advocate of salvation through truth, it has been compared to Henrik Ibsen's *The Wild Duck*. Because it takes place in a bar and has a philosophic observer at the center of it, it has

357

even been compared to William Saroyan's *The Time of Your Life*.[8] The comparisons are valid ones, and useful to some extent, but they tend to draw our attention to superficial likenesses. If it is valuable to go outside the play to help describe it, the analogy that seems most appropriate to me is Anton Chekhov's *Uncle Vanya*. Although the Chekhov play opens at about the point O'Neill has reached at the beginning of Act II, the action of the two plays is essentially similar. In both cases, an enclosed group, sufficient unto itself, is invaded by an outsider, a presumably known and admired quantity who turns out to be very different from what was expected: Serebryakov in *Uncle Vanya*, Hickey in *Iceman*. In both plays, the intruder upsets the domestic calm, temporarily for some of the characters, and departs, at peace with himself, leaving the protagonist—Uncle Vanya in Chekhov, Larry Slade in O'Neill—painfully aware of the shambles around him. In making the comparison between *The Iceman Cometh* and *Uncle Vanya*, I am not suggesting that O'Neill borrowed the form of his play from Chekhov, but that, like the Russian playwright, he is using one of the perennial dramatic situations. In any case, O'Neill has his own story to tell.

When the play opens, it is early morning of Harry Hope's birthday. He and his sponging friends and tenants have been waiting all night for Theodore Hickman, for Hickey has always used Harry's birthday as an excuse for an extended drunk. Their expectation stems, in part, from the fact that Hickey's arrival means free whiskey. More important, however, Hickey brings jokes (the one about his wife and the iceman is the favorite); he comes, an envoy from the outside world, and by his acceptance shores up their illusions. He is late this year, however, a fact that sends disturbed ripples through the calm that Larry describes, and when Cora and Chuck come in with the news that they have seen Hickey and that he is on his way, their report plants seeds of doubt, in the audience, if not in the other characters. Cora brings a message from the salesman: "Tell de gang I'll be along in a minute. I'm just finishin' figurin' out de best way to save dem and bring dem peace." Although she agrees with Harry that Hickey must be kidding, she adds, "But he was funny, too, somehow. He was different, or somethin'." Chuck explains that he was sober. Hickey's entrance, following on the heels of their descrip-

tion, is a beautiful character turn. He comes on in a burst
of one-of-the-boys heartiness, singing bits of convivial songs,
calling for drinks, and moving among them, shaking hands,
greeting them by name, blessing them with unanswerable questions: *"How's the kid?"* *"How's the boy?"* There is genuine
affection in his behavior, but there is calculation, too. He *is*
a salesman, and the audience, warned by Cora's words, sensing
that something is wrong, suspect that he has brought a bill
of goods to peddle in this unlikely market. He has certainly
not brought the comfort that the dreamers have come to expect
from him, and their suspicion builds from the moment he refuses to drink with them: "Cora was right, Harry. I have
changed. I mean, about booze. I don't need it any more."

Hickey has come to save them:

> I meant save you from pipe dreams. I know now, from my experi-
> ence, they're the things that really poison and ruin a guy's life and
> keep him from finding any peace. If you knew how free and con-
> tented I feel now. I'm like a new man. And the cure for them is so
> damned simple, once you have the nerve. Just the old dope of hon-
> esty is the best policy—honesty with yourself, I mean. Just stop lying
> about yourself and kidding yourself about tomorrows.

His method is disruptive. His insistence that everyone face the
truth breaks the group into pieces. He will let no one practice
what he considers the wrong kind of pity, Larry's kind, the pity
that feeds illusions. Stripped of their mutual dependencies, they
all become defensive, irascible, suspicious. The harmless jokes
with which they once teased one another become wounding attacks. There is even violence or the possibility of it. The Boer
War veterans, friendly enemies, are suddenly at one another's
throats; Joe Mott flourishes a knife and Rocky draws a gun to
meet his threat. To Hickey, all this is temporary, a necessary
adjustment before they come to rest, at peace with themselves
and the world. He nags, needles, digs at them until, if only to
escape him, each of them acts on his tomorrow dream, goes out
only to return beaten. "Dey're all licked," says Rocky. "I
couldn't help feelin' sorry for de poor bums when dey showed up
tonight, one by one, lookin' like pooches wid deir tails between
deir legs." Not that Rocky is an objective observer, for he, too, is

defeated. He has agreed to call himself a *pimp* rather than a *bartender,* but he can face his truth only by soliciting others— Parritt and Larry—to join him in the trade. For most of Hickey's converts there is nothing at all. "You look funny. You look dead," says Hugo, when Harry Hope, unable to take the promised walk around the ward, stumbles back into the bar and finds that he can neither get drunk nor reawaken his pipe dream.

It is Larry who turns Hugo's comment into an accusation that is at once an attack on Hickey and a summing up of his influence: "It's the peace of death you've brought him." When Hickey's peace settles on Harry Hope and Larry puts a label on it, there is no surprise for the audience, for Hickey has been identified with Death since the first act when Willie Oban, unable to cadge a drink from Parritt, says, "Let us join in prayer that Hickey, the Great Salesman, will soon arrive. . . . Would that Hickey or Death would come!" At the end of Act II, putting the final damper on Harry's party, Hickey tells the would-be revelers that his wife is dead and Larry reacts with an involuntary outburst: "Be God, I felt he'd brought the touch of death on him!" The words that Hickey uses in his attempt to persuade the group are "killing your pipe dreams," a phrase that looks forward not only to the inevitable revelation that he has murdered his wife but to the corpse-like state in which he is going to leave the presumably saved.

In the last act, distressed at the results of his missionary work, Hickey delivers his confession in the hope that it will reinvigorate his unhappy converts. It does so by providing an escape hatch rather than an example. They clutch at the possibility that he was insane when he killed Evelyn and use that assumption to dismiss all that he has done and said since the murder. Their own actions, their own failures, become attempts to humor their friend. No real test of their tomorrow dreams has been made. Tentatively they rebuild their illusionary world. Rocky conveniently remembers the nonexistent automobile that almost ran Harry down when he tried to leave the bar. "Sure, I seen it! Just missed yuh! I thought yuh was a goner," he says and adds, hesitantly, "On de woid of a honest bartender!" Harry, understanding, gives him the answer that lets him forget he is a pimp. "You're a bartender, all right," Harry admits, and he uses

Rocky's adjective to go into a familiar and acceptable joke: "But, bejees, don't pull that honest junk! You and Chuck ought to have cards in the Burglars' Union!" The others begin to rebuild their bridges, the whiskey starts to work again, and it becomes clear that in more ways than one, since Harry provides the drink and since "to spring" is slang for "to treat," Hope springs eternal.

If we focus, as in the description above, on the group as the center of the action, the play might almost be seen as a fable that could end with the oldest comfort line in the history of story-telling: and so they lived happily ever after. Unhappily happily, perhaps, but, still, *The Iceman Cometh* is a neat parable about man's inability to live without illusions. It is more than that, however. It is fascinating as a kind of cautionary tale, but its dramatic strength lies in its three central characters who play their painful truth-illusion game against the pattern of community lost and gained. They are Hickey, Parritt, and Larry, and none of them is ever quite at home at Harry Hope's.

Ironically, of the three, Hickey most belongs in a pipe-dream palace. A charter member of "the Tomorrow Movement," he has always come to Harry's to feed dreams as unlikely as the one he shared with his wife, the certainty that someday he would re-form, quit drinking and whoring, and be the perfect husband to Evelyn's perfect wife. Having killed that dream when he killed his wife, he arrives, wearing his new truth proudly, but it does not take the audience long to see that his freshly scrubbed face is just another mask. From the moment that Hickey steps on stage, it is clear that he is being driven by a desperate need of his own, that his desire to save his friends is a great deal more than mis-guided charity. O'Neill indicates this in the way he flaws Hickey's smooth hard-sell speeches with hesitation, hints that are leading toward the final revelation. In the Quintero production, this quality in Hickey was emphasized by Jason Robards, Jr., who played the role with a nervous intensity that found outward manifestation in fingersnapping, a good-fellow gesture so com-pulsive that it became a tic. To sustain his motive for having killed Evelyn—to bring her peace, to free her of the constant disappointment of his relapses—Hickey convinces himself that he killed her deliberately and that her murder was the act that

finally freed him of self-deception, of dependence on an illusionary tomorrow. His conviction, however, like Rocky's decision to call himself a pimp, cannot sustain itself without external support. He must destroy all the dreams at Harry Hope's,
as he did his own, and use the testimony of his friends' newly
found peace to shore up his own uncertain illusion. His long confession speech in the last act, made over the protests of men who
do not want to hear, is really for himself, an attempt to hold on
to the new pipe dream that tells him he is free of pipe dreams.
He loses control of his story, however, and when he reaches the
climax, the murder itself, he blurts out all the bottled-up resentment of Evelyn, all the years of guilt at having failed her over
and over only to be forgiven again and again: "Well, you know
what you can do with your pipe dream now, you damned bitch!"

Hearing his own words, he stammers a protest, "No. I never—"
and then snatches for the nearest comfort, "You know I must
have been insane, don't you, Governor?" At first reluctant to give
up his mission, Hickey tries to deny that he has been "crazy ever
since," but Harry's bar runs on illusionary trades and Hickey
gives them back their tomorrow dreams in exchange for his new
insanity pipe dream.[9] The important thing about Hickey at the
end of the play is not that he is presumably on his way to actual
death, for no character gets executed after the curtain comes
down; it is that the last we see and hear of him, he is still
protesting that he has not got "a single damned lying hope or
pipe dream left" and, in almost the same breath, busily building
his fantasy about Evelyn. He emerges as the best dramatic example of the philosophic point exemplified by the group at Harry
Hope's. Spiritually, he belongs there, but, since his is a destructive illusion, he has to be rejected. They do give him a little
comfort to take with him on his last journey.

Dan Parritt is in many ways analogous to Hickey, but very
different in the need that brought him to Harry Hope's. He is
full of excuses rather than illusions and there is no comfort in
them. He has come to find real death, rather than the death-in-
life that Hickey is peddling as peace, and to make Larry Slade his
executioner. When Parritt and Hickey first meet at the end of
Act I, Hickey assumes that they must have met before. Assured
that this is impossible, he persists, "But still I know damned well

I recognized something about you. We're members of the same lodge—in some way." They have committed similar crimes and with the same motivation. Parritt has turned police informant and put his anarchist mother, Rosa, and her political associates in jail. This is surrogate murder since Rosa is characterized by Parritt himself as a woman so attuned to freedom that imprisonment would be death to her. At first, he pretends he is a fugitive from the same police roundup. Then, admitting that he is the stool pigeon, he excuses himself by insisting that his mother's arrest was an accident, that he informed on the movement out of patriotism or out of greed. Finally, in a burst of echo statements, interruptions of Hickey's confessional monologue, he admits that he acted out of the guilt that he could no more live up to his mother's expectations than Hickey could to Evelyn's: "You know what you can do with your freedom pipe dream now, don't you, you damned old bitch!" He has come to Larry, once his mother's lover and as close to a father as he ever had, to find peace which, in his case, is the courage to commit suicide. In anger and pity, Larry sends the boy to his death.

Larry is the only character in the play who undergoes a real change. When we first meet him, he comes on as the "old Foolosopher," the man who has taken "a seat in the grandstand of philosophical detachment." He has apparently been sitting in Harry Hope's waiting for easeful death ever since he left both Rosa and the movement years before, a single desertion for, as Parritt says, "To hear her go on sometimes, you'd think she was the Movement." It is obvious, early in the first act, that Larry is a kind of den mother to this collection of derelicts, that he wears his compassion on his sleeve. It is also clear that his pessimism is rhetorical—he quotes Heine, "The best of all were never to be born"—and that he is doing nothing to hurry himself into the "fine long sleep" of death for which he is presumably eager. One of the reasons that Parritt is in the play is to indicate one of the roads to peace closed to Larry. In his sales pitch to Larry, Hickey insists "that all that grandstand foolosopher bunk and the waiting for the Big Sleep stuff is a pipe dream." Although Hickey fails to persuade Larry with words, he forces Larry to become his antagonist, to let the pity come to the surface. The act of sending Parritt to his death is Larry's admission that he has been a poseur and his recognition that his pipe dream is gone. Unable to join the rest of his friends in their return to whiskey-soaked illusion or to follow Parritt off the fire escape, he sits at the end of the play, a quiet spot in a stage full of noise, and mourns his new self-knowledge, "Be God, I'm the only real convert to death Hickey made here. From the bottom of my coward's heart I mean that now!"

If *The Iceman Cometh* is a microcosm, as I assume it is, it posits a world in which most men live on illusion and in which only anguish awaits the man who can see through to the truth. "Use your head, can't you, use your head," says Hamm in Samuel Beckett's *Endgame,* "you're on earth, there's no cure for that!" O'Neill's bar, unlike Beckett's "Bare interior," has an identifiable relation to a world outside, for O'Neill is writing a social as well as a philosophic play. *The Iceman Cometh,* with all its talk about pipe dreams, becomes a comment on the American Dream, which may be the greatest pipe dream of all. Harry Hope's bar, like the ships in O'Neill's early sea plays, is stocked with national types, not because it represents the world, but because it is America in small, a saucepan-size melting pot; even the two foreigners who want to go home, the veterans of the Boer War, are here because they came to take part in the St. Louis Exposition, that very American world's fair, celebrating the centennial of the Louisiana Purchase, which Theodore Roosevelt, in his dedication speech, called "the event which more than any other . . . determined that we should be a great expanding Nation." O'Neill's characters are a cross section of that nation in more than their national and racial origins. Their illusions are rooted in the reality outside the bar, but that reality has its own illusions about success, progress, expansion. The American business world is represented by Hickey, the salesman, and Jimmy Tomorrow, the publicity man, and by Willie Oban, whose father was a successful financier until the police closed his bucket-shop operation. American government, at least on the municipal level, can be seen in Harry Hope, "a former minor Tammanyite," as O'Neill calls him, and Pat McGloin, the ex-police lieutenant, kicked off the force for taking bribes. The American Left is present in those two veterans of the anarchist movement, Hugo and Larry, and in Parritt, its most recent betrayer. Not the ideal representatives, perhaps, but here in a desiccated form are success dreams, democracy dreams, revolution dreams, all manifestations of the big dream of a wealthy, happy society. That presumably is why so many of the characters in the play look back nostalgically [10] to the turn of the century, the golden age of American optimism. As Larry says, sardonically, "It's a great game, the pursuit of happiness." Yet, the play is set in 1912, just before the First World War, an event which shattered the nineteenth-century faith in progress for most of the world, if not for the United States. *The Iceman Cometh* is an oblique comment on the years between Theodore Roosevelt speaking at St. Louis in 1903 and Eugene O'Neill talking to an interviewer in 1946.[11] President Roosevelt promised that "we shall make of this Republic the freest and most orderly, the most just and most mighty, nation which has ever come forth from the womb of time."

Eugene O'Neill said:

I'm going on the theory that the United States instead of being the most successful country in the world, is the greatest failure. . . . it was given everything, more than any other country. . . . Its main idea is that everlasting game of trying to possess your own soul by the possession of something outside of it, thereby losing your own soul and the thing outside of it, too.

The Iceman Cometh is, then, not simply a fine play and an exercise in compassionate nihilism, but an American document as well.

Notes

1. "Dry Ice," *Partisan Review*, XIII (November–December 1946), 577–579. The review was reprinted in her book *Sights and Spectacles* (New York, 1957).

2. *Kenyon Review*, XIV (Summer 1952), 476–492. Bentley's article is based on his experiences directing the play in Zurich in 1951; it was reprinted in *In Search of Theater* (New York, 1953).

3. In "Hugo of *The Iceman Cometh*: Realism and O'Neill," *American Quarterly*, V (Winter 1953), 357–366. The originals of most of the characters in *Iceman* have been identified by Miss Alexander in *The*

Tempering of Eugene O'Neill (New York, 1962) and by Arthur and Barbara Gelb in *O'Neill* (New York, 1962).

4. The noisiest was John Mason Brown, whose review appeared in *The Saturday Review of Literature*, XXIX (October 19, 1946), 26–30. For a man so beset by the length of O'Neill's play, Brown took an unconscionable space to make his few points about *Iceman*. The review is reprinted under the title "Moaning at the Bar" in *Dramatis Personae* (New York, 1963). Bentley boasted that he cut an hour out of the play in his production and that, as a result, "Zurich was offered a more dramatic evening than New York."

5. In *The Magic Curtain* (New York, 1951), pp. 397–409. The O'Neill letter quoted at the beginning of this chapter is reproduced in the same chapter.

6. "Postscript to a Journey," *Theatre Arts*, XLI (April 1957), 27–29, 88.

7. "Some of the comedy writing is irresistible," Nathan wrote in his review of the 1946 production in *The Theatre Book of the Year, 1946–1947* (New York, 1947), pp. 93–111. Not simply a review, this essay includes, with slight alterations, a summary of O'Neill's career that appeared in *American Mercury*, LXIII (December 1946), 713–719. Bentley reported that "Nothing struck my fancy more, in our production, than the little comedy of the Boer general and the English captain."

8. The similarities between *Iceman* and these plays were apparent to many of the first reviewers. Even Robert Garland (New York *Journal American*, October 10, 1946), whose review was both impatient and inept, mentioned *The Lower Depths;* Richard Watts, Jr. (New York *Post*, October 10, 1946), found "an alliance between Saroyan and Gorky." Both John Mason Brown and George Jean Nathan cited all three plays. Probably one of the reasons for the Saroyan analogy is that Eddie Dowling, who directed *Iceman,* earlier directed and played Joe in *The Time of Your Life*. Perhaps another reason why some of the reviewers saw Saroyan in O'Neill is that the bar in *The Time of Your Life* is the same kind of self-protective sanctuary as Harry Hope's in *Iceman*. There have been a number of lengthy articles comparing *Iceman* to *The Lower Depths,* of which Helen Muchnic, "Circe's Swine; Plays by Gorky and O'Neill," *Comparative Literature*, III (Spring 1951), 119–128, is the most interesting. So far as I know, none of them has noticed that the characters in the two plays can only be compared by complicated cross-switching. Hickey, who, as an advocate of truth, is presumably the ideational equivalent of Satin in the Gorki play, has the function of Luka in the dramatic action; Larry, an illusion-monger, like Luka, is functionally one with Satin. The best brief comparison between *Iceman* and *The Wild Duck* can be found in the O'Neill chapter of Robert Brustein's *The Theatre of Revolt* (New York, 1964), p. 340.

9. Miss McCarthy opens her review by calling Hickey "a mad hard-

ware salesman" and Bentley says that he turns out to be "a maniac." This assumption seems to ignore the pattern of shifting illusion of the character and to turn the play into a conventional, if windy, melodrama.

10. In *The Plays of Eugene O'Neill* (Carbondale, Illinois, 1965), pp. 66–75, John Henry Raleigh suggests that nostalgia, which he calls "the only kind of sentimentality that is honest," is central to *Iceman;* he makes an attempt to set the historical scene against which the memories of some of O'Neill's characters would necessarily be played.

11. The O'Neill interview was with John S. Wilson in *PM* (September 3, 1946), p. 18. Theodore Roosevelt's speech at the dedication ceremonies of the Louisiana Purchase Exposition, St. Louis, April 30, 1903, can be found in *Presidential Addresses and State Papers* (New York, 1910), I, 341–353. Both this speech and Roosevelt's brief opening-day remarks (April 30, 1904) are reprinted in David R. Francis, *The Universal Exposition of 1904* (St. Louis, 1913).

32 JOHN F. KENNEDY: *PROFILES IN COURAGE*

John William Ward

The back cover of the memorial edition of *Profiles in Courage* shows John F. Kennedy, with that infectious grin, finger pointing, arm about to be thrust out, standing with the seal of the President of the United States before him and the draped flag of the United States behind. The energy, the youth, the shining confidence, the zest to engage in debate leap out of the picture. They leap out of a background of solid black. John F. Kennedy is dead.

To sit now with the image of the living man in one's hands, it is still hard to believe he is not still living, dead before he was forty-seven years old. But out of the blackness of death Kennedy still lives, larger than life, in the memories and the emotions and the minds of his fellow Americans. After death, the real Kennedy is now the symbolic Kennedy, the figure about whom has clustered the yearnings, the ideals, and the aspirations Americans have for themselves and their country. That symbolic Kennedy also stands between the reader and Kennedy's book. We know what happened, and we cannot undo that knowledge. We read *Profiles in Courage* now with a different eye. The present changes the meaning of the past. We can get the record straight, as historians like to put it, but the meaning of that straightened record is inextricably involved in the meaning we also try each day to discern in the confusion of the living present. The memory of John F. Kennedy is part of that present.

In 1955, Harper and Brothers published *Profiles in Courage* when John F. Kennedy was "Jack" Kennedy, the junior senator from the state of Massachusetts. If Kennedy had not gone on to be President of the United States, further, if he had not been

sures, who did stand for their independence, who did place their own judgment before and above all else. Now, the easy way to admire these eight men would have been to admire their courage because they were right, but the remarkable thing about Kennedy's book is that he does not take that easy and sentimental way out. He does not admire these men because they were right —quite the opposite. He admires them because, right or wrong, they had the guts to stick by their own sense of what was right or wrong. Courage is his subject. It is courage, not wisdom, he extols. At one point, describing the opposition of the liberal but isolationist senator, George W. Norris of Nebraska, to the internationalism of Woodrow Wilson, Kennedy remarks, "It is not now important whether Norris was right or wrong. What is now important is the courage he displayed in support of his convictions." The remark is characteristic and variations on it appear throughout Kennedy's book. What is one to make of it? To take a cruel example, are we to admire the bestial act of political assassination simply because the assassin had the courage to do the deed? What standard does Kennedy's admiration of courage provide?

His chosen heroes have, of course, their own standards, most of them estimable to most men. Edmund G. Ross of Kansas, during Reconstruction, deserts the radical wing of the Republican party in its attempt to impeach the President of the United States, Andrew Johnson. Senator Ross was no friend of the South, and no friend of Andrew Johnson, but in the Senate, against incredible pressure from all sides, he refused to give the vote which would have provided the two-thirds majority necessary to convict. He stood firm out of his commitment to the doctrine of the separation of powers in the American Constitution, out of his belief that if Johnson were to be removed on such weak charges the executive office would become a plaything at the whim of Congress, and that this would unbalance the system established in the Constitution by the founding fathers.

Robert Alonzo Taft, "Mr. Republican," the conservative senator from the state of Ohio, gratuitously went out of his way to attack the legality of the Nuremberg trials which condemned the perpetrators of Nazi atrocities. There was no necessity, no occasion, which demanded that Taft speak out. Doing so, he weakened his chance to become his party's candidate for the presidency of the United States, the one great ambition of his political life. But the *ex post facto* nature of the laws under which Nazi criminals were tried offended Taft's high regard for the decorum of legal procedure and his primary commitment to the rule of law, even in cases where he despised those the law protected.

Young John Quincy Adams, another junior senator from Massachusetts, outraged New England and defied the Federalist party which had sent him to the Senate by siding with Thomas Jefferson, the enemy of his own father, President John Adams, in support of Jefferson's continental expansionism, which weakened the political hegemony of New England, and in support of Jefferson's embargo against trade with England, which destroyed New England's commerce and its prosperity. Adams did so, not just because his vision went beyond New England's regional interests, but because he had been taught by his father the old Puritan doctrine that "the magistrate is the servant not . . . of the people, but of his God." Adams acted in obedience to a higher law, confident as only an Adams could be that he knew God's will, and disdained, as he put it later when he was President himself, to be "palsied by the will of [his] constituents."

The integrity of the political system embodied in the Constitution, respect for the rule of law, belief in the supremacy of a law higher than the wishes of a transient majority: all these are estimable grounds on which to base one's actions, grounds on which many Americans may comfortably stand. Kennedy clearly shares respect for many of the motives that gave his lonely heroes the courage to act, but not all. He recognizes that Taft's commitment to legal procedure could frustrate justice in the higher sense Adams had in view, and says of Taft, as he had of George W. Norris, "we are not concerned today with the question of whether Taft was right or wrong." We are concerned, insisted Kennedy, with "Taft's unhesitating courage in standing against the flow of public opinion for a cause he believed to be right." To insist again, it is not the wisdom or the rightness of an action which is Kennedy's subject. It is the courage to act.

One may understand the appeal of Kennedy's insistence on the importance of individual action, and the courage to take that

374

action, by remembering the time in which he wrote. Kennedy published *Profiles in Courage* in 1955. The decade of the 1950's already seems a long time ago. That was the decade of the "silent generation," the decade of the great success of books like David Riesman's *The Lonely Crowd* and William Whyte's *The Organization Man*. Today, as students take to the streets in the United States, it is hard to recall that the dominant fear of observers of the American scene in the 1950's was that American youth had opted for security and comfort, for adaptation to the system, for conformity, and had turned their backs on the ancient tradition of independence and dissent. Mass society and mass conformity were the themes of serious as well as journalistic critiques of the quality of American culture. The American, it was said, had changed from the inner-directed man who looked to himself and had become the other-directed man, sensitively attuned to the expectations of those around him. He was the faceless man in the crowd. That was the mood of the time, as quickly as that mood has changed in so few years. Kennedy's appeal, the appeal which is the subject of *Profiles in Courage,* was against this mood, this mood of acquiescence and cynicism. He held up an older ideal, the ideal of resistance to the mood of the mass man.

The context is important. The immediate moment in which Kennedy wrote goes far to explain much of his appeal. He spoke for the confident belief that one man counted, that one man could change the course of events, that one man could have an effect, if only one had the courage of one's convictions. This is the message of *Profiles in Courage,* a message which John F. Kennedy dramatized in his own person, in his lean and eager presence and rapid and clipped speech, a message he later summed up as the "New Frontier." Kennedy's appeal, especially to the young, was that the world was still an open and plastic world, open to change and renewal, if only one had the courage to resist the tyrannous weight of mass conformity.

But there is a curious conclusion to the celebration of resistance, the celebration of the courage to stand, as Kennedy said of Taft, against the flow of public opinion. There is, at least, when that celebration becomes the celebration of an act simply because it shows the courage to be different. To put it another way, the man who takes a course because it is opposite to the popular mood is as much a creature of the crowd as the man who chooses to follow the crowd. He just marches in a different direction. But the way the crowd is going still determines his direction. To state it more precisely, although more ponderously, he becomes a negative function of the crowd. If a man resists the dominant mood simply because it is the dominant mood, then he is indistinguishable, except for strategy, from the man who goes along simply to go along. We can no more admire the one than the other. Which brings us back to the critical question, the question Kennedy himself finally had to come to at the end of his book: What standard do we have to measure the meaning of courage? Why is courage in and of itself an admirable quality?

If Kennedy appealed to an older tradition of independence and self-reliance, he did not, however, share the assumptions which had once provided support for that position. When, for example, Thomas Jefferson defended the rights of the minority, he did so in the trust that the truth is great and will prevail, in the trust that reason would finally manifest itself in conflicts among men. Or, for another example, when Ralph Waldo Emerson wrote the sentence every schoolboy knows, "Trust thyself: every heart vibrates to that iron string," he wrote in the assurance that "to believe your own thought, to believe that what is true for you in your private heart is true for all men." Emerson's assurance depended on the trust that all men share a common nature, that beneath the crust of convention and circumstance, if men had the courage to break through that crust, all men would discover the same truths.

There is none of this in Kennedy, none of the sanguine assurance in the rationality of man or in the moral order of the universe. Yet, stripped of the old supports which bolstered the courage to be one's self, Kennedy still affirmed that courage. For his eight senators, he thought that the situation which especially demanded courage of each of them was the desire to serve the national interest, but he was even skeptical of that large abstraction. He quotes John Adams to the effect that it is not true "that any people ever existed who love the public better than themselves." To what, then, does one turn to affirm one's admiration of those who have the courage of their own convictions?

Kennedy's answer was simple. It was not because his senators "loved the public better than themselves." On the contrary it was precisely because they did *love themselves*—because each one's need to maintain his own respect for himself was more important to him than his popularity with others—because his desire to win or maintain a reputation for integrity or courage was stronger than his desire to remain in office—because his conscience, his personal standard of ethics, his integrity or morality, call it what you will—was stronger than the pressures of public disapproval—because his faith that *his* course was the best one . . . outweighed his fear of public reprisal.

"It was precisely because they did *love themselves*." As an older book has it, "Love thy neighbor as thyself." But that wise counsel means that one must love one's self before one can begin to know how to love one's neighbor. Charity begins at home. The bedrock of Kennedy's admiration of courage is the glimpse he has of the simple fact that if one does not act out of self-love, out of one's necessity to please one's self, then what follows can only be self-hatred and impotence and disgust. What is primary is the necessity to be one's self, and to take delight in that act of being. Whether one is right or wrong, whether action leads to success or failure, such considerations are secondary. They are not essential. What is essential is the primacy of the self and the courage to be that self.

Norman Mailer, in a famous article, once hailed Kennedy as the "existentialist" in politics, although later Mailer thought that Kennedy had let him down. The epithet is fashionable, but still useful. Kennedy, at bottom, insisted that the beginning of everything else was the courage to accept what one was and act on that self-acceptance, that love of self which finally makes it possible to love others. One will not do violence to others because that would violate one's own self. It is this image of Kennedy which somehow reached the young, which still lives in the spirit of Kennedy. As the young put it today, "Do your own thing." Don't get seduced by comfort or raped by power. Love yourself enough to be what you are, whatever that may be. If you don't do your own thing, if you start doing someone else's thing, then you become alienated from your own self. The rest is ashes.

One can put the position in more seemly language, perhaps, but it is this sense of the courage of the single individual to be what he is that lies at the heart of John F. Kennedy's book,

Profiles in Courage. Perhaps, as I said at the start of this essay, it is the blackness of death, that ultimate negation of the self, which makes this quality in Kennedy seem so strong to us today. We might not have seen it in 1955. But despite all the trappings of glamor, despite the wealth, the Harvard education, the handsome wife, despite the presidency, the sweet smell of success itself, the quality that emerges most is the spirit of a lonely man, yet finding courage to be the man he was alone with. In a sentence I much admire, the late Joseph Schumpeter once wrote that the mark of a civilized man is his ability to stand unflinchingly for the relative validity of his beliefs. It took a civilized man to write *Profiles in Courage.*

33
THE AMERICAN
AS INVOLVED AND DROPOUT:
AN AFTERWORD

Hennig Cohen

The "writings" that have been considered in the foregoing chapters of this book span the history of the United States from Plymouth Rock to the New Frontier of John F. Kennedy. Their range is wide—literature, language, history, biography, science, politics, sociology, economics, architecture, music. Some of these writings and their authors are familiar throughout the world. Others, though significant, are still little known even in the land that produced them. Yet despite this range of time, subject matter, and degree of familiarity, they are only a sampling and introduction to what has emerged thus far from a large, diverse, and complex nation, a nation, incidentally, which tends still to look upon itself as in an emerging state. All of which is by way of noting the limitations of this selection as the basis for generalizations. But generalization is in order, even though the evidence is not as complete as we would like and even at the risk of oversimplification. Within this volume of thirty-two discussions, in subject matter rather wide-ranging but limited to the compass of the introductory essay, configurations do appear and patterns of similarity and contrast do occur.

The parlance of the hippie provides terms for a pattern of contrast which is conspicuous in the various writings in this book. The terms are *involved* and *dropout*. To be involved is to be committed to the society, the establishment—conforming to it or seeking to exist within it or to reform it. To drop out is not only to question the relevance of the answers of society but to question the questions, to make a radical and total break. The language may be new; the antithesis, of course, is not. One might even argue that a characteristically American experience consists of an original condition of involvement, a radical dropping out, and a return, sadder and wiser, to involvement in society. And it is characteristic of Americans whether they have stayed within the establishment, whether they have dropped out, or whether they have dropped out and returned, at once to idealize and to be wary of the dropout and his way of life. When this pattern engaged the writer, the dropout is usually portrayed as youthful and his sanctuary is often pastoral, sometimes even primeval, and invariably remote, distant in time or space.

The protagonist who accepts involvement is generally more mature and his habitat usually urban. (Cain, the original drop-out, became in his later years the first man to build a city, a fact that Melville, for one, liked to emphasize.) The important thing, however, is not the setting or the age of the protagonist. These are relative matters. It is the process of rejecting the original situation for an alternative, reconsidering the decision of rejection in the light of the experience provided by the alternative, and then deciding whether to adhere to the alternative or to return. The third phase with its elements of choice is what differentiates the American pattern from archetypal journeys such as Dante's descent into the Inferno or from what the Germans call the *Bildungsroman*. Traditionally, the hero's descent into Hell results in his return to the world matured and enlightened. In the American version the choice is not always so clear-cut. Sometimes the world has become so corrupt and disordered that the protagonist rejects it categorically. Sometimes Hell is so soft and enticing that he chooses to remain. Sometimes he is himself inadequate, though not necessarily as a result of some fault of his own. The price he pays, the punishment for dropping out, is immaturity or death, the equivalent to the hippie's childishness and experimentation with drugs. Of course this pattern or any other may be applied so loosely as to be meaningless.

The various writings we have considered were not selected to demonstrate this pattern though many of them do; and the pattern appears even more obvious when the examples are essentially literary. Without reexamining in detail works already analyzed, but merely shifting focus somewhat, who among the earlier writers were involved? Who among the dropouts, factual or fictive, remained dropouts and how did they fare? Who dropped out and then returned?

As Pilgrim Fathers and Founding Fathers, epithets applicable to both, William Bradford and Benjamin Franklin were establishment figures and involved. Bradford in *Of Plymouth Plantation* assumed that his history of the founding of the Plymouth colony was fundamentally an account of man's progress, through heavenly grace but with occasional backsliding, toward the predestined achievement of spiritual salvation. Franklin was Bradford's secular godchild. His *Autobiography,* among other things, is the personal history of the progress of an apprentice lad who achieved, by means of his own efforts and also with occasional backsliding, worldly success in the new nation he helped to establish. If Bradford's history is provident in one sense, Franklin's is in another. Both books are exemplary of the committed life. Observe, however, that Bradford was a Separatist from the Established Church of England and a leader of a voluntary emigration, and Franklin was the elder statesman of the American Revolution. Is there not here a kind of dropping out and returning? Comparable questions arise in connection with *The Federalist.* This series of political essays by Alexander Hamilton, James Madison, and John Jay is likewise a document of commitment. Speculative and hopeful and at the same time shrewdly realistic about mankind's shortcomings, its purpose was to promote the ratification of the United States Constitution. It was establishment propaganda. But even so there are some troublesome questions. The young men who wrote *The Federalist* helped to make a revolution. In their radical break with the *British* establishment were they dropouts? Did their revolutionary experience elicit a return to society with a commitment more meaningful than before? As a national experience, to what extent does the American Revolution constitute a parallel?

St. John de Crèvecoeur also lived through the American Revolution, and its disturbing effects becloud his *Letters from an American Farmer.* We know the *Letters* as an early, sensitive inquiry into the American experience: "What then is the American, this new man?" he asks. The initial answer is a kind of vernacular pastoral poem. His spokesman, Farmer James, lives in an ideal world. He is close to nature, free from old restraints of state and church, expansive, generous, with a sense of personal and national destiny. But he discovers the lawlessness and brutishness of the western frontier and the luxury and cruelty of a southern city sustained by slavery and controlled by merchants and lawyers. When the American Revolution erupts, he is forced to give up his farm and seeks refuge with the Indians. Crève-coeur's Indians abound in simple virtues and live close to nature. Their life is devoid of urban corruption. But they are childlike primitives, their virtues are cloistered, and their future uncertain. Is Farmer James a dropout? Does he perceive the risk and the cost?

Farmer James is a rudimentary character in a book that is only incidentally literary. Rip Van Winkle and Leatherstocking, the literary creations of America's first major men of letters, Washington Irving and James Fenimore Cooper, are more subtle, more richly complex. In Irving's tale, Rip runs away to the Catskill Mountains to escape his familial responsibilities. He meets a stranger, drinks a hallucinogenic potion, and for twenty years sleeps a sleep of death. When he does awaken and return, in conformance with the third phase of our pattern, he is a childish old man, unsure of his identity. He lingers on to exist at the fringes of a society that has passed him by. In the Leatherstocking saga we follow the career of a partially Indianized white man, a plebeian who is one of nature's noblemen. Constricted by the laws of society and requiring the spiritual sustenance of nature, he moves ever westward ahead of the line of settlement. We see him finally in *The Prairie,* an old man silhouetted against the western sunset. In the weakness of his declining years, a context which should not be overlooked, he professes a need for the social laws he has spent a lifetime trying to evade. So much for this late gesture of commitment. Without family ties, Leatherstocking lives his last years with but somewhat apart from his Pawnee Indian friends. How curious it is that the two most notable characters of the first cycle of American literature should respond so ambiguously to American civilization, should drop out, and should return in so reserved a fashion.

The historian Francis Parkman was less equivocal. In his Boston Brahmin eyes, the American Indian was the equivalent of a dropout. He was a savage dwelling in savage surroundings, incapable of civilization. This is enough to assure his doom. Hence in the long view the Indian was less a threat than an object of pathos, and so was the wilderness itself. As the twenty-three-year-old Parkman followed the Oregon Trail with a zeal approaching neurotic compulsion, he could let himself be caught up in the picturesque aspects of wilderness life because they were transitory and because he was an onlooker and a wayfarer who would return in due course to civilization. The wilderness was no refuge for Parkman. It was the place where he proved his stamina and confirmed his convictions.

Our glance at the first seven chapters of this book reveals a progression with qualifications. Those patriarchal figures, William Bradford and Benjamin Franklin, were by definition involved, as were the authors of *The Federalist*. But they all broke with the British establishment. So much for the first phase of our pattern. Crèvecoeur's Farmer James represents the second phase. He was a dropout but with another kind of qualification: the possibility existed that the Indians with whom he sought a haven, in their natural virtue, might be able to achieve a better society than the American colonials caught up in fratricidal turmoil. Irving's Rip Van Winkle runs away from the obligations of society and eventually returns, but his return is qualified by the fact that while he was away a revolution had taken place and the country had changed, and not entirely for the better. Leatherstocking is another dropout who eventually makes a return of sorts. He lives out his last years in a wilderness setting, finally admitting to the need for civil laws, maintaining his racial integrity, and adhering to his natural Christianity. For all practical purposes, Parkman's Indians are dropouts. He himself, in the current terminology, was a "plastic" dropout, a weekend or summer vacation hippie. Rip, Leatherstocking, and Parkman represent, with qualifications, the third phase.

To indulge his excessive artistic sensibility, Roderick Usher of Poe's "The Fall of the House of Usher" withdraws from the world into his moated, stone-walled mansion. The setting, in a phrase Poe uses elsewhere, is "Out of Space—Out of Time." We recognize it as appropriate to Roderick who is, in our phrase, a dropout. Here he remains until his fantasies and projections grow to such proportions that he is overwhelmed by them. His end is madness and death. In Hawthorne's *The House of the Seven Gables,* Clifford Pyncheon and his sister, Hepzibah, are similarly disaffected and withdrawn. Though wronged by their cousin, Judge Pyncheon, in their own generation and sharing the original family sin inherited from Colonel Pyncheon who built the house and established their line, they are also personally defective—Clifford through a certain shallowness and aestheticism and Hepzibah through ineptitude and false pride. Their own efforts to reenter society are pathetically ineffectual, and they are grateful to return to their house, at which point Clifford says: "A dreary home, Hepzibah! But you have done well to bring me hither!" Removed from the house by a new generation which learns how to escape its baleful influence, they live on in a state of carefree childishness.[1] Motivation aside, to call Roderick Usher or Clifford Pyncheon a dropout seems a jarring anachronism. Nevertheless, the situation if not the term applies.

Hemingway's *The Sun Also Rises* concerns American expatriates and uprooted Europeans in France and Spain, yet the setting is much more immediate than the symbolic landscape of the House of Usher or the history-haunted New England house of the Pyncheons. Badly hurt by a "dirty war," they behave with a mixture of irresponsibility, self-pity, wit, and style. In a superficial sense and to some extent all these characters—the narrator Jake Barnes; Lady Brett Ashley whom he loves but cannot possess; Mike, the drunken bankrupt whom Brett plans to marry; and Robert Cohn, the incurable romantic—are dropouts. They are, in the words of Gertrude Stein that Hemingway adopts as one of his epigraphs (and despite his subsequent qualifications), members of "a lost generation." It is Robert Cohn, the young American who attaches himself to Jake, who exemplifies the failed dropout. Romantically naive and given to self-deception, he has come to Europe to write novels. He is attractive, talented, anxious to please, and terribly in earnest. Unlike Jake, to whom he is a foil, he is unable to learn how to function within the limitations of the human condition. Early in the story one of the cosmopolitans ask Cohn: "Tell us right off. Don't think. What would you rather do if you could do anything you wanted?" Cohn replies: "I don't know. . . . I think I'd rather play football again with what I know about handling myself now." Willful and self-centered, Cohn even botches his role as a dropout, ending up as an embarrassment, "a case of arrested development." Hemingway called the type the "American boy-men." [2]

By dictionary definition a "Babbitt" is "a business or professional man who conforms unthinkingly to prevailing middle-class standards." [3] He is, in short, a great American square. The word derives from the title of Sinclair Lewis' novel whose principal character is one George F. Babbitt. Babbitt conforms all right, but he also serves his time as a dropout, his "rebellion" as the book has it. Sensing the sterility of his life, he takes up with a "Bunch" who consider themselves sophisticated and bohemian and he has a fuzzy flirtation with liberal politics, but his gesture is feeble and inglorious and he recants. Still, unlike Robert Cohn, in an elementary way, he has gained from his experience. The novel ends with his defying righteously indignant friends and family by accepting the runaway marriage of his son who wants to drop out of college. He tells this scapegrace: "I've never done a single thing I've wanted to in my whole life! . . . you knew what you wanted to do and did it."

At sixteen the boy Ike McCaslin in Faulkner's "The Bear" undergoes an initiation into the social order of "men, hunters, with the will and the hardihood to endure and the humility and skill to survive." He learns at the same time that his personal inheritance and, by extension, his society, is tainted. When he legally comes of age, he renounces it. He earns his livelihood as a carpenter and the respect of the community for his prowess as a hunter. But the woman he wanted to marry refuses him because he will not accept his legacy. We see him, finally, an old man of almost eighty, childless but known as "Uncle Ike" to the sons and grandsons of the men who taught him to hunt.[4] In renouncing his legacy, Ike shows a nice sense of moral responsibility but he is also renouncing his society and stepping aside from it. He is dropping out, and he fails to return. His is a private act, somewhat selfish and evasive.

A vein of selfishness and evasion, in fact, characterizes our array of dropouts. Roderick Usher, the introverted artist, destroys himself. Clifford Pyncheon, weak and pleasure-seeking, seems headed toward a life of doddering self-indulgence. Robert

Cohn, the adolescent romantic, apparently returns to the harsh lot of a man who must live with the woman he scorned. The cowardly, bumbling Babbitt's own life is a waste, and he must depend upon living vicariously off the life of a son whose promise is less than bright. Ike McCaslin suffers because his concerns are personal and backward-looking. They focus inward upon themselves rather than outward toward the community and the future. In short, there appears to be a direct ratio between the severity of the exaction and the extent to which the dropout is able to return to society. Roderick Usher, the complete dropout, is in effect a suicide. Ike McCaslin, who understands what he must do to cleanse himself (and his society) as fully, as instinctively as he understood what he had to do in order to see Old Ben, the bear, but cannot bring himself to do it and thus cannot completely return, spends his life in an agony of frustration. In contrast—one might even say in shining contrast—are the affirmations of those who dropped out and returned, returned without reservation or qualification.

Two examples must suffice, the personae of Thoreau's *Walden; or, Life in the Woods* and Whitman's "Song of Myself." Both books are autobiographical accounts of men who deliberately turned inward, separating themselves from society, in order to learn how to live more completely within society. Both center upon the self but in a way that ultimately extends outward toward the universal. But, though they are fundamentally alike, they differ in important respects that make them serviceable as representatives of the characteristic American experience of dropping out and returning. The principal difference is that *Walden* is forthrightly factual and down to earth while "Song of Myself" is forthrightly mystical, an observation which is not intended to diminish the symbolic import of the facts of life in the woods or the firm validity of the rhapsodic insights of "Song of Myself." The difference is more one of tone, of approach.

Thoreau was a practical man, almost cantankerous in his insistence on facing the facts. There was no nonsense about him, nothing inflated and nothing pretentious. While Walden is a spiritual biography, it is earthy and lighthearted. "When I wrote the following pages," Thoreau begins, "I lived alone, in the woods, a mile from any neighbor, in a house I built myself. . . .

At present I am a sojourner in civilized life again." At Walden Thoreau made a daily ritual of waking up, greeting the dawn, bathing in the pond. He methodically observed the facts of the natural world—the diurnal cycle and the round of the seasons; seeds that fell to the ground took root and grew; the thaw of the pond in the spring; a torpid snake that came alive in the warming rays of the sun. The emphasis is on regeneration and return. Thoreau was a sojourner at Walden Pond in order that he might become "a sojourner in civilized life again." In his solitude he came to realize his commitment to society.

Whitman was a visionary who could write a mystical poem with the exalted title, "Song of Myself." His mystic way does not abase or mortify. It elevates the ego and glorifies the flesh, and it is not sin that he seeks to purge but the sense of guilt. "I celebrate myself, and sing myself," his Dionysian incantation begins. An ecstatic flight takes him first inward into the solitude of self, but ultimately the movement is "Outward and outward and forever outward." From the self he reaches out to touch, to embrace, and then to embody and fuse. The climactic vision is one of "form, union, plan." This mystical union is presented as sexual union, for Whitman saw in the sexual act the essence of both selfishness and mutuality. The mystical element is rendered substantial by embodiment in flesh; the flesh can be spiritualized because, rendered guiltless, it has returned to a state of original innocence. Whitman's journey begins in withdrawal and ends in return, in an affirmation both of the individual identity and identity with all other selves, and in a mystical union of the body and soul that permits the retention of the integrity of each.

Writings such as those discussed in these thirty-two chapters are in several senses "landmarks." They represent artistic and intellectual achievement; they indicate the aspirations, directions, attitudes, and values of the society which produced them; they characterize the locality and the people who dwell there; and they provide points of orientation. We have seen that many of these writings have in common a pattern to which we can appropriately apply certain terms from the current American lexicon—dropout and involved. It is significant that these words are Americanisms, that they are borrowed from the idiom of the young, and that they are applicable to a configuration discernible in a variety of American writing from the period of the first settlement to the present. What generalization can be derived from this? What does this tell us about the national experience and the national character?

We Americans are committed to freedom not only as an end but as a means of achieving social responsiblity, but we see risk in this and it tends to make us uneasy. Thus we recognize rejection of the establishment as a normal phase of the educative process. We even associate in art and life certain settings and movement in certain directions with this phase: backward into childhood, inward into the self, faraway into the physical spaciousness of the western frontier or the psychic spaciousness of the Old World. But we are fearful in our permissiveness that our dropout may not choose to return, to accept the responsibilities and demands and uncertainties of our society.[5] So our response to the dropout of fact and fiction is ambivalent. We revere the Founding Fathers and find inspiration in Thoreau and Whitman because, in their fashion, they dropped out and returned. The adventures of Leatherstocking and Rip Van Winkle we remember with affection and read to our children but do not take seriously because their return was only partial. Poe frightens us a little with the dark implications of his tales of those who did not return. In sum, we have chosen the risk of freedom in order to attain maturity and responsibility, but it hasn't been an easy choice and sometimes our uneasiness shows.

Notes

1. Their deliverer, Phoebe, instinctively describes Clifford to Judge Pyncheon as a "gentle, child-like man" (Chapter Eight). At the end of their abortive flight from the house, Hepzibah prays: "O God,–are we not thy children?" (Chapter Seventeen).

2. "The Short Happy Life of Francis Macomber": "It's that some of them stay little boys so long, Wilson thought. Sometimes all their lives. Their figures stay boyish when they're fifty. The great American boy-men."

3. *Webster's Seventh New Collegiate Dictionary.*

4. See Faulkner's "Delta Autumn."

5. We are even more fearful of elements of the American population that indicate they might not want in. See Parkman's Indians who are prototypes of the Black Nationalists, Amish, Hasidic Jews, and others who choose to remain outside the establishment. When such elements are a threat like Parkman's Indians, the response of society can be vicious. Otherwise they are tolerated though considered perverse or patronized as "colorful."

Index